FRONT-PAGE PITTSBURGH

Front-Page Pittsburgh

Two Hundred Years of the *Post-Gazette*

CLARKE M. THOMAS

University of Pittsburgh Press

Published by the University of Pittsburgh Press, Pittsburgh, PA 15260
Copyright © 2005, University of Pittsburgh Press
All rights reserved
Manufactured in the United States of America
Printed on acid-free paper
10 9 8 7 6 5 4 3 2 1

Library of Congress Cataloging-in-Publication Data

Thomas, Clarke M.
  Front-page Pittsburgh : two hundred years of the Post-gazette / Clarke M. Thomas.
     p. cm.
  Includes bibliographical references and index.
  ISBN 0-8229-4248-8 (hardcover : alk. paper)
  1. Pittsburgh post-gazette (Pittsburgh, Pa. : 1978) 2. Journalism—Pennsylvania—
Pittsburgh—History. 3. Press—Pennsylvania—Pittsburgh—History. I. Title.
  PN4899.P565P588 2005
  071'.4886—dc22   2004019671

CONTENTS

ILLUSTRATIONS

PREFACE

As with any long-lived person or institution, a history of a long-surviving newspaper such as the *Pittsburgh Post-Gazette* inevitably invites the question: Why? What circumstances and events have allowed this newspaper, the first west of the Alleghenies, to endure? The clues can be discerned from its founding in 1786 and followed through its many permutations, editors, publishers, able competitors, and mergers to the present.

Perhaps, however, the most important and interesting answer to the question is found in the history of the community (both the local surroundings and the larger public) that this newspaper has served for many years. The *Post-Gazette*'s story is intertwined with that of Pittsburgh, southwestern Pennsylvania, and the nation. It parallels the development of two centuries of the country's journalism as a vital part of the American experiment.

Obviously, a history of a newspaper this venerable cannot encompass in detail every change of ownership or editorship. Fortunately, there is an able account of the early years, written by J. Cutler Andrews and published in 1936 as *Pittsburgh's Post-Gazette*. This book is especially indebted to that source, as well as to Leland Baldwin's early histories of Pittsburgh and the Whiskey Rebellion, the memoir of Frank Hawkins, onetime editor of the *Post-Gazette,* and Frank Brady's biography of Paul Block, *The Publisher.* A full list of sources is provided in the bibliography.

While this book incorporates elements of the history of the community and of American journalism, it does not claim to be comprehensive regarding either subject. Instead, this history concentrates upon those occasions when events in Pittsburgh and its region, as reported by the *Post-Gazette,* captured major national and even international attention.

One focal point will be the divergent history of the two "parents" whose combined name the newspaper has borne since 1927. The *Gazette* traditionally was friendly to business and, before the Civil War, to the anti-slavery cause; the newspaper and its editors played key roles in forming the Republican Party. On the other hand, the *Pittsburgh Post,* from its founding in 1842, was a Democratic and prolabor paper, and was, for many decades, discriminatory toward African Americans. Such clashing views on the great social issues of each era made a natural rivalry inevitable.

Nevertheless, echoing the story of journalism in most communities across the United States, competing, and even adversarial, papers found themselves subject to surprising marriages—often shotgun weddings. These mergers are part of the complex equation for figuring how the *Post-Gazette* survived.

———•◦•———

Editorial emendations have been used sparingly in primary source documents to remedy obvious typographical and grammatical errors. The spelling of "Pittsburgh" has been made uniform, even though from 1890 to 1911, in particular, the variant "Pittsburg" was often used. Exceptions to this rule occur where "Pittsburg" appears in the title of a newspaper or business. Varying methods of capitalization in headlines and other similar matters of style have been preserved.

The author is grateful for the cooperation of the many people interviewed for this book, especially the staff of the *Post-Gazette* and the Block family. Thanks in particular are due to Angelika Kane and Stephen Karlinchak of the *Post-Gazette* library and to the staff of the Pennsylvania Department of the Carnegie Library of Pittsburgh in Oakland, notably Barry Chad. My thanks also go to Ken Neal for his editing help and to Cynthia Miller and Deborah Meade of the University of Pittsburgh Press for their counsel and editing advice. Finally, my everlasting gratitude goes to my wife Jean for her computer and editing skills and especially for her moral support.

FRONT-PAGE PITTSBURGH

Painting by George W. Mengelson depicting the printing of the first issue of the *Pittsburgh Gazette* on July 29, 1786
(From Stefan Lorant, *Pittsburgh: The Story of an American City*, Author's Edition, 1964; Courtesy Rowman and Littlefield Publishers)

Chapter 1

The Beginning

J ULY 29, 1786, WAS an exciting day for the village of Pittsburgh, a collection of huts and taverns around Fort Pitt inhabited by three hundred people, at most. On that Saturday, the initial issue of the *Pittsburgh Gazette* emerged, one page at a time, from a hand press. The first newspaper west of the Allegheny Mountains, it was three columns wide and 15 x 9¾ inches, with a front page that was a solid mass of advertisements.

Behind this triumph for two printers, John Scull and Joseph Hall, both twenty-one years old, was one of the most colorful characters in Pittsburgh's history. Princeton-trained lawyer Hugh Henry Brackenridge, born in Scotland in 1745, had moved from York County, Pennsylvania, to Pittsburgh in 1781, and, according to his eulogy, determined "that a newspaper was indispensable to the future of the community and going to Philadelphia he engaged John Scull, a young printer, a member of one of the finest Quaker families in the community, as well as a man of splendid business capacity and most engaging in manners and deportment." Brackenridge's connections to journalism dated back to 1779. After service as a chaplain in the Revolutionary Army, he settled in Philadelphia and founded a periodical, the *United States Magazine*, which focused on the value of literature in American life. That venture

Front page of an early issue of the *Pittsburgh Gazette*

Num. II]　　　THE　　　[August 12, 1786

PITTSBURGH GAZETTE

Price Six-Pence.]　　　SATURDAY, August 12, 1786.　　　[VOL. I.

Foreign Intelligence.

HAGUE, April 18.

PARIS, April 18.

MADRID, April 4.

NAPLES, (Italy) March 15.

LONDON, April 27.

ON NEGROES.
A FRAGMENT.

STERNE.

Hugh Henry Brackenridge,
from an oil painting by Gilbert
Stuart
(Courtesy Carnegie Library of
Pittsburgh)

had closed after one year when it ran out of money, and Brackenridge blamed the magazine's demise on the large class of people who "inhabit the region of stupidity and cannot bear to have the tranquility of their repose disturbed by the villainous jargon of a book."[1]

Although Brackenridge never had any official connection to the *Gazette*, other than as a contributing writer, he helped to bring the paper into existence when he facilitated the purchase of an old wooden hand press from Andrew Brown, proprietor of the *Philadelphia Federal Gazette*, and its transport across the mountains in the autumn of 1785. The press had been designed by Adam Ramage, the most celebrated of the early American pressmakers. It was so small that it was necessary to print a newspaper in sections; eight pulls were required to make four pages. A printer and apprentice would have to work at top speed to pro-

Pittsburgh Gazette masthead of settler and Indian

duce seven hundred copies in a ten-hour day. Of course, a printing press alone was not sufficient to spread the word about this developing community. The Scull and Hall printing shop at the corner of Market and Water Streets thus expanded its newspaper enterprise.

From the outset, the *Gazette* reflected the propensities that would run through its history: a serious nature, a friendly attitude toward business, involvement in community affairs, and openness to varying opinions—within limits. Under Scull, the *Gazette* was basically conservative in tone and in political leanings. While Pittsburgh was still a raw frontier community, its crucial position in the Ohio River system made it a boarding station for travelers sailing farther west. Scull's *Gazette* proved to be a good match for the region.

Unexpected problems soon mounted for Scull, however. first, John Hall died on November 10, 1786, of an unknown disease. Furthermore, John F. Boyd, a replacement for Hall recruited by Brackenridge from Philadelphia, hanged himself in February 1789 on what became known as Boyd Hill, later the site of Duquesne University. Delivery difficulties already had prompted Scull to take on the role of Pittsburgh's first postmaster when postal service was inaugurated in 1788. Thereafter, Scull utilized the *Gazette* to publish lists of people whose letters were lying uncollected in his shop. In a letter to subscribers in the August 1, 1789, issue, Scull complained of the expense of "the carriage of paper from the east of the mountain" but wrote that he hoped to lower the price as soon as paper became available locally. Scull's letter scolded, "Surely in a couple of years a man may find two dollars worth of information, but if not, he will consider that in time it may improve." At one point, he was forced to borrow cartridge paper—an essential for firing flintlock weapons—from the commander at Fort Pitt, Major Isaac Craig. No precise circulation figures were ever made available for early newspapers such as the *Gazette,* but the first federal census, taken in 1790, showed a Pittsburgh population of 376.

Despite the increasing difficulties facing the paper, Brackenridge found in the *Gazette* an outlet for his view on how Pittsburgh's development should proceed. In the August 26, 1786, issue, in an article titled, "Observations on the Country at the Head of the Ohio River," Brackenridge wrote presciently: "This town must in future time be a place of great manufacture. Indeed the greatest on the continent, or perhaps in the world. The present carriage from Philadelphia is six pence for each pound weight, and however improved the conveyance may be and by whatever channel, yet such is our distance from either of the oceans, that the importation of heavy articles will still be expensive. The manufacturing then will therefore become more an object here than elsewhere. It is a prospect of this, with men of reflection, which renders the soil of this place so valuable." Brackenridge understood the need to overcome impressions such as those expressed after a 1784 visit by Arthur Lee of Virginia, who described Pittsburgh as a town of "paltry log-houses, [which] are so dirty. . . . There are in the town four attorneys, two doctors, and not a priest of any persuasion, nor church, nor chapel; so that they are likely to be damned without the benefit of clergy. . . . The place, I believe, will never be very considerable."[2] On September 2, 1786, Brackenridge countered such sentiments in an article urging the state legislature to fund an institution of higher learning in Pittsburgh: "The situation of the town of Pittsburgh is greatly to be chosen for a seat of learning: the fine air, the excellent water, the plenty and cheapness of provisions render it highly favorable."

While such pointed articles appeared regularly in the *Gazette,* technically, the early paper carried no editorials. Many opinion pieces authored by Scull and Brackenridge were signed with pseudonyms such as "Democritus," "Vindex," "Observer," and "Farmer," and others were printed as unsigned letters or dispatches. Some letters were addressed from actual subscribers, usually circulation complaints. Scull welcomed contributions from many disparate voices, and allotted space to long proclamations, whether from the president, Congress, or Pennsylvania's General Assembly. In a September 9, 1786, response to a letter from Gilbert Gichen of Peter's Creek, asking about the *Gazette's* policy on receiving articles, Scull attached this note:

As the above correspondent wishes to be informed whether we are confined to the publication of essays of one, two or three authors, or whether the plan is more general: the Printers are happy to acquaint him that the *Pittsburgh Gazette* shall never be a vehicle for conveying abuse abroad, either on public or private matters, they also inform him, they will thankfully receive (from any person) essays which may tend to the entertainment or improvement of the readers of this paper. They are sorry to add, that many pieces already have been received for insertion, which, if complied with, would have tended greatly to the injury of the *Pittsburgh Gazette.*

Most news appeared in the form of letters or dispatches, some from foreign sources. This policy was in keeping with an opinion piece from Brackenridge asserting that a newspaper should print distant rather than local news: "Who would not give half a guinea to know, exactly as he knows his own calf pasture, what is going on everyday when he rises, at Smyrna and Amsterdam, the armies that are on foot in Europe."[3] Already, the September 2, 1786, issue, under the heading "Foreign Intelligence," had letters from Constantinople (dated April 10), Copenhagen (May 30), London (June 13), and The Hague (May 13).

"Distant news" could also include items from Philadelphia, which had become the state capital in 1790. "A principal advantage," Brackenridge wrote, "will be to know what is going on in our own state; particularly what our representatives are doing: Heretofore, like boys creeping into a hay stack at such a remote distance, we could see only their heels, while their heads were hidden away amongst the cabals in Philadelphia."[4] On September 23, 1786, the *Gazette* reported, for example, that the state government had passed a resolution allowing a William Butler more land for a ferry landing "opposite the town of Pittsburgh" for "the accommodation of the public" because the present site had a tendency to flood.

Scull refrained for more than three decades from assuming the title of editor, but he certainly shaped the *Gazette* with his views. Sometimes his ambivalence on an issue was apparent. For example, he became known for his aversion to horse racing, calling it a "fruitful seminary of all vice."[5] He refused to accept any advertising for jockeys and their mounts, but his front pages during horse-breeding season contained many ads for noted stud horses. Scull seemed to struggle, too, with larger issues such as slavery. Although the fight for abolition—led, in Pennsylvania, by the Quakers—was well underway, the *Gazette* published advertisements for runaway slaves, such as this one: "Runaway on the 19th instant, from the subscriber, living on Plumb creek, Allegheny County, a Negro man named Jack. He is about 40 years of age, and his hair is not so curly, nor so much like wool, as the most of Negroes. It [*sic*] is supposed to be lurking about Pittsburgh. Whoever will take up said Negro and deliver him to his master, shall receive two dollars reward, paid by Thomas Girty." Despite the occasional presence of these kinds of advertisements, Scull published several pieces that raised serious questions about slavery. A particular example, from the July 25, 1789, issue, is the text of a speech to the Maryland Legislature by member William L. M. Pinckney of Harford County, which included this statement: "that this inhuman policy was a disgrace to the colonies, a dishonor to the legislature, and a scandal to human nature, need not at this enlightened period be labored. . . . We may talk of liberty in our public councils, and fancy that we all feel a reverence for her dictates; we may declaim with all the vehemence of animate rhetoric against oppressions, and flatter ourselves, that we detest the ugly monster, but so long as we continue to cherish the poisonous weeds of partial slavery among us, the world will doubt our sincerity. Call not Maryland a land of liberty!"[6]

Scull was a religious man, believing in supernaturalism, but not narrowly so; he agreed, for example, to advertise the writings of Emanuel Swedenborg (1688–1772), the Swedish religious mystic. Although the *Gazette* gave room to news about the gradually developing community of churches in Pittsburgh, at times Scull was accused of unfaithfulness and deism—charges that were also brought against such defenders of religious liberty as Thomas Jefferson.

If slavery and religion were important issues of the day, then no less so was the young government of the United States. On June 8, 1789, the *Gazette* published the entire text of the Bill of Rights amendments proposed by James Madison. Just a few months later, on September 26, the newspaper printed this reminder of apprehensions undoubtedly shared by Scull and many others: "The world is waiting with anxious expectation to see the operation of the new government: Much is justly expected from the legislature of the United States. The people of America having set an original example by adopting in peace, without force, fraud, or surprise, a constitution, simple, plain, and competent to their exigencies, a doubt cannot remain but that all acts and doings of the legislature will be such a comment upon its principles as will give it that complete force and operation, which will crown the wishes of this great people."

Scull's choices of articles often reflected changing American attitudes, and he, like most, hailed the advent of the French Revolution as an expansion of the tide of liberty emanating from the American Revolution. However, Scull looked askance at the French Revolution as it continued; an August 1 dispatch from London in the *Gazette* reported: "The city is tolerably quiet and the utmost precautions are taking for its continuance, but so alarmed are all ranks of people, natives as well as foreigners, at the late riots, that it will be long before confidence is restored among them: great numbers of persons are emigrating from Paris every hour, and would flock still faster to this country [England] but there are not horses or carriages to bring them." The early accounts of the revolution tended to be pro–King Louis XVI and anti-mob, but many Americans of the democratic constituency so enthusiastically championed the French cause that they changed their knee breeches for trousers, addressed each other as "citizen," and began to form "democratic" societies for the promotion of the ideals of the French rebellion. Naturally, this caused dismay among conservatives, Scull among them. The divide in American opinion became deeper as the bitter civil war in France was complicated by military attacks on the new government by other European nations determined to snuff out this threat to the royal concept. By 1793, the acceleration of rebel executions by the guillotine caused enthusiasm for the rebels to wane in many quarters. Dispatches in the *Gazette* played upon these doubts, such as one from London telling of contradictory reports about Robespierre, including a plan to declare him dictator of France. That particular report proved to be all too true as Maximilien Robespierre's ascension to power set off the bloody Reign of Terror until the dictator himself was consumed by the fury and guillotined on July 28, 1794. The *Gazette*'s sympathies by that time were clear, as this article of January 1, 1794, illustrates: "By yesterday's mail from Philadelphia. Paris. Oct. 16 [1793]. Yesterday morning the once all powerful and beautiful Marie Antoinette, consort of the unfortunate Louis, king of France, was brought like the meanest malefactor from the vile prison of Conciergerie, and placed at the criminal bar of the revolutionary tribunal. . . . At the place of execution this morning (the 16th) this unhappy victim of democratic fury was ignominiously carried to the place of execution in a common cart . . . and on the scaffold preserved her natural dignity of mind."

Events in France complicated political matters in the new United States. By 1794, the overpowering prestige of George Washington as the new president could not stop fissures from forming among the Founding Fathers. Washington and those who later would become the Federalists were being confronted by less conservative politicians such as Thomas Jefferson and James Madison, despite Madison's previous warnings against factionalism. Federalists and others who worried about the trends of the French Revolution labeled the more liberal elements typified by Jefferson as pro-French, with all the ills therein cited against them. Conversely, the Jeffersonians painted anti-France leaders such as Washington, Alexander Hamilton, and John Adams as too pro-English, even to the point of being monarchical.

The matter was exacerbated in western Pennsylvania, which abounded in citizens who feared the central government was becoming too strong. The historian Leland Baldwin noted: "Pittsburgh's enterprise and prosperity thus made it the cynosure of western eyes, [but] with the French Revolution's popularization of radical democratic ideas it actually became hated as the local exemplar of corrupt aristocracy and soulless materialism. The time was not far distant when this attitude was to be translated into action."[7] Also, many western Pennsylvanians were concerned about the continued presence of British troops in forts at Detroit and other western locations that the English were supposed to vacate under treaties ending the American Revolution. Moreover, the British were suspected of surreptitiously arming the Native American tribes and fomenting their resistance to the steady encroachment of American settlers coming across the Alleghenies.

John Scull was a Federalist who favored the new Constitution as a necessary antidote to what he considered the near-anarchy that prevailed under the Articles of Confederation devised in 1778. During the battles over the ratification of the 1787 document, Scull stood shoulder to shoulder with Brackenridge in attempts to persuade their centralization-wary compatriots of the benefits offered by the proposed Constitution. Brackenridge, as a newly elected member of the state legislature, had been barely able in 1788 to head off an effort by many of his fellow western legislators to block ratification. Led by William Findley of Westmoreland County, a number of legislators had fled the chamber to preclude a vote by the necessary quorum. Guards had to bring enough legislators back from the streets of Philadelphia to restore the required number. This incident essentially ended Brackenridge's career as an elected official; he and Findley remained inveterate foes from that time forward. Still, Brackenridge was chosen to give the oration at a celebration in June 1788, hailing the ratification of the Constitution by New Hampshire, the ninth and final state needed to make the Constitution effective. Brackenridge's audience gathered on the slopes of Grant's Hill, then well outside of Pittsburgh.

Whatever Scull's feelings were on this issue, as A. Warner dryly noted in his history of Allegheny County, one can find no direct trace of it in the pages of the *Gazette*.[8] Nor were there editorials promoting the establishment of an institution of higher learning in Pittsburgh, only opinion pieces from Brackenridge and also short news items about meetings on the subject, both before and after the incorporation in 1787 of the Pittsburgh Academy, ancestor of the University of Pittsburgh. Likewise, no editorial attention was given to the elevation of Pittsburgh on April 22, 1794, to the status of borough. That milestone, though, was to be overshadowed within months by one of the seminal events in the history of southwestern Pennsylvania and, indeed, of the new nation. Scull's policy of fairness would be strongly tested as growing unhappiness about a federal excise tax exploded in the Whiskey Rebellion.

Chapter 2

The Whiskey Rebellion

— ◆ —

Oɴᴇ ᴏꜰ ᴛʜᴇ ꜰɪʀꜱᴛ signals in the *Pittsburgh Gazette* of the impending storm known as the Whiskey Rebellion came in a proclamation from President Washington, which was repeated in several issues in March and April 1794.

Whereas by information given on oath it appears that in the night time of the 22nd day of November [1793] a number of armed men having their faces blackened and being otherwise disguised, violently broke open and entered the dwelling house of Benjamin Wells, collector for the revenue arising from spirits distilled within the United States, in and for the counties of Westmoreland and Fayette in the district of Pennsylvania, and by assaulting the said collector and putting him in danger of his life, and his dwelling house aforesaid, in the said county of Fayette did compel him to deliver up to them his commission for collecting the said revenue, together with the books kept by him in the execution of his said duty, and did threaten to do further violence to the said collector, if he did not shortly thereafter publicly renounce the further execution of his said office . . .

The announcement went on to "offer a reward of TWO HUNDRED dollars" to anyone bringing to justice "said offenders."

In contrast, the viewpoint of the aggrieved citizenry was presented on March 21, 1794, in a letter from the pseudonymous "J. R. Distiller."

This letter, addressed to General John Neville, federal collector of revenue for Allegheny County, further outlines the issues at stake in that momentous year: "You, sir, may think light of it, but my employment has taught me to believe that the burden would be intolerable if country stills were subjected to all the regulations of large town distilleries—the legislature, I believe, has thought so, but it appears the head of your department thinks otherwise, and is determined to make it otherwise."

These are just two examples of the ways in which the *Gazette* covered the rebellion, by letting the various factions make their cases through proclamations, opinion articles, and letters. At the epicenter of the controversy was an increasingly prosperous Pittsburgh, which had sixteen industries and thirty-six mechanics in 1792. In only a few cases did Scull's newspaper carry news stories in the modern sense, let alone editorial comments. This demonstration of caution, however, would contrast with Scull's personal involvement in the unfolding events.

In 1756 the General Assembly, Pennsylvania's legislature, passed a tax on all distilled spirits. This act in itself seems to have occasioned little controversy, but in 1781, the government established a system of collectors. The first taste of the events to come occurred not long after William Graham, a Philadelphia tavern keeper, was appointed in April 1783 as a collector for Washington, Fayette, and Westmoreland counties. More despised than feared at first, Graham was the victim of such pranks as finding hot coals in his boots and having the tail of his horse bobbed. These pranks escalated, and Graham received numerous serious threats. Then, on April 6, 1786, a mob of about one hundred people attacked Graham in open daylight near Cross Creek in Washington County. His pistols were broken in pieces, one side of his hair was cut off, and he was marched across the county while onlookers jeered. It is interesting, in light of later events, that Hugh Henry Brackenridge was retained by the leaders of the rebels to defend the suit Graham brought against them; he lost the case, and twelve of the rioters were found guilty and forced to pay damages.

Matters intensified further when, under the new U.S. Constitution of 1787, the states delegated to the federal government the power of imposing excise taxes. On March 3, 1791, Congress passed an excise tax on distilled liquors of domestic manufacture. Farmers were most irritated by provisions for inspectors to earn one-fourth of the tax collected and for illegal whiskey to be forfeited, with one-half of the proceeds going to anyone divulging information. Since all stills had to be registered, a system of surveillance and espionage arose, something liberty-loving citizens detested.

A *Gazette* article printed after the rebellion had fizzled remains perhaps the single most concise outline of westerners' grievances to appear during the entire affair:

A meeting of Committees from the several townships of the County of Fayette held at Union town the 10th day of September, 1794. Twenty one members present.

In the Western Country, our poverty, our distance from market and their uncertainty were not the only objections we had to the duty. We felt its effect in a more essential manner, both as manufactures, and as consumers; as manufactures, because the number engaged in the manufacture was larger here than in any other part of the Union; as consumers, because, partly from habits which could not be changed by the mere enactment of a law, and chiefly from our situation from not having yet beer and cyder to use as substitutes, spirits distilled from domestic materials are the only common drink of the mass of the people; and of course they consume more in proportion to their numbers than in most parts of the U.S. To this may be added, that, by the law, no provision has been made by which we could obtain a drawback on the spirits exported to the Spanish settlements on the Missipi [*sic*], in the craft that navigate our rivers.

It was not the excise law itself, but one of its consequences, which gave rise to the unfortunate events, that have taken place since. Their immediate cause was [to take citizens] to be tried a distance of 300 miles by juries unacquainted with the character either of parties of witnesses, and thus to put in operation the dangerous power given by law, to the federal courts, of oversetting that inestimable privilege, which the citizens of Pennsylvania had always enjoyed, of being tried in their own counties. . . . John McGaurraugh, chairman. Albert Gallatin, secy.

Swiss-born Albert Gallatin went on to become President Jefferson's secretary of the treasury.

Frontiersmen traditionally had felt they should be exempt from taxation because of their poverty and the hard conditions of life in the West. The problem, in economic terms, was very specific: most western products were too heavy to ship across the mountains to markets in the east. Rye grain, selling in Philadelphia at $0.40 a bushel, was manageable. A packhorse could carry four bushels, meaning a $1.60 return. However, a bushel and a half of rye could produce a gallon of Monongahela whiskey, selling for $1.00. A packhorse could carry two eight-gallon gourds of whiskey, netting $16.00, or ten times the value of unprocessed grain.

James Veech, a Presbyterian historian writing in 1876, when the temperance movement was gaining strength, highlighted the important social value that whiskey had held a century earlier: "Whiskey was the indispensable emblem of hospitality and the accompaniment of labor in every pursuit, the stimulant in joy and the solace in grief. It was kept on the counter of every store and in the corner cupboard of every well-to-do family. The minister partook of it before going to church, and after he came home. At home and abroad, at marryings and buryings, at house raisings and log rollings, at harvestings and huskings, it was the omnipresent beverage of old and young, men and women; and he was a churl who stinted it. To deny it altogether required more grace or niggardliness than most men could command, at least for daily use."[1]

At first, opposition to the tax took the form of public meetings, the first of which was held at Redstone Old Fort (now Brownsville) on July 27, 1791. Later meetings in Washington, Pennsylvania, and Pittsburgh produced resolutions to repeal the tax, which were published in the August 23 and September 7, 1791, issues of the *Gazette*. Pennsylvania legislators responded and repealed the state's excise tax—but the federal levy remained. More conferences ensued without results in Congress, and events began turning uglier. In June 1793, revenue inspector John Neville was burned in effigy. Then came the attack on revenue collector Benjamin Wells that provoked the proclamation by President Washington cited above. Meetings continued in the Monongahela Valley region, and on February 28, 1794, at Mingo Presbyterian Church in Union Township, Washington County, those assembled established the Mingo Creek Democratic Society.

In its own fashion, the *Gazette* began paying attention to events. The June 28, 1794, issue included these resolutions:

Resolved, that any attempt to create causeless jealousy or mistrust, or to inflame the minds of the less informed in a government under the above circumstances, is inimical to its true interests and real happiness, and that the patriotism of such although arrogating the titles of Democrats, Friends to Liberty, &c. ought to be as much doubted, as the friendship of the savage who at the time he salutes you brother, applies either the knife or hatchet.

Resolved, That democracy which formerly meant that form of government in which the sovereign power is lodged with the body of the people, now means quite a different matter—it now means supineness, lethargy, and sometimes a little toryism in times of real and necessary danger; and violent threats, defiances, meetings, mobs, and feathers in times of peace—it now means abuse of the federal government formed by collective wisdom; it now means scurrility against the President (that best of men) and accusations against the superior officers without supporting a single charge.

These two resolutions, with no source given, obviously emanated from Federalist pro-government views, which were favored by Scull. The same issue of the *Gazette* also published a contrary view, signed by "Democritus":

I am surprised that so little notice has been taken of what was done by the society which met at the mouth of the Yough [Youghiogheny River]. And that the measures they recommended have not been adopted.

I am too well acquainted with mankind to suppose everyone would agree to any one system either of a judicial or civil nature, but I hope there are few Americans who would adopt that British maxim taught by and supported by ecclesiastical authority, viz., that it is not for people of ordinary capacity to argue but to obey.

Secretary of the Treasury Alexander Hamilton had stirred the pot with what westerners perceived as a double cross. Congress, on Hamilton's recommendation, had passed an amendment to the excise tax law allowing persons arrested for breaking that law to have their cases heard in a state court if they lived more than fifty miles from a federal district court. This measure was designed to address the complaint of western Pennsylvanians, who had previously been required to travel three hundred miles to Philadelphia for trial. This legislation was signed on June 5; in July, however, the government began serving processes that had been issued on May 31 under the old law. This state of affairs aroused suspicion among many western Pennsylvanians, and would ultimately lead to charges that Hamilton provoked the violent crisis that followed.

Matters heated up considerably; soon signs began appearing throughout the Pittsburgh region bearing threats to revenue collectors and their allies, signed by "Tom the Tinker." A man named John Holcroft was credited with coining the term, an oblique reference to those inspectors who "mended," or "tinkered with" stills by shooting holes through them. These threats turned to actions as the harassment of revenue collectors heightened in June. John Lynn, deputy collector in Washington County for General Neville, was tarred and feathered and tied up in the woods. Even that was only a presage of more serious matters to come. The story appeared in this "Public Notice" in the August 2, 1794, *Gazette*:

In my house at Bower Hill, on Chartiers creek, which was attacked, plundered, and burnt by the rioters on Thursday evening last, were $4,611.60 funded debt of the U.S. in my own name in two certificates. . . . This is to caution the public lest they may be offered for sale with forged powers or conveyance. If they are fallen into the hands of an honest man, he can return them to Col. Presley Neville, in Pittsburgh.

John Neville. July 20, 1794.

On the same day, the front page announced:

By a respectable number of citizens who met on Wednesday the 23rd inst. at the Meeting house on Mingo creek, it is recommended to the townships of the four western Pennsylvania counties, and the neighbouring counties of Virginia, to meet and choose not more than five nor less than two representatives, to meet at Parkinson's ferry, on the Monongahela, on Thursday the 14th day of August next, to take into consideration the present situation of the western country.

Below this notice ran the following:

Pittsburgh, July 20, 1794

Finding the opposition to the revenue law more violent than I expected, regretting the mischief that has been done, and may from the continuation of measures, seeing the opposition changed from disguised rabble to a respectable party, think it my duty and do resign my commission.

ROBERT JOHNSON

The day before Johnson's resignation announcement appeared in the *Gazette*, the largest gathering of rebels in the entire insurrection took place at Braddock's Field. For the most part, the whiskey rebels were Scotch-Irish—either first-generation immigrants from Northern Ireland or their descendants, whose ancestors had emigrated to the Ulster sector of Ireland from Lowland Scotland or western England. As Kevin Phillips has observed, "By the time they started migrating to American in large numbers, the Scotch-Irish were already a toughened frontier breed, quite different from other Britons. The melting pot of seventeenth-century Ulster also foreshadowed the feisty politics that Scotch-Irish stalwarts in America would bring to the Revolution. Independent-mindedness, because they had brought no lairds to tell them what to do; hardiness, imbued by two or three generations on a bloody and rugged frontier; and an intense Presbyterian religion and sense of persecution that made them hostile to the Crown and to established Anglicanism."[2]

Conflict mounted over other grievances, as well. The same August 2 issue of the *Gazette* featured a dispatch from the *Kentucky Gazette* of Lexington, urging "our right to the free navigation of the western waters." It trumpeted: "To you the inhabitants of the west is reserved the display of those virtues once the pride and boast of America—Uncontaminated with Atlantic luxury, beyond the reach of European influence; the pampered vultures of the commercial country have not yet found access to your retreat. No power on earth can justify, palliate, or excuse the marked injustice done to the inhabitants of the west, by the insidious policy of eastern America."

Just before this issue of the *Gazette* appeared, on the night of July 31, a Pittsburgh town meet-

In 1794, as the violence of the Whiskey Rebellion increased, the *Pittsburgh Gazette* printed the resignation letter of tax collector Robert Johnson above a letter from distillery owner John Reed requesting the reprinting of a "Tom the Tinker" notice that had been pasted to a tree outside his business.

Pittsburgh, July 20, 1794.

FINDING the opposition to the revenue law more violent than expected, regreting the mischief that has been done, and may from the continuation of measures, seeing the opposition changed from disguised rabble to a respectable party, think it my duty and do resign my commission.

ROBERT JOHNSON.

Mr. Scull,

I am under the necessity of requesting you to put the following in your next paper—It was found pasted on a tree near my distillery.

JOHN REED,

July 23, 1794.

IN taking a survey of the troops under my direction in the late expedition against that insolent exciseman John Nevill, I find there were a great many delinquents, even among those who carry on distilling; it will therefore be observed that, I Tom the Tinker, will not suffer any certain class or set of men to be excluded the service of this my district, when called to attend on any expedition carried on in order to obstruct the execution of the excise law, and obtain a repeal thereof.

And I do declare on my solemn word, that if such delinquents do not come forth on the next alarm, with equipments, and give their assistance as much as in them lies, in opposing the execution and obtaining a repeal of the excise law, they or they will be deemed as enemies, and stand opposed to virtuous principles of republican liberty, and shall receive punishment according to the nature of the offence.

And whereas a certain John Reed, now resident in Washington, and being at his place near Pittsburgh, called Reedsburgh, and having a set of stills employed at said Reedsburgh, entered on the excise docket, contrary to the will and good pleasure of his fellow citizens, and came not forth to assist in the suppression of the execution of said law by aiding and assisting in the late expedition, have, by delinquency manifested his approbation to the execution of the aforesaid law, is hereby charged forthwith to cause the contents of this

ing was held. As a result, twenty-one leading citizens—including
Scull—were appointed to create resolutions to counter a proposal by
David Bradford. Bradford, rapidly emerging as a leading figure in the
rebellion, was, at thirty-four years of age, a popular attorney, a state legislator, and a deputy attorney general for Washington County. He suggested that federal mails to Philadelphia should be intercepted in order
to determine which citizens were urging the government to take strong
action against the rebels. Three citizens whose letters had been opened
by Bradford—prothonotary James Brison, Edward Day, and Abraham
Kirkpatrick—were asked to "exile" themselves from Pittsburgh to ease
the tensions. It was agreed that a committee of respected citizens, including Brackenridge, should travel out to Braddock's Field, not to
fight, but, rather, to gather information and seek to pacify the insurgents. The committee instructed John Scull to print six hundred copies
of its resolves in the form of handbills to pass out the next day at
Braddock's Field, and Scull stayed up all night to accomplish the task.[3]

On August 1, at Braddock's Field (now Braddock), the rebels talked
of invading Pittsburgh and capturing Fort Fayette, the only significant
garrison following the decline of Fort Pitt. One small band of Pittsburghers had decided to mingle in the crowd and do their best to dis-
suade the dissenters. Historians mention the handbills printed by Scull
as helping to calm the crowd. Albert Gallatin was a voice of reason, and
Brackenridge used his oratorical skills to highlight the grievances of
those present, while at the same time counseling caution. Brackenridge
seemed to play the role of a double agent in this conflict, which later
made him suspect with Secretary Hamilton and federal leaders and re-
viled by the rebels. In particular, Brackenridge gave some advice to the
supporters of Tom the Tinker types that may have turned the tide for
that day and the next. While voicing his support for the rebellion,
Brackenridge predicted casualties of about one thousand men in a sly
attempt to give the rebels pause before committing violent acts.

The rebels, still unsure about whether or not they would storm the
fort, decided, in any case, to march the next day on Pittsburgh. On the
banks of the Monongahela, the citizens of Pittsburgh laid out a feast for
the invaders, including lots of whiskey. Brackenridge later wrote, "I
thought it better to be employed in extinguishing the fire of their thirst,
than of my house."[4] The Pittsburghers had made sure that after the
meal there would be enough ferryboats to carry the men across the

Monongahela and had found a ford where horsemen could cross. The day ended with the rebels full of food and drink safely across the river and on their way back to their homes to the south.

Shortly thereafter, Scull's true feelings on the insurrection emerged in one of the few direct editorial comments of those early years. As J. Cutler Andrews wrote, "Scull waited long to express his real feelings; and when at length he did so, his voice simply harmonized with a swelling chorus."⁵ In the August 30 *Gazette,* Scull wrote: "If every man would now speak out his real sentiments, there would be very few found to approve the late opposition to the law. It cannot be supported without a separation from the United States—a thing that could not be effected, and if it could, would enfeeble and ruin the Western Country." Historian A. Warner wrote a much more skeptical account: "It has been stated, with a flourish, that the *Gazette* took a firm stand against the whiskey rebellion, but its 'firm stand' must have consisted of saying and doing nothing. Its influence may have been felt on the right side, and doubtless it was, but its columns can not be cited as proof. Down to 1830, and perhaps afterward, this characteristic of the press was maintained, and one cannot but wonder, in looking back, how the papers of the day made their impression on the public mind. The contrast between that day and this, in that respect, is marvelous and noteworthy."⁶

Perhaps Scull's resolve had been bolstered by twin proclamations he had printed in full on August 23, 1794. The first, from President Washington, asserted that the mounting of a military expedition was necessary. The second came from the governor of Pennsylvania, Thomas Mifflin, and affirmed that all officers were "hereby required and enjoined to employ all lawful means for discovering, apprehending, securing, trying and bringing to justice, each and every person concerned in the said riots and unlawful proceedings."

These proclamations were followed by action. Washington, Mifflin, and the governors of New Jersey, Maryland, and Virginia issued orders calling up their militias. It proved difficult to enlist enough men; Revolutionary War veterans, in particular, complained about being called back to service. Eventually, 12,950 men were assembled. This mission is noteworthy in American history as the only time when a president personally led an army. It was the seventh time that Washington had visited Pennsylvania, starting with his scouting expedition against the French in 1753. The whole affair has been called the first civil war, because it was the only such domestic conflict between the commencement of the new nation under the Constitution in 1789 and the Civil War of 1861–1865. As it turned out, resistance melted away so quickly that Washington came no farther west than Bedford, eighty-five miles from Pittsburgh. He transferred command to the head of the Virginia forces, Governor Henry "Light Horse Harry" Lee—later the father of Robert E. Lee, born in 1807—and stressed the importance of suppressing the insurgents.

On August 14, 1794, discussion at the meeting at Parkinson's Ferry (now Monongahela) focused on a resolution that called for a Committee of Public Safety to guard against any invasions of the rights of the people. Even though Gallatin had been named secretary of the session, he clearly wanted to head off an organized military resistance. Brackenridge later said that while he admired Gallatin's courage, he thought nothing would be gained by a frontal attack on a resolution that obviously expressed the sentiments of those present. He ostensibly opposed Gallatin by agreeing to the resolution but also suggested that, to ensure proper phrasing, the document should be referred to a redrafting committee. The result was that eventually this resolution and others were watered down enough to make them feasible as bargaining tools in negotiations with commissioners sent to Pittsburgh by President Washington. After those negotiations were held on August 20, the insurgents' leaders carried news of a possible agreement back to their followers. In a climactic meeting of August 28 held at Redstone Old Fort, seventy Westmoreland County riflemen looked on from across the stream as the precarious negotiations continued. Speeches by Gallatin, seconded by Brackenridge, apparently made the difference. Gallatin's biographer, John Austin Stevens, contended that Gallatin thereby "saved the western counties of Pennsylvania from anarchy and civil war," because the assemblage later that day adopted a resolution declaring it to be "to the interest of the people of the country to accede to the proposals made by the commissioners on the part of the United States."7

By a fascinating historical coincidence, the August 20 negotiations occurred on the very same day that the federal government, so despised by the whiskey rebels, was winning the crucial Fallen Timbers battle in northwestern Ohio against Native Americans who threatened western Pennsylvania residents. The success of General "Mad" Anthony Wayne in the struggle near present-day Toledo opened the way for white settlement in what became Ohio, Indiana, and Illinois. Pittsburghers first received printed word of the battle on September 20, in an indirect sort of report not unusual in the *Gazette* of that era: "We are informed that there is a letter in town from a gentleman in Canada, informing that the advance of the American army, on the march to the Miami, had encountered and defeated a party of Indians and took 40 prisoners; that upon the approach of the army to the fort lately [held] by a detachment of British soldiers, the garrison retired, without opposition. Leaving 4 pieces of cannon, and that it was destroyed by the order of General Wayne. Not having obtained sight of the letter, we are unable to state particulars."

Meanwhile, negotiations between the federal commissioners and the rebels remained unsettled. According to Baldwin, "Tom the Tinker renewed his literary activities and John Scull did not dare refuse him space in the *Gazette* of September 13, 1794."[8] The item read:

You will please have this printed in the Pittsburgh paper this week, or you may abide by the consequence.

Poor Tom takes this opportunity to inform his friends throughout all the country that he is obliged to take up his commission once more, though disagreeable to his inclination. I thought when I laid down my commission before that we had got the country so well united that there would have been no more need for me in that line, but my friends see more need for me now than ever—they chose a set of men whom they thought they could confide in but find themselves much mistaken, for the majority of them are proved traitors four or five big men from below has sceared [*sic*] a great many, but few is killed yet, but I hope none of these are any that ever pretend to be a friend to poor Tom, so I would have all my friends keep up their spirits and stand to their integrity for their rights and liberty, and you will find poor Tom to be your friend—This is fair warning, traitors take care for my hammer is up and my ladel [*sic*] is hot, I cannot travel the country for nothing. From your old friend TOM THE TINKER.

However, cautious men, and especially the Presbyterian clergy, advocated a peaceful resolution under the terms proposed by President Washington's representatives. The ministers did not favor the excise tax, but had continually advocated for peaceful solutions. At this point, the Reverend John McMillan, who held great authority in the region, even delayed the date for when he would administer communion, implying that those who refused to sign the terms of the agreement would be ineligible to participate in this holy rite. Eventually, enough representatives signed, but Washington's army continued its marching preparations. Spirited meetings in the Monongahela Valley continued, but Tom the Tinker's ladle was being decisively cooled.

As the rebellion wound down, Secretary Hamilton came to Pittsburgh in November. One purpose for his visit was to investigate his suspicions of Brackenridge's conduct at the time of the Braddock's Field episode. Hamilton left convinced that Brackenridge, rather than fomenting the uprising, had been instrumental in dampening it. This acquittal of Brackenridge greatly upset some of his enemies.

Others were not as fortunate as Brackenridge. On November 13, 1794, just four days before the bulk of the troops were pulled out of western Pennsylvania, General Lee's troops arrested 150 to 200 men. They were dragged from their beds in the middle of the night—later called "The Terrible Night"—and forced to walk half-naked through mud to makeshift prisons, including an open pit in Pittsburgh. Those compelled to trudge across the mountains for trial in Philadelphia faced mocking crowds when they arrived. However, despite a year of treason trials, all eventually escaped punishment

David Bradford was the only rebel not ultimately pardoned by President Washington. As the rebellion collapsed, Bradford escaped into Natchez, Spanish territory, where he lived in exile. However, he was later pardoned by President John Adams on the day of George Washington's death, December 14, 1799. Congress finally abolished the whiskey tax in 1802, when Albert Gallatin was secretary of the treasury.

The alliances, factions, and personal vendettas that bloomed during this first major internal threat to the new nation were to flavor Pennsylvania politics and Pittsburgh life for many years. Brackenridge and his adversary within the anti-Federalist ranks, William Findley of Westmoreland County, wrote reams as they tried to set the record straight according to their unique perspectives. The subsequent parting of the ways between Brackenridge and his onetime protégé, John Scull, was to have consequences for the *Gazette* as the turn of the century approached.

Chapter 3

Competition

ㅡ◆ㅡ

J OHN SCULL UNDOUBTEDLY did not realize it at the time, but the
Whiskey Rebellion was to be the peak of his thirty-year career as
editor of the young *Pittsburgh Gazette*. Those years represented the
high tide of the Federalist cause that Scull espoused, marked by President Washington's bloodless quelling of the Monongahela Valley insurgents. After that, the region—and the nation—began moving toward
anti-Federalism, led by Thomas Jefferson, James Madison, and the
Democratic-Republican Party, and culminating in the election of
Jefferson as the third president in 1800.

This development was to be personally painful for Scull as some of
his peace-seeking comrades during the Whiskey Rebellion, including
Brackenridge and Gallatin, advocated the anti-Federalist movement.
The rupture between old friends and allies would become increasingly
evident to all as it was played out in public forums—first the columns of
the *Gazette*, then the courts. As the debate forced Scull out of neutral
territory, his Federalist leanings inevitably aligned him more clearly with
the Pittsburgh business community's interests at a time of both commercial and cultural growth. Quite crucially for the history of the *Gazette*, the political split brought newspaper competition to Pittsburgh
for the first time, thanks to Brackenridge.

Up until the Whiskey Rebellion, Scull and Brackenridge had remained on good terms. In fact, in 1793, Scull printed the third volume of *Modern Chivalry*, a novel that Brackenridge wrote and published in six volumes over thirteen years. This political satire, generally acknowledged as the first book published in the Pittsburgh region, earned Brackenridge a national reputation and only thinly disguised his personal views on who should govern. His conclusion, it seemed, was that he should—he pursued several campaigns for public office, and then accepted, in 1799, a lifetime appointment to the Pennsylvania Supreme Court.

It was indicative of a growing rift between Brackenridge and Scull that the *Gazette*'s editor chose not to publish any of Brackenridge's 1795 book, *Incidents of the Insurrection,* an account of the Whiskey Rebellion in which the author attempted to erase any damage that had been done to his reputation by his involvement in the affair. Instead, Scull printed excerpts from a 1796 account by Brackenridge's political rival within the anti-Federalist ranks. William Findley's *History of the Insurrection, in the Four Western Counties of Pennsylvania* furnishes some fascinating insights, including the view that federal officials—specifically Hamilton—and their policies were to blame for much of the violence that had occurred.

Another point of friction between Federalists and anti-Federalists within the region was the Washington administration's handling of Native American affairs. Only five months after the Battle of Fallen Timbers, on January 24, 1795, the *Gazette* published a message "submitted" to President Washington from his secretary of war, Henry Knox:

The desires of too many frontier white people to seize by force or fraud upon the neighbouring Indians lands has been, and still continues to be, an unceasing cause of jealousy and hatred on the part of the Indians, and it would appear upon a calm investigation that until the Indians can be quieted upon this point and rely with confidence upon the protection of their lands by the U.S., no well-grounded hope of tranquility can be entertained.

The encroachment of White people is incessantly watched, and in unguarded moments, they are murdered by the Indians. Revenge is sought, and the innocent frontier people are too frequently involved as victims in the cruel contest. This appears to be a principal cause of Indian Wars. That there are exceptions will not be denied. The passion of a young savage for war and fame is too mighty to be restrained by the feeble advice of old men.

The message went on to suggest several solutions: establishing a string of military posts; that the Indians surrender for a military court-martial any Indian who committed murder or theft against whites; and that whites warring or looting against the Indians should "become liable and subject to the rules and acts of war which are or shall be established by the government of the troops of the U.S." Knox asserted, "government would then have made the fairest experiments of a system of justice and humanity, which it is assumed could not possibly fail of being blessed with its proper effect, and honorable tranquility of the frontiers."

This indication of the Washington administration's policy did not sit well with many westerners, many of whom wanted to keep options open for settling in "neighbouring Indians lands" and did not favor efforts at reconciliation. Such announcements only fanned anti-Federalist sentiments ignited in the whiskey tax controversy of 1794. Politicians like Brackenridge and Findley felt the need to justify—or cover up—their actions in the Whiskey Rebellion precisely because they wanted to ally themselves with the growing Democratic-Republican impetus. The intensifying political climate made it more difficult for John Scull to maintain his policy of neutrality, though as late as 1797, he was still working to hold that ground. In the August 12 edition of the newspaper, he somewhat disingenuously wrote: "The *Pittsburgh Gazette* has never deserved or obtained the epithet of a party paper; because the Editor is of no party, not being greatly versed in the abstract science of politics, and not having the ambition or the skill to be any thing but a printer."

Scull's personal sensibilities may have begun to gnaw at him. He was essentially a religious man and was bothered by the way in which the Jeffersonians vigorously championed the irreligious French Revolution. Scull was a staunch Protestant—so much so that he would not accept anything for publication from Roman Catholics—and was deeply concerned with the condition of the Presbyterian Church, which was the dominant Protestant sect in Pittsburgh. The *Gazette* of October 24, 1800, included a number of questions directed toward Presbyterians, related by J. Cutler Andrews: "Could they hope for good morals without religion or the fear of God? Could religion be maintained without tax support? Were they not able to erect a respectable and commodious church building? Would not money so employed be more beneficial to the town than horse racing, billiard playing? The implied rebuke was understood. On April 2, 1802, the *Gazette* announced that the contract for a 'Brick Meeting House' for the Presbyterian congregation of Pittsburgh had been let."[1]

In the late 1790s, Scull's personal and political convictions began to diverge more and more from those of Brackenridge, Findley, and their faction, and move instead toward those of Federalists like revenue collector General John Neville. Neville's supporters included a lawyer named John Woods, who ran as a Federalist candidate for Congress in 1798. Brackenridge, in a sly countermove, enticed General Neville's son Presley also to run, and no one could convince Presley to withdraw. As a result, the Federalist vote was split and the Democratic-Republican candidate, Albert Gallatin, won instead. He proved to be one of the most capable men ever to enter the young Congress, moving from there to become not only Jefferson's secretary of the treasury but later a foreign envoy of considerable stature.

The Federalists were livid about Brackenridge, and became even more so by Brackenridge's support in the 1799 gubernatorial election for Jeffersonian candidate Thomas McKean, then chief justice of the Pennsylvania Supreme Court. Anger was doubled when the newly elected McKean immediately rewarded Brackenridge by appointing him to the high court.

As the 1800 election approached, Scull decided to give up any pretense of neutrality. Undoubtedly, Scull was further provoked when a small Jeffersonian newspaper, the *Herald of Liberty,* was launched in Washington, Pennsylvania, by John Israel and backed by McKean. Scull began refusing to publish columns by anti-Federalists, and printed unflattering comments about McKean, such as the story that he had forced his daughter to renounce her religion in order to marry her to a Spanish nobleman.

That kind of advocacy would prove to be too much for the Jeffersonians to swallow. As early as 1797, Brackenridge had suggested to his anti-Federalist cohorts the advisability of starting an opposition paper in Pittsburgh. By November 30, 1799, Scull was able to detail the plans for a new paper in town. Of explanations from Brackenridge,

Scull declared: "That his is a mere pretext, will not be questioned, when the public are informed, that ANOTHER Press last long since been talked of by Mr. Brackenridge. For upwards of 13 years my best endeavors have been exerted to preserve the freedom and impartiality of the Pittsburgh *Gazette,* and to render it useful. But my offence is of a nature not to be pardoned—My paper has not teemed with abuse of the government, its officers, and its supporters—on the contrary I discountenanced publication of that kind—in this I have offended—that is the unpardonable sin—and for this we are to be vilified with what is modestly termed ANOTHER Press. THE EDITOR." A week later, on December 7, Scull plaintively wrote: "What Printer prints cheaper than I do? What sheet is better filled than mine? He may indeed get a Printer to publish what may be more agreeable to himself—but I submit to my readers, whether any can fill the sheet with more useful intelligence."

Scull's attempts to maintain an editorial monopoly were, finally, in vain. John Israel quietly moved his operations to Pittsburgh, installed a press, and on August 6, 1800, began printing a small four-column opposition sheet, renamed the *Tree of Liberty.*[2] Scull was not above reflecting the latent anti-Semitism of the community, and on August 23, leveled the favorite Federalist charge of irreligion: "I reverence the Bible, and do not like . . . to see the word of God profaned. Messrs. Brackenridge and Israel have taken a motto to their paper from Revelation 22:2, where the Holy Spirit speaking of the Tree of Life says, 'And the leaves of the Tree were for the healing of the nations.' These sacred words they have profanely applied to their paper."

Scull was happy to print letters from sympathizers who supported him against the new rival. One such was an article from A.W. of Robinson's Run, who commented on August 23, 1801, "You have laboured faithfully among us. And I, for my part, whatever others may do, cannot forget this." Another letter of support, which must have particularly delighted Scull, came from Dr. Andrew Richardson and was published in the October 2, 1801 edition:

I warmly interested myself in establishing a paper at this place, entitled the *Tree of Liberty.* I expected that it would have been conducted on pure Republican principles, but on my sending a refutation of falsehoods published against me, by William Gazzam and Company, to my astonishment the editor shut his press against me and refused to publish in my favor. Is this the Liberty of the press? Is it Republicanism? No sir, it is a Tyranny of the darkest nature, and every independent man must disapprove of such conduct.

I cannot trouble you with my publication for nothing, after supporting the other press against you, but if you will insert the enclosed, I will pay you for it.

Bitterness continued to flare from both sides. Brackenridge breached decorum by firing an angry shot in the *Tree of Liberty* at a fellow judge, Alexander Addison. The two had worked together in 1794 to quell the Whiskey Rebellion. At that time, Addison guided the grand jury to accept President Washington's terms. Later, however, on November 15, 1800, Brackenridge wrote: "It . . . is a strong proof of the love of order, and respect for the laws among the people, that under a sense of groundless and degrading LIBEL, they were not fired with sudden indignation, and did not drag you from your seat, and tread you under foot."

This diatribe apparently convinced Scull that a revolution was planned. The November 28, 1800, *Gazette* carried one of the rare inflammatory headlines of that era: "Insurrection." In a backhanded phrase, the public was advised that if tumult, violence, and insurrection did not take place, such a failure could not be ascribed to Brackenridge. Scull apparently thought that Brackenridge had lost his sanity, for he had a letter on hand to the effect that on Brackenridge's "late Mad circuit" throughout Washington County, the judge had become "terribly drunk" in Canonsburg, had walked around the tavern naked, and had induced the local boys to throw buckets of water over him. This seemingly was a variation of another story about Brackenridge riding into town naked in the rain, explaining that he had placed his clothing under his saddle to keep it dry.

In 1801, Scull printed President Jefferson's March 4 inaugural address on the front page. Perhaps he was mollified by Jefferson's conciliatory clause, "But every difference of opinion is not a difference of principle. We have called by different names brethren of the same principle. We are all Republicans, we are all Federalists." On March 20, the *Gazette* proclaimed that "it relieves the Federalists from their apprehension [about the] Democrats, who go prowling about like ravening wolves seeking what they may devour." Scull's true reaction, however, may have been represented by a dispatch "from a correspondent at Beaver Town," carried in the same issue:

Wednesday the 4th of march being the day appointed by law for the inauguration of the Chief Magistrate of the United States, a number of the
friends of anarchy and confusion, commonly called Democrats, from the
town of Beaver and vicinity, assembled at the house of Jeffe Harte at
Brady's run, and did then and there erect a whiskey alias sedition pole, to
testify their joy on the occasion, on the top of which was hung a white (or
nearly white) pendant, supposed to be part of an old table cloth. After performing many Indian dances, and singing the favorite Jacobin songs "Ca
Ira" and "Carmignole" and recounting the many wonderful achievements
and hair breath escapes they had made during the revolutionary war (by
the bye there was but one who had ever pulled a trigger in the cause) and
after settling the affairs of the nation and enjoying the loaves and fishes in
imagination, and reprobating the hateful alien and sedition laws, the
scourge of such renowned patriots, they took a very plentiful dole of the
juice of the grain, and reeled home to recount to their wives and children,
the wonderful exploits of the day.

Scull also printed articles disparaging Thomas Paine as a freethink-
ing agitator and linking him to Jefferson whenever possible. Paine
(1737–1809) had stirred colonial spirits with his 1776 *Common Sense,*
followed by *The Crisis,* a series of pamphlets that led with the memorable phrase, "These are the times that try men's souls." Paine returned
to England 1787 and five years later moved to France, where he served
as a member of the National Convention. Because he favored the exile,
rather than the execution, of Louis XVI, he drew the anger of
Robespierre and was imprisoned between December 1793 and November 1794. During that time, Paine wrote *Age of Reason,* in which he expressed objections to organized religion. The book, published in two
volumes, was widely read as an atheist work, and caused many of
Paine's friends and supporters in both Europe and America to turn from
him.

Scull attacked Paine as an underhanded way of attacking Jefferson,
as is evidenced in this unsigned article of August 21, 1801, on the pend-
ing presidential invitation for Paine's return from exile: "To countenance the man is to approve of his principles. And is it come to this? Do
we live under a government where a reviler of the Christian Religion,
where a scoffer at the Sacred Scriptures, and a defamer of Jesus Christ
(whose precious blood and sufferings were an atonement of our sins) is
encouraged and publicly patronized by the administration? It will not,

nor can it come to pass—Friends to Religion! Ought we not to show our disapprobation of the measure . . ."

This was followed by a "communication" on September 11, 1801: "Should the president's affectionate letter to Thomas Paine succeed in bringing him to America, the following extract will throw what evils may probably result both to civil and religious society from his residence among us." After a lengthy discourse about Paine, the article ended with a sly nudge toward Scull's competitor: "The editor of the *Tree of Liberty* is requested by the author to give the above communication a place in his paper." Although Jefferson arranged for Paine's safe return to the United States, Paine died poor and a social outcast.

Despite his disapproval of Jefferson, Scull joined his fellow westerners in joy at the news of the Louisiana Purchase in 1803, declaring on July 22, "no event so important to the western country has ever happened since the British treaty which surrendered the western posts, as the cession of New Orleans to the United States. By this every man who owns a farm may reckon it one half more valuable than before, and every man on the western waters may reckon himself one half richer."[3] However, Scull was unwilling to credit Jefferson for this coup, instead acknowledging Napoleon's resistance to the British government, which forced the French to sell what they could not keep.

One immediate result of the acquisition of the huge western territory was that quotations from the New Orleans market, as well as advertisements of New Orleans wares, began appearing in the *Gazette*. As more western land became open to American settlers, "gateway" cities such as Pittsburgh realized a great benefit. The increasingly wealthy population of Pittsburgh increased from 1,565 people in 1800 to 4,787 only ten years later.

Local politics continued to elicit partisanship in the newspaper. In the 1808 election for Pennsylvania's governor, Scull supported the campaign of Federalist James Ross. On September 21 of that year, almost the entire front page and the first column of the second page were devoted to extolling Ross's merits. On October 10, Scull ran a front-page spread under this two-column head: "Farmers Look Here!! Americans, let not a single vote be lost—Your Constitution is at stake. Vigilance only can preserve your rights. Be at your posts—Your enemies are seeking your destruction. . . .Will you have for Governor—James Ross—the friend of the Constitution or Simon Snyder, who will call a Convention, destroy the trial by jury & and independence of the judiciary."

Yet Scull's agitating was to no avail. On October 19, the *Gazette* announced the results of the election in Allegheny County: Ross, 1,249, and Snyder, 2,118. A week later the *Gazette* reported, with a sarcastic twist at the end: "Simon Snyder is elected governor of Pennsylvania. His majority far exceeds what his most sanguine friends calculated on. Almost in all the counties of the state, the Democratic ticket for Congress, Assembly &c. has succeeded. The Legislature will be more Democratic this year than it has been for a number of years past. What a blessed *prospect!*"

Scull's attitude about the 1808 campaign represented his overall unhappiness about the rise of the Democratic-Republican Party. As the years went by, Scull could no longer blame the rise of anti-Federalism on Brackenridge, who had moved to Carlisle, nor on John Israel, as the editor of the *Tree of Liberty* had died of blood poisoning on October 7, 1806. Federalism was out of step with the changing West, and John Scull and his friends represented a view of politics that was destined to undergo a temporary eclipse.

When the War of 1812 commenced, Scull promoted an antiwar policy to which the *Gazette* would hold until the Civil War. Several years earlier, Scull had opposed the Jefferson administration's imposition of the Embargo Act, which forbade U.S. ships to carry goods to other nations. The 1807 embargo was devised in response to seizures of American ships by British blockaders of Napoleon's Continent and by the French counterblockade. In New England and the Mid-Atlantic states, this measure caused exports to pile up in the warehouse, and many men to lose their jobs. These areas included Federalist strongholds, and there was soon talk of secession from the Union. Because the British navy had more control of the seas, Americans saw England as the greater offender, and these hostilities eventually led to the War of 1812.

As usual, the news that the war had commenced was reported in a roundabout way in the June 25, 1812, issue, using the "extract of a letter to a gentleman in this town, dated Washington City, June 18, 1812." The *Gazette* quoted: "I embrace the first opportunity to inform you that WAR has this day been declared, and the injunction of secrecy taken

Declaration·of
War, a *Pittsburgh
Gazette* broadside,
June 25, 1812

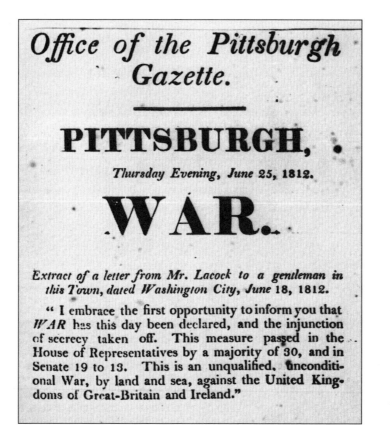

*Office of the Pittsburgh
Gazette.*

———

PITTSBURGH,

Thursday Evening, June 25, 1812.

WAR.

*Extract of a letter from Mr. Lacock to a gentleman in
this Town, dated Washington City, June 18, 1812.*

" I embrace the first opportunity to inform you that
WAR has this day been declared, and the injunction
of secrecy taken off. This measure passed in the
House of Representatives by a majority of 30, and in
Senate 19 to 13. This is an unqualified, unconditional War, by land and sea, against the United Kingdoms of Great-Britain and Ireland."

off. . . . This is an unqualified unconditional WAR, by land and sea, against the United Kingdoms of Great Britain and Ireland." For the first time, the *Gazette* began publishing extra editions.

Early in the war, Scull urged a political solution. He energetically supported a group of war-weary Pittsburghers who met to form a peace ticket for the 1812 congressional election. Perhaps because of the *Gazette*'s backing, the peace ticket carried Allegheny County by a majority of nearly two hundred votes. Butler County, however, the other part of the congressional district, amassed enough votes to return the incumbent, Adamson Tannehill, to Congress.

On the subject of presidential politics, Scull's reverence for the Founding Fathers did not stop him from railing against James Madison. On October 9, 1812, he thundered, "Instead of fortifying the country, and ordering it impregnable to attack, the fortresses on the frontier have been suffered to moulder into ruin: New Orleans open to the first invaders—Chicago, Michilimachinac, Detroit, Niagara, neglected, left destitute of military garrisons, supplies, and repairs, so as to afford neither protection nor resistance in the hour of distress." Scull's point was that Jefferson, in his abhorrence of having a standing army, had let the defense sector slide, despite inner-circle concerns on the part of such as Secretary of the Treasury Gallatin. Madison, a parliamentary genius, had been much less successful as a chief executive. The truth was that Scull had little stomach for war activities, anyway.

Scull's antipathy to the war, including his anti-French sentiments, even extended to an announcement about his introduction of a new typeface on January 29, 1813. He described it as "A new coat, not a turncoat trimmed at the treasury—not a fancy coat finished with French lining—but an honest American coat, warp and woof, durable in its texture, and creditable to the owner."

The *Gazette* achieved its first "scoop" when it published the earliest news of Oliver Perry's September 10, 1813, victory on Lake Erie. When Scull learned that Perry was a Federalist, his joy overflowed from the pages of the October 8 issue: "We state this with the greater pleasure, as all the disgrace and defeats which our armies have met with, were solely owing to the treachery, cowardice, or incapacity of their Democratic commanders."

Finally came the word of Andrew Jackson's January 8, 1815, victory at New Orleans, about which the *Gazette* printed an extra on February 6. For several weeks, the paper had grumbled that neither the western mails nor the *National Intelligencer* of Washington, D.C., had brought tidings of what had happened at that Mississippi River port. On February 26 the *Gazette* published the full terms of the Treaty of Ghent, which actually had ended the war on December 24, 1814, although word had not reached the combatants in time to forestall the battle at Chalmette, just south of New Orleans. Gallatin, Scull's friend-then-adversary, had been one of the commissioners who fashioned the peace treaty. Scull might have been sobered about the victory had he realized it was to launch Jackson's political career. Jackson's efforts to build the new Democratic Party and his subsequent election in 1828 marked the end of the Federalists, and prompted their metamorphosis into the Whig Party.

In 1815, however, Scull and the *Gazette* joined in the general exuberance over a military victory—finally—and the end of the war. Pittsburghers celebrated with a public illumination on February 28 and general merriment. Later in the year, the *Gazette* published the news of the Battle of Waterloo and the banishment of Bonaparte to St. Helena in the South Pacific. However, Scull was worried about rumors that Napoleon might be coming to America. In the August 26, 1815, issue, he declared: "We most fervently pray that our soil may never be polluted by the landing on it of this demon of discord, this fiend in human shape."[4]

The War of 1812 caused massive economic growth in Pittsburgh; by 1817, the city was home to 259 factories employing 1,637 men. By 1820, the federal census set Pittsburgh's population at 7,248, a 53 percent gain over 1810. As the frontier moved away from Pittsburgh, Scull's *Gazette* continuously stressed the city's potential as the workshop for the "New West" and the necessity for an active newspaper toward that end. Thus, from the earliest years the *Gazette* was sympathetic to and cooperative with the business community. New service-oriented businesses were founded to serve the expanding population, such as the Bank of Pennsylvania branch that was established on Pittsburgh's Second Avenue.

Historian Catherine Reiser explained that Pittsburgh's principal ambition was "to secure an economic development which would relieve her binding dependence upon eastern manufacturys."[5] Instead of being just a commercial center and outfitting outlet using eastern goods, Pittsburgh sought to become a producer itself. Multiple Pittsburgh-area factories arose, building upon the region's natural abundance of wood, coal, and, for a time, price-competitive iron ore. These resources gave Pittsburgh dominance in the production of iron (and later, steel) well into the twentieth century. The area's wealth of coal afforded cheap fuel for the production of steam power, the benefits of which had been discovered in 1769 by Englishman James Watts. Among the first applications of steam power was a steam engine-powered flourmill on the Monongahela River. Before long, low-pressure engines themselves were being manufactured in Pittsburgh, and Fulton engines for steamboats were not far behind. In its July 10, 1812, issue, the *Gazette* carried advertisements such as this combative one from George Evans: "The public are hereby informed that the subscriber is ready to contract for the supply of STEAM ENGINES on Oliver Evans's principles. He will warrant and uphold them to be far superior to those on the principles of Bolton and Warr." Along with manufacturing, service industries also grew as Pittsburgh developed.

With economic expansion came cultural growth. In 1795, just eight years into its institutional life, the Pittsburgh Academy (later the University of Pittsburgh) had this expansive curriculum: "English Grammar; Writing, Arithmetic, and Book-keeping; the Latin, Greek, and French Languages; Rhetoric, and the Belles Lettres; Geography, and the most useful parts of the Mathematics; to which will be added an Introduction to Natural, Civil and Ecclesiastical History, Astronomy, Natural Philosophy, Logic, Moral Philosophy, and Chronology."[6] From time to time the *Gazette* printed notices of meetings of the academy's board of trustees. Smaller schools of reading, writing, music, and art also flourished. Zadok Cramer, who arrived in Pittsburgh in 1800, established a bookstore called "Sign of the Franklin Head." Before long, Cramer placed an advertisement in the *Gazette* signaling an important new contribution to the life of Pittsburgh: a circulating library.

Theater and music productions were also on the rise in Pittsburgh. A group called the Apollonian Society gave concerts, and students at the Pittsburgh Academy staged performances of *Cato* and *The Anatomist* in local taverns. In 1803, a private theatrical company used the courthouse to present several plays, including *Trick Upon Trick, or, the Vintner in the Suds.* Shortly thereafter, local authorities, perhaps prompted by the Pittsburgh Moral Society, imposed a ten-dollar license fee upon theatrical performances. By 1808, the fee seems to have been rescinded, and two new recreational drama groups were formed.

While some leisure activities were the province of particular societal classes, others, like horse racing, spanned all boundaries. Races were held twice each year at the county fairgrounds, northeast of Pittsburgh. As the community spread eastward, the races were moved to McKeesport. This move drew the applause of some letter-writers to the *Gazette,* who had complained that the races attracted the worst characters from all quarters and corrupted Pittsburgh's young people. The October 10, 1808, issue carried a notice of another event that crossed all social lines: "Elephant may be seen in the Borough of Pittsburgh from Wednesday the 12th to Saturday the 15th instant. A living elephant. Admittance 15 cents, children 12½ cents." Accompanying the notice was an engraving of the beast.

Long before, Scull had begun using block-print illustrations to help his advertisers. For example, he used a drawing of a horse, along with a caption such as "The Famous Horse," to draw attention to breeding stallions. This advertising feature was used to announce, on June 28,

1794, that "Young Shakespear [*sic*] will cover mares this season" in Peters Creek. Similarly, drawings of farm tools appeared for an advertisement in the same issue, which read: "Scythe and sickle maker. William Dunning, fronting the Diamond." The *Gazette* also printed a variety of public notices, presumably without cost, judging by a charge policy announced much later, in 1830. A typical notice of February 28, 1795, announced a meeting of the Pittsburgh Mechanical Society "at the usual place," and another noting a session of the trustees of the Pittsburgh Academy "at Mr. Morrow's."

As the city developed, Scull continually improved the format of the *Gazette* to appeal to a more sophisticated readership. By the early 1790s, Scull had enlarged the size of the four-page *Gazette*, and had picked up the four-column format common to newspapers east of the Alleghenies. By 1793, Scull had removed the paper's logo—a rifle-wielding settler and a Native American separated by a book—presumably to allow more front-page space for advertisements. In 1799, Scull again increased the size of the *Gazette*, gothic head and all, making it larger than any other paper in the western United States. In 1811, the *Gazette* adopted a super-royal sheet—33 x 38 inches. At 13¼ x 18¾ inches, the *Gazette*'s page size ranked with those of Philadelphia's newspapers.

As the years went by, Scull had to face more and more new rivals, and his bitterness increased. In 1803, before the death of John Israel, Scull had sued the rival publisher, claiming that articles in the *Tree of Liberty* were too violent. Scull won that quarrel, but he would have a more difficult time with his new and sturdier competitors. The *Commonwealth*, first published by Ephraim Pentland on August 24, 1805,[7] was an even more radical Democratic political paper than the *Tree of Liberty*. Under the motto "Virtue, Liberty, and Independence," Pentland sought to maintain "a press in the western part of Pennsylvania that should speak the people's will . . . support their supreme authority . . . and counteract the base, insidious endeavours of their unprincipled opponents."

On January 10, 1810, Pentland was succeeded as editor by Benjamin Brown, who formerly had been connected with the *Reporter* of Washington, Pennsylvania. In that day's issue, Brown outlined his political creed: "Be it known that I am a democratic republican; one of that unfashionable class, which by the *lords* of the land, are despised for their adherence to the cause of the 'rabble.' I know not, nor will I ever acknowledge, any other government under Heaven than that of the people. I will oppose, with all my might every system which tends to undermine their supremacy; and I will, if in my power, 'lash the rascals' who dare traduce them." Although Brown remained with the paper only four years, the *Commonwealth* continued until 1818, when it was succeeded by the *Statesman*. The *Gazette* took frequent potshots at the *Commonwealth*, such as this comment in the June 29, 1816, issue: "We are sometimes amused by that facility of declamation, with which the thorough-going editor of the *Commonwealth* rails thro' his columns."[8]

In 1816, on the thirtieth anniversary of the founding of the *Gazette,* Scull stepped down as editor in favor of his second son, John Irwin Scull. The senior Scull was only fifty-one years old; his retirement may have been prompted by the steady decline, both locally and nationally, of his beloved Federalist Party. The Democrats had co-opted many features of Federalist policies, and however flattering that might have been to Federalists, the fact remained that the Democrats held the power. As the seemingly inevitable victory of James Monroe in the upcoming presidential election approached, on March 30, 1816, Scull mourned, "To what a pitiable pass has democracy come!"

A tribute to the outgoing editor, written by his son, appeared in the August 9, 1816, issue.

The *Pittsburgh Gazette* under the original proprietor, Mr. John Scull, was the first establishment of the kind, west of the mountains. On its first appearance, it was viewed as a meteor of the moment, whose existence would terminate with the second or third number; and the idea of deriving a subsistence from its publication, was classed among the chimeras of a too sanguine temper. Our country was then a "howling wilderness," and the Ohio, whose fair bosom is now covered with the "white sails of commerce," was then disturbed only by the yell of the savage, who lay ambushed on its bank, or glided o'er its surface, in his solitary canoe. But these obstacles, though disheartening, were not sufficient to destroy the enterprise of the Editor. He had turned his back on the civilization and comforts of his native place; he had deliberately subjected himself to the inconveniences of emigration, and his was not the ardour to be damped at the outset . . . . He became a citizen of Pittsburgh, when it was little more than an Indian village; his interests grew with its growth; he saw it rise into a manufacturing town; he has heard it emphatically called the "Birmingham of America"; and, finally, he has the triumphant satisfaction, of beholding in his own days, the village of the desert, changed into the city of the west. He has succeeded even beyond his expectations; he has run his moderate, unostentatious course. The patronage he has received, was sufficient for his desires; his editorial life here ends; with feelings acutely sensible of the favors he has received, he now relinquishes to his son and successor the *Pittsburgh Gazette,* unstained by corruption, and free from venality, but ever firm, he trusts, in supporting our palladium, the freedom of the Press.

Scull retired to a rural area in Westmoreland County, not far from Irwin. He later served as the president of the Farmers' and Mechanics' Bank. Upon his death on February 8, 1828, he bequeathed $13,600—a tidy sum for that period—to his wife, Mary Scull.

The new editor had attended Princeton University, returning to Pittsburgh to enter law. During the War of 1812, John Irwin Scull stayed at home, perhaps swayed by his father's prejudice against the war. Without a military record and with indifferent success in the legal profession, John was happy to take over active control of the weekly *Gazette.* He moved the establishment to a point opposite the post office on Front Street, and changed it to a semi-weekly to be published on Tuesdays and Fridays. The subscription rate was set at $3.00 per year in advance or $3.50 "on time."

In the same August 9 issue in which he bade farewell to his father, John Irwin Scull expressed his vision for the *Gazette.*

The prospectus of village journals, has heretofore been as little attractive, as a "tale thrice told," or as the periodical ebullitions of the fourth of July. A country Editor, when sitting down to announce his intention, and to explain his principles, commonly does it more for the sake of form, and of complying with established custom, than from the anticipation of being generally read, or from the still more delusive hope of increasing, by these means, the list of patrons. Provincial gazettes have been destined to be viewed as village appendages, too much in the light of an alehouse, or blacksmith's shop; as these are necessary for the temporary accommodation of individuals, so are *those* considered merely as convenient vehicles, for announcing to the world, the important intelligence of stray cattle, runaway apprentices, and cheap stores. But the present Editor feels happy, that at the moment he enters on his duties, a new era is commencing in the western country. His predecessor began his publication before science had even dawned, o'er the "wild," and before politics were thought of as a system; he, on the contrary, commences his career, at the instant Pittsburgh takes her place among the Cities of the Union.

John Irwin Scull's high hopes, however, would not be fulfilled. After the war, half of the five hundred newspapers being printed in the United States were struggling to meet their expenses. The *Gazette* had a good-sized staff, and its circulation was apparently insufficient to cover the high overhead expense. So the *Gazette* was forced to give an increasing prominence to advertising material.[9] On January 30, 1818, Scull apologized for the fact that the front page had become a solid bank of advertisements: "Our advertising custom, though necessary for our support is already too great for our limits: and is daily encroaching upon that portion of our paper which we would wish to devote to useful and interesting matter."

Within two years, Scull announced the sale of a half interest in the paper to Morgan Neville, grandson of General John Neville and son of Colonel Presley Neville. Soon it was evident that Neville had assumed editorial control. In 1819 Scull was elected to the office of Allegheny County sheriff; subsequently, a large share of legal advertising appeared in the *Gazette*.

Early in 1820, the firm of John I. Scull and Morgan Neville was dissolved. The debts had grown to four thousand dollars during the twenty-one months since Neville had joined the staff. Longtime citizens wondered whether the *Gazette* could continue without one of the Sculls in control or if the paper was doomed.

Chapter 4

An Editor for a Contentious Era

Bоth names of the man who became editor of the *Gazette* in 1829 spoke volumes to Pittsburghers, particularly those conscious of the town's history. Neville Craig was the son of Major Isaac Craig, the deputy quartermaster at Fort Pitt (the very same man who had once loaned cartridge paper to John Scull). Isaac had married into the wealthy and influential Neville family. Neville Craig had served in the military as a young man and came to his new position at the newspaper with a certain amount of prestige. Yet Neville Craig's cousin, Morgan Neville, had already proved that a famous name did not necessarily lead to journalistic success. When the partnership of John Irwin Scull and Morgan Neville dissolved in 1820, the printing firm of Eichbaum and Johnston purchased the newspaper and hired Morgan Neville as editor. One result was that the paper became known as the *Pittsburgh Gazette and Manufacturing and Mercantile Advertiser.* Before long, Neville "stepped out with seeming reluctance."[1] In 1824, he moved to Cincinnati, where he founded the short-lived *Commercial Register,* the first daily published west of Philadelphia. In the summer of 1822, Eichbaum and Johnston turned over editorial direction of the newspaper to Benjamin Evans, a lawyer. By October, Evans was gone, too, as the journal's fortunes declined. It looked as if the *Gazette and Manufacturing and*

Mercantile Advertiser was to vanish along with so many other Pittsburgh periodicals of different eras. Eichbaum and Johnston lamented the fact that in the two years they had owned it, the paper had brought in scarcely enough to pay the cost of labor and materials. Because this low point in readership came in a decade when Pittsburgh's population was booming—12,565 by 1830—it is difficult to assess the blame. Perhaps it was due to faulty leadership or a surplus of publications: the number of American newspapers burgeoned from two hundred in 1801 to twelve hundred in 1835.

The floundering continued as the paper changed hands once again. David MacLean of Westmoreland County, who had served as an apprentice to John Scull in 1805, bought the *Gazette* in 1822. After his apprenticeship with Scull, MacLean had worked for, and then owned, the *Greensburg Gazette*, a Federalist organ. At the *Pittsburgh Gazette*, MacLean and his brother Matthew practiced what later would be called "counting-house journalism," operating on the basis that providing twenty columns of advertisements and a minimum amount of news was sufficient. On the plus side, the brothers returned the paper to its original title and expanded the journal to imperial size—a width of six columns. In September 1828, they added a semi-weekly edition at a subscription rate of four dollars per year to supplement the weekly.

Given the MacLeans' proclivity for revenue over substance, it is not surprising that they were apathetic toward domestic politics. Although the *Gazette* claimed to be the only Federalist paper left in the district, the editors did not express dismay in 1824 when Pittsburgh residents cast 1,385 votes for Democrat Andrew Jackson and only 18 for John Quincy Adams. The election was deadlocked nationally, however, and Adams emerged victorious from the House of Representatives selection process. Democrats charged that this result was obtained by some horse-trading of votes involving Henry Clay. They drummed upon this issue for the next four years, until Jackson won a resounding victory in the 1828 elections. The MacLeans scored one of the important journalistic scoops of that period by printing President Jackson's inaugural message. At 12:35 p.m. on March 8, 1829, express riders left Washington with the message, reaching Pittsburgh just twenty-four hours later. Within a few hours, the speech was in type, ready for the next *Gazette* edition.

The usually conservative *Gazette* expressed sympathies for the efforts of revolutionaries abroad, such as Simón Bolívar and José de San Martín, struggling for independence in South America, and Greek patriots seeking to overthrow Turkish control. In 1827, the newspaper was involved in raising nearly two thousand dollars for Greek relief.

In 1829, however, a very different editor took charge of the *Gazette's* helm. Neville Craig's past included some encounters with the law and several nearly fatal encounters. As a child during the Whiskey Rebellion, he had thrown a cannonball from the window of his home into a group of rebels on the day they marched into Pittsburgh. Surprised and provoked, one member of the group had whirled around and pointed his gun at Craig. Fortunately, an officer struck the gun with his sword, saving the boy's life. At seventeen, Craig was sent to Princeton, but his tenure there suddenly ended when he sided with fellow students in a fight against police and wounded one of the officers with a sword cane. He was arrested and held for a trial, which his father attended. Although clearly guilty, the memory of his father's gallantry at the Battle of Princeton in 1777 influenced the court and resulted in acquittal. Expelled, Craig stopped at Philadelphia on his way home and got into an argument with an old schoolmate, which led to a duel. Fortunately, neither was harmed, and they parted friends. Much later, after Craig had been appointed deputy attorney general for Allegheny County, he got into a legal dispute with another practicing attorney, John Henry Hopkins. The squabble led to heated words, name calling, and finally a scuffle right in the courtroom. Not surprisingly, this behavior led to Craig's arrest and a heavy fine.

Why a man with such a quick temper turned to journalism is not clear. Perhaps it was because his previous career ventures had not proved successful. He had been admitted to the bar in 1810 after reading law with Alexander Addison, the jurist of Whiskey Rebellion fame. Craig married Jane Fulton, daughter of merchant Henry Fulton, but his meager income with the law firm of Walter Forward and Henry M. Watt prompted him to try storekeeping in Ohio. Although Craig returned to Pittsburgh to accept a commission with the Pittsburgh Blues during the War of 1812, the entreaties of his aging father kept him from marching away with them. Upon returning to private law practice, he had the MacLean brothers as clients. This acquaintance led Craig to become a contributing writer for the *Gazette* and, later, its owner.

Craig quickly made a mark on the newspaper. In the left-hand col-

Neville B. Craig. In addition to being the editor of the *Gazette* from 1829–1841, Craig wrote the first history of Pittsburgh, published in 1851.
(Courtesy Carnegie Library of Pittsburgh)

umn of the third page, often under the heading, "Various Matters," he began to run a string of assorted short articles into which, on occasion, he would insert editorial opinions. For instance, in the December 22, 1829, issue, this item appeared concerning the recent congressional election: "In choosing Mr. Denny, we believe, the yeomanry of this district have selected a gentleman who is superior to Mr. Stevenson. . . . We have the utmost confidence that the interests of this district may be safely confided in Mr. Denny." Four days later, the editor commended Governor George Wolf on his inaugural address: "From a hasty perusal, we have resolved that the address is quite a credible and orthodox production." On March 18, 1831, the column contained a funny anecdote: "To a pert young man who inquired, 'What is the price of this cousin of yours?' (pointing to a little pig). 'One dollar,' replied the woman, 'but here is a twin brother of yours (taking up a goose) that you may have for half the money.'"

Craig created a new precedent for the *Gazette* by occasionally attaching his name to an editorial. Beginning on March 31, 1838, he began printing the editorials in larger type than the rest of the paper as a way of drawing attention to them. He also departed from tradition in one way that many an editorial writer since has wished he could enjoy: on the morning of August 6, 1839, Craig wrote, "We do not feel much disposed to write an editorial this morning, and having nothing to say, we have deliberately concluded to say nothing."

Craig ordered a new imperial-size, one-pull press from Philadelphia to replace the old Ramage machine that had printed the newspaper's first issues. The public was very excited about the arrival of the new press. Meanwhile, with little fanfare, a weekly called the *Pittsburgh Times* was launched on January 12, 1831. Devoted to the anti-Masonry cause arising in American politics, the *Times* shared the *Gazette's* offices. In 1832, yet another weekly entered the Pittsburgh arena. The *Advocate* had editorial policies roughly similar to those of the *Gazette*.

On March 15, 1831, perhaps as a reaction to the competition, Craig announced that he was "converting the *Pittsburgh Gazette* into a Daily Paper." However, it took many months of stop-and-go preparation before the new daily was launched on July 30, 1833, as an afternoon paper, priced at six dollars a year, "strictly in advance." In 1837, Craig added a Washington, D.C., correspondent, "Junius," to send along gossip in the form of random letters. The *Gazette's* news columns otherwise continued to rely extensively on selections from such eastern journals as *Poulson's Daily Advertiser* and the *United States Gazette* of Philadelphia, the *Boston Atlas,* and the *National Intelligencer* from the nation's capital. Craig began to shape the paper in the image of what he idealized it to be: a schoolmaster "bound to give publicity only to those matters which intend to inform the mind, or improve the heart."[2] He adopted some of the MacLeans' policies, such as avoiding sensational crime stories and printing advertisements for various lotteries accompanied by engravings of a wagon hitched to dancing horses and overflowing with coins. Despite the appearance of these advertisements in the *Gazette,* when the state legislature abolished lotteries in 1833, Craig wrote an editorial strongly endorsing the decision.

Craig modified some of the *Gazette's* fiscal policies, perhaps made

Front page of the first daily
edition, July 30, 1833

more confident by the increased volume of advertisements in the early
1830s. At a meeting of Pittsburgh's newspaper publishers in May 1836 it
was decided that everything except obituaries and political notices
would thereafter require payment. No longer would material concerning railroads, canals, societies, fire companies, or weddings be printed
free of charge.

Advertisements were not only subject to fees, but also to Craig's
approval. Unfortunately for the arts, Craig's list of prohibited subjects

extended to coverage of the theater, which he considered a school of vice. When the August 11, 1834, issue of the *Gazette* advertised a panorama of the battle of Waterloo, the sponsors thought it wise to add: "The public are most respectfully informed that the above is nothing of a theatrical exhibition, so that no religious scruples need prevent any from visiting it." A *Gazette* employee who enjoyed going to the Drury Theater told later of being summoned to Craig's office and handed a letter to give to his mother. When the mission had been performed, the employee learned that the editor had written an ultimatum—either give up the theater or depart from the paper. As late as 1841, Craig editorialized: "The fact is, there is not enough of a drama loving population in this city to support a respectable theatre, and we are glad of it. We think it speaks well for the good taste and morality of our inhabitants."[3]

On other matters, however, Craig was determined to be positive. For example, he argued that air pollution—already a serious problem by the 1830s—was a *good* thing. On April 13, 1830, Craig wrote: "Many persons of our city, ourselves among them, have long entertained the opinion, that the smoke of our stone-coal contributes to the health of our population. In an article in another column of our paper today, upon 'The former Unhealthfulness of London,' it is asserted that the present healthfulness of that city is, in part, owing to the general introduction of stone-coal as fuel. If in addition to economy, comfort, and safety, our coal also contributes to health, we should cheerfully submit to the inconvenience which is created by the coal and dust." He showed a similar disregard for the obvious in his reaction to one of the periodic cholera epidemics that struck cities with primitive sanitary arrangements. A poorly operating water system had been installed in 1828, drawing water from the Allegheny River to a reservoir at Fifth and Grant. In August 1834, the *Gazette* reported forty-four deaths from cholera in the previous ten weeks. Nevertheless, it proceeded to attribute the good health of the citizens to "our coal smoke, our air, and excellent hydrant water." This attitude was in keeping with a civic booster approach in cities that vigorously denied epidemics, a practice that the Norwegian playwright Henrik Ibsen much later was to pillory devastatingly in his 1882 play, *An Enemy of the People*. More than half a century later, this posture would delay the establishment of a purification plant for the city's water supply.

Even in a time when newspaper writers hurled insults at each other of a nature astonishing to today's presumably shockproof readers, Craig was a master of invective. Epithets like "vile and speckled reptile" and "scalded hound" were typical of the era in which Craig traded attacks with such local Democratic papers as the *Allegheny Democrat,* the *American Manufacturer,* the *Mercury,* and the *Pittsburgher.* Like the *Gazette*'s founder, Craig could not resist an opportunity to remind the Democrats of the "infidel" Thomas Paine. More than three decades after the height of Paine's activities, on December 25, 1829, Craig reprinted excerpts from an article in *Blackwood's,* an English magazine: "Paine had fallen into disrepute, and was shunned by the more respectable of his friends on account of his drunken habits." Well before the 1832 presidential election, on October 28, 1831, Craig made his views plain: "We think the election of General Jackson has been seriously injurious to the character of our country. . . . We think that the reelection of General Jackson would be an event greatly to be deplored."

Angered at the *Mercury*'s sudden attachment to U.S. Senator William Wilkins after his desertion of the cause of the United States Bank, Craig reminded readers on January 25, 1834, that the *Mercury* was "the selected sewer through which all kinds of filth was poured upon the devoted head of 'our present distinguished Senator.'. . . Every charge that could be raked up from the filthiest kennels, were [*sic*] freely, nay cheerfully, belched forth from the office of the *Pittsburgh Mercury.*" Some months later, on June 20, the *Mercury* borrowed a reference from the new and widely popular works of Charles Dickens to frame the following barrage at Craig: "If the abuse of the ruffianly editor of the *Gazette* was any disgrace, who would have a character left? He attacks every one who crosses his path. . . . He has a malignant ferocity, a sanguinary appetite, such as 'Boz' has delineated in Bill Sikes's dog." Craig used classical terms in a similarly ironic fashion, as he did, for instance, in an article of May 27, 1836, to chide the *Advocate* for its withdrawal from the struggle against President Jackson. "What has befallen that war?" Craig wrote. "Is it carried on so quietly no person can hear it? . . . Or have our neighbors—those modern Hannibals, who have sworn an interminable war against the old *Roman,* concluded an inglorious peace with their enemy? . . . We will call again—in the meantime we leave our card."

Curiously, no action for libel was brought against the *Gazette* while Craig was the editor. On the other hand, Craig filed two libel suits of his own. In one case, in 1834, he compelled the editors of the *Advocate* to retract what he considered charges of treason against him. In the other instance, in 1839 he forced the *Manufacturer* to write a letter of apology and pay the legal costs.

The "Era of Good Feeling," which had peaked during the Monroe's administration (1817–1823), faded into bitter factions during Andrew Jackson's rise to power, and the *Gazette* explored different ways to fight "Old Hickory" and the Democratic Party he led. In this contentious era, however, Craig acted admirably toward a rival newspaper, the *Statesman*. Late one night, loud knocking at the door awakened John B. Butler, the *Statesman*'s editor. When Butler answered, he was quite surprised to see Neville Craig. Having overheard rumors that the Butler home was to be burned to the ground that night, Craig had arrived before the troublemakers to warn his adversary.

In this era, too, Craig's political activities followed a slightly new direction. The anti-Jackson movement with which Craig had been previously connected had become, essentially, an embarrassing fringe group. Hoping to oppose Jackson's work in a more mainstream way, Craig joined in the efforts to form a new Whig Party out of the remnants of the onetime Federalist Party. Craig and his allies felt especially provoked by Jackson's attempts to eradicate the United States Bank. When Jackson removed government deposits, Craig, a director of the Bank of Pittsburgh, was especially incensed. Craig and his friends prepared a great public demonstration of protest, prepared resolutions, and forwarded copies to Congress. A Pittsburgh delegation went to Washington to petition for the return of the deposits. Jackson would have none of it, loosing a tirade against the national bank: "I will not bow down to the Golden Calf; the Spanish Inquisition could never make me bow down to the monster."[4]

While Craig had his doubts about starting a new party, he consented to serve as vice president of a May 1834 jubilee celebration of the newly convened Whigs of Pittsburgh to mark some recent victories in New York State. A few days later he journeyed to Harrisburg for the first state convention of the Whigs and allowed himself to be named its secretary.

Craig was much more cautious in revealing his thoughts on the burgeoning question of race in American politics. In 1837 and 1838, the issue of color rose sharply in Pennsylvania politics because a constitutional convention was being held to update the 1790 Constitution. In that document, the wording of Article III gave the right of suffrage to "every freeman of the age of twenty-one years, having resided in the state two years . . . and within the time paid a state or county tax." The 1838 convention revised the wording to read: "In elections by the citizens, every white freeman of the age of twenty-one years . . . " This changed wording extended the reasoning of a July 1837 Pennsylvania Supreme Court opinion, *William Fogg v. Hiram Hobbes,* which found that nominally free blacks could not be considered freemen and were therefore already disenfranchised under the existing state constitution. On February 26, 1838, just four days after the convention in Harrisburg completed its work, the *Gazette* carried a "Message from Convention Leaders" that explained the proposed constitutional revision. Craig did not comment on this constitutional matter or, in fact, any other. Yet he chose, the following week, to reprint the entire Pennsylvania Supreme Court decision on disenfranchisement. On the eve of the October 1838 election, the *Gazette* carried an article opposing the constitutional revisions, which observed that the Supreme Court's decision in *William Fogg v. Hiram Hobbes* had already settled the question of black suffrage and that the proposed revision would not actually alter the constitution. As it turned out, the constitutional alterations were approved by a narrow margin of state voters—113,971 for, 112,759 against. Significantly, however, voters of Allegheny County opposed the revisions—4,460 for, 5,049 against.

Race-related issues continued to make news. On October 30, 1838, the *Gazette* printed an article with the headline: "A report from Cincinnati. The anti-slavery cause." It noted that two synods of the Presbyterian Church, meeting in that Ohio city, had "made strong anti-slavery declarations—twelve months ago, the same assembly shunned any expression of opinion. The *Gazette* heralds that and other [aspects] of recent transaction, in terms of its own selection." Like many of his contemporaries, Craig felt the solution to the slavery question was to ship blacks back to Africa. In 1836, Craig had personally pledged one hundred dollars a year to help the cause of colonizing Liberia with freed slaves. The next year he made his position even clearer by refusing to reprint from the *Cincinnati Whig* an advertisement for a slave who had escaped from a Tennessee master. That decision was quite in contrast

Typical advertisements in June 1834 included ads offering rewards for the capture of runaway slaves.

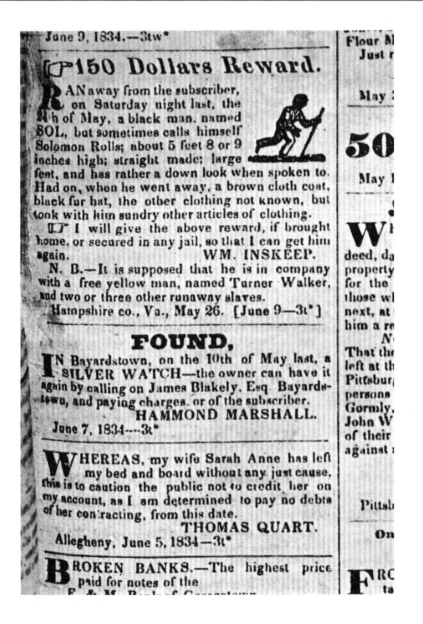

June 9, 1834.—3tw*

☞150 Dollars Reward.

RANaway from the subscriber, on Saturday night last, the 24th of May, a black man, named SOL, but sometimes calls himself Solomon Rolls; about 5 feet 8 or 9 inches high; straight made; large feet, and has rather a down look when spoken to. Had on, when he went away, a brown cloth coat, black fur hat, the other clothing not known, but took with him sundry other articles of clothing.

☞ I will give the above reward, if brought home, or secured in any jail, so that I can get him again.   WM. INSKEEP.

N. B.—It is supposed that he is in company with a free yellow man, named Turner Walker, and two or three other runaway slaves.

Hampshire co., Va., May 26. [June 9—3t*]

FOUND,

IN Bayardstown, on the 10th of May last, a SILVER WATCH—the owner can have it again by calling on James Blakely, Esq. Bayardstown, and paying charges, or of the subscriber.
HAMMOND MARSHALL.
June 7, 1834----3t*

WHEREAS, my wife Sarah Anne has left my bed and board without any just cause, this is to caution the public not to credit her on my account, as I am determined to pay no debts of her contracting, from this date.
THOMAS QUART.
Allegheny, June 5, 1834—3t*

BROKEN BANKS.—The highest price paid for notes of the

with the case only sixteen years earlier when John Irwin, the father-in-law of John Scull, had advertised in the *Gazette* for the return of his own runaway slave.

While the nation faced turbulent times, Pittsburgh was also changing. The municipal charter of Pittsburgh, which had been designated a city in 1816 by the state legislature, was changed in 1833 to allow the people to elect the mayor. Each of five wards chose eight councilmen.

In the economic sphere, the city benefited from the completion in 1834 of the Pennsylvania Canal from Philadelphia. Earlier, on April 13, 1830, the *Gazette* had proudly announced, "The western division of the Pennsylvania Canal is now open for navigation." By the mid-1830s, however, waterways were already taking a backseat to the advent of steam railroads. In some cases the two technologies were combined; to travel between Philadelphia and Pittsburgh, for example, one would start out riding the Columbia Railroad from Philadelphia to the Susquehanna River, and then continue the journey via canal to Hollidaysburg. At that point, one would pick up the Portage Railroad in order to traverse the Allegheny Mountains, noting that sections of canal boats were also being transported using inclined planes. From Johnstown, a canal extended to Allegheny City (now Pittsburgh's North Side) and then an aqueduct spanned the Allegheny River, ending in Pittsburgh.

Craig showed a great deal of interest in the workings of the new transportation systems. In 1831, he printed a map, later called "Craig's Spider," in which he delineated his vision of a great system of roads, canals, and railways radiating outward from Pittsburgh. Eight years later, Craig used the *Gazette* to suggest the viability of a railroad from Pittsburgh to New Orleans, although he tried to preempt ridicule by printing an apology for his outlandishness alongside the article. Not long after, it became apparent that the Pennsylvania Canal would never be profitable, and that most of the twenty-five million dollars that had financed the canal's construction had vanished due to graft. The United States Bank of Pennsylvania, the reluctant backer of the canal project, went bankrupt in 1841. Worse yet, years went by in which no buyer could be convinced to take on the Pennsylvania Canal and the equally foundering Portage Railroad. The burgeoning Pennsylvania Railroad finally purchased both systems in 1857 at a cost for $7.5 million, in order to remove the lingering weak rivalry that the Portage Railroad presented.

As he was picturing Pittsburgh's future, Craig was also making some decisions about his own. He had experienced enough of being both the publisher and the editor of the *Gazette*. On June 25, 1840, he sold ownership to bookseller Alexander Ingram Jr., but remained the editor. On New Year's Day, 1841, another printer, David N. White, bought the paper and changed the time of issue from afternoon to morning, but retained Craig. Only six months later, on July 29, 1841, the fifty-fifth anniversary of the founding of the *Gazette,* Craig announced his resigna-tion. His enemies were happy to project the image of a wounded Craig leaving under duress. From William H. Smith, editor of the newly com-bined *Mercury* and *Democrat,* came the maliciously joyous observation that Craig "retreated snarling and snapping, more like a half-starved wolf when scared and driven from his prey than a vanquished combat-ant retiring from an honorable and well-fought field."[5] Many others, however, praised Craig in tributes to his honesty and ability. At the time of Craig's retirement, the *Gazette* clearly led Pittsburgh's numerous newspapers in both circulation and advertising. Under his stewardship, the *Gazette* had become something more than a tradition—it was now a strong force in the community.

Chapter 5

The *Post* Arrives

I N AN EVENT portentous for the already fifty-six-year-old *Gazette,* two editors of rival papers joined forces to found the *Daily Morning Post.* On September 1, 1842, William H. Smith, editor of the weekly *Pittsburgh Mercury and Democrat,* and Thomas Phillips, editor of the *American Manufacturer,* merged their papers and announced plans for publishing a daily. Not only did this development create a strong ideological adversary for the conservative *Gazette,* but also launched an honorable and venerable career for a newspaper with which, eighty-five years later, the *Gazette* would be merged.

On September 10, two thousand copies of the first edition of the *Post* rolled out from the Mansion House at Wood and Fifth Streets. In the inaugural issue, the editors wrote: "We present to our patrons and the public the first number of the *Daily Morning Post.* Of course our arrangements are not perfect and it will take us a few days to get our 'new' harness to work with ease and comfort." They also promised "a paper that will faithfully follow . . . the principles of the democracy—our opponents can depend on having their cause treated of with respect and courtesy." This sentence communicated the political tendencies of the *Post;* in the nineteenth century, the phrase "the democracy" almost always referred to the Democratic Party.

The advent of the *Post* came at a time when Pittsburgh was changing from a commercial city that imported goods from the east and sold them to businesses in the west into a factory town making those products itself. Such a change required labor force adjustments, and Pittsburgh was indeed growing. The city's population in 1840 was 21,515 people, a number that showed an 89 percent increase since the previous census of 1830. By mid-century, Pittsburgh had become solidly established as the Iron City, with thirteen rolling mills and thirty foundries.

The *Post* played a particularly important role in the political sphere of an increasingly industrialized Pittsburgh. The paper's Democratic and pro-labor editorial policies provided an important foil for the *Gazette*'s Whiggish, and later Republican, tendencies. The political tendencies of the papers did not always divide along the same lines that are currently assumed. For instance, the *Gazette* was pro-business and suspicious of labor, particularly during strikes. The *Post* was much more sympathetic to the cause of labor. On the other hand, the *Gazette* and its editors during these crucial years before the Civil War were involved in the anti-slavery movement and in extending federal programs for roads, canals, and railroads under the "American System" championed by Henry Clay. The *Post* favored states' rights, which put them in opposition to anything that would strengthen the federal government. In keeping with the zeal of Southern Democrats to head off federal efforts to abolish slavery, the paper resisted even those elements of the American System that would have aided the economic development of the South and the West.

One event, however, brought about the same response from both newspapers. On April 10, 1845, a blaze that would come to be called the Great Fire swept through a large part of downtown Pittsburgh, and raised doubts about the city's ability to recover. The next morning, Friday, April 11, the *Gazette* ran headlines, "Awful Conflagration! Most Dreadful Calamity! Pittsburgh in Ruins!!" The editor confessed:

Our paper presents rather a rare appearance this morning. The great fire must be our excuse. Our office is also in great confusion, as the fire was raging close by us on two sides, and we had packed up our materials preparatory to moving. Fortunately our office was saved, and we shall get underway again tomorrow. Those of our subscribers who are burnt out, will

please call at the office for the paper, and leave word where they will have it left. . . .

At 6 o'clock p.m. Thursday evening, we sat down to our desk with a sad heart, to record the most fearful calamity which ever befel [*sic*] any city the size of Pittsburgh. While we now write, an awful fire is raging, consuming the fairest portion of our city, and no human being can tell where it will stay its ravages. It has now been burning for six hours, and confusion reigns extreme, and it cannot be expected we shall give any thing like a particular statement of a calamity so extensive and involving such fearful ruins. . . . The fire absolutely appeared to dance from roof to roof and in an incredibly short space of time, the three immense squares, composed mostly of warehouses, bounded by Market and Wood and extending from Third to the river, were a sea of flames. . . . Twenty squares are entirely destroyed. . . . The loss of property must be immense. We shall not attempt to compute it. . . . Among the public buildings destroyed, are the Pittsburgh Bank, the Monongahela House, the Merchant's Hotel, the Mayor's office, and all our Pittsburgh Insurance offices. . . . The *Chronicle* lost its presses. The *Presbyterian Advocate* and *Protestant Unionist* offices are both destroyed. . . . For extent of loss and wide-spread desolation, no fire in this country ever equaled it.

The *Post* on April 11 devoted its front page, as usual, to advertisements, but its second page blazoned: "Tremendous Conflagration. Twenty squares of the city in ruins!! From 1000 to 2000 houses destroyed! Loss estimated at Ten Million!" The news story lamented: "It is our painful duty to record one of the most terrible fires that ever devastated any city on this continent—a great portion of our busy and populous town is in ruins. More houses have been destroyed by this single and horrible conflagration, than have been consumed by all the fires that have ever occurred in the city before." The article went on to praise the firemen: ". . . nothing in the shape of reward can compensate them for the incessant toil they had to undergo—and for the unyielding, heroic firmness, which they manifested under the appalling terrors which surrounded them on every side. . . . We write in the hurry, confusion, and excitement of the terrible time, and under the physical weariness caused by laboring to save the furniture of the house of one of the editors, which was burned to the ground—therefore, we may omit much that we ought to notice—but we have endeavored to give as full an account of the calamity as we could."

While reporting "Incidents of the Fire," ward by ward, the *Gazette* insisted, "although the city is terribly shaken, it is neither ruined nor totally prostrated." On April 14, along with a large map showing the fire-swept district, it proclaimed that business continued "on the wharf and even from the burnt district," and added: "We therefore cordially invite western and country merchants to come on as usual. Their presence in our market will be received with pleasure and we think they will not be disappointed in meeting with the customary facilities." The same issue carried a notice that city officials "at the request of a number of clergymen have set aside Friday next as a day of fasting and prayer. Truly it becomes us to humble ourselves beneath the rod of God's chastisement, and bewailing our many errors, acknowledge the source whence comes all blessings." However, by the next day, April 15, the editor had had second thoughts about the Fast Day, arguing, "It is entirely *too soon*. . . . Many of our citizens have not yet heard of it—most of our churches have not had an opportunity to give notice to their congregations, and making their arrangements, and such is the general confusion, no concert of action can be had by the people." This advice went unheeded.

In the end, Pittsburgh made a remarkable recovery. The *Gazette* continued to stress the need for precautionary measures against another such occurrence, such as building with bricks and improving the firefighting facilities with more apparatus, new fireplugs, and larger water mains. The fire certainly did not slow the city's growth. By the next census, in 1850, the population had more than doubled, growing to 46,601. In the following year, railroad trains began operating out of Pittsburgh, and by 1852, travelers could make the trip between Pittsburgh and Philadelphia in fifteen hours.

David N. White
(Courtesy Carnegie Library
of Pittsburgh)

Despite the massive changes that enveloped Pittsburgh in the 1840s and 1850s, the *Gazette's* policies remained remarkably consistent. At the core of this stability was David N. White, who, except for a period of illness in 1847–1848, served as the *Gazette's* editor from 1844 to 1856. Arriving in Pittsburgh in 1827 from Massachusetts, White worked for the *Gazette* for thirteen years before moving on to Illinois. Shortly thereafter, White returned to Pittsburgh and became part owner of the *Gazette*.[1] In 1844, White made a shift significant for the future of the *Gazette* and its successors by changing it to a morning paper. During this period, the *Gazette* published a daily (at a subscription rate of six dollars per year); a triweekly (four dollars); and a weekly (two dollars in advance, three dollars at the end of a year). White made technological advances, as well. He replaced Neville Craig's hand press with a Napier steam press—the first one used in Pittsburgh to print a daily—to keep up with the amount of news that the Great Fire produced, and made use of the new magnetic telegraph. Lapses in the mail made it difficult for White to keep up with the most current reports, so when a telegraph line was completed from Washington to Pittsburgh in late 1846, White made the most of it. Readers in eastern cities praised the *Gazette* for publishing daily reports of the markets in Baltimore, Philadelphia, and New York. Because the telegraph line ended at Pittsburgh, newspaper editors farther west inundated White with requests for exchange copies of the *Gazette*. In order to meet these demands, White negotiated an agreement among several papers to split the cost of telegraphic news. Thus the *Gazette* was a pioneer in initiating a telegraphic news service west of the Allegheny Mountains.

White also moved the *Gazette* into new, three-story offices on Third Street in downtown Pittsburgh. The new accommodations included facilities for the *Christian Advocate,* a Methodist publication for which the *Gazette* had the printing contract. Due to failing health, however, White yielded his interest in the *Gazette* to Erastus Brooks in 1847 and briefly left the paper. Brooks, who had been a Washington correspondent to various eastern newspapers and later a European correspondent for the *Advertiser* of Portland, Maine, brought his experience with larger dailies to the *Gazette*. Perhaps because of his vast travels, though, Brooks proved too restless to remain in Pittsburgh for long, and so White, when he was fully recovered, returned to his position as editor and proprietor of the *Gazette*.

The *Gazette*'s staff continued to grow; by the eve of the Civil War there were twenty-two employees. Distribution, however, was handled by only one adult carrier. Subscriber complaints about the removal of papers from front stoops prompted White to write on December 11, 1844: "We wish the public to *take notice*—None of our papers are placed in the hands of the boys to sell. If any boy offers to sell them, he has *purloined them,* and we wish the boy detained, and notice given to us immediately."

The *Post* simultaneously secured a steam press and a telegraphic news service. In honor of these developments, the *Post* originated a new department that bore the powerful name, "Received by Lightning; Printed by Steam." Another newspaper appeared on the Pittsburgh scene with the first issue of the *Dispatch* on February 8, 1846. The *Dispatch* was ostensibly nonpartisan but eventually became sympathetic to

Republican doctrines on the tariff and protectionism. In 1882, however, it joined in a revolt against the corruption of the state Republican machine, resulting in the election of Governor Robert Emory Pattison, the only Democratic governor elected in Pennsylvania between the Civil War and 1935.

In the face of these competitors, the *Gazette* remained the city's leading newspaper in the 1840s and 1850s. During this period, the *Gazette* went through a succession of enlarged sheet sizes and other changes in appearance, but never increased the page count over the traditional four. In 1851, White instituted larger type in a departure from the practice of most newspapers of the time, which used smaller type in order to cram in more reading material. For the most part, illustrations were confined to the advertising sections. White also made efforts to reach untapped sources of advertising revenue, remarking on November 19, 1844, "The general advertising of the city is mostly confined to Wholesale Grocers, Produce dealers and Commission Merchants. Our Dry Goods, Hardware, Queensware and Shoe merchants, and our manufacturers of all descriptions with few exceptions, make no use of this means of extending their business or exhibiting the amount of business done here." Many Pittsburgh businessmen, however, were not persuaded by White's entreaties. The editor tried a different approach, hoping that increased circulation figures would affect potential advertisers. In the summer of 1845, a year in which the *Gazette* had a combined daily and weekly circulation of about 5,500 readers, White informed readers that the *Gazette* would sell both advertising and subscriptions in various cities, including Philadelphia, Baltimore, Boston, New Orleans, and, a little later, Cincinnati. Only nine years later, in 1854, White announced that the daily circulation had increased by about seven times and the weekly by about five times.

One ingenious innovation by White to boost circulation was the organization of "campaign clubs" during election years, starting in 1848. The concept was to mail to a subscriber, starting June 10, copies of the weekly *Gazette* in packages of ten copies for five dollars; fifteen copies for seven dollars; twenty copies for nine dollars; and one hundred copies for thirty-five dollars. By the 1858 election, the weekly *Gazette* was circulating not only in western and central Pennsylvania but also in Ohio, western Virginia, Kentucky, Indiana, Illinois, and sections of Wisconsin, Iowa, Missouri, plus the Kansas, Nebraska, and Minnesota territories. The combined circulation of the daily and weekly editions exceeded twelve thousand copies. Acquiring advertisers was no longer a problem; in fact, the *Gazette* did not even solicit. This practice became *Gazette* tradition, and was explained this way on January 8, 1859: "We are sometimes asked, 'Why did you not come in and ask us for an advertisement?' We will answer briefly: Our business-manager may always be found at our counter, to attend to the business of his department. We have always acted upon the principle that this was the proper place to make contracts with our friends, and shall not change until convinced that they prefer being bored by us."

As mentioned previously, the editorial policies of the *Gazette* under White and other editors in that antebellum period remained fairly constant. At one point, White, while admitting that the newspaper had never quite caught the public imagination, attributed that minus, as well as some pluses, to his faithful allegiance to certain principles. J. Cutler Andrews cataloged these as: "on the one hand, an opposition to secret oath-bound societies, to the encroachments of slavery, and to the pretensions and demands of the Roman Catholic hierarchy; on the other, to the advocacy of a protective tariff and the rights of the workingman and to the encouragement of local industrial enterprises."[2] White favored penal reform and, in a limited fashion, the cause of women's rights. Yet he considered it wrong to drop all distinctions between the sexes. The policies of the new *Post* also remained consistent under the editorship of Smith and Phillips, providing an interesting contrast for Pittsburghers.

American politics was chaotic by the time David White became editor of the *Gazette*. The Whigs had seen the 1840 victory of William Henry Harrison snatched away when he died within a month of his presidential inauguration, bringing the ascension of the vice president who had been chosen to balance the ticket. John Tyler, a Virginia Democrat turned Whig, reverted in many ways to his earlier anti-Federalist principles. To the consternation of the Whig leadership in Congress, he vetoed most of the platform issues that they had jubilantly assumed would be law with the election of "Tippecanoe and Tyler, too." Tyler turned down plans for a new Bank of the United States, for higher tariffs, and for federal road building and other elements of the "American System." The conflict got so bad that the Whigs tried unsuccessfully to impeach Tyler, an effort supported by the *Gazette*.

For conservatives like White, the situation was a disaster. Clearly, the Democrats were profiting from the split within the Whig Party over President Tyler. In the first senatorial election after the great Harrison victory, Pennsylvania's Whig Party came away with only twelve of Pennsylvania's twenty-four seats in Congress. At that point, Pittsburgh's Whig leaders evaluated the *Gazette*'s leadership and made a decision. Both of the *Gazette*'s owners, Matthew Grant and David White, were supporters of the waning Anti-Mason Party. Grant, however, was more fervent, while White might be persuaded to endorse a Whig candidate in the upcoming election—after all, most Anti-Masons had, by this time, gone over to the Whig Party. In January 1844, fifteen Whig leaders advanced two hundred dollars each to enable White to buy out his partner's interest. Grant was gone by the end of the month, leaving White in sole charge.

The rival *Post* took some apparent pleasure in proclaiming that the fifteen purchasing Whigs were "members of the lodge" and would run White's show. Angrily, White retorted that the *Post*'s allegation was "false in its conception, false in its details, false in every particular." Yet the *Post* must have felt even more certain that something unusual was occurring when, two months later, one Judge Baird sold the recognized Whig newspaper, the *Advocate,* to White. The *Gazette* changed its name to the *Pittsburgh Daily Gazette and Advertiser* and picked up the patronage of its previous rival.

As the 1844 election campaign began, White was also very concerned about the annexation of Texas that had been proposed by President Tyler and advocated in the campaign by Democratic presidential hopeful James Polk. Many residents of southern states worried that their power in Congress would continue to be diminished by the creation of new free territories, and eventually of free states. Blocked by Mexican territory to the west, these southerners welcomed the uprisings by American settlers in Texas against Mexican rule. Democrats saw annexation as a welcome solution, whereas Whigs such as White saw it as expansionism that could easily develop into a war.

The latter became all the more probable after Polk defeated the Whig candidate, Henry Clay, who had run for president for the third and last time. On the day of the election, White excused himself from editorial duties for the reason that "we are too weary and fagged out with our vigils to say anything today." Although a majority of Allegheny

County voters—2,369—voted for Clay, Polk carried Pennsylvania and, when the New York State returns finally were counted, the nation.

When the Texas Congress accepted the terms of annexation, White was particularly bitter, thundering on July 8, 1845: "This monstrous iniquity, this most stupendous fraud upon the free states of the Union is accomplished." White sarcastically proposed to the winners that they drown by their shouts "the wailings and groans of the fathers, mothers, husbands, wives and children, whom their accursed instrumentality has torn from fond embraces of earth's dearest ties, to sweat and groan and bleed and die, upon the burning soil of Texas."

White's concerns about an expansionist war for the acquisition of Mexico were compounded when, on May 12, 1846, the news that war had been declared reached Pittsburgh. In that day's *Gazette,* White indignantly demanded to know what justification Polk had for sending General Zachary Taylor's army into the disputed territory. To invade the country of a foreign power, White asserted, was absolutely beyond the constitutional powers of the executive.

The *Post* accused the *Gazette* of a pro-Mexican bias and a lack of patriotism. Not so, White snapped back. To attack President Polk's policy was not to attack the government. White continued to hammer away at the administration, predicting (accurately) that the "pestilential climate" of the Mexican country would prove deadly to the army. Moreover, White argued, if Mexico were to be conquered, the United States would have another Ireland on its hands—too weak to make war, too weak to make peace.

Whatever negatives could be said of the war, it was definitely good for news. Every newspaper edition, including extras, sold out. Moreover, the astonishing military victories of Generals Taylor and Winfield S. Scott made it hard for many Americans to repress a sense of pride. In April 1847, Pittsburgh city officials decided to hold a "public illumination" to celebrate the war's successes. Some readers, such as the author of a letter published in the April 24 edition, urged the *Gazette* to stick to its antiwar stance: "So we are to illuminate, are we? For one, I shall not do it on the present occasion. So long as blood is flowing in torrents, not only of soldiers and those whose trade it is to kill, but of helpless and innocent women and children, I cannot, will not illuminate." The *Gazette,* while sympathizing with such sentiments, decided to support the celebration, which was brilliantly held on that same April 24.

Eventually, the *Gazette*'s attitude toward the Mexican War began to clash with its political leanings; the Whig newspapers in Philadelphia were supporting General Taylor for the presidency. Erastus Brooks, the editor during White's hiatus, balked at such a prospect, convinced that the military spirit rampant in the land must be curbed. Eventually, the discipline of party loyalty won out, and in the September 14, 1848, issue, the *Gazette* touted the Whig choice with this poem:

> The glorious name of Taylor
> Has spread from sea to sea
> And Mexico (his field of fame)
> His monument shall be.
> His name's a talisman to us,
> The dread of every foe;
> The synonym for victory,
> From Maine to Mexico.

Taylor carried Allegheny County by 3,500 votes and the state by 13,500 votes over Democrat Lewis Cass. As it had in the case of William Henry Harrison, though, death again thwarted the Whigs with the sudden demise of President Taylor on July 9, 1850. The timing was especially unfortunate because the nation was in a state of nervous tension over congressional debates on the famous Compromise of 1850, which was supposed to answer the slavery question. The issues left unresolved tore apart the Whigs at their national nominating convention in Baltimore in June 1852. White had gone to Baltimore in a pleasant mood, but a deadlocked balloting and divisiveness between northern and southern Whigs prompted sharp forebodings in the editor's mind as to the future of the party. In fact, although Allegheny County recorded 2,389 votes for Scott, the state went for the winning Democrat, Franklin Pierce, by 20,000 votes. Robert Riddle, editor of the outright Whig paper, the *Pittsburgh Daily Commercial Journal,* thought the Whig Party ought to be dissolved.

The Compromise of 1850 was an attempt by Henry Clay and other congressmen to keep North and South together. Under the terms of the compromise, money would be paid to the Republic of Texas to settle boundary disputes; the territories of Utah and New Mexico would be organized without slave legislation (the question would be decided later by each territory upon applying for statehood), California would enter the Union as a free state, the slave trade would be prohibited in the District of Columbia (though slave ownership would still be permitted), and a rigorous Fugitive Slave Act would be implemented. That final provision called upon the federal government to require, and assist with, the return of a slave caught anywhere in the nation to his master. Fugitive slaves who had counted themselves safe in Pittsburgh began departing in droves for Canada. Northerners were astounded by the sight of women, children, and men being dragged from their homes and forced to return to bondage in the South. The cause of the abolitionists found new, fertile ground. The *Gazette* was full of warnings that the new law was dangerous to the South, dangerous to the Union, and dangerous to the very existence of slavery itself. In 1850 White was certainly not a proponent of abolition; rather, he was a conservative anxious about the fate of the Union. When invited to report the proceedings of a Nashville convention called to consider the advisability of secession, White prophesied that if such a doctrine were acted upon, "nothing can prevent a most bloody Civil War."[3]

The next attempt at compromise, the Kansas-Nebraska Act of 1854, caused more alarm at the *Gazette*. The Missouri Compromise of 1820, which admitted Maine as a free state and Missouri as a slave state to maintain representational balance, had drawn an imaginary line at 36 degrees 30 minutes north latitude. Land north of the compromise line was to be free. The Kansas-Nebraska Act called for the elimination of the Missouri Compromise Line, and opened those areas, at least potentially, to slavery. Under the terms of the 1854 act, two territories, Kansas and Nebraska, rather than one, would be organized. Each would have the opportunity to decide whether to allow slavery—though in fact, most legislators assumed that under the provision, one territory would be slave, and the other free. The *Gazette* had grave concerns over the new law and warned of the danger of violating the Missouri Compromise. When the 1854 measure passed the Senate, the editor exclaimed on March 6: "Workingmen of the North, arouse! You who expect to go or send your children to obtain your portion of the fertile lands of the great West look to it that you are not robbed of your inheritance . . . tell the slaveholding conspirators that this outrage upon justice, humanity and freedom shall not be."

The *Post* strongly disagreed with its rival over the Kansas-Nebraska question. It editorialized sarcastically, on February 6, 1854: "Another assault on Freedom. Such is the alarming cry of the *Pittsburgh Gazette* on Saturday last. We were frightened to read it. We thought 'The British were coming.' But as we read on, lo, and behold! It was only an assault on McClintock, our Democratic Senator at Harrisburg. And it illustrates either the ignorance or malice of the *Gazette*. . . . If such is the course of the *Gazette* on this subject, what confidence can be placed in his statements and representations in regard to the Nebraska Bill? What cares the *Gazette* for the Missouri Compromise? Except to make it an excuse for assaulting the Democracy."

J. Cutler Andrews recounts the *Gazette*'s response to such sentiments: "Indicative of the fire that the *Gazette* flung at the 'Kansas iniquity' was an editorial called 'Let us alone,' which likened the attitude of the *Post* and its friends to that of the evil spirits who cried out when encountered by Christ. 'Blessed be Sharp's rifles!' said White on another occasion. 'They are the only peacemakers which such villains can understand or respect.'"[4]

Opposition to the Kansas-Nebraska Act proved futile. On May 25, 1854, the *Gazette* conceded sadly, "The deed is done." All the newspaper could do was to print the names of the free-state representatives who had voted for the bill, in a box bordered in black, titled the "Black List of Traitors" or "Nebrascals." The *Post* was incensed by that development. It leveled this blast at its competitor on May 30: "A Base Fraud— the *Gazette*. Were the people of this county made fully aware of the systematic deception practiced upon them by a certain Whig paper published on Third Street, in our city, they would give little heed to its assertions hereafter. . . . All this clamor against the Nebraska Bill, by Whigs and abolitionists, is a false alarm—a humbug attempt to make political capital out of a measure that, so far as slavery is concerned, is of no practical importance. . . . The remarks of the *Gazette* that we would favor the extension of slavery are simply a falsehood."

As if mounting tensions over slavery were not enough, the *Gazette* was faced with the emergence of the Know-Nothings as a potent third-party force. Because the Know-Nothings were basically anti-immigrant and anti-Catholic, its Pennsylvania leaders expected support from the *Gazette*. After all, White had opposed the local Catholic bishop on educational issues, and once had gone so far as to call Negro slavery and the Roman Catholic Church "the two great systems of oppression in the civilized world."[5] White soon realized, however, that the Know-

Nothings traced their origin to a secret society called the Order of the Star Spangled Banner. The *Gazette*'s tradition of opposing such societies continued, as White wrote on March 30, 1855: "*We* stand where we always have stood; in determined opposition to all secret political organizations. Nothing can tempt us from this position. Dearly as we love the anti-slavery cause, not even the prospect of doing *it* a benefit could induce us to yield one inch in this regard."

If the Know-Nothings were to be shunned, the problem for conservatives remained. Both the Whigs and the Anti-Masons were lost causes. In a May 29, 1854, editorial, White had asked why the defunct Whigs should not be replaced with a ticket of those opposed to the Kansas-Nebraska Act. The *New York Tribune* later broadcast the idea as though it were the first time anyone had proposed it. Heartened by this response, White prophesied that a regrouping must take place soon and continued editorially to smooth away possible obstacles. Such a synthesis seemed extant in the new Republican Party. This precarious combination included outright abolitionists, disgruntled northern Whigs, and former members of the short-lived Free-Soil Party. By the summer of 1855, White was publishing calls for both a county and a state convention to promote the organization of a state branch of the Republican Party. This action provoked interest outside of Pennsylvania. Governor Salmon P. Chase of Ohio, later to become President Lincoln's secretary of the treasury, came to Pittsburgh in November 1855 and invited White to his hotel to confer about plans to make the effort in Pennsylvania part of a nationwide movement to challenge the Democrats.

From there it was full speed ahead. On January 23, 1856, the *Gazette* editorial column carried a notice signifying the general desire for an informal convention of the Republicans of the Union to meet in Pittsburgh on February 22 to organize the party and make plans for a nominating convention. Both White and ex-editor Neville Craig were on the welcoming committee to greet such notable attendees as *New York Tribune* editor Horace Greeley, abolitionists Owen Lovejoy and Joshua R. Giddings, and an Illinois lawyer already attracting attention—Abraham Lincoln.

The momentum continued into a national nominating convention in Philadelphia, for which the *Gazette* began in early in June to advertise half-fare excursions. The *Gazette* started touting Governor Chase for the presidency. Chase and other hopefuls were passed over, however, and White had to resign himself to the selection of John C. Fremont, a soldier who had gained attention with his explorations of the West. By 1856, the formation of the new party caused even more dissention between the *Gazette* and the *Post*.

———·•·———

Given Pittsburgh's rapid industrial growth in the nineteenth century, it is not surprising that labor disputes also became a part of the picture. In 1806 Pittsburgh's tailors went on strike, and evidently won their demands. Tensions heightened in 1815 when a group of shoemakers were tried on grounds of conspiracy to organize a "society" and appoint a "tramping committee" to inspect shops and wages. With a judge's instructions that left no room for the jury other than conviction, the defendants were found guilty—but fined only one dollar each.

The *Gazette* and most of the city's newspapers supported the employers against their workers. An article published by the *Gazette* made clear its view that Pittsburgh was getting a bad name because of its labor views. One contributor wrote: "No wise man will risk his capital in the uncertain and dangerous [business] of manufacturing in a place where his interests are exposed to increasing newspaper attacks, and himself made an object of continual abuse. . . Here capitalists are reproached, their business interfered with, violence excited against them, their property hazarded by mobs, and every evil passion stirred up against them." For the *Gazette,* the future of Pittsburgh lay in the hands of its manufacturers, whose only hope to beat cutthroat competition was to hire cheap workers and drive them for as many hours as possible.

Of the major papers, as historian Leland Baldwin commented, "only the intransigent *Post* dared to hold out against the popular stand."[6] The *Post*'s pro-labor attitude was presumably influenced by the working conditions. In factories, employees' days varied from eleven hours in the winter to fourteen hours in the summer, and store clerks worked twelve-hour days during the week and up to eighteen hours on Saturdays and market days. Wages often ranged between $1.00 and $2.00 dollars per day, but women in the cotton mills received only $2.50 a week.

The different positions of the *Gazette* and the *Post* were highlighted in 1848 when women working in cotton mills clashed with management over implementation of a new ten-hour workday law that had been passed in the state legislature. What had seemed a remarkable victory contained a loophole that management was quick to exploit—a provision allowing an exception if, by special contract, the workers agreed to longer hours. Management insisted that if workers, or their parents or guardians, did not sign such contracts, the mills would have to close and move elsewhere.

The employees did not buy that argument. The business community was shocked when workers defied public concepts of female behavior by parading in the streets with a banner inscribed with the Whig Party's 1840 campaign promise to workers: "Two dollars a day and roast beef."

As the women stuck to their demands all through the long, hot summer, the *Gazette* chastised the "infuriated Amazons," but tried, in its own way, to be fair to the strikers. On August 5, 1848, the *Gazette* announced: "One of the charges alleged against your employers is that they have gone into the newspapers with their statements, while you are precluded from doing the same on account of the expense! Now we promise you that, while we will make your employers pay for every line published in our paper, we will publish your replies, of equal length for nothing."

The *Post,* on the other hand, rallied to the side of the workers. On July 27, 1848, it launched a sympathetic treatment of the cotton-mill "operatives," as the employees were termed: "The factory operatives had another large meeting in the Diamond, Allegheny, on Tuesday night. A great many speeches were made; but we have not heard that a single dollar has been contributed to the support of the suffering women and children. Nor has any plan been proposed by which they can be relieved from the necessity which seems to press them back to the slave mills." Matters soon came to a head in Allegheny City, as reported in the *Post* on August 1:

THE OPERATIVES—The bells of some of the factories were rung yesterday morning, which attracted great crowds of men, women, and children, to the vicinity of the mills, whether they gathered to notice the girls who were willing to enter on the old system of "Twelve Hours." There was necessarily considerable excitement. As a few girls passed to enter the mills, the crowds hissed; and many were, no doubt, kept back by this means. Some did go into the Penn [Factory], and the machinery was started; but whether a sufficient number were induced, or forced, back to warrant the proprietors in continuing in operation, we do not know. No other mill was started, we believe. . . .

After we had written the above, we were informed that there was a great row at the Penn Factory. . . . We found thousands of people around the premises. . . . The object of the outside girls was to get those inside to stop work. The insiders were willing to do this, judging from their conduct in throwing out bobbins, and waving handkerchiefs to the crowd below. It seems this demonstration was anticipated; for the proprietors had furnished bread and cheese for dinner.

Some time towards noon the attack was made. A large yard gate was broken open, and in rushed the crowd. The east door was broken down by one girl who wielded *one* axe. . . . The sheriff and his aids were on the ground, but made no arrests. The Mayor and police of Allegheny were also there, and they did nothing.

Stories of the July 31 fracas at the mill continued to build. On August 2, the *Post*'s "Local Matters" column reported: "INDISCREET— While the crowd rushed into one of the doors of the Penn Factory on Monday, one of the proprietors, or a twelve hour foreman, or someone appeared with a double barreled gun, and aimed it at the girls and men who stood before him. Not one flinched. One or two of the girls deliberately gathered up some mud and daubed the hero a little. Whoever held this gun should be the first one arrested, if any arrests are to be made."

On August 4, for whatever reason, the *Post* tried to balance its reporting by publishing a "Statement of the Manufacturers." It was signed by the heads of seven mills—Pitt, Hope, Eagle, Union, Penn, Star, and Allegheny. In it, the managers agreed to the new law's limitation on labor, affirming that at no time had the twelve-hour system been in their interest or that of their employees, "but that the practice originated through the entreaties of indigent parents, whose wants were supplied by their earnings." On August 7, however, the *Post* took a stronger position than ever:

It is a fearful state of affairs when girls and children are driven by hunger to work as repugnant to them as must be that offered in those cotton mills. The crisis calls for further and more rigid measures by the Legislature. The special contract clause should be—*must* be—stricken out of the law, so that no minor shall be permitted to work more than ten hours, and no *child* should be permitted to work at all. . . . The 15 or 20 factory proprietors in our county have an idea that legislation should aim at giving protection to them and their profits; and pay no heed to the suffering bodies and souls of the thousand poor people who are goaded by fear of want to enter these establishments! They must be taught more correct ideas of American institutions than this.

The next paragraph described the appointment of committees, ward by ward, "for collecting funds in aid of these operatives, who need assistance in standing out against the 12 hour system."

When, several days later, the owners of one mill attempted to run the machinery themselves but gave it up after five hours, the *Post* promptly and sarcastically labeled the effort "the five hour system." On August 9, the *Post* reported: "Two or three of the proprietors, or 'bosses,' started the machinery. They exhibited a remarkable degree of skill and proved conclusively that they could work some. But did they put in the 12 hours of 'mere play' which have heretofore been required of the real operatives? *No, ser-ee.* In five hours they proclaimed physical exhaustion, and demanded refreshments! The engine stopped, and the fires were extinguished. Not a girl appeared during this interesting ceremony." The strike effort, however, was in vain. The *Post* reported on August 10 that at the Star factory, "which is owned by Germans, a large number of German girls have gone to work." A large crowd had gathered but "no violence was attempted." On August 28, the *Post* further reported, "Factories started work yesterday under the 10 hour system. Reduction of 10–16 percent. Girls had a large meeting and resolved they would never go to work at the reduced wages. The Star and Allegheny factories are filled now. We presume, however, that the mills will continue, short-handed as they are, until they can be gradually filled up." By the end of the month the workers had returned to the mills after a compromise by which they took 10 to 15 percent reductions in pay in return for the 10-hour day.

Four years later, the newspapers themselves faced labor issues when the printers' union went on strike. Interestingly enough, the *Gazette* did not print negative comments about the strike, but only mentioned it in the context of an advertisement. The editor posted a wanted notice for several compositors, and explained that because he had refused to surrender the management of his office to the control of the printers' union, his entire staff, save two reporters and three apprentices, had walked off the job. The editor even hinted that should no other options be available to him, he might even consider hiring women!

In 1853, one year after the printers went on strike, another issue captured the attention of Pittsburgh newspapers. In both that year and the next, elections included questions of prohibition. The *Gazette*'s interest in the temperance movement, which dated back to John Scull and Neville Craig, had been enthusiastically carried on by editor David N. White. The *Post* took the opposite view and came out victorious. Temperance was defeated by only a narrow margin in a statewide referendum in 1854, but the *Gazette* had to admit complete defeat. In Allegheny County, residents voted against outlawing liquor by a larger margin than other Pennsylvanians. The issue, of course, was to continue as a major political battleground throughout the rest of the century and up until the prohibition of liquor was placed in the U.S. Constitution in 1919.

The 1854 defeat did not dampen the fervor David White had for the temperance movement. In fact, he had become involved in its revival aspects, speaking up for such famous temperance lecturers as John B. Gough and Neal Dow when they came to Pittsburgh. The *Gazette*'s support of the anti-alcohol movement was one of the reasons why it came to be known as a religious paper: the causes that it championed were likely to support the aims and purposes of the church. This predilection may have even been a boon to the paper in a city where, in 1840, a visitor had counted sixty places of religious worship and commented on the fact that on the Sabbath the streets were filled with churchgoing people. The paper noted on February 11 of that year that religious fervor, once isolated to one denomination or congregation, had spread so that "almost every denomination, and nearly every congregation in Pittsburgh, Allegheny, and Birmingham [later the South Side], are enjoying a season of religious refreshing. . . . These are the Lord's doings, and are marvelous in our sight."

The *Gazette* did not extend such a positive attitude, however, to atheists. The newspaper tended to group atheists, deists, and Unitarians together, and treated each with equal disdain. With regard to Catholics, Craig had noted his misgivings in the 1830s, when the population around St. Patrick's Church on Pittsburgh's eastern edge, founded by Irish immigrants in 1806, had grown to include so many Catholics that Pittsburgh had become the seat of a bishopric. Moreover, Roger B. Taney, a Catholic, had been named Chief Justice of the U.S. Supreme Court. The *Gazette* was not alone in its concerns. The

Pittsburgh Daily American took a crack at the Irish Catholics on April 24, 1841, after noting that they were holding meetings in different parts of the United States: "If these officious foreigners were so anxious for the liberation of their country, why did they not stay at home, and endeavor there to effect it?"

The arrival of seven Sisters of Mercy and the establishment of a Catholic hospital and of Catholic schools further disturbed the *Gazette*. Led by Mother Frances Warde, the "Mercies" emigrated from County Carlow, Ireland, on December 20, 1843, at the invitation of Bishop Michael O'Connor. They would come to play an important role in Pittsburgh.

The 1850 mayoral election pitted street preacher Joseph Barker, who ran on the Reform ticket, against Whig Robert McCutcheon and independent John B. Guthrie. The *Gazette* and the *Post* battered each other in the days just before the election. The *Gazette,* on January 4, accused the Democratic Party of hand-selecting candidate Guthrie, and then "recommending" him as an "independent" candidate. "One of two things is certain, they are ashamed of their flag, or they fear defeat under it," the *Gazette* chided, adding that the Whigs should "rally for the election of Mr. McCutcheon . . . notwithstanding the defection of some who support Barker, on the one hand, and Guthrie on the other." On the same day, the *Post* gave prominence on its front page to a headline, "John B. Guthrie, independent candidate for mayor."

Despite the attempts of both papers to influence the vote, it was Barker, the candidate who was not endorsed by either the *Gazette* or the *Post,* who emerged victorious. A September 26, 1936, article in a series by George Swetnam on Pittsburgh's mayoral history included this colorful description of the events of that election day: "The *Gazette*'s animus toward Catholics and liquor was more than 'rewarded' with the outcome of the 1850 city election when an unordained street preacher named Joseph Barker was elected mayor while sitting in jail for shouting anti-Catholic epithets on the steps of old St. Paul's Cathedral. It was part of his preaching against foreigners, Catholics, Masons, politicians, slavery, intemperance and 'other evils of America' and, later, against judges and churches in general. Sentenced to a year's imprisonment, Barker told the jury to go to hell and warned the judge that he might be hanged from a lamppost."

The day after the election, on January 8, the *Post* chortled, "Barker's friends rallied early in the morning, and made extraordinary efforts throughout the whole day for the 'martyr.' Towards noon, the Whigs, finding that there was no prospect of electing McCutcheon, generally abandoned their man and turned to Barker. The election of the latter was the result. . . . Although a large portion of our citizens appear to think that the election of Barker will give a license to rowdyism, violence and indecency, yet we hope such will not be the case. . . . But if our worst fears are realized, the responsibility must rest with the Whigs who abandoned their own candidate, and voted for Barker."

The *Gazette* tried to make the best of Barker, observing on January 9, 1850, that he was "a strong Whig" and an original supporter of President Zachary Taylor and expressing the hope that he would properly discharge the duties of his office. However, a few days later, White insisted that the result of the election showed "less of a personal regard for Barker, than of opposition to the Catholics" and the Democrats. Swetnam later observed: "Barker's term was doomed to virtual failure from the start. He quarreled with council over police appointments. Fined Bishop Michael O'Connor and the head of Mercy Hospital $20 for blocking a sewer. But also closed brothels, banned prizefights, drove hucksters from the streets and closed bars on Sunday. He mediated an iron puddlers' strike and instituted a 10-hour work day, except 13 hours for clerks."[7]

By the time of the next mayoral election, even the *Gazette* had had enough of Barker. Just before the 1851 election, on January 12, it declared that reelecting the incumbent "would inflict an indelible stain upon the credit and character of the city, and would be a cause of deep mortification to every respectable citizen." John B. Guthrie, this time running unabashedly as a Democrat, defeated Barker to become mayor, and on January 15, the *Gazette* sighed in relief: "The defeat of Barker, and the complete and final prostration of Barkerism, is a matter of sincere and heartfelt gratulation [*sic*] with every true friend of Pittsburgh and her interests. We hope this sad lesson will never have to be repeated to convince our citizens that when they lay aside their own self-respect, and exercise the sacred right of suffrage, by voting for such a person as Joe Barker, at the time expiating his offenses in jail, they sow the wind only [to] reap the whirlwind." As it turned out, the 1851 election had finished Barker's political career. He was killed by a train in Manchester on August 3, 1862, while returning from a speech in Ross Township to promote the Civil War effort.

The "sad lesson" that the *Gazette* referred to may have been the impetus for the paper to make an exception to its usual bias toward Catholicism, when it went to the defense of Bishop O'Connor against an "atrocious" (but unspecified) libel being circulated by Barker. On August 12, 1854, the *Gazette* declared: "It is our duty to warn that no confidence can be placed in any reference by Barker to any society or party or individual he may choose to oppose. He is a disgrace to the community. . . . Our readers know our opinion of Roman Catholicism, and how freely and frankly we have opposed it and how completely we differ with Bishop O'Connor and the Roman Catholic hierarchy. But we oppose principles and measures and not persons. . . . Common humanity and a sense of justice should prompt the community to protect him against the vile libels of such a walking pestilence as Joe Barker, who disgraces Protestantism and humanity by his ribaldry and blasphemy."

The story of mixed and changing party allegiances in the Barker affair was typical of the chaos that enveloped many communities as the country moved inexorably toward a cataclysmic civil war. In Pittsburgh, the major newspapers would square off over one of the last-minute conflicts leading to the final rupture.

Chapter 6

The Civil War

As the nation inched closer and closer to the Civil War, tensions ran high in Pittsburgh. In the waning days of 1860, huge crowds of Pittsburghers gathered on the northeastern outskirts of Pittsburgh (later the Lawrenceville neighborhood) outside the government's Allegheny Arsenal to block the shipment of artillery weapons to the South.

The way in which Pittsburgh's newspapers approached the subject of the artillery-transfer effort tells much about the hardening of their contrasting policies in the months preceding the onset of the Civil War. When the war did come, it would bring tremendous changes to the newspapers and to the city of Pittsburgh, whose war-aided economy would fuel an explosive population growth—from 49,217 in 1860 to 121,977 a decade later.

Just weeks before the citizen uprising, the election of Republican Abraham Lincoln as president had sent secession-minded southerners into convulsions of anxiety and anger. South Carolina had officially seceded from the Union on December 20, and six more states would follow before the March 4, 1861, presidential inauguration of Lincoln. On January 29, 1861, Kansas was scheduled to be admitted as a free state, convincing the slave states that they eventually would be outnumbered sufficiently in Congress to open the way for the abolition of slavery. So by the closing days of December, it was becoming apparent to almost all that the breach was unbridgeable, and that war was inevitable if secession were to be halted. Therefore, Unionists in Pittsburgh saw the artillery order by John B. Floyd, President Buchanan's war secretary, as a contribution to the efforts of a potential enemy.

In the fiery words of the *Pittsburgh Dispatch:*

It is not enough that we are to be sold out to the Secessionists—the Administration would bind us hand and foot, deprive us of arms, and deliver us tied neck and heels to the traitors who would dissever the Union. It has already ordered one hundred and twenty-four heavy guns from the Allegheny arsenal to the south, not to defend the Stars and Stripes, for which our skilfull [sic] mechanics made them, but to batter down the battle flag of some Lone Star or Rattlesnake government. . . . To take these [to Galveston] would strip us entirely of cannon and leave us disarmed (so far as cannon are concerned) at the mercy of traitors. For months muskets have been sent to southern points where rebels have seized them by the thousands. Shall Pennsylvania be disarmed and Charleston be allowed impunity to seize the federal arms with which to overthrow the Union? Shall our people submit to this?[1]

The indignation boiled into a mass meeting around the Allegheny Courthouse in downtown Pittsburgh at 2:00 p.m. on December 26. After several speeches advocating moderation, Thomas J. Bigham, editor of the *Commercial Journal,* wriggled through the crowd with a telegraphic dispatch announcing that Fort Moultrie, South Carolina, had been evacuated. From that point on, Pittsburghers were determined that no artillery would be shipped from their river docks to arm the South for the impending conflict. President Buchanan was deluged with telegrams and letters decrying the Floyd order, and the weapons and their military escorts were halted or delayed without violence.

The staunchly pro-Union *Gazette* was under new ownership. The conflicts of the 1850s had proved to be too much for White, who left newspaper work and sold the *Gazette* to a new firm, S. Riddle & Co., with Samuel Riddle as chief owner and Russell Errett as editor. The elevation of Errett brought to the fore one of the most extraordinary figures in the history of Pittsburgh journalism. Born November 10, 1817, seven years after his family emigrated from Ireland, Errett had only two years of formal schooling. In a Horatio Alger–like career, he climbed the professional ladder to become clerk to Pittsburgh mayor Alexander Hay in 1842 and the editor of a small penny journal, the *Daily Sun,* from 1842–1845. In 1845 he went to Washington, Pennsylvania, to be editor of the *Washington Patriot,* established by Dr. G. LeMoyne and other Washington County abolitionists. After that paper closed, he eventually returned to Pittsburgh in 1852 to become commercial editor of the *Gazette.*

Because his anti-slavery views clashed with the prevailing Whig view, Errett joined the Free-Soilers and on August 11, 1852, was chosen as one of the secretaries of their national convention, which was held in Pittsburgh that year. After becoming the editor of the *Gazette,* Errett served on Pittsburgh's Common Council from 1855–1859 and was council president in 1857 and 1859. Active in forming the Republican Party, Errett was elected as both city controller of Pittsburgh and clerk of the Pennsylvania Senate in 1859. His subsequent careers included not only newspaper work, but also time spent in the Union Army, the Pennsylvania Senate, and the U.S. Congress.

Under Errett, the *Gazette*'s anti-slavery remarks were powerful enough to be noticed in the South. According to J. Cutler Andrews: "Around June 1, 1857, the *New Orleans Commercial Bulletin* referred to some remarks in the *Gazette* concerning a national crime wave and asked why this 'abolitionist paper' did not pay more attention to such things in the North and take its mind off slavery. Errett replied to this by advising the *Bulletin* to remove the beam from its own eye and by printing a list of crimes of violence culled from various issues of the *Bulletin.*"[2] Despite Errett's sympathy for the slaves, he, like so many other northerners, refused to be labeled an abolitionist. He adopted the stance of the Republican Party, which held to non-interference with the domestic institutions of the southern states.

Even so, Errett's opposition to slavery became more extreme as the crisis approached. In 1859 when abolitionist John Brown of "bloody Kansas" fame had attacked the federal arsenal at Harpers Ferry, Errett called it "a foolhardy adventure of a handful of monomaniacs . . . a purposeless and senseless riot."[3] He felt personally provoked, however, by the language of southern papers about the incident. When Brown was hanged for his deed, the *Gazette* declared that, Samson-like, he had dragged down the pillars of slavery in his fall. As church bells tolled unceasingly across the northeast throughout the execution day, December 2, 1859, many northerners felt that Brown had been unjustly put to death.

Errett was at first concerned that Abraham Lincoln lacked the aggressiveness and impetuosity for national leadership, but after the 1858 debates in Illinois between Lincoln and Stephen Douglas, Errett decided that he had underestimated Lincoln. Upon learning that the candidate was to follow Douglas on a speaking tour through Ohio, Errett in an editorial asked eagerly if Lincoln could not be persuaded to come to Pittsburgh, too.

When Lincoln eventually did come to Pittsburgh, on February 14, 1861, he was en route to his inauguration in Washington. Allegheny County had given Lincoln a plurality of ten thousand votes, the highest recorded by any county in the Union. When Lincoln read the returns in Springfield, he is said to have asked, "Where is this State of Allegheny?"[4]

Meanwhile, the *Pittsburgh Post* was exhibiting conflicting emotions. On February 12, it expressed sympathy for the president-elect: "Mr. Lincoln has started on his way to the White House. Never did a president elect make progress towards the National capitol at a time when the country was in such a condition as it is now. The question is now to be decided whether Abraham Lincoln is to be the President of 'these United States,' as we have been bound to term them heretofore, but now alas, seven of the sisterhood have declared that they will no longer be held by the bonds of Union. The times are out of joint. . . . What a weight of responsibility must accumulate upon the head of Abraham Lincoln."

By the next day, however, the *Post*'s attitude was quite different: "Mr. Lincoln's remarks at Indianapolis, on Monday . . . strike us as singularly weak and inconclusive. . . . [In the past] he certainly made some fine speeches, and showed that he possessed a considerable amount of forensic and controversial talent. But since his election he has been as silent as an owl until the present time, and now he speaks as a doubter."

The *Post*'s opinions were likely shaped by those of James P. Barr, who had become the paper's editor and proprietor on May 1, 1857. Barr had entered the Pittsburgh newspaper scene in 1841 as an apprentice to the printers in the office of the *American Manufacturer.* Involving himself in election politics, he was elected surveyor-general of Pennsylvania in 1863.

All of the newspapers detailed the events as the "state of Allegheny" turned out in full force for the president-elect. Shops closed and a procession was planned to meet the train in Allegheny (later Pittsburgh's North Side) and conduct Lincoln to the Monongahela House, the major downtown Pittsburgh hotel. For the planners, however, there was double misfortune. First, the train was delayed in Freedom, Beaver County, for several hours. Second, when the train arrived, it had begun to rain. However, the parade went ahead as planned. Several elite military companies under General James S. Negley led the way, but one such company, the Duquesne Grays, refused to parade in honor of a Republican. The crowd was so thick that Negley's soldiers had to fix bayonets to clear a path for the president's party into the hotel. Despite the rain, the crowd stayed until Lincoln had made not one but two balcony appearances. In the second, a half-hour speech, he expressed the opinion that the crisis was an artificial one that could be solved if both North and South addressed the issue calmly.

The next day the *Post* grumbled about Lincoln's late arrival, and on February 16 subjected him to searing criticism:

The Honorable Abraham Lincoln has come and gone. On the whole, he has made a favorable impression upon the people; but as Allegheny is the boasted banner county of the banner state, it is natural that those who have a 10,000 majority of Mr. Lincoln and the Chicago [Republican national convention] platform, should be pleased with their representative man. Neither is Mr. Lincoln as ungainly in personal appearance, nor as ugly in the face, as he has been represented. He is by no means a handsome man, but yet he possesses an intelligent countenance and a gentlemanly mien, and his facial angles would not break a looking glass . . . But the people have ceased to look for any good results from the progress of Mr. Lincoln through the country. . . . The country is bleeding at every pore for the Union, and yet Mr. Lincoln goes on with his rare show, and says there is no crisis.

The *Post* continued to be hopeful that the "non-crisis" would go away. On February 18, it reported a speech of "Alexander H. Stephens of Georgia, now vice president of the Southern Confederacy [who] has always been regarded as a fair man in politics, and a true lover of his country. Even in the position which he now occupies, we believe he would gladly embrace any reasonable compromise of the questions which divide the North and South which might be offered." The next day the *Post* threw a left-handed spear at the abolitionists. "The Sufferers in Kansas. Poor Kansas! She has suffered deeply from the politicians. They induced people to go there who had no business there, and now, when they cannot eat their Sharp's rifles, and are starving, those who sent them there render them no efficient aid."

Scarcely two months later, the Confederate bombardment of Major Robert Anderson's federal garrison at Fort Sumter proved that there would be no peaceful end to the crisis. On April 12, 1861, the *Gazette* editorially declared, "The secessionists have drawn upon their own heads the fearful responsibility of inaugurating civil war, and a tremendous war it is likely to be." For the *Post*, however, even the news of events at Fort Sumter was not quite convincing at first. Although the front page of its Saturday, April 13 issue proclaimed: "War commenced!" the editorial on the next page insisted, "A secession movement of the most extraordinary character now threatens the integrity of the Government. Armed men are in the field, navies upon the sea. And yet the majority of the people of the nation are still hopeful. . . . They want the Government of their country preserved, and its honor to remain untarnished." The *Post* then wondered, "But what are all these great military preparations for? We are content to hope that they are not to initiate a civil war, and we are content to wait and see what they are for. . . . Those who control the Government are Christian men with human hearts and we do not believe that they will attempt anything in the shape of coercion or an aggressive warfare against the seceded States."

On April 17, the *Post* accepted that war had indeed come, and proclaimed its loyalty to the Union in an editorial beneath a cut of an eagle and a flag bearing the slogan, "Fidelity to the Union": "For two days, the country has been in a condition of the most intense excitement. The awful catastrophe so long anticipated has at last fallen upon us. The die is cast. The choice between compromise and battles has been made. Civil war is upon us. 'Unto the end of the war desolations are determined.' . . . However much we may deprecate the political causes which have driven the South to this insane madness—this fratricidal war— the time is past for crimination and recrimination as to what might have been done and what ought to have been done. The Flag of Our

Front page of the *Pittsburgh Post*, April 13, 1861, "War Commenced"

Country—the glorious Stars and Stripes must be supported and defended by every American."

Once the war erupted, Pittsburgh responded wholeheartedly in terms of volunteers for military service and the tooling up of industry to meet the demand for material of all kinds. Many of the *Gazette*'s employees were among the volunteers, so much so that by the summer of 1862 the *Gazette* was apologetic for the handicaps placed upon its operations by the absence of so many men off to military service. All the newspapers were likewise affected. Errett himself was soon called to Washington to assist with the enormous correspondence that had deluged the War Department. Not willing to remain desk-bound, he engineered an appointment as a major in the Port Royal expedition in South Carolina.

In the spring of 1861, local young men began drilling in Camp Wilkins, later the Oakland neighborhood of Pittsburgh. A Committee of Public Safety was formed to attend to tasks such as searching out traitors and gathering information about what the local Democrats were up to and to what extent they were tied to the so-called "Copperheads," the term for northerners sympathetic to the southern cause.

For Pittsburgh and its industrial future, the war was a boon. Leland Baldwin's history of Pittsburgh captures the industrial scene:

Locomotives and freight cars, heavy artillery, small arms, ammunition, clothing (too often shoddy), steamboats, coal, and thousands of head of cattle and hogs left the vicinity in a steady stream. The Mississippi ram fleet [that eventually helped break the Confederate hold on the Mississippi River] was largely Pittsburgh built, it was armed with Pittsburgh guns, and the engines were fired by Pittsburgh coal. . . . The manufacture of armor plate became a leading industry . . .

Pittsburgh's cannons were the giants of that day. The Fort Pitt Foundry alone furnished 1,193 cannon (or fifteen percent of the government's artillery), which were valued at about $1,600,000. . . . The cannon were regularly tested at Tarentum, and that Allegheny River town gained the nickname "Bangtown-on-Allegheny." . . .

About ten per cent of the projectiles bought by the government were manufactured in Pittsburgh. Gun carriages, wagons, harness, blankets, tents were among the other contributions. During the four years of the war nearly 5,500,000 tons of coal were mined in the vicinity of the city.

Shortly before the war, the *Gazette* had experimented with separate morning and evening editions. The conflict had barely commenced before the *Gazette* merged with the *Commercial Journal,* so that for two years it labored under the ambitious title of the *Daily Pittsburgh Gazette and Commercial Journal.* Early in 1864 it was transferred to new ownership led by Josiah King, E. H. Irish, and Robert Ashworth. The Gazette Publishing Association, as they called their organization, continued to publish the paper until after the war. Throughout the conflict, the evening edition specialized in the latest news bulletins, while the morning edition focused on the discussions of public problems. To meet the demand for news, the paper added special reporters in Washington, D.C., and Harrisburg as early as January 1861. Within three weeks after the start of the war, the *Gazette* had appointed two correspondents to visit the volunteer Pennsylvania regiments and to write daily articles from the camps. The *Gazette*'s Washington office was located on Fourteenth Street, opposite the Willard Hotel where much of the political activity during the war took place.

During the Civil War, Pittsburghers waited outside the offices of the *Pittsburgh Dispatch* for the latest war news.

In the latter part of 1862, in order to further extend its coverage, the newspaper added several assistants to help correspondents collect news. The *Gazette* also teamed up with certain Detroit, Cincinnati, Louisville, Indianapolis, and St. Louis papers to form the Western Associated Press to supplement the services of the Associated Press, which was, at that time, basically a combination of New York dailies. The *Gazette*'s editors frequently complained about the conduct of the Associated Press, its favoritism, its illegibly transcribed dispatches, and its fragmentary reports. Even under the new arrangement, the *Gazette* had to be alert to prevent its competitors from profiting at the expense of its own newsgathering. Repeatedly, the newspaper criticized the *Chronicle,* in particular, for borrowing news without acknowledgment. All of these efforts involved spending more money; the *Gazette* boasted that the extra cost exceeded, by many hundreds of dollars, the budget of its entire news department before the war began, and that it paid more for news per week than all the other Pittsburgh dailies combined.

Circulation increased dramatically during the war. By 1863, the *Gazette* claimed to have the largest circulation of any of the city's papers, but the delivery of papers outside of the city was a problem because the movement of troops and arms along the railways choked the shipment of other articles. Newspapers had to take their chance along with other commodities of a non-military nature.

At the same time, the *Gazette* cost more than ever to publish—approximately fifty thousand dollars in 1862. Labor was expensive and hard to get. Taking advantage of that fact, the compositors at all the newspapers went on strike for higher wages; before the war was over, they would be paid as high as twenty-five dollars a week. No wonder that in November 1862, the four English-language dailies—the *Gazette, Evening Chronicle, Dispatch,* and *Post*—announced new schedules of advertising rates necessitated by the depreciation of the currency, the implementation of new taxes, and the greatly increased cost of everything used in the printing business. Paper, ink, telegraphic dispatches, gross revenue—each carried a tax. The scarcity of cotton rags was driving up the cost of paper. Advertising revenues were shrinking. The entire income of the *Gazette* from state, county, city, and borough advertising did not pay the cost of the paper's special telegraphic service for three months. The upshot was that in December 1862, the *Gazette* raised the annual subscription rate of the morning edition from $6.00 to $8.00 and of the evening edition from $3.00 to $4.50. In the summer of 1864, the *Gazette* was forced to raise rates again to $10.00 a year for the morning edition and to $6.50 for the evening edition. The pressures of competition, meanwhile, escalated with the appearance of two more newspapers—the *Evening Telegraph* in April 1863 and the *Sunday Leader* in December 1864.

During the war, newspapers were subject to military censorship. Early in 1862, the *Gazette*—for the most part a loyal supporter of the war—protested a War Department order forbidding the press to publish any war item except officially authorized military dispatches. Later that year, military authorities delayed definitive information regarding the September 17 Battle of Antietam from getting to papers for several days. This was the first major Civil War engagement fought on northern ground—but it was not the only reason Pittsburghers heeded the date. On that same September 17, an explosion took place at the Allegheny Arsenal, killing seventy-five people. As early as July 1861, the arsenal had engaged four hundred employees to make bullets, cartridges, and equipment for horses. The danger of explosion was always present, and at one point the commandant had discharged two hundred young men on the grounds that they were persistently careless with matches, and had hired young women in their places. His fears proved warranted when the arsenal's laboratory blew up. The cause of the disaster was never determined, but public indignation was high and a coroner's jury severely censured arsenal officials for neglect.

Although the *Gazette* and the *Post* both supported the Union, the latter was more critical of the government's conduct of the war. From time to time it reprinted articles from other newspapers affirming the people's right to criticize public officials. Undoubtedly, it was smarting from the tendency of pro-Lincoln newspapers to label all criticism of war strategies or tactics as partisan politics. Pittsburgh's Republicans must have been upset by the *Post*'s June 11, 1863, issue, which included a reprint of a *London Times* article lauding the name and memory of Confederate General Thomas "Stonewall" Jackson, killed in the previous month's Battle of Chancellorsville. The *Times* described him "not only as a brave man fighting for his country's independence, but as one of the most consummate generals that this country has produced"—an implicit criticism of the Union generals. Elsewhere in the same issue, the *Post* took an editorial swipe at the Lincoln war administration in a comment about a "Peace Convention" taking place in Washington, D.C.: "That the people who pay the taxes and furnish the fighting material for the army, and not the contractors and others who are growing opulent upon the nation's distress are anxious for peace, there can, of course, be no question." Yet the *Post* then criticized the peace movement with further comment: "Desirable as peace is and anxious as we all are for the speedy return to distracted firesides, there is one price the people will not pay for it—the separation of the States of the Union, under any circumstance. . . . At the present time, overtures to be at all attractive should come from those in rebellion against their government."

The *Gazette*, meanwhile, continued its strong support of Lincoln's efforts, illustrated in this excerpt from an editorial of May 31, 1863, entitled "Freedom of Speech": "One Daniel Tuttle, of Bucyrus, Crawford county, Ohio, lately posted a placard in the following words: 'Resistance to tyrants is patriotism! The minions of Lincoln . . . have invaded our soil, to drag from their homes 600 freemen of Crawford county. To arms, ye men of Crawford! Have a bullet ready for the dastards who order one drafted man to leave his home and county against his will.' This is the kind of stuff which politicians of the copperhead stripe are trying to entrench among the constitutional immunities of free speech. . . . We know the country is full of such men as he, who have neither heart nor brains sufficient to raise them above the low range of mere partisans."

The *Gazette* and the *Post* disagreed vehemently about the role of African Americans in the war. The *Gazette,* in an editorial published on June 12, 1863, at a time when Pittsburgh feared an attack by General Lee, observed: "It is likely that some of our people, whose sensibilities were so outraged some months ago at the bare idea of suffering colored men to help us in this war, will now when a vigorous conscription stares them in the face, be entirely willing to 'count them in.'" In the same period, the *Gazette* carried regular reports about the use of African American troops in the battle for Vicksburg. A June 13 article with a Memphis dateline stated: "The federal force at Millikens Bend consisted of three negro regiments and the 23rd Iowa. The rebels made a desperate charge at daylight. The negroes broke in confusion, but finding their captured companions slaughtered, they rallied with great desperation, and drove the rebels back."

The *Post* disapproved, ostensibly for humanitarian reasons. It lamented the use of black troops at Port Hudson on the Mississippi River, part of the Union's attempt to close in around Vicksburg. "Fanatical cant and professional philanthropy" and "Driven dumb and desperate upon their death" were the headlines of June 18, 1863, over text that included the sentence: "The simplest humanity revolts when the lives of hundreds of unoffending human beings, whatever be their color or their station, are thus ruthlessly sacrificed to vindicate a point of fanatical policy and fortify a partisan 'reason of state.'"

As an abolitionist paper, the *Gazette* supported Lincoln's January 1, 1863, Emancipation Proclamation, and expressed editorial outrage when ninety-six ministers of various denominations in Richmond, Virginia, published "An Address to Christians throughout the World," urging a protest against the proclamation. The ministers argued that "the Union cannot be restored" and that "the Confederate Government is a fixed fact." The clergymen asserted that Lincoln's actions would instigate a general rebellion by slaves, and that the result would be to "make it absolutely necessary for the public safety that the slaves be slaughtered." On June 10, 1863, the *Gazette* fired back: "Slaveowners are saying 'that unless they can bind the negro down to slavery, they will slaughter him? That he shall either live as a slave, or not live at all?'" The newspaper's editor further stated, "The men who signed this abominable sentence will yet learn that they made the strongest appeal to Europe in behalf of the Union cause which has yet been issued from this country."

Even the pro-Union *Gazette* was sometimes critical of the conduct of the war. As early as October 28, 1861, the newspaper had particularly harsh words to say for the commander of the Army of the Potomac, General George McClellan, bitterly alluding to Shakespeare in a comment about the "divinity that doth hedge—a General." Reflecting upon military mistakes that had cost the lives of many soldiers, the paper continued: "We tell those in authority that if they will not fight the enemy they shall not murder our men. . . . Many of us have sons and brothers and husbands in the ranks, and it is horrible to think that they are in the hands of a set of incompetent blunderers." Sadly, Lincoln was to have a succession of such "blunderers" before he finally found a winning general in Ulysses S. Grant. Even then, the Union general's success came at a fearful loss of life on both sides as he ground the Confederates into final submission at Appomattox.

Small wonder that when the Democrats in 1864 nominated McClellan as a peace candidate against Lincoln, the *Gazette* became almost apoplectic. On November 7, it regaled readers with tales of cowardice on the part of the dismissed general and declared that the vote would be "more important than was ever cast by man since the world began, and for a thousand years there may not be the like of it again." Whether or not the *Gazette*'s campaigning had a hand in the results, Lincoln won in Allegheny County, by an eight thousand-vote margin, and in the Union as a whole.

In June 1863, when General Lee abandoned his position at Fredericksburg, Maryland, and headed north, the *Gazette* and the *Post* voiced concerns that Pittsburgh was in danger. The major question was whether Lee would move toward Philadelphia and the major cities of the northeast, or, as Pittsburghers feared, veer west toward the Allegheny Arsenal and the industries of Pittsburgh that manufactured supplies for the Union. Unlikely as it seems in retrospect that the Confederate Army would attempt to fight its way across the Allegheny Mountains, Pittsburghers at that time were taking no chances. Besides, a lightning raid by J. E. B. Stuart's redoubtable cavalry was not implausible. After all, raiders earlier in the year had penetrated as far west as Morgantown, located in the western part of Virginia that had refused to secede and that would, on June 20, 1863, be admitted into the Union as the new state of West Virginia.

On June 12, the *Gazette* sounded the siren. "We are not alarmists; but we have sufficient information in regard to current military events to believe that *our city is now in imminent danger of a rebel attack,* by a strong force of cavalry and artillery, under a bold and desperate leader." The *Post* concurred. On June 13, it asked: "Is Pittsburgh in danger?" It then quoted from a *Pittsburgh Chronicle* editorial: "It is of vital importance that Pittsburgh shall never fall into Rebel possession," and added, "It is scarcely necessary to observe that in this, as in nearly everything else of a military nature, we entirely agree with the *Chronicle.*"

The *Gazette* was less sure on June 15 that an attack was imminent, indicating that General Lee's ability to move troops swiftly foiled even the ability of a telegraph-equipped society to keep track. The paper sought to allay the public's fears: "West Virginia may be in danger, but we have no apprehension of any serious attempt being made upon either Maryland or Pennsylvania." However, by the next day, the *Gazette's* anxiety had increased again. The paper issued "an urgent call to the militia" and declared, "The watchword of the hour: Action." On June 17 came the shrill headline, "An appeal to manhood," over the admonition, ". . . long years hence, it will be asked, *who bared his bosom to the foe, and who skulked, in June, 1863?*"

Following this appeal, on June 19, the *Gazette* reported: "Movement among the colored men. We are informed that the colored men of the two cities [Pittsburgh and Allegheny] sent a deputation to the military authorities, tendering their services in any capacity, for the present emergency, whether to labor on the defenses now building near the city, or to act in any other capacity the military authorities may think fit to place them. . . . We know not the reasons why their services were declined." The *Gazette* lamely suggested that perhaps they were not in "harmony" with the plans of the general in charge. It concluded, "The offer, however, was honorable to them, and we hope that matters can yet be so arranged that they may have an opportunity to render their assistance."

The "defenses now building near the city" were the result of a meeting on Sunday, June 14, in which manufacturers and businessmen agreed to defer work in order to send their men to build emergency defenses for the city. The next morning, several thousand men, to be paid $1.25 a day by their employers, met to be assigned to their sectors. Boys received $0.75 a day to carry free beer and hard cider to the workers. A defensive boundary was constructed around both cities, especially the Allegheny Arsenal, and cannon foundries were emptied so that their products could be placed on the line. As this work proceeded, the *Gazette* was forced to discontinue its usual "Pittsburgh Markets" column. On June 19, 1863, it explained: "Owing to the fact that business was entirely suspended to-day, we are of necessity compelled to omit our usual market report. The only thing thought of or talked about was the war news, and business, for the time being, may be considered suspended." Still, not every business was closed, as the *Gazette* bitingly noted on June 24: "While around the line of fortifications yesterday, and amongst the citizen soldiers in Camp Howe and elsewhere, we have one subject of a general and bitter remark—the selfish and unpatriotic conduct of those churlish few who persist in keeping their stores open, while so many thousands of their fellow citizens are spending time and money, laboring for the public defense. A stern public indignation should compel the general closing of the stores, in both cities." On June 25, under the headline, "Excitement on Liberty Street," the *Gazette* reported that a party of men had started up that street for the purpose of compelling certain shopkeepers to close up their stores. Presumably, the mission was accomplished.

Lee's intentions remained obscure. The *Gazette* anxiously admitted, "Of the exact whereabouts of the main body of Lee's army it is impossible to get any accurate information." Although it reported on June 27 that Gettysburg had been "occupied by a portion of [Confederate General] Longstreet's corps," on June 29, it was still wondering. On June 30, the *Gazette* expressed astonishment at the news that Joseph Hooker, commander of the Army of the Potomac, had been replaced by George Meade. As late as July 3, the turning point in the Battle of Gettysburg, the *Gazette* headlined, "Big news of fighting around Carlisle," which actually was miles away from the action. Below was a much smaller article headlined, "The Battle at Gettysburg, Pa."

Meanwhile, activity on the line of fortifications was spurred to even greater heights by a telegraph operator's message on June 25, which stated that a Confederate cavalry unit was on its way from McConnellsburg, Pennsylvania, to Pittsburgh. This advance, however, proved to be nothing more than rumor. In all, ten thousand men contributed to the local defenses throughout June and early July. Ironically, the day the labors came to an end also marked the end of the closest threat, as Lee began to retreat southward from Gettysburg.

News of the Union victory at Gettysburg was slow in coming. On that July 4, four columns of the *Gazette*'s front page were consumed with sheriff's sale notices, and the second page carried an article called "Details of the Gettysburg Battle," which reported on the opening skirmishes of July 1. By Monday, July 6, the *Gazette* had received word of the Confederate retreat. The paper tried to be cautious, stating that *if* the news were true, "we shall have had a glorious and memorable Fourth of July." However, on the second page, restraint fell away, and the paper exclaimed: "Glorious victory. The enemy successfully resisted." By July 8, the other great Union victory on July 4 had registered. The *Gazette* responded: "Thank God! With the fall of Vicksburg, the lately lowering cloud of danger has passed away forever." And on July 9, the paper was finally able to give "A full Account of the Three Days' Conflict" at Gettysburg.

After that decisive battle had removed invasion threats, Pittsburghers could settle back to the main order of business, supplying the tools of war for the Union Army for the nearly two years more that the war lasted.

The Civil War brought changes to the Pittsburgh area beyond fortified defenses. One of the area's biggest events of the day was the Great Sanitary Fair of 1864. When the war started, there was no standard medical organization for the military. Even Florence Nightingale's example of nursing care for British soldiers during the Crimean War (1853–1856) had not spread across the ocean into military circles. As a stopgap, President Lincoln reluctantly established the U.S. Sanitary Commission in 1861 to advise the overwhelmed Army Medical Corps on measures that could prevent deaths from disease and infection. The commission became a sort of early-day Red Cross, supplying doctors and nurses, equipping hospital ships, and coordinating the collection and dispersion of supplies. Yet in the bursting military budgets of the era, no tax money was provided to the Sanitary Commission. Many communities sent supplies on a voluntary basis to their local soldiers in the field. That haphazard approach, however, was not sufficient to meet the army's growing medical needs. As the Sanitary Commission's need for major funding became more critical, two energetic Chicago women conceived the idea of putting on a benefit fair of unprecedented proportions. So spectacularly successful was the Chicago Sanitary Fair in October 1863, that "fair fever" swept the North. Within nine months, at least thirty-seven cities had conducted Sanitary Fairs, variously titled "Great" or "Grand," the proceeds from which totaled nearly five million dollars.

The fair in Pittsburgh, as elsewhere, was an epochal event in the life of a community weary and stressed by endless costly battles and feelings of helplessness in the face of the ongoing war. As the Army of the Potomac engaged in battles throughout Virginia and approaching to Atlanta, the fair offered an opportunity for all elements of the Pittsburgh community to pull together. Men constructed temporary buildings on a large square in Allegheny City, women acted as organizers, farmers brought in free loads of produce to be cooked and sold to the

Sanitary Fair of 1864. The women of Pittsburgh held the bazaar to raise money for medical aid for Union soldiers. (Courtesy Carnegie Library of Pittsburgh)

crowds, exhibitors arrived with a variety of arts and crafts, and performers staged concerts, lectures, and cultural activities of all kinds.[5]

Pittsburgh's newspapers gave all-out coverage to the eighteen-day fair, from the first meeting of an organizing committee on March 1, 1864, through its closing on June 18. At one point, there had been talk by the fair's organizers of publishing a daily newspaper on the grounds, but that idea was abandoned because the Pittsburgh papers had contributed so generously both in advertising space and editorial content. The *Gazette* and the *Post* both carried columns of names of contributors to the fair, and notices of meetings of the various committees, which, in an era before telephones, were crucial. On May 23, the *Gazette* included a report of preliminary flag-raising event at Floral Hall, along with the full text of the four addresses given by notables on the occasion.

As the June 1 opening day approached, the *Post* expressed anxiety. On May 26, it carried the plea, "The patriotic people of Western Pennsylvania and Eastern Ohio are urged to provide articles for the 'Old Curiosity Shop' at the Sanitary Fair to make it successful." The paper further observed, "though the buildings of this Fair are rapidly approaching completion, yet the time for the opening ceremonies is coming as rapidly, and it will require all the exertions of the mechanics employed to have it prepared for the reception of the many contributions now arriving." Although people living in the wooded sections of Westmoreland and Fayette counties voluntarily brought in wagonloads of woven evergreens for decorating the buildings, there was still too little material, and the *Gazette* sent out a last-minute appeal for more in the June 1, opening-day edition. That issue also featured front-page advertisements for the fair, plus a rapturous editorial inside: "No effect has been spared by our patriotic citizens of both sexes to make it a complete success. . . . The attractions which the Fair will present to the visitor have been so fully explained in our local columns that any mention of them would be a work of supererogation. We may, however, say that never before in the history of Western Pennsylvania has an opportunity been presented to look upon so many, so rare and exquisite attractions as will be exhibited in the various halls and booths of this Sanitary Fair." The *Post* was equally laudatory, but expressed concern, on the fair's second day, about crowd control: "If this estimate is correct [22,000] and as large a crowd attend today as the opening of the Fair, it will be impossible to keep any kind of order, and damage to the stands and goods may result from the eagerness of the excited tumult to witness the sights in the different apartments of the Fair." The editor need not have worried so much—the chairman of the fair had invited 120 West Chester cadets to camp on the square for the duration of the activities.

Day after day abundant stories and advertisements described the range of goods for sale, as well as the variety of entertainment, including classical concerts, a large art exhibition, gymnastics, military exhibitions, a stereopticon display, tableaux, programs by school children, promenades, and a ball. The newspapers duly carried reviews of the concerts, including one of the first Pittsburgh performances of Handel's "Messiah" on June 11. Admission to concerts ranged from twenty-five cents to one dollar. In the end, the fair was an outstanding financial success. Including the proceeds from end-of-fair auctions, the benefit fair made more than three hundred thousand dollars, an enormous sum at the time. The executive committee proudly announced that the total amounted to a per capita contribution of $3.47 for every man, woman, and child in the two cities and all adjacent boroughs. Moreover, that was the highest per capita rate for any of the Sanitary Fairs up to that time.

During this period, the *Gazette* also had cause to celebrate its own progress. On May 26, 1864, the newspaper proudly announced: "The New Press." It explained, "Workmen are now engaged in putting in place for us one of Hoe's four cylinder presses, which is capable of printing ten thousand copies of the *Gazette* in an hour. The press cost us about $12,000. Its purchase was rendered necessary by the large increase in our circulation, which has almost doubled since our enlargement in the month of December last."

The *Gazette*'s increased circulation reflected the public's hunger for constant news of the war's unfolding. Finally, the conflict drew to a close. Three days after the fall of Richmond on April 4, 1865, the *Gazette* printed a false rumor that Lee had surrendered. The actual event followed two days later, and was met with celebration throughout the Pittsburgh region. Whatever reservations the *Post* had held about the Republican administration's conduct of the war were swept away in joy: "It is difficult to comprehend the magnitude of the nation's rejoicings, over the prospects of a speedy peace and Union, and what is particularly gratifying is the tone of moderation used toward the vanquished. . . . Our war was actually necessary in order to give us an idea of our greatness; now that it is over we can place a proper estimate upon our prowess and resources, and with a thoroughly united country, may defy the world in arms. The South fought bravely and long, and continued the struggle until her resources were exhausted. Her gallant bearing against superior numbers entitled her to our admiration, while her desolate and powerless condition should extort our pity. In rebelling against the government she sinned most grievously, and most grievously has she answered for it."[6]

Then, in the midst of rejoicing, came the worst possible news. The *Gazette* of April 15 in headline after headline broke the tidings: "Most Startling News! President Lincoln and Secretary Seward Assassinated —The President Dying! The Secretary Will Probably Die! The President Shot in the Theatre! Seward Stabbed in his Bed! Narrow Escape of Gen. Grant—Escape of the Assassins—Wild Excitement in Washington." On the same day, the *Post* published an unsigned but highly personalized account: "About two o'clock this morning, we were startled by the awful announcement of the assassination of President Lincoln and Secretary Seward, detailed in the following telegraphic dispatches. We are so petrified at this awful intelligence that, at this early hour in the morning, we are unable to speak of its damnable enormity as it deserves." A lengthy dispatch from Washington followed, similar to the *Gazette*'s account. As it turned out, both newspapers were in error on one point—Seward had survived a stabbing attempt.

The postwar era had begun on a note that confounded all expectations and plans. Sorrow for the president's death was as universal as had been the rejoicing. Both the *Gazette* and the *Post* had very clear views on what should happen next. The papers were at odds once again.

Chapter 7

Reconstruction, Railroads, Riots

I N THE EDITORIALS of the fateful week between General Lee's sur-render at Appomattox and the assassination of President Lincoln, readers could see the outlines of the political fissures that were to de-velop in the triumphant North.

The *Pittsburgh Post* advocated magnanimity toward the South and was incensed at a suggestion by Union General Ben Butler that Con-federate officers should be hanged. Butler was a somewhat ineffectual military leader, but was kept in place by the Lincoln administration as a Democrat whose presence mitigated the Republican predominance in the war effort. He eventually became one of the most ardent Republi-cans. On April 14, 1865, the *Post* disgustedly wrote: "General Butler and his stripe of patriots, who looked to the broad acres of the South as fine pickings to be used for compensating their 'loyalty,' will be terribly dis-appointed if the President acts with the slightest liberality in the settle-ment of our difficulties. But let them fret till their corrupt hearts break; the country can get along without them." The next day it referred to Butler as a "beast" and a "monster."

Over at the *Gazette*, the mood was much less conciliatory. On the same April 14, under the headline "Peace—Reconstruction," the *Ga-zette* noted that there was now no southern nation. With no one therefore to deal with, the national government "should reduce the rebellious States to the condition of territories—the proper power of the states being, meanwhile, not extinct, but in abeyance. But we can see no other way." Two days later it blamed the South for Lincoln's assassination and called for vengeance: The editorial column was led by a short paragraph. "Apologetic—Owing to the circular form of our press and forms, it is not in our power to turn our rules and put our paper 'into mourning,' as it is termed. We regret this, but cannot help it." (Turning the rules refers to a practice of flipping the rules between the columns of type upside-down, so that a funereal-looking set of thick, black lines run up and down the page.) The *Gazette* then editorialized: "It is a fearful way in which to teach this nation a needed lesson; but probably it would have been too blind to learn it in any other way. That lesson has now been taught as by an overruling Providence, and we learn by it that Slavery is *not* dead. It was slavery aimed that blow at the life of the President, and he is not a true man who does vow that he will give himself no rest until Slavery and the spirit of Slavery are thoroughly rooted out of this land. . . . The South has provoked its doom, and it cannot be averted. We must wipe out every vestige of Slavery, whatever, or in whatever shape it exists. We must teach the rebellious people of the South that there is nothing for them but submission or expatriation; that there is no door open through which they can come back and be as they were before."

The *Gazette* continued to stake out territory as a radical Republican newspaper, supporting those in Congress whose policies included harsh treatment of the defeated South, efforts to give the freed blacks political rights and status, and the election of black state legislators and members of Congress. This cemented African Americans from both North and South to the Republican Party for generations and, conversely, created the "solid south" for the Democratic Party. Lincoln's successor, Andrew Johnson, fell from grace with the *Gazette* when his temperate attitude toward the rebellious states became apparent. Not surprisingly, the *Post* swung to his support; after all, Johnson was a Tennessee Democrat paired with Lincoln to balance the ticket in the 1864 election.

There is no question but that support for clemency to the South was often accompanied by overt racism. The *Post* demonstrated this in an September 17, 1866, editorial titled, "The Mulatto Convention," which sneered: "The black and tanned gathering of burly negroes, long-nosed Abolitionists and toothless old maids who assembled last week in Philadelphia, was the most disgraceful and profane known in the history of popular assemblies. The organs of the Radicals feel that it has damaged their cause and are disposed to say nothing about it. Defeat stares them in the face, and their courage has consequently forsaken them."

Pittsburgh continued to be strongly Republican, in keeping with the business-oriented climate that enabled the city to thrive in the post–Civil War era. As an ever-expanding industrial center, the city became a magnet for immigrants from eastern and southern Europe. That growth was reflected in the census figures, a nearly seven-fold increase from 49,217 in 1860 to 321,616 in 1900. Not surprisingly, it was accompanied by labor strife as workers and management squared off over shares of the economic pie—another subject for editorial sparring between the *Gazette* and the *Post*.

In May 1866, a quartet of respected businessmen—F. B. Fenniman, Josiah King, Thomas Houston, and Nelson P. Reed—took over the *Gazette*. As matters developed in the succeeding years, three of the partners retired or sold their interests. Therefore, Nelson Reed emerged as so powerful a figure that by the time of his death from grippe in 1891, that period in the life of the *Gazette* had become known as "The Reign of Reed." Indeed, because Reed was succeeded by his nephew, Alfred Reed, that "reign" actually extended until the *Gazette* again changed hands in 1900.

A major development during Nelson Reed's tenure was the shift in responsibilities: in a time when journalism was becoming impersonal and commercial, the editor no longer had supreme control. While the *Gazette* had a succession of editors, Nelson Reed, from his desk as business manager, ran the show. In 1883 the scope of his influence was formalized when he became the head of both the business department and the editorial page. Reed's imprint on the paper was significant, as J. Cutler Andrews noted: "[E]very division felt the impress of his control. It was his forte to bear responsibilities with unruffled poise and unshaken nerve. Yet his manners were simple and frank, and his kindness of heart was proverbial. At all times he conversed freely with and was closely in touch with all members of his staff. An excellent judge of men, he kept around him a continuous corps of trusted employees, who enjoyed his remarkably keen sense of humor and liked him all the more for his hearty booming laugh that echoed and reechoed through the office corridors."[1]

Nelson P. Reed

The *Gazette* in those years needed Reed's touch. While the Civil War had impressed upon local citizens the value of a daily newspaper for news, Pittsburgh businessmen were still woefully indifferent in terms of advertising support. Reed was born in Butler County on August 14, 1841, and, after a preliminary education at Butler Academy, he started working for his father, Major George Reed, county treasurer. When war came, Reed joined the local company of volunteers and fought diligently until a shot at the Battle of Antietam incapacitated him. At home, recovering from his wound, he decided to take up business and enrolled at Duff's Commercial College in Pittsburgh. He worked at the provost marshal's office, which led to a position as the business manager at the *Pittsburgh Dispatch.* He increased the prosperity of that newspaper so well that he was asked to join the entrepreneurial foursome in purchasing the *Gazette.*

One of Reed's major accomplishments was the purchase in 1877 of the *Commercial,* a morning competitor that had been launched in the 1850s by C. D. Brigham. To reflect the change, the *Gazette* changed its name to the *Commercial Gazette.* During the *Commercial*'s short life it had become quickly known both for its outspoken Republicanism and for a distinguished editorial page. After the acquisition, the man largely responsible for the latter, Russell Errett, returned to the *Gazette* to supervise its editorial work. This merger added 6,000 subscribers to the *Gazette*'s circulation, which had been seriously hurt by the financial panic of 1873. In 1870, the daily *Gazette* had 9,000 subscribers and the weekly edition had 14,000. The daily skidded to 4,500 in 1873 and continued decreasing, to reach a low of 3,500 in 1875. Yet Pittsburgh's economy was starting to improve. The city's post–Civil War prosperity and industrial growth was emphasized by the 1880 census, showing a population of 156,389, a 28 percent gain over ten years. By the turn of the century, the *Gazette*'s circulation figures reflected this prosperity: 35,267 people subscribed to the daily in 1900 and 17,000 to the weekly.

Errett had been busy since his days as the activist *Gazette* editor in the 1850s. After the war, he worked for the *Commercial,* but in 1867 ran for the state senate against James P. Barr, editor of the *Post,* and was elected. Starting two years later, he served as President Grant's U.S. assessor of internal revenues until the post was abolished. In 1876 Errett ran against a three-term member of Congress, General James G. Negley, and defeated him. At that point, even the formidable Errett found being a member of Congress and a newspaperman at the same time to be too much. So he resigned from the *Gazette* when he was re-elected in 1878 to the twenty-second congressional seat—all of Allegheny County south of the Ohio and Allegheny Rivers. He served until an independent Republican candidate defeated him in 1882. He died April 7, 1891.

Besides Errett, another unusual choice made by Reed for the editorial page was the Reverend Jonathan Vannote. Andrews paints a picturesque scene around this clergyman's role at the newspaper: "The life of a newspaper editor in the 1870s hardly conformed to modern conceptions of what it should have been. The conveniences of arrangement to be seen in the newspaper office of today were for the most part unknown. The large egg-shaped stove, the ample coal box, and the equally ample wood box half filled with sawdust and toby [cigar] stubs were the familiar furnishing of the composing room, which, as the one place in a morning newspaper office that was always occupied, was in winter the most comfortably heated room in the building. Not infrequently Vannote, while associate editor, would enter a city pulpit on Sunday morning and then, after the sermon, make his way to the *Gazette* office to write a leader for Monday morning's paper."[2]

As time went on, fashions in journalism changed. Perhaps because the public was more indifferent, the newspaper's editorials no longer carried the weight they once had. By 1885, the editorial page was running small feature columns such as "Paragraphic Pencilings of Passing Events Pertinently Put," "Terse Telegrams," "Near-town Notes," "Jocular Jottings," and "The Quiet Observer." The latter eventually won a nationwide reputation. Its author was Erasmus Wilson, who had grown up on an Ohio farm, served in the Civil War, and then become a country doctor. He began his journalistic work with the *Pittsburgh Leader,* then shifted to the *Commercial Gazette* from 1877 to 1880 before moving to the *Telegraph* and then the *Dispatch.* He later loved to tell of how, during the election year of 1884, he submitted a report of a political gathering that the *Dispatch*'s managing editor angrily denounced as neither news nor editorial. Wilson was dismissed with the words "your head is off" ringing in his ears. Fortunately, friends intervened so that, as Wilson whimsically put it, "I was permitted to go around town with my head off for several weeks." He was allowed to continue a special column of comment, whose popularity prompted Reed to bring him back to the *Commercial Gazette* in January 1888. Wilson's column focused on "manners and events," discussing such subjects as the obnoxiousness of male flirts, the public attitude toward bachelors, politics in the public schools, and the intricacies of social etiquette. His keen vision and gentle humor so delighted thousands of readers that once, when it was hinted that the "The Quiet Observer" might be discontinued, the *Gazette* was flooded with so many indignant letters that the idea was hastily shelved.

Wilson's column had even more effect than he perhaps intended. A young Elizabeth Cochran wrote an angry letter to the *Dispatch,* complaining about a particular "Quiet Observer" column entitled "What Girls Are Good For." Wilson had suggested that women should be confined to domestic tasks only, and called a woman working outside the home "a monstrosity." Cochran's letter vigorously defended the women of Pittsburgh who needed to work in order to make money to live. Her letter so impressed the *Dispatch*'s editor that he hired her as a staff reporter. Her articles, which focused especially on the working women of Pittsburgh, poverty, and divorce, appeared under the pen name "Nellie Bly," taken from a song by Stephen Foster. Bly would go on to become world famous as a New York journalist and the woman who traveled around the world in seventy-two days, beating the mythical record of Jules Verne's hero.

Although the Pittsburgh newspapers of that era were stiff competitors, there was also a certain amount of solidarity among the staffs. This was illustrated in 1878 upon the death of Joseph S. Lare, coeditor of the *Post.* Lare's family, Philadelphia printers, owned the A. J. Holman Bible Company, one of the largest Bible printing companies in the United States at the time. In 1866, Lare had entered a joint partnership with

Elizabeth Cochran, better known as Nellie Bly, got her start in journalism at the *Pittsburgh Dispatch* and went on to write for the *New York World*. (Courtesy Carnegie Library of Pittsburgh)

James Barr, who had been editor and proprietor of the *Post* since May 1, 1857, as well as with Edwin A. Mayers and William A. Schoyer. When Lare died at the age of forty after two years of illness, an organization calling itself the Newspaper Fraternity of Pittsburgh issued a statement on March 8: "In Memoriam of Joseph S. Lare, late one of the editors and proprietors of the *Pittsburgh Post*. It is the sense of the representatives of the daily journals after a meeting called for the purpose of giving expression of the same . . . that we have lost an able, devoted, conscientious and exemplary member." The signers were men from seven papers—the *Commercial Gazette*, the *Telegraph*, the *Freiheit Freund*, the *Chronicle*, the *Post*, the *Dispatch*, and the *Leader*.[3]

All of these papers were affected by the technological innovations of the late nineteenth century. In 1882, the *Commercial Gazette* announced its purchase of a large new press, capable of printing fifteen thousand impressions per hour instead of the six thousand of the discarded four-cylinder Hoe press. Both sides of the paper could be printed at once, and each complete issue could be cut, pasted, and folded before leaving the press. In 1894, the management introduced the new Mergenthaler machine, or linotype as it came to be called, which changed typesetting from a hand to a machine operation. An operator could set a line of type at a time using typewriter-like keys. The machine turned each line of type into a slug made from hot lead, and a set of successive slugs containing a story or advertisement was then placed in a shallow metal form to create a page, proof sheets of which could be pulled for proofreaders to correct mistakes. The forms were then taken to the stereotype department where an impression was made on a mat—a special kind of thick, cardboard-like paper that could be shaped into a half-cylinder to fit on a rotary printing press. A hot metal impression of the curved mat was made, producing a stereotype that could be placed directly on the press.

During that era, too, there were important innovations regarding paper stock. For several hundred years all paper had been made by hand from rag pulp. In 1840, however, a German named Friedrich Keller invented a process for grinding wooden logs into a fibrous pulp, and in 1867, an American named B. C. Tilgham found that the fibers in wood could be separated if the wood were dissolved in a solution of sulfurous acid. Various European chemists improved on this sulfite process so that by 1882, wood pulp was made by processes similar to those in modern paper mills.

In 1894, the *Commercial Gazette* dropped its subscription rate to two cents per issue (or five dollars per year) and in 1895 to one cent per issue (or three dollars per year). These changes undoubtedly resulted from the competitive success of a major local "penny paper," the evening *Pittsburgh Press,* launched June 23, 1884. Designed to tap a reservoir of readers designated "the common people," penny papers circumvented the customary subscription charge of six to ten dollars a year in advance, a price that was more than most skilled workers earned in a week, and that few people would have as a ready lump sum. By the time the *Press* was inaugurated, the penny press concept was a half-century old in America, having been launched in 1833 with Benjamin H. Day's *New York Sun,* which first utilized sensationalism to attract readers, but gradually broadened offerings to attract readers from higher social and economic brackets. A Pittsburgh version of the penny paper, the *Daily Sun,* operated in Pittsburgh from 1842–1845 under none other than Russell Errett, but after its unsuccessful run, no other such paper had arrived in the city until the *Press.*

Like many Pittsburgh papers, the *Press* evolved out of another daily. In the early 1880s, Thomas J. Keenan was practically the entire staff of the *Pittsburgh Times.* When he discussed with his employer, Robert Nevin, his hopes of having a paper of his own, Nevin surprised him by offering to sell him the *Times* for forty thousand dollars. Although he was able to cobble together twenty-five thousand dollars from friends and Colonel Thomas M. Bayne, North Side political leader, a thorough inspection of the *Times* showed it was losing money and had dilapidated equipment. So Keenan and his backers decided to start a new paper, thinking it might succeed as a penny paper in a field crowded with dailies selling for two and three cents.

Because printing equipment had not arrived on the day scheduled for publication, the presses of the *Times* were used for several weeks to print small, four-page issues of fewer than ten thousand copies each, which were delivered by wheelbarrow. The first issue carried local items, such as men being thrown out of saloons and bachelors having troubles finding living quarters. The penny-price idea quickly caught on, so much so that some of the subscription solicitors were able to make their quotas by merely sitting in saloons and signing up the men who came in. By August, the *Press*'s newly arrived four-cylinder Hoe press could hardly keep up with the demand as circulation within a month had soared to 13,500.

In 1888, the paper's name was changed to the *Pittsburg Press,* dropping the "h" from the end of "Pittsburgh." The *Post,* the *Dispatch,* the *Leader,* the *Times,* and other newspapers echoed that move after a decree from the U.S. Geographic Board in December 1891. This was a standardization move to require post offices in all municipalities ending with "burgh" to become "burg," and for every "borough" to become a "boro." That ruling, creating considerable confusion in newspaper names and stories from that era, finally was rescinded in July 1911. The overturning of the standardization in 1911 occurred, in part, due to the political muscle of U.S. Senator George Oliver, at that time the

Gazette's publisher. Interestingly, the *Gazette,* even while changing names in those years, always retained the "burgh" spelling.

In 1889, the Sunday *Press* was born, selling for two cents in Pittsburgh and Allegheny City, three cents elsewhere. The *Commercial Gazette, Post, Leader,* and *Dispatch* also added Sunday editions at this time. In the 1890s, this development almost brought ruin because of the blue laws in Pennsylvania that prohibited businesses from operating on Sundays. An organization called the Law and Order Society began swearing out warrants every Monday for the business managers of the five local Sunday papers. The managers paid their two-dollar fines and went ahead publishing the Sunday papers. Then the society began swearing out warrants for every employee of each paper, which could have broken the papers financially. However, the *Gazette*'s Thomas Houston discovered the promoters of the Law and Order Society were racketeers wanted in several other cities for shady deals, and so squelched their campaign.

The *Press* impacted the city in both obvious and subtle ways. In the days before radio and television, newspapers drew attention to their forthcoming editions by placing huge bulletin boards in front of their offices, headlining the latest news and often attracting large news-hungry crowds during periods of tension. In 1892, the *Press* began to post their bulletins in black ink on gold paper. Black and gold became the *Press*'s colors, and were later adopted as the official colors of the city of Pittsburgh and, even later, of its professional sports teams. Also in the 1890s, the *Press* began a long, commendable career of sponsoring charity and youth events, beginning with a campaign that raised fifty thousand dollars for a home for orphans, and extending to the establishment of the Press Young Folks League, which held picnics and sponsored activities of many kinds, and the Press Cadets, a semi-military group that held regular drills and a two-week summer camp for approximately one thousand young Pittsburghers. This kind of civic activity was to continue through the decades, and later included the Old Press Newsboys organization, which raised money for the Children's Hospital of Pittsburgh. Moreover, the *Press* became the first newspaper in town to furnish typewriters for its reporters and editors and to use an automobile—a loud three-wheeled model—for delivery service.

With one of the most modern news plants in its five-story building at

325 Fifth Avenue and three hundred employees, Keenan thought of adding a morning paper. Before that plan could be initiated, however, Keenan sold the paper for $750,000 to a syndicate headed by Colonel Oliver S. Hershman. Hershman also purchased the *Daily News,* formerly the evening edition of the *Pittsburgh Times,* and merged it into the *Press.* The combined newspaper forged ahead with innovations, including colored-ink comics, such as "Happy Hooligan," "Maud," and "Little Ah Sid, the Chinese Kid." By 1904, the *Press* announced that it had passed the one hundred thousand mark in daily circulation, and in 1907 the daily *Press* broke the national record for advertising volume with twelve million lines of paid advertisements. Hershman sold the paper to the Scripps Howard chain in 1923.

The *Commercial Gazette,* perhaps in response to the new challenge, began to reach out to a broader audience, including the female newspaper reader. In 1884 the *Commercial Gazette* began providing a resumé of current society events every Friday. Later, management designated Cara Reese as a full-fledged editor, and her "Cara's Column" came to serve as the women's department of the *Gazette.* In the early 1880s, the *Gazette* also tried to attract sports fans by printing box scores for baseball games and increasing attention to "Our Own," as the Pittsburgh Pirates were commonly known.

Another change made at the *Commercial Gazette* in the Reed era was in the size of its pages. When the "quartet" of which Nelson Reed was a member took over in 1866, the *Gazette*'s sheet size measured twenty-six by twenty inches in a folio—or four-page—edition eight columns wide. Two years later the number of pages was doubled, but the sheet size was cut to twenty-three by fifteen inches, with each page only six columns wide. Evidently, the reaction of the public was negative, for the *Gazette* dropped the idea, returning to a four-page journal. It wasn't until 1882 that Nelson Reed once again adopted the eight-page, smaller page format. In 1885 the *Gazette* enlarged its Saturday edition to twelve pages. The *Post* also adopted an eight-page format in the 1880s.

When the *Commercial Gazette* lowered its prices to the penny-press level, businessmen as well as the *Gazette*'s competitors were impressed that, in the obvious effort to increase its circulation, the paper apparently had strong enough advertising revenues to warrant such a sacrifice. The quantity of advertising in the *Gazette* increased steadily during the years from 1866 to 1900. The most startling change was in department-store advertising, from the use of two or three squares of space in 1866 to full-page illustrated spreads by Joseph Horne and Company, Kaufmann's, Grand Depot, Gusky's, Campbell's and other businesses by 1900. The *Gazette* staff also began to realize the advantages of placing ads next to news.

In the post–Civil War period, the first major event with national implications in the life of Pittsburgh and its newspapers was the railroad riot of 1877. What began as a garden-variety strike by railroad employees over management's 10 percent cut in wages unleashed a dammed-up fury that surprised everyone involved. For Pittsburgh's newspapers, it brought to the fore different views on political, labor, and social issues.

In mid-July, the *Gazette* began to take notice of disturbances on the Baltimore and Ohio Railroad that threatened to spread to the Pennsylvania Railroad. The paper was mildly critical of the strikers but hardly expressed concern. Then, suddenly, on July 20, it was startled to discover that the "railroad war" had broken out in Pittsburgh itself. That day huge crowds continuously watched the *Gazette*'s bulletin board and snatched up extra editions as soon as they appeared. The front-page headlines on Monday, July 23 related the disastrous events of the weekend in headlines stair-stepped downward—

Mob law rampant
　The reign of anarchy in the smoky city
　　An attempt to quell the strike by the military power disastrously fails
　　　The Philadelphia troops attempt to clear the tracks
　　　　They are assaulted and return the fire
　　　　　Men, women and children fall victims to the bullets. The wildest excitement ensues
　　　　　　The passions of the workmen are inflamed. Reason is thrown to the winds
　　　　　　　Mob law inaugurated. The authorities powerless before the fury
　　　　　　　　The incendiary's torch leads to fearful destruction. A night of horrors
　　　　　　　　　The troops beleaguered in the Round House. The desperate defense. The building fired
　　　　　　　　　　They march through the streets and escape. The men who fell by the way. A day of riot, vandalism, pillage and arson
　　　　　　　　　　　The whole city stricken with alarm. The citizens assemble.
　　　　　　　　　　　Vain pleading with the rioters

Over thirty lives lost and ten millions of property destroyed. Thousands of cars and hundreds of locomotives fall a prey to the flames

The magnificent Union Depot goes down. The grain elevators in ashes. The fire line extending for miles. The work of ruin complete

On the editorial page that day, the *Gazette* excoriated the behavior of the mob and demanded stern reprisals: "In the afternoon of Sunday there were hundreds of persons that could be seen on the streets rolling barrels of flour, carrying hams, dry goods, and articles of every description taken from the freight cars. It was a mob, made up of the vicious elements of the city, that simply seized on the occasion for pillage and incendiarism. . . . With the spirit of lawlessness there is but one way of dealing. It must be stopped and the depredators punished, at whatever cost. . . . And if there are, as rumored, some reputable citizens who are disposed to applaud and favor them, we have only to say that they will have the pleasure of paying the cost of this display of Communism." Several days later, on July 26, the *Gazette* invoked the Civil War rhetoric of a dozen years earlier in this sarcastic comment: "It is calculated to make the reader open his eyes to find the Southern papers denouncing what they call the 'present great rebellion' at the North, and advocating the strengthening of the powers of the Federal Government by increasing the regular army to enable it to deal with such outbreaks."

Although the *Gazette* admitted, in a follow-up story of August 2, that management was to some extent responsible for the strike, it placed most of the blame on the workers' side: "The leaders in this movement are clearly demagogues, and are of no value whatever. Were the working people to cultivate close and friendly relations with their employers, and have less to do with demagogues, who earn their salaries by developing troubles, bad blood, and antagonisms between labor and capital,

(*Opposite, top*) The railroad riot of 1877, as depicted in *Frank Leslie's Illustrated Newspaper*
(Courtesy Carnegie Library of Pittsburgh)

(*Opposite, bottom*) *Harper's Weekly* portrayed the burning of the Union Depot and Hotel while crowds gathered to watched "in wild anxiety," according to *Harper's* reporter.
(Courtesy Carnegie Library of Pittsburgh)

they would serve their own interests, and it would be better in every way." The paper also took the opportunity to criticize its old enemies, the Democrats: "The recent strikes, with the attendant unreliability of State militia, have proven the necessity of a strong regular army, and the criminal folly, not to say worse, of the Democratic majority in Congress that sought to paralyze and destroy, and did injure the regular army to gratify political spite."

The *Post* initially shared the *Gazette*'s consternation. On Monday, July 23, its front-page top headlines screamed: "Reign of the Mob! A Black Sunday for Pittsburgh." On the editorial page, it commented: "The terrible story of mob supremacy in Pittsburgh for the best part of two entire days is told elsewhere. It is written in blood and ashes—desolated households and streets swept as with the besom [broom] of destruction. We realize for the first time in our history what mob rule is and that when once we pass the line that divides the law breaker from the faithful citizens, how fearfully rapid is the descent to scenes of the most brutalizing and inhuman character. . . . A redress of grievances can never be reached by weakening the bonds that hold society together." The *Post* editorial then shifted gears: "Another lesson the events of the last few days emphasizes, and this is that a great corporation, possessed of boundless wealth and resources, with its thousand arms stretching to the remote parts of the land—a corporation that is omnipresent with legislatures and governors, and tenderly coddled by the judiciary—cannot in the usefulness of its power pursue systematic injustice and opposition without experiencing a day of reckoning. . . . It took a decade and more of injustice and wrong to every business man of Pittsburgh to bring about this rendition of public sentiment. We grieve to say it, but under no other circumstances could the mob have worked out such a terrible result." The *Post* editorial went on to condemn the state government and the mayor, and declared that "the [Republican] sheriff of the county seems to have lost his head, and what little brains there is in it, early in the troubles."

On July 26, the *Post* printed on the front page an exchange of letters between Colonel Thomas A. Scott, president of the Pennsylvania Railroad, and the editor. Scott wrote, "You will speedily discover that the strike of a few of our railway employees is simply being used by the mob violence which some of you people are permitting or encouraging, to offset other purposes, which if successful, will destroy many of your leading local interests."

In his reply, the *Post*'s editor, James Barr, said: "I implore you not to assume the ground that the military can settle anything but defiance of law. Have this compromise [arbitration] effected at once and the country will owe you a debt of gratitude." On the editorial page, the *Post* reiterated its call under the headline, "Why not arbitration?"

By Friday, the *Post* was joining other papers in exhibiting a persecution complex. In "Punishing Pittsburgh" it expressed resentment: "The Philadelphia papers are advocating a terrible vengeance on Pittsburgh. It is that the Pennsylvania Railroad shall 'go around the city,' so as 'to avoid this turbulent centre in the future.' . . . Philadelphia newspapers, with the chivalry of the jackal, seem to have a fancy for lingering over the recent unfortunate events to insult, and slander Pittsburgh and its citizens."

The *Gazette* declared on August 2 that the state militia "did their duty in a most commendable manner," but the *Post* heaped sarcasm upon both the militia and the regular army. Its July 30 edition read: "Our city is doubly honored. We have here a force of regular soldiers larger than we have had here for many years. Then we have two or three thousand of the National Guard from different parts of the state. . . . To be sure there doesn't appear to be much for this extraordinary concentration of men and muskets to do, other than appear in dress parade and prance around to the lascivious tootings of the fife and bass drum. . . . The trains are running on the railroads, not exactly because the soldiers are here, but as the result of measures adopted by our authorities, civil and military, to maintain order. We extend a hearty welcome to the boys in blue, and gray, yellow and green; hope their sojourn here will ever be a delightful remembrance, and an inheritance to their children, and their return to their homes garlanded with flowers and laurels, and moistened with lager. We couldn't say more if we tried." On the editorial page that day, the tone was more serious. Under the headline, "Treat Them Like Men," the *Post* asserted, "Underlying the question of wages involved in the recent railroad strikes is the question of the treatment of employees as human beings, having rights to courtesy, and some sense of their own manhood. The fact has cropped out in all the manifestations around here; the petty tyranny of railroad officials had quite as much to do with the dissatisfaction culminating in the strike as the question of a fair day's pay for a fair day's work."

Elections, predictably, provoked bitter rivalry between the *Gazette* and the *Post*. In the presidential election of 1880, the *Commercial Gazette,* which initially had backed the ambitions of ex-President Grant to go for a third term after a hiatus during the Rutherford Hayes presidency, swung in line behind James Garfield when he won the Republican nomination. The *Post,* of course, became the only Pittsburgh paper to back the Democratic nominee, dubbed "Slippery Sam" Tilden by the *Gazette*. As the election campaign heated up, the *Gazette* volleyed on October 28: "The *Post* has voluntarily rated itself among the most unscrupulous Democratic papers in the country. It has reached the lowest stage of journalistic depravity, and should not hereafter be permitted to enter a Republican dwelling or house of business." When Garfield won, the *Gazette* celebrated with illustrations of a raccoon and a rooster, symbols of the Republican and Democratic parties respectively, with a legend reading, "The Hurricane Strikes the Office of the *Pittsburgh Post* and Scatters Its Poultry in All Directions."

Eight months later, the *Gazette* obtained one of the greatest scoops in its history with the shocking news of the assassination of the new president on July 2, 1881. The story is that a Western Union Telegraph Company employee in Pittsburgh took the first dispatch on the subject and rushed over to the *Gazette* office with the news. The staff was incredulous at first but took the gamble and put out a short bulletin. A crowd that had gathered murmured that the story could not be true, since no other newspaper office had any such notice. The men at the *Gazette* were about to tear down the notice when their Western Union informant came running over with full information of the shooting by Charles J. Guiteau, a disappointed patronage seeker. The *Gazette* furthered its "beat" with a second bulletin, followed by a hastily printed extra edition.

In terms of scoops, the *Post* was to have its revenge in spades nearly twenty years later during the Spanish-American War by publishing the nation's first account of Commodore George Dewey's great naval victory over a Spanish squadron in Manila Bay on May 1, 1898. Actually, the desire for a scoop got the better of journalistic integrity in an enterprising example of sleight-of-hand, imaginative writing on the part of the *Post*. The story, appearing under a Hong Kong dateline with the by-line "G. Schlotterbeck, Hong Kong correspondent," was actually written in Pittsburgh. The bulletins from across the Pacific indicating that a battle had been fought and won were just enough to be tantalizing. All day Sunday and late Sunday night the *Post*'s managing editor, Joe Myers, sat waiting for the complete story. Suppose the story were to arrive after the *Post*'s morning edition had gone to press? Or suppose one of the other morning papers, the *Commercial Gazette* or the *Dispatch*, had the story and was waiting to spring it in the final edition? Or would the evening papers get the first opportunity to print the news? What happened next is best related by Schlotterbeck himself in a story that ran decades later in the *Post*'s successor newspaper:

At 1:30 Monday morning, Joe Myers . . . called me into his office and said, abruptly: "I appoint you our special correspondent at Hong Kong. You have a lively imagination," the managing editor continued, "now weave these few bulletins into a connected story. We will set it in 10-point and triple-lead it, so as to fill the entire front page." I went to my task with high enthusiasm . . . and within an hour had the story complete. Demand for the *Post* was so tremendous on Monday morning that the presses were kept running until noon. The old *Pittsburgh Dispatch*, owned by the O'Neils, was flabbergasted, and for months showed its grief at being scooped out of its boots. On Tuesday forenoon a letter from Uniontown arrived, reading as follows: "Your correspondent was so accurate in his details that he must have been on both flagships at the same time."[4]

This scoop must have been particularly galling for the *Commercial Gazette* since it had backed Republican President William McKinley's resistance to going to war with Spain. Even the February 15, 1898, explosion in Havana harbor that sent the *U.S.S. Maine* to its grave did not sway the *Gazette*'s loathing for the war-drum efforts by Hearst's *New York Journal* and the rest of the "yellow press." The *Gazette*'s editor characterized these papers as full of "partisanship and sensationalism run mad." He tartly observed, "Compared with the promoters of such journalism, the vultures wheeling above the sunken *Maine* may command admiration."[5]

Occasionally, the rival papers cooperated with each other and presented a united front. This happened on the evening of May 31, 1889, when news came by telegraph that an inadequate dam had broken on the property of the elite South Fork Fishing and Hunting Club and destroyed the city of Johnstown, seventy miles east of Pittsburgh. The front page of the *Commercial Gazette*'s June 1, 1889, edition told the story: "Extra—A Stupendous Calamity—The Conemaugh Valley Scraped Bare and the Town of Johnstown Wiped Out by an Overwhelming Deluge from a Mountain Lake."

Although the rainy season of the past several weeks had practically suspended rail service east of Pittsburgh, Pittsburgh's newspapers joined forces to charter special trains to the scene. The first carried newsmen from the *Dispatch* and the *Times*. The second carried journalists from the *Commercial Gazette,* the *Post,* and the *Chronicle-Telegraph.* The trains got no farther than a washed-out bridge at Bolivar, but some of the reporters somehow made their way the last twenty miles to Johnstown. They sent back tales of horror—accounts of white-faced messengers giving the alarm, of panic-stricken people fleeing to higher ground, and the terrible scenes that ensued when the wall of water rolled into the town.

On June 3, in an editorial called "Relief for the Sufferers," the *Commercial Gazette* declared: "Never in the history of Pittsburgh, not even when one-third of the town was in ruins and hundreds of families were left houseless was there such a pressing need for assistance as is occasioned by the calamity at Johnstown." The editorial advised those most in need to come to Pittsburgh to be better cared for, and four trainloads of Johnstown citizens accepted that offer, receiving open-handed hospitality from everyone. Gusky's, a leading Pittsburgh department store, purchased two columns of advertising space in the *Gazette* and then, with telling effect, left the entire space bare except for a small card in the center conveying the management's sympathy. At that point, the *Gazette* offered to take charge of all monetary contributions for the benefit of the sufferers. The community, including magnates Andrew Carnegie and George Westinghouse, donated generously—Carnegie was himself a member of the South Fork Fishing and Hunting Club. The *Gazette* management pledged five thousand dollars to start a subscription loan and it asked all western Pennsylvanians to participate. The paper printed an honor roll of all the names of those who responded to the appeal, but the subscription loan was abandoned when Philadelphia banks came forward with funds, making loans to private individuals unnecessary. The *Gazette* was rewarded by a demand for its editions so enormous that the supply of paper on hand was nearly ex-

Johnstown Flood.
June 2, 1889.

hausted. Indeed, the regular size of each issue was reduced temporarily until an express order for additional supplies could be filled.

Across the country, many papers, such as the *New York Sun,* the *Cincinnati Enquirer,* the *New York Daily Graphic,* and the *Chicago Herald* editorially lashed the South Fork Fishing Club and its members for negligence. Within Pittsburgh, the pro-business *Commercial Gazette* defended the members, who, in addition to Carnegie, included Henry Clay Frick and Andrew Mellon. The *Post,* despite its quite different social bias, rose to their defense as well. On June 7, 1889, it noted: "There is no evidence of even carelessness or indifference by the officers and members of the Conemaugh club as to the safety of those below the dam. On suggestion of possible danger they set about to test the matter, and did so to the satisfaction of those who thought there was danger. They were not derelict in duty, and the awful calamity is a shock to them as it is to few others, because in all aspects of the case they must

Pittsburgh journalists gathered on June 2, 1889, in Johnstown, Pa., to report on the flood that killed more than three thousand people. (From Stefan Lorant, *Pittsburgh: The Story of an American City,* Author's Edition, 1964; Courtesy Rowman and Littlefield Publishers)

feel a certain responsibility; innocent, but none the less grievous for that." The *Press* also felt that too much scorn was being heaped upon the club, since the dam had been built years before and could have broken at some earlier time.

It is not hard to believe that the populist resentment against the wealthy Pittsburghers in the South Fork Club contributed to the ill will that boiled over three years later in one of the great events in the history of Pittsburgh and, indeed, of the nation—the bloody Homestead Strike. At this point, the *Gazette* and the *Post* resumed their differing editorial viewpoints. As with the 1877 railroad strike, wages were the issue at the Carnegie steel works at Homestead, up the Monongahela River from Pittsburgh. On June 7, 1892, a *Post* news story on the subject was headlined, "Will be a fight to the finish. Manufacturers and the Amalgamated Association [of Iron and Steel Workers] will have trouble." The *Gazette* watched anxiously as both sides stood firm. As labor leaders talked of a strike, Henry C. Frick, acting for Carnegie, said nothing—but word went around that he was erecting a nine-foot palisade around the plant as though for defense in case of a siege. On June 30, 1892, newspapers reported the discharge of the entire labor force at Homestead, but added that employees were thoroughly organized to forestall any invasion by "black sheep" from Pittsburgh.

On Wednesday, July 6, however, the *Commercial Gazette* reported the introduction of an entirely new element in the situation with the headline "Pinkertons at Homestead." The Pinkerton detective agency had been organized in 1850 by Scottish immigrant Allan Pinkerton and had made its early fame by exposing counterfeit gangs, guarding President Lincoln on some of his journeys, and smashing several western gangs. After the Civil War it especially became known for the organized groups of armed men whose services were available to employers at a daily fee. Union members hated them because they often were used to break labor strikes. By Thursday, July 7, the Pinkerton story had exploded all over the *Commercial Gazette*'s front page with large headlines over the lead story. "A bloody fight. Strikers and Pinkertons do battle at Homestead. Ten men are killed. Hordes of angry workmen." In the fourth column of the page, another big headline trumpeted: "The Big Battle. Bullets flew fast." The sixth column continued the story with these headlines: "Both hands up. After surrendering the unfortunate Pinkertons were compelled to run a terrible gauntlet. Women as well as

"The Bloody Battle at Homestead, Pa. Wednesday's Deadly Conflict Between Pinkerton Men and the Locked-Out Employees," as depicted in the *Saturday Globe,* Utica, New York, July 9, 1892.

men belabor them." The story in the eighth column reported: "To rescue them. On how Pinkertons were rescued, shipped out of city, except 18 sent to hospitals."

The coverage was ably enhanced by drawings scattered throughout the page, such as "The scene of battle" and "Little Bill," the tugboat that had towed the two barges carrying the Pinkerton strikebreakers up the Monongahela into the resistance by the Homestead workers. Other drawings that placed the workers in a dismal light were: "Firing from ambush," "Strikers firing over the [river] bank," and "Attacking Pinkertons after the surrender."

On the editorial page that day, under the headline, "The Bloodshed at Homestead," the editors commented: "The situation at Homestead is most deplorable. Owing to the attitude voluntarily assumed by both parties to the controversy, rioting and bloodshed were inevitable. Things had been conducted in an orderly way up until the interference of the sheriff, at the request of the mill-owners. It is true the locked-out men had taken virtual control, if not possession, of the works. . . . It is high time that reason, humanity and law take the place of passion, violence and lawlessness. The law must assert itself." Later the editorial demanded greater efforts for a truce, noting that otherwise, "more

Great Battle of Homestead, a broadside by Pittsburgh artist Edwin Rowe

blood shall follow." The next day, July 8, the *Gazette* front page carried an article headlined, "Frick explains. By improved machinery introduced wages will not drop." Frick was managing the enterprise while Carnegie was vacationing in Scotland. A story inside the paper headlined, "No food in sight. The terrible treatment Pinkerton men received." However, quite a different twist came in another story inside: "With One Voice. Men of all parties denounce the hiring of Pinkertons. A murderous gang. Strong terms applied to them by speakers in congress. . . . A great pity that Carnegie . . . . was not at the head of the Pinkerton squad. [U.S.] Senator Voorhees through Senator Palmer argues that the strikers had a legal right to do as they did. Preparing for a thorough investigation of the trouble."

If the *Commercial Gazette* was somewhat equivocal, the *Post*'s attitude was quite clear—pro-labor, anti-Pinkerton. The previous month, on June 7, the *Post* had asserted, "The members of the Amalgamated Association of Iron and Steel Workers are fortifying themselves for the most desperate struggle known in the organization's history. There can be no mistaking the situation; the manufacturers are determined upon a general reduction of wages, and the association is just as determined that it will not stand the proposed cut." On June 28, the *Post* carried a cartoon depicting a dwarfish Benjamin Harrison trying to avert a conflict between labor and capital that might ruin his chances for renomination to the presidency. Four days later, on July 2, the *Post* proclaimed: "Evidently a finish fight against organized labor."

Like the *Commercial Gazette,* the *Post* covered the front page on July 7 with stories and drawings about the bloody events of July 6. Its bank of headlines told readers: "The news in town. It creates the most profound sensation throughout the city. Business almost suspended. Everybody discussing the great Homestead tragedy." The *Post*'s news sense was sufficiently strong enough to allow a story under this headline, "Pinkertons much abused." However, in a story inside the edition, the *Post*'s political proclivities were evident: "Special to the *Pittsburg Post* from Washington. Republicans despondent. The Homestead trouble ends the party's hopes. Every person denounces the action of the firm. The use of Pinkertons condemned. That Carnegie and Pinkerton's Hessians are carrying Pennsylvania and Ohio for the Democratic party is the opinion here today."

That forecast proved to be wrong, as the two states were not part of the tide that swept Grover Cleveland back into the White House in the fall elections. Benjamin Harrison carried Pennsylvania by 516,011 votes to Cleveland's 452,264 and Ohio by the much narrower margin of 405,187 to 404,115.

Also on July 7, the *Post* published an editorial, "Outbreak at Homestead," which conceded that the Homestead mills belonged to the Carnegie Steel Company and that "their right to put into these mills non-union workers if they should see proper to do so is undeniable. . . . Order at Homestead, which should never have been disturbed, must be restored, and it will be." However, it went on to assert: "But there is another aspect from the moral point of view. Powerful capital, such as is involved in this matter, could afford to pursue a different policy toward labor than the cold and arbitrary one it has seen proper to take. All means to a satisfactory settlement had not only not been wholly exhausted, but there had not been a serious effort to utilize these means."

An ancillary editorial commented: "The trouble at Homestead has demonstrated the fact that there is a very fair knowledge of military tactics among the men who follow peaceful occupations as a rule. It is a pity this knowledge was not used against a common enemy instead of against men who were probably nearly all American citizens."

The rancor between the two morning rivals heatedly broke forth in a *Post* editorial on July 12, entitled "1877 and 1892." It blasted: "For intense and narrow partisanship the *Pittsburgh Gazette* is always entitled to the cookie. The Republican party can do no wrong, the Democratic party no right is its shibboleth." The point of the editorial was to defend Governor Robert Pattison, a Democrat, for delaying the calling out of the National Guard. "He acted with caution, prudence and moderation, but with all necessary firmness when the emergency was reached he all along proclaimed would compel the intervention of the State military. . . . Go back to 1877 and compare the needless and reckless way disorganized and inefficient troops were thrown into the disturbed district with the killing and destruction of property that followed. . . . Yet the only words that the *Gazette* in its utter shamelessness and beastly partisanship can find to describe [Pattison] is that 'he has prostituted the executive chair to the base purpose of a demagogue.' This is the talk of a political anarchist." On July 14, the *Post* fired another shot in discussing an editorial in the *New York Sun:* "It even goes farther than the *Gazette* in defending the Pinkerton thugs as a useful and proper institution."

In the end, management prevailed, the strike was squashed, and the men had to return to work on company terms. Organized labor nationally suffered a setback that lasted more than four decades until Franklin Roosevelt's New Deal produced the Wagner Act of 1935 that made collective bargaining more feasible. The general feeling of bitterness toward Carnegie and Frick was diffused by two major subsequent events. One was the attempted assassination on July 23 of Frick in his office in downtown Pittsburgh by a Russian anarchist, Alexander Berkman. The wounded Frick's brave demeanor after the attempt, and a wave of indignation across the country, undercut the cause of the strikers, even though they had nothing to do with the solitary Berkman's crime. The twenty-one-year-old Berkman was found guilty of attempted manslaughter and served fourteen years in the state's Western Penitentiary in Pittsburgh.

The second factor that undermined antipathy was the opening in

1895 of the Carnegie Institute, one of numerous endowments by Carnegie that set the standard for the arts and culture in Pittsburgh. Not surprisingly, the *Commercial Gazette* was full of praise, especially in a November 4 editorial called "An Interesting Week," printed on the Sunday before the Institute's opening: "The election will be of minor importance this week so far as Pittsburgh is concerned, which will be engaged in celebrating the formal opening of the Carnegie library, the music hall and art galleries, grouped in the magnificent structure at the entrance of Schenley Park. In all respects relating to the improvement, the broadening and the culture of the mental and artistic faculties of our people, it is not too much to say it will be the most important week in the history of our city. . . . The munificence of Mr. Carnegie gives Pittsburg what it has never had and has long waited for."

But the *Post's* November 4 editorial on the subject definitely marked Carnegie's rehabilitation in view of that newspaper's stand during the Homestead strike: "Some may be disposed to ask, What would have induced Mr. Carnegie to found such [an institution], at an outlay running into the millions?" The writer listed a number of reasons and then adds: "It is to be regretted that so gorgeous a temple reared for the common benefit of this populous community and devoted to the various uses of literature, science, art and music could not be accepted without a carping few trying to discover whether there is not concealed somewhere in the substantial walls or beautiful adornments, some traces of human weakness, some tinge of personal vanity."

Chapter 8

The Twentieth Century Opens

———◦◦◦———

A S THE TWENTIETH century opened, important changes were coming to the *Commercial Gazette*. The "reign of Reed" ended in June of 1900, when the paper announced its new ownership. Nelson P. Reed & Co. had sold the newspaper for an undisclosed price (estimated at around six million dollars) to George T. Oliver, a prominent local business and industrial leader. Oliver had been born in Ireland and reared in Pittsburgh. He had graduated from Bethany College in West Virginia and then tried his hand at teaching, law, and the wire business, with success in each case. From 1881 to 1888, Oliver had served as president of the Pittsburgh Central Board of Education.

The change in the *Gazette*'s ownership would affect Pittsburgh journalism, in developments that would parallel national trends: advancements in the composition of newspapers, the use of wire services, and the proliferation of evening newspapers. The *Gazette*'s new direction would also reflect a shift in Pittsburgh's politics as the nation headed into an era of reform involving women's suffrage, temperance, and the limitation of business trusts. The city itself was growing—the population of 321,616 in 1900 would reach 533,965 only ten years later.

The Oliver purchase of the *Gazette* added substance to the rumors in Pittsburgh that a big steel merger was stirring—a topic on which

George T. Oliver

Andrew Carnegie was mysteriously silent. In May, Oliver had sold his Oliver Wire Company holdings to the American Steel and Wire Company—a move that foreshadowed the series of corporate consolidations that would result in the formation of U.S. Steel in 1901. When Oliver purchased the *Commercial Gazette*, it seemed that this fifty-two-year-old industrialist was looking for new worlds to conquer.

It was also rumored that either George Oliver or his brother Henry aspired to a seat in the United States Senate. Just before purchasing the *Commercial Gazette*, George had declined the Republican nomination for congressman-at-large. The newspaper purchase could be viewed as a political move, and there was speculation that the new owner might soon seek election as a senator from Pennsylvania. Oliver consistently denied any such motivation, however, and made no move to do anything other than run the *Gazette.* In this vein, Oliver took care to assure the public that he planned to maintain the paper's essential presentation and focus.

Nevertheless, the *Commercial Gazette*'s new owner did begin to reshape the newspaper in numerous ways. In 1896, the rival *Post* had introduced a special cable and wire service that was the envy of competing papers. Oliver continued to subscribe to the Associated Press, but he also added the cable and wire service from the *New York Tribune*—the best of the time. Encapsulating his mission of improvements without fundamental change, the new publisher announced a new motto: "Watch the Old Lady Grow Young."

Later that year Oliver added an evening newspaper to his fleet, the *Chronicle Telegraph.* In 1906, the *Post* followed suit by inaugurating the *Sun,* an afternoon paper that would figure prominently in the 1927 set of mergers that altered the nature of Pittsburgh journalism. The *Sun* was an immediate success, selling over 118,000 copies on the first day.

These developments were in keeping with a nationwide trend as publishers realized the importance of evening newspapers. Between 1880 and 1900, the evening field claimed seven-eighths of the increase in the number of daily newspapers. By 1890, two out of three papers were evening editions. There were two reasons for this shift. Publishers discovered that women readers, who made up more and more of the total readership, and to whom retail-store advertising was directed, favored newspapers delivered in the afternoon. Moreover, innovations in newsgathering and technology permitted the evening papers to carry news on the same day that it occurred, including events of Europe and Asia.

In 1901, the *Commercial Gazette* moved into an architecturally significant new home at 335–339 Virgin Alley (later Oliver Avenue). Designed by D. H. Burnham, one of the nation's most prominent architects and a favorite of Pittsburgh's wealthy elite, the building was large enough to accommodate the *Commercial Gazette* as well as the *Chronicle Telegraph,* the *Volksblatt,* and *Der Freiheits Freund,* all recently acquired Oliver properties. Oliver also chose this moment to restore the paper to its historic title, the *Pittsburgh Gazette*. He had always considered the world "commercial" in the title to be a misnomer because even though the paper had a long reputation for its full commercial reports, it provided more than just the business news. Moreover, Oliver was ready to publish a Sunday edition—practically a necessity in view of the public demand for it. In 1892, the *Post* had celebrated its fiftieth anniversary by launching a Sunday edition. To Oliver and his associates, however, a *Commercial Gazette* seemed out of place on the Sabbath, a day noted for abstention from business activity and for the leisure it afforded for reading of a broader nature. The name change might mollify those for whom Sabbatarian sentiments still prevailed. On November 10, 1901, the first edition of the Sunday *Gazette* emerged from the updated presses. Each copy contained six sections and fifty-two pages, and sold for five cents. The "Humorous Section" included six full pages of comic strips, some of them in color.

Oliver scored another impressive coup in 1906 when he acquired the *Pittsburgh Times* despite the efforts of a group headed by Philander P. Knox to obtain it. Knox was a prominent Pittsburgh lawyer who had served as U.S. attorney general under President McKinley and had been appointed to the U.S. Senate in 1904. The result of Oliver's victory was the *Gazette Times*. Following the death of *Times* owner Christopher Magee in 1901, the paper had been operated by the Magee estate and run by a highly efficient staff. There was ironic justice in the merger in that the *Commercial Gazette* had perennially opposed Magee, a local political boss. In a February 22, 1893 editorial, the paper had described his "ring" as "one of the most corrupt combinations that ever ruled a municipality."

Magee and colleague, William Flinn, had figured prominently in the chapter on Pittsburgh in Lincoln Steffens's 1903 six-city expose, *The Shame of the Cities*. What is particularly surprising about Steffens's influential book is that it failed to mention that Magee was owner of the *Times* and that Flinn owned the *Pittsburg Leader*. This was partly how the Magee-Flinn political machine held power—by directly owning many of the levers of authority. Steffens wrote: "Boss Magee's idea was not to corrupt the city government, but to be it; not to hire votes in councils, but to own councilmen; and so, having seized control of his organization, he nominated cheap or dependent men for the select and common councils. Relatives and friends were his first recourse, and then came bartenders, saloon-keepers, liquor dealers, and others allied to the vices, who were subject to police regulation and dependent in a business way upon the maladministration of law. For the rest he preferred men who had no visible means of support, and to maintain them he used the usual means—patronage. And to make his dependents secure he took over the county government."[1]

The *Gazette* did not exactly have clean hands in terms of political machines. For many years, it sided with a foe of Magee's, U.S. Senator Matthew Quay of Beaver, one of a string of ruthless Republican bosses who dominated Pennsylvania's politics from 1866 to 1921. The *Gazette*'s relationship with Quay was not just a case of "the enemy of my enemy is my friend." It had grown out of a singular Civil War occurrence, when Quay had confronted enemy fire in order to drag editor Nelson Reed's wounded brother to a place of safety. Quay remained friends with the Reed family from that time forward, and usually stayed overnight at the Reed home when he visited Pittsburgh.

When the *Gazette* and the *Times* merged in 1906, each paper had a readership of about 70,000 people. The circulation of the merged newspapers soared beyond expectations to reach 131,000 a year later. This figure was greater than the combined circulation of all the other morning papers and far ahead of any other newspaper between the Alleghenies and Chicago. However, when the daily doubled its price to two cents from one at the end of the year, the result was noticeable, a drop to 80,000, where it lingered for a decade.

The *Times* was a good match for the *Gazette*. It was conservative, ardently Republican, and relatively free of sensationalism. Moreover, the acquisition furnished the *Gazette* with some of Pittsburgh's most talented newsmen. One was Morgan Gable, whose reputation was such that the joke in newsrooms was that "George T." had purchased the whole *Times* establishment in order to recapture Gable, who had joined the *Commercial Gazette* in 1887 as telegraph editor, then as city editor before jumping to the *Times*. Gable, born in Lancaster County, had one of those amazing rags-to-riches nineteenth-century careers: he had begun working as a slate picker in the anthracite mines of Tamaqua, Pennsylvania, at the age of nine, and used his skills and hard work to become managing editor of the *Reading Herald* at age nineteen.

Gable could write vitriolic editorials, usually at the expense of Democrats. His talents were directed against his fellow Republicans in the 1912 election, however, when the *Gazette Times* sided with incumbent president William Taft against the insurgent Progressive challenge of ex-president Theodore Roosevelt. That pitted Oliver, Gable, and the *Gazette Times* against William Flinn, who was leading the Roosevelt backers in Pennsylvania, and his newspaper, the *Leader*. The *Gazette Times* repeated stories of Flinn's flirtations with Standard Oil funds and his attempts to buy a U.S. Senate seat in 1904. Gable's editorials denounced Flinn's "slimy trail" across the records of city, county, and state and mercilessly stressed the irony of "such a creature" serving as Roosevelt's lieutenant in a crusade for "social justice."[2] The *Gazette Times* found itself opposing not only Flinn, but also many of its own readers who supported Roosevelt. Many of the letters that poured into the paper were so virulent that the editor deemed them unfit to reprint in a "family newspaper." When an insane man wounded Roosevelt with a pistol shot in Milwaukee, the *Gazette Times* had to defend itself against charges of having unwittingly instigated the attempted assassination. In the end, the split among Republicans led to a national victory for Democrat Woodrow Wilson. Both Pennsylvania and Allegheny County went Progressive in the election—Roosevelt carried the county by twenty thousand votes.

As the popularity of Roosevelt and Wilson testified, the early twentieth century was a great age of reform. As before, the *Gazette* and the *Post* often took opposite sides in the debates of this period. The *Gazette*, for example, was a leader in the fight for Prohibition. As early as 1854, when a statewide referendum on the subject was held, the *Gazette* supported the Prohibition cause, while the pro-labor, anti-temperance *Post* took the opposite side. Even though the reformers lost by a narrow margin, the *Gazette* had to admit outright defeat, for the margin by which Prohibition was defeated in Allegheny County was wider than in the state as a whole.

In 1907, George Oliver shifted the *Gazette Times*'s stance away from promoting outright Prohibition to advocating a local option—the right of a locality to abolish the sale of liquor by special referendum. In 1914, the Oliver papers began refusing liquor advertisements, perhaps because of the rising tide of Prohibition sentiment. In 1909, Oliver had been selected by Governor Edwin Sydney Stuart to fill out the term of U.S. Senator Knox, who had become secretary of state in the Cabinet of President Taft. Oliver was then elected to a full term, beginning in

1911, and so became an even greater power in his own right. Because of Oliver's influence, the editorials in the *Gazette* were closely followed not only in Pittsburgh but also across the country. In April 1915 Oliver presided over a mass meeting to urge the passage of a local-option prohibition bill by the Pennsylvania legislature. However, the local-option bill was defeated two years later, partly because the U.S. Congress had written the Eighteenth Amendment with stronger restrictions on liquor, and had referred it to the states for ratification.

At that point, Oliver dictated a milestone editorial in the *Gazette Times*. He had retired from the Senate after declining to run again in 1916 under the popular-election procedure mandated by the Seventeenth Amendment, passed in 1913. That was a reform that the *Gazette* had not favored, asserting on June 14, 1911, that the appointment of senators by state legislatures was a wise provision to counteract "temporary gusts of popular passion." Now Oliver turned his full attention toward Prohibition. His editorial conceded that while his newspaper had long felt that Prohibition should be handled at the local level, the growth of public sentiment in favor of outlawing liquor at the national level had reached a point requiring special treatment: "The *Gazette Times* is, therefore, of the opinion the amendment should be ratified and the liquor traffic abolished." The newspaper continued to support Prohibition after it became law with the passage of the Eighteenth Amendment in 1919. The *Post*, on the other hand, maintained its opposition to Prohibition and, in 1925, brought to light the glaring weaknesses of local prohibition enforcement and the swarms of speakeasies thriving in the self-described city of churches. When the *Post* and the *Gazette* merged in 1927, the paper carried the sentiment of its publisher, Paul Block Sr., that Prohibition should be repealed—and in 1933, it was.

The *Gazette* took strong stands on other reform issues, as well. As early as 1884, the *Commercial Gazette* demanded that vendors of suspicious grades of meat be prosecuted. Four years later, the Chicago meat industry offered to pay the expenses of Pittsburgh businessmen to come and inspect the packing houses in question. Although the *Pittsburg Leader* liked the idea, the *Commercial Gazette* thought this was an attempt to conceal the facts, and preferred that meat be inspected at the time of its arrival in Pittsburgh. In 1895, the *Commercial Gazette* demanded the enactment of a national pure-food law to safeguard the public's interest. It took eleven years for such a law to be passed; after conscientious people in the food industry such as Henry J. Heinz of Pittsburgh applied pressure, Congress finally passed the Federal Food and Drug Act in 1906.

Over the decades, the *Gazette* and other local papers pushed for changes to secure a safe water supply. Early Pittsburghers drew their water from rivers, ponds, and cisterns. An 1802 ordinance provided for construction of four public wells and the purchase of private wells; in 1826, the Pittsburgh Select and Common Councils approved the construction of a waterworks, which was completed in 1828. A steam pump drew water from the Allegheny River and raised it to a million-gallon reservoir on Grant Hill. Yet for a growing city like Pittsburgh, the demands for infrastructure improvements were constant. Thanks to Pittsburgh's continuous annexation of adjacent municipalities between 1868 and 1900, its land area had increased from 1.77 square miles to 28. On June 11, 1866, the *Gazette* stressed the close connection between a pure water supply and public health, with a particular emphasis on population growth in the Allegheny Valley: "Year by year the waters become more unfit for drinking. Ultimately they must become prolific of disease and death." The warning proved all too true, as typhoid fever plagued Pittsburgh in the years to come. Still, nothing was done.

In early 1894, a commission assembled by a group of civic agencies, including the Engineers' Society of Western Pennsylvania, the Allegheny County Medical Society, and the Chamber of Commerce Committee on Water Supply found the water supply for the municipalities of Pittsburgh and Allegheny City to be "not only not up to a proper standard of potable water but . . . actually pernicious."[3] It recommended a slow-sand filtration system. During this period, the *Pittsburg Dispatch,* in particular, took a leading role in focusing attention on the issue. The *Commercial Gazette,* too, was involved, especially when a filtration commission appointed by the mayor in 1896 seconded the slow-sand recommendation in an 1899 report. The cost would be steep—three million dollars—but the *Gazette* asserted on February 7, 1899, "As to cost, though a part of the amount named is contingent and may not be required, it is to be considered that the provision of filtration for the water supply of a city of Pittsburgh's size is at the cheapest no inexpensive undertaking. Whatever is worth having is worth paying for—and filtration is worth having."

Still, despite recurrent typhoid epidemics, the matter dragged on, even though the voters approved a bond issue for plant construction in 1899. The *Pittsburg Leader,* the *Pittsburg Dispatch,* and the *Gazette* all pointed the finger directly at the politicians. The November 12, 1901, edition of the *Gazette* declared:

The rival factions in the city each are making a vigorous attempt to charge on the other the delay in securing filtration. . . . The Department of Public Works has during that time been in control of both factions. The money for the work has been lying idle in the city depositories for two years, and at this date the record is that not a pick-stroke of actual construction has been made. . . .

The importance of fighting over the control of city patronage and contracts has been more pressing to the political mind that that of stopping the wholesale ravages of water-borne diseases among the people.

Two years later, the impasse continued, prompting the *Pittsburg Leader* to print a June 6, 1903, editorial under the headline, "An Appalling Death List." It read: "The simple statement that 865 persons died from typhoid fever in the city of Pittsburg in the past two years . . . ought to rouse the people to demand from councils action in obtaining pure water."

Many factors delayed the construction of the filtration plant:

One involved individuals who refused to accept the validity of the scientific analysis concerning the relationship between typhoid and the city's water supply. Edward Bigelow, director of the Public Works Department, argued that the city's water did not cause typhoid and warned that impugning its quality would discourage investment in the city. In addition, disputes between political factions within the Republican Party over control of the construction contracts brought further delay and political battles. Bigelow also played a key role here, insisting that the filtration contracts, rather than being awarded to the construction firm of political boss William Flinn, be granted in open bidding. And a third factor involved disputes over source and technology choices, with some advocating bringing water to the city by aqueduct from Indian Creek, while others argued for a mechanical rather than slow sand filtration system.[4]

The matter finally came to a public vote on July 12, 1904, as part of a five million dollar bond issue that included money to eliminate a "hump" on Grant Street, downtown. Perhaps as a way to boost support for the bond issue, on July 9, the *Post* ran an article on artesian wells, an alternative being pursued by municipalities unhappy with polluted river supplies. The *Gazette* responded on July 10, with an editorial warning: "It is probable that, if either proposition fails tomorrow, it will not be revived during this generation, and Pittsburgh will continue to be a by-word for filthy water and the never-ending typhoid fever epidemic. The Hump will be with us evermore."

To the surprise of many politicians, the filtration part of the bond issue carried but the "hump" section failed. Indeed, most post-election news stories focused on the latter. Whether that reflected a greater business interest in improving downtown than in pure water can only be conjectured. For instance, the *Gazette* assessed the election on July 13, 1904, under the heading, "Hump improvement turned down." There had been some excavation work on the hump in 1832 and 1846, but the failure of that portion of the 1904 bond issue halted the project until it was resumed on April 5, 1912 and finished on November 17, 1913.

Because the filtration part of the bond issue carried, a new water plant was constructed north of the Allegheny, just east of the borough of Aspinwall. In 1911, disinfection was added to the water purification system through the use of chlorine.

The year 1906 saw the fruition of a number of other causes that the *Gazette* championed. A long fight to have the railroad tracks removed from Liberty Avenue was won. Pittsburgh and Allegheny City were consolidated, despite the latter's resistance. Even the election of Democrat and reformer William Guthrie to the position of mayor pleased the *Gazette,* as the editors predicted a welcome change from the former reign of the Magee-Flinn stronghold. However, the anti-reform forces bided their time and soon returned to office. Meanwhile, the annexation of Allegheny City across the Allegheny River had compounded the absurdity of the existing council system. The membership of Common Council swelled to 101 and of Select Council to 59, numbers that were clearly unworkable even if everyone had been clean.

They were not. An investigation uncovered that bribes were being paid to city council members by "interested" parties, The Municipal League resorted to a "sting" operation by bringing in Robert Wilson, superintendent of the Municipal League of Scranton, who posed as a contractor. A retrospective article in an April 1, 1936, anniversary edition of the *Pittsburgh Sun-Telegraph* explained how Wilson operated. He let it be known that he sought street-paving contracts by whatever means necessary, and soon was holding conferences with the "Big Six," as the ruling clique on the council was called. Wilson learned of one way a bribe was handled. The bankers in the scheme placed $17,500 in a shoebox in a hotel room and then left. A few minutes later a councilman would enter the room, pick up the box, and leave. When the lid blew off in 1908, two bankers and seven councilmen were indicted. The *Sun-Telegraph* story recounted how one member of the "Big Six" had contemptuously said that some of the "hoodlums" on the councils could be bought for a suit of clothes or a couple of streetcar tickets.

Wilson's revelations undoubtedly helped bring about the banner year for reform, 1911, when a single city council of nine members elected at large was substituted for the two unwieldy councils. On May 29, after the state legislature had mandated the change, the *Gazette Times* idealized a configuration: "Nine councilmen who will not be too small to grapple with the larger problems of municipal progress nor too big to work out the smaller details of better city conditions. Nine men who will work their politics for Pittsburgh's good instead of working Pittsburgh for selfish political advantage." Two days later, in a gracious gesture, the *Gazette Times* paid tribute to the old councils after their last meeting: "It is due to the old councils of Pittsburgh to say that the dignity and good humor with which they terminated their service on Monday night were greatly to their credit. . . . The manner in which members acknowledged the force of events and prepared to make way for the new order of things municipal was both gracious and sensible." Shortly thereafter, though, on June 14, in an editorial called "Open and above board," the *Gazette Times* issued a reminder to the new council: "Since the organization of Pittsburgh's new Council there has been more or less discussion, both at city hall and in the newspapers, of the subject of open sessions, as if this were a question for council to determine, or to be advised upon. The law is so plain on the point in controversy as to permit of no doubt. All sessions of the Council and of all committees and sub-committees therefore shall be public." The at-large feature of the nine-member city council continued until 1987, when the voters approved a change to election by districts.

The reforms of 1911 also swept over the public school board, reducing its size from thirty-one elected members (one from each ward) to fifteen members selected by the Allegheny County Court of Common

Pleas. This was part of a comprehensive statewide bill reforming the free-school law of 1834 (the first in the nation), as amended by the school code of May 8, 1854. Roadblocks on the way to its passage, however, provoked the editorial indignation of the *Gazette Times,* which, on March 9, 1911, had complained: "The scheme evolved at Harrisburg, to complicate the battle which is being waged for a new public school code by introducing a rival bill, deserved to be discountenanced from the start. Plainly this counter proposition is an ill-conceived makeshift to which little thought has been given. Its evident purpose is to retard reform rather than to promote it, and its ultimate object undoubtedly is to avert the adoption of any code at all. . . . Expenditures for popular education in Pennsylvania are lavish; our total outlay is enormous. We are not, however, getting a dollar's worth of results for the children for every dollar paid out." The tide of reform sentiment was strong enough, though, that a new code was enacted on May 18, 1911. Ten days later, the *Gazette Times* exulted: "The people of Pennsylvania, and particularly those of Pittsburgh, are to be heartily congratulated upon the final passage of the School Code. . . . As for Pittsburgh the code does away with our Central Board, over the demise of which few tears will be shed. For many years it operations have been a scandal and a reproach, hampering educational programs and weakening faith in popular government. . . . Well, the central board goes, and a more compact body, with real authority centralized, removed from the contamination of politics by judicial appointment, takes its place. The ward boards, the original source of the political bacilli, also go; no longer will Nepotism elect its nieces as schoolmarms, nor Ignorance decide that it needs a change in text-books." The newly appointed board took office on November 13, 1911, naming David B. Oliver (George T. Oliver's older brother) as president and Taylor Allderdice as vice president. The next day, the *Gazette Times* had a front-page story with a big picture of the board members—twelve men and two women (Mrs. Alice Carmalt and Mrs. Mary Crowley)—with only "Miss Julia Morgan Harding absent as she was abroad."

Over the years, populist sentiment for an elected board rose from time to time. The Pittsburgh Chamber of Commerce on March 28, 1931, condemned two measures, the Rooney and Root bills, designed to provide for an elected board. Both bills, it said, had been concocted "by some politicians to furnish them with additional office-holders to be made the pawns and favors of political factions" and reminded Pittsburghers that before 1911 the "incompetency and corruption" of elected school boards had "occasioned such scandal that the legislature ripped out the whole system." However, a problem kept cropping up that eventually helped doom the appointive system. On February 1, 1942, *Pittsburgh Press* writer Douglas Naylor complained that two labor leaders, Phil Murray and George Walters, seldom, if ever, attended board meetings. In later years there would be similar complaints that members selected by the Court of Common Pleas for their "blue ribbon" status in the community often seemed too cavalier to attend school board sessions. The appointive system lasted until 1978, when a grassroots wave of sentiment in Pittsburgh led to a legislative act giving the right of selection of a nine-member board to voters on a district basis. The newspapers opposed the change, but the measure was passed.

Despite its passion for reform, the *Gazette Times* was distinctly cool toward the idea of allowing women to vote. The newspaper waited until 1915 to support the women's suffrage movement in its final moves toward victory with the adoption of the Nineteenth Amendment to the Constitution in 1920. During the pre–Civil War tenure of editor David White, the *Gazette* had taken a mixed position on women's rights. White was willing to concede that the law regarded women as having little more capacity for caring for themselves than children or idiots had, but he asserted that it was wrong to drop all distinctions between the sexes.

Susan B. Anthony, a leading suffragist, had spoken back in 1880 "before a small audience of men and women in Pittsburgh in what was then known as Lafayette hall, Wood street." When the Wilkinsburg Woman's Suffrage Club, perhaps the first such club in the area, organized in February 6, 1889, it found its cause so unpopular that it changed its name to the Women's Civic Club of Wilkinsburg. "By 1904, clubs had been established in Bellevue, Allegheny City, Homestead, and Coraopolis."[5]

In June 1904, the women in these groups joined together to form the Allegheny County Equal Rights Association, and this marked a turning point for Pennsylvania. By 1913, the Equal Franchise Federation of Western Pennsylvania, founded in 1909, had branches throughout the region. Nevertheless, newspaper coverage of the movement was sporadic at best, and support almost nonexistent. An exception was the

Singer and actress Lillian Russell married Pittsburgh newspaperman Alexander P. Moore on June 12, 1912, and settled in Pittsburgh. Moore was editor of the *Pittsburgh Leader* and part owner of the *Pittsburgh Telegraph* and the *Pittsburgh Chronicle Telegraph.*
(From Stefan Lorant, *Pittsburgh: The Story of an American City*, Author's Edition, 1964; Courtesy Rowman and Littlefield Publishers)

Pittsburg Leader, whose publisher, Alex Moore, was the devoted husband of the famed actress Lillian Russell. Russell was solidly for women's rights. Her beauty advice column in the *Leader*, titled "Lillian Russell's Philosophy," offered women readers such insights as: "Our Creator never intended lovely women to be angular any more than he did the planet earth, from which she, together with all living things spring and under whose fostering all living things take form; roundness is the order of the universe, and all beauty is contingent upon the prevalence of circling lines."

The *Gazette Times,* however, took a different approach to the issue. Its editorial attitudes were evidenced in the extensive coverage it gave to the Pittsburgh Association of Women Opposed to Woman Suffrage, founded on February 11, 1912. Included among the fifty women at the initial anti-suffragist meeting were women bearing prominent names in early Pittsburgh history, such as Mrs. Harmar D. Denny, Mrs. James Hay Reed, and Julia Harding, a member of the new Pittsburgh school board, who was elected as the association's president. On February 12, the *Gazette Times* outlined the association's strategy, including "a publicity bureau, as it depends largely upon publicity for its success. It will arrange for a series of lectures by men and women of note, and will further its cause, the annihilation of sentiment which would give women the ballot, by distributing literature broadcast throughout the city and county."

The women went right to work. Julia Harding, in a speech at the second meeting of the association, declared, "woman suffrage and socialism go hand in hand."[6] On March 29, a *Pittsburgh Post* article, headed, "Event extremely fashionable," set the tone for its coverage of a meeting at the Pittsburgh Conservatory of Music: "A double row of automobiles lined Dithridge street for blocks yesterday afternoon while their mistresses attended the anti-suffrage lecture. . . . Young society girls and debutantes acted as ushers." The following day the *Gazette Times* aired the views of the lecturer, Minnie K. Bronson, who criticized the suffragettes for a lack of charity: "The suffragists want to vote for better laws but we, the antis, believe we have a greater power without the vote. Now, the suffragists in New York are pledging themselves neither to work for nor give money to any other object until they obtain the ballot. That means all forms of charity and philanthropy. In the meantime we will go along as we have been doing and will help the unfortunate who need us and who but for us would have no one to help them."

Nearly a year later, on January 5, 1913, the *Gazette Times* published a long editorial in which it accepted that "the present feminist movement . . . is undoubtedly here to stay," before adding:

But women's entrance into politics and her precipitate rush for honors in the field of forensic and executive achievement will not change radically the nature of the sex. There is a great deal of fearful prophecy as to the hardening and debasing influence of public life upon the character of women. One of the strongest arguments put forth by the "anti-suffragettes" and the critics of the militant women is that the home and our social order will be displaced by women's entry into the arena of government. The weight of all these objections and criticisms may be left to be settled by those whom they most affect. It may however, be pretty safely assumed that the present feminist movement lacks the terrifying aspects that its enemies would give it. . . . If all the suffragettes in the U.S. should be called together in convention and asked to promulgate new laws, who is so foolish as to believe that they would tackle the tariff or the currency question? Government in its profounder aspects is man's duty, and no one recognizes

Pennsylvania College for Women (later Chatham College) demonstration in support of women's suffrage, 1914 (Courtesy Chatham College Archives)

this more thoroughly and willingly than women themselves, even though they be "suffragettes."

This consideration . . . should rob the thought of "equal suffrage" and the women in politics of some of its terrors. It is a house cleaning the dear women want, just as they always are wanting to save the children, make vice less easy of existence, and punish the destroyers of home. Child labor, the white slave traffic, unequal wages and the exposure of boys and girls to the temptations of life, are the subjects upon which women legislate and orate when they foregather in any of the modern feminist movements. The leopard cannot change his spots nor the Ethiopian his skin, but it would be easier for these things to happen than for women to lose her divine sense of motherhood for the race and her obligation to maintain unharmed the home in which she may rear rightly the children that God has given her, or, if denied her, vouchsafed her more fortunate sisters.

As the movement advanced, the tone of the *Pittsburgh Post* became enthusiastic, as evidenced in its report on a May 2, 1914, gala. This date was hailed as Suffrage Day across the nation, and Pittsburgh joined the celebration with more than one hundred automobiles making a circuit of the city and more than 1,500 women marching downtown. The *Pitts-*

burgh Post was ecstatic in its May 3 report, called "Equal Franchise workers give Pittsburgh a beautiful street demonstration." The article exulted: "Men and women of all ages and stations in life and the social scale joined in the parade; so did Boy Scouts and a squad of Camp Fire girls. . . . Society matrons and misses, clad in beautiful gowns of latest fashion, shop girls, mothers, grandmothers and one or two great-grand-mothers—all were there, to say nothing of the men and boys, many of the former world-famed in their professions, for the parade was a rep-resentative gathering. Race, creed, and social standing were eliminated in the common cause. . . . As a climax to the double parade of automo-biles and marchers, was the great open-air meeting on the old Frick property at Oliver Avenue and Cherry Way."

On June 4, 1919, Congress sent the proposed Nineteenth Amend-ment to the states, after rejecting efforts to restrict its application to white women. Suffragist leaders descended in force on Harrisburg, and on June 24, Pennsylvania became the seventh state to ratify the amend-ment. Finally, the fight culminated in Tennessee where a forty-eight to forty-eight tie in the House of Representatives was broken when twenty-four-year-old Harry Burn switched sides at his mother's request. Tennessee provided the thirty-sixth state necessary for ratification, which was declared August 26, 1920, just in time to give women the right to vote in the November election that year.

As suffrage and other reform issues occupied the domestic news, the beginnings of war were stirring abroad. In the 1890s, as the Spanish-American War approached, the *Commercial Gazette* demonstrated the same aversion to conflict that it had shown throughout much of the nineteenth century, until the Civil War. The *Gazette* supported Presi-dent McKinley, a Republican, against the efforts of Democrats and of the "yellow press" headed by publisher William Randolph Hearst to push the country into war against Spain over the issue of its colonial abuses in Cuba. However, when war came on April 22, 1898, the *Com-mercial Gazette* broke out with a streamer headline six inches deep across the front page—"WAR WITH SPAIN NOW ON"—and gave its full support to the war effort. In the months that followed, the paper tried to reassure its readers. An article of June 20 read: "There need be no fear that this country is about to enter upon a land grabbing policy

Pittsburgh Commercial Gazette's Spanish-American War Extra, 1898

and become a competitor of old world nations in that kind of imperialism. It is not the sentiment of the nation and will never find expression in action."

The newspaper joined the general relief on August 14, 1898, that the war had been won so quickly and painlessly, but ten days later reiterated its anti-imperialist position. In an article in the *North American Review,* Andrew Carnegie had expressed opposition to the acquisition of the Philippines. The *Gazette* published its approval of Carnegie's stance, but later had to work to reconcile such statements with the support the paper extended to a peace treaty that included the annexation of the Philippines. The paper contradicted itself once again in 1899, when the

Philippine insurrection prompted an editorial stating that the sooner an honorable withdrawal from the archipelago was made, the better it would be for all sides.

When World War I began in 1914, most papers asserted that there was no reason for the United States to become involved. For Democratic papers like the *Pittsburgh Post,* this position led to support for President Wilson, whose 1916 renomination campaign centered on the slogan, "He kept us out of war." When the German government, early in 1917, recommended all-out submarine warfare against Allied shipping interests, the *Post* backed Wilson's change of heart and America's entrance into the war in April. The *Post* became Pittsburgh's preeminent war paper and was given a large share of the credit for the success of local Liberty Loan campaigns. In one night an open-air entertainment sponsored by the *Post* and held in front of its building raised $750,000.

The *Gazette Times,* from the start, kept a neutral attitude about the war. When it ran an anti-neutralism article by correspondent Richard Harding Davis, entitled "German Fights Foully/Knowing Cause Wrong," the newspaper carefully advised readers that the opinions of Davis were his own, and not those of the editorial board.[7] On August 13, 1914, shortly after the war began, the *Gazette Times*'s lead editorial, "Fair Play for Teutons," called on readers to be skeptical of the flood of atrocity stories about German army activity in Belgium and France coming from Allied sources. Perhaps this policy reflected an honest desire to be objective, but the Olivers may have been thinking of the large German population on Pittsburgh's North Side and of the business arrangements with Pittsburgh steel companies made by foreign countries on both sides of the war.

To the staunchly Republican *Gazette Times,* Woodrow Wilson was a longtime adversary, even though he had enacted many reforms that George T. Oliver had favored. This led to a breach of good taste when Wilson died on February 3, 1924. One of the staff members wrote an editorial the following day that focused on Wilson's perceived weaknesses, including his "excessive love of adulation." The editorial went so far as to say that the Democratic president "had been weighed in the balance as a statesman and found wanting." Pittsburghers lashed out in disapproval at the *Gazette Times.* On February 7, in a daring and unprecedented move, the *Gazette Times* apologized with "keenest regret"

and claimed the offending editorial had never been approved by the paper's publishers.

By 1900, all of Pittsburgh's newspapers had a modern appearance, with multicolumn headlines and stories enhanced by large photographs. During the Oliver era the *Gazette Times* added many new departments, each headed by a specific editor, including Sunday, drama, literature, finance, sports, and society. In 1911, the *Gazette Times* added the most complete art department in Pennsylvania, with photo-engraving equipment and the most recent camera models. Its Sunday magazine section boasted more artists than the combined staffs of all other Pittsburgh newspapers. In a separate department the editorial writers shaped and applied the newspaper's policy on public questions.

An increasing amount of attention went to both sports and women's pages. From 1900 to 1927, the amount of space given to sports increased three times. Writing became more colorful as sportswriters described

Photograph by the *Pittsburgh Sun-Telegraph* shows a World War I regiment of engineers marching in parade near the corner of Fifth and Smithfield as onlookers welcome them home. (Courtesy Carnegie Library of Pittsburgh)

Pittsburgh's baseball heroes in the World Series of 1909 and the football stars of "Pop" Warner's University of Pittsburgh Panthers. For women readers, dress patterns were added to the *Gazette Times* in 1912, Winifred Black's syndicated advice column appeared in 1917, and a feature called "Changing Fashions" was introduced the following year.

Although advertisements had vanished from the front pages, they continued to be an important source of revenue, and so rated prominent placement. Locally, department stores were especially important advertisers. The increased use of brand names for household goods, such as Coca-Cola and Postum, also made national ads a liberal source of income. Newspapers continued their nineteenth-century tradition of accepting advertisements for patent medicine, and ads for chewing gum and cigarettes began to gain momentum.

In an era when news writers switched back and forth from one paper to another, the *Gazette Times* obtained its share of the stars. Moreover, the Olivers kept no clear distinction between the *Gazette* and the *Chronicle Telegraph,* so superior journalists such as Henry Jones Ford served as editor in charge of both periodicals from 1901 to 1905. Ford also wrote scholarly books, which brought him to the attention of Woodrow Wilson, then president of Princeton, who secured him for the faculty in 1908 as a professor of politics. Later, as U.S. president, Wilson named Ford to the Interstate Commerce Commission. Another fabled newsman, the satirical poet Arthur Burgoyne, was with the *Gazette Times* for a short period, writing a column called "Short Shots" and later "Snap Shots." Burgoyne's most famous contribution to Pittsburgh had been made earlier, at the *Leader,* where he was credited with creating the figure of "Pa Pitt" in colonial garb to visually represent the city, replacing the previous image of a dainty but uninteresting "Miss Pittsburgh." "Pa Pitt" was to have a continued presence in the cartoons of the *Gazette* for decades until the end of the tenure of political cartoonist Cyrus Hungerford in 1976.[8] The first daily comic strip in the *Gazette Times* was published on February 7, 1910, on the sports page, under the title "With Mutt in Germany—by 'Bud' Fisher." This later metamorphosed into the well known "Mutt and Jeff."

The *Post* kept in step with these innovations and introduced some of its own. For instance, it hired Sidney Smith, the creator of the comic strip "The Gumps" as a political cartoonist. His duties included producing illustrations for the Sunday magazine section and retouching all photographs and line drawings used in the paper. Smith became an in-famous character in Pittsburgh when he kidnapped his young daughter in violation of a court visitation order. He drove the Allegheny County sheriff to distraction because a man who had vanished without a trace somehow was able to send daily cartoons to the *Post*'s editorial office from scattered points in West Virginia, then Ohio, then New York, and finally Maryland. Eventually, Smith returned home after the governor of Pennsylvania announced he would honor no extradition papers if the cartoonist were caught.

Early on, the *Post* emphasized aeronautics; it had Pittsburgh's first aviation editor and garnered a reputation as "the aviation paper of Pitts-burgh." To further the cause, in 1918 it held an airplane circus in Schenley Park. In another appeal to young readers, it had launched the Fair Play Club, in which over 125,000 children took the "fair play" pledge administered by the *Post*'s Uncle Walt (Garett Geerlings) and contributed material for a whole section of the Sunday edition reserved specifically for them.

When George T. Oliver died on January 22, 1919, his sons George S. and Augustus K. Oliver succeeded him. By 1920, the *Gazette Times* had a daily circulation of 80,977 and a Sunday figure of 78,211. The compa-rable figures for the *Post* were 66,963 and 105,549. The *Pittsburgh Press* beat them both at 110,683 and 116,396. By 1927, the circulation of the *Gazette Times* topped the 100,000 mark and the Sunday issue had reached 143,432. The *Post*'s comparable figures were 142,385 and 187,132 and the *Press* had 181,360 and 235,279.[9]

In 1923, it became evident that Pittsburgh had too many newspa-pers. The publishers banded to reduce the costs of publication, and two papers, the declining *Dispatch* and *Leader*, were dissolved. Shortly thereafter, Colonel Oliver Hershman sold the *Pittsburgh Press* to the national Scripps Howard syndicate. To many, that transition seemed natural, given that both the *Press* and the Scripps Howard chain had long portrayed themselves as representing the interests of "the common man." Edward Wyllis Scripps (1854–1926) worked in circulation at the *Detroit Evening News,* which his half-brother James had founded in 1873. Going the "penny press" route, the Scripps family had newspapers in Cleveland, Cincinnati, St. Louis, and Buffalo by the end of the 1880s. The chain's early successes followed the general pattern of "new jour-nalism." Scripps's newspapers "were low-priced evening publications,

In 1924, staff correspondents from the *Chronicle Telegraph* and the *Gazette Times* covered the Democratic National Convention in New York City.
(Courtesy Carnegie Library of Pittsburgh)

small in size but well written and tightly edited, hard-hitting in both news and editorial-page coverage of the local scene. Above all, they were distinguished for their devotion to the interests of working people." As low-cost dailies that relied principally on circulation revenue, they had to be edited carefully. "Scripps saved newsprint costs by insisting on small headlines and short, concise stories. . . . Word economy also meant that after the essential news had been told, there would be plenty of space for editorial opinion and features."[10]

E. W. Scripps rose in the post–Civil War era of prosperity and growing business conglomerates, which often caused dire economic conditions for farmers, laborers, and immigrants. "New journalism" proclaimed itself as the champion of the working people, and readers responded in droves. One of E. W. Scripps's mottos was "I have only one principle, and that is represented by an effort to make it harder for the rich to grow richer and easier for the poor to keep from growing poorer." Scripps's health failed in 1917, and he gave control of his newspaper holdings to his son Robert. In 1922, Robert Scripps hired Roy W. Howard to be manager of the chain, and renamed it Scripps Howard. Howard had previously led the United Press Association, a news service founded by E. W. Scripps to aid his own papers and others. Howard proved to be an able manager, making just one mistake: he reported the unverified news on November 7, 1918, that World War I had ended. The armistice actually came on November 11, and Howard was always remembered as the man who ended the First World War four days early. In his new position, Howard would have a great impact: "Howard was held responsible by his critics for a rightward shift in the outlook of the . . . Scripps Howard dailies. . . . The complaints were not of the same character as those made against Hearst and [Colonel Robert] McCormick; rather they reflected the disappointment and dismay of the liberals that the 'people's papers' of Edward Wyllis Scripps had in many respects become conventionally conservative in tone."[11] Moreover, under Howard's management, the chain engaged in a nationwide purchasing spree, buying up newspapers and dissolving many of them. Between 1923 and 1934, Scripps Howard closed fifteen papers. Yet one of their most complex mergers was still to come: in 1927, the *Gazette* and the *Post* would become one.

Chapter 9

The Block and Hearst Deal

THE 1927 TRANSACTION that resulted in the union of the *Gazette* and the *Post* was one of the most mysterious in the history of Pittsburgh and, indeed, of national journalism. Without any warning to the staffs involved, four newspapers were combined into two, and then, within minutes, reconfigured to form completely different combinations. All of this activity was the work of press barons William Randolph Hearst and Paul Block Sr.

Of the two, the best known and the most flamboyant was Hearst. Born in 1863, he was the only son of wealthy California mining pioneer George Hearst. In 1880, George, seeking political power, purchased the debt-ridden *San Francisco Examiner,* converted it into a Democratic Party organ, and became a U.S. senator. William returned to California after an undistinguished career at Harvard—he was expelled for indulging in too many pranks—and, at age twenty-four, became the *Examiner*'s editor.

William's work at the *Examiner* embodied what came to be known as "yellow journalism." By featuring sensationalism of all kinds, including crime and sob stories, Hearst doubled the paper's circulation in one year. His technique also included crusades against businesses such as the Southern Pacific Railroad, the bulwark of the Republican state machine. Hearst soon took on the East Coast, purchasing the *New York Journal* in 1895. Not only did he bring the best of his *Examiner* staff to the *Journal,* but he also hired as many stars as he could from his sensationalist rival, Joseph Pulitzer's *New York World.* Before long, Pulitzer had to cut his price to a penny an issue to match the surging Hearst paper. In one month, the *Journal*'s circulation jumped by 125,000, thanks to such headlines as "Real American Monsters and Dragons," "Why Young Girls Kill Themselves," and "Strange Things Women Do for Love."

Yellow journalism reached new heights in the days leading up to the Spanish-American War, when the *Journal* led the New York newspapers' outcry over the Spanish army's tactics in crushing an insurrection in Cuba. When the warship *U.S.S. Maine* was sunk in the Havana harbor on February 15, 1898, and 266 American lives were lost, Hearst's hysterical anti-Spain campaign was influential in pushing a reluctant President McKinley to go to war on April 22.

Flushed with his success, Hearst began to style himself as "the people's champion." In early 1899, he announced an editorial policy calling for the public ownership of public franchises, the dissolution of trusts, a graduated income tax, the popular election of U.S. senators, and the improvement of the public schools at all levels. Before long he was urging the nationalization of coalmines, railroads, and telegraph lines. Moreover, he gave encouragement to labor unions, including striking miners in the anthracite coalfields of Pennsylvania who battled with management in 1897, 1900, and again in 1902. However, Hearst's bitter attacks on President McKinley backfired in September 1901 when an anarchist in Buffalo who was rumored to have a copy of the *Journal* in his pocket fatally wounded the president. Whether or not Leon Czolgosz really had the *Journal* on his person, the story was enough to prompt strong criticism against Hearst. He soon changed the name of the newspaper to the *New York Journal-American.*

Hearst successfully ran for Congress in a Democratic district in New York City, and served from 1903 to 1907. He sought and won the Democratic nomination for governor of New York, but lost the 1906 election to Republican Charles Evans Hughes, partly because major Republican speakers reminded the public of the McKinley assassination episode. With his political career over, Hearst continued empire-building in his original field, adding eight papers, including four in large cities—Chicago, Boston, Atlanta, and Los Angeles. He led technical innovations in journalism that made possible flaming banner headlines and captivating illustrations, and hired major editorial cartoonists. Hearst also gathered a stable of comic strips, such as "Katzenjammer Kids," which proved to be a major moneymaker for his organization through the decades.

In contrast to Hearst, Block was the child of a poor Jewish immigrant family, which arrived in Elmira, New York in 1885, having fled Germany due to anti-Semitism. The fact that Block had been born in East Prussia in 1875, however, did not come out until his death, as he had always named his birthplace as Elmira. Paul's father, Jonas Bloch, changed his name to John Block after arriving in America, where he worked as a peddler. Four of nine Block children died of diphtheria during the 1890s.

Soon after arriving in Elmira, Paul went to work as a messenger boy and news carrier at the *Elmira Sunday Telegram* to help support his family. Harry S. Brooks, who had founded the *Telegram* in 1879, became a mentor to Block, training him in each department at the paper. After Paul finished school at the Elmira Free Academy at the age of seventeen, he successively became a printer's apprentice, cub reporter, advertising solicitor, and, eventually, advertising director.

In 1895, when Paul Block was twenty, he went to work for the *Telegram*'s New York advertising representative, A. Frank Richardson. As national advertising became more important, papers hired firms such as Richardson's to sell their space by directly contacting advertising agencies, account executives, and advertisers. Paul Block's move to New York City came at a time when brand names were just beginning to be recognized and sold nationwide, and when retailers and business people were coming to realize the power of advertising to help them market their products and services. Block quickly became a leading salesman for Richardson, taking on responsibility for all of New York State and later of all New England.

As part of this job, Block became caught up in the debatable business of advertising patent medicines. These promotions proclaimed cures for headache, neuralgia, alcoholism, deafness, and even crossed eyes—many products, such as tonics for losing weight and for growing and removing hair, were aimed specifically at women. The ad placements often were coupled with a requirement that the newspaper run so-called news stories and pictures heralding the wonderful results of taking such medicines. These practices disillusioned Block, as did the delay in his progression through the ranks of the agency.

Toward the end of 1900, Richardson named as chief operating officer his nephew, Wallace C. Richardson, a relative newcomer to the business. Paul had expected the job himself—by now he was bringing in the largest amount of company income through his sales, and was actually serving as de facto office manager. Many years later, Dina Block, Paul's wife, conjectured that Richardson was slightly anti-Semitic and therefore did not want to promote Block. Paul decided to leave Richardson's firm and go into the special representative business for himself.

Although Block's new occupation was difficult, he soon achieved a major triumph by securing the *Washington Post* as a client. The *Post* had been the first major daily in Washington to merge with a Sunday weekly and publish seven days a week, helping set off a decline of Sunday-only papers across the country. Block began shaping advertising in a new way that had a profound impact on American commerce. For example, Palmolive soap, which had been sold simply as a soap to clean one's hands, was now to be touted as a way of "achieving that schoolgirl complexion." Because Block-originated advertisements succeeded in selling more products, advertisers increasingly placed more ads in the papers he represented.

In 1906, Block extended his business to magazines, becoming the director of advertising at *Pictorial Review*, a women's periodical that would later claim the largest circulation in the United States. Perhaps because of his earlier experiences, Block decided to remove all patent medicine advertising from *Pictorial Review*. This was a bold step, considering that practically every other publication in America, including the *Washington Post*, still carried the patent medicine ads.

Block also served as advertising manager of one of the first Sunday magazine supplements, the now-forgotten *Illustrated Sunday Magazine*, a precursor to *Parade*. It was the first Sunday supplement to be produced by an independent staff; no reporters or artists were employees of a newspaper. It filled a gap for many newspaper publishers who saw the need for such a supplement with a more literary bent to attract new readers' attention, but found that their own staffs were unqualified or unwilling to fit that need. Block's advertisers for the supplement included such important national names as the Cream of Wheat Company, Nestlé's Foods, Coca-Cola, Pond's, Quaker Oats, Bon Ami, and Carter's Inc. Among the newspapers that made *Illustrated Sunday Magazine* the official Sunday supplement was the *Pittsburgh Gazette Times.*

The recession of 1907 lowered the prices of newspapers up for sale, and Block saw a new opportunity. Henry I. Stoddard, an old acquaintance of Block's, bought the *Evening Mail* in New York and hired Block as vice president in charge of all advertising. Block played a large part in boosting the circulation from 25,758 to 200,000. This whetted Block's appetite for owning a newspaper in the New York area. To that end, he went across the Hudson River and bought two Newark newspapers, combining them to create the *Newark Star-Eagle.* These purchases began a round of acquisitions that made Block a major newspaper magnate by 1930. He purchased the *Detroit Journal* from E. D. Stair in January 1917 for eight hundred thousand dollars, then bought the *Memphis News-Scimitar* and the *Duluth Herald* in 1921. Partly because of resistance in Memphis to his expressions of support for minorities, Block accepted a purchase offer in 1926 from E. W. Scripps and sold the *News-Scimitar.*

In 1923, Block bought the *Lancaster New Era,* an evening newspaper in the heart of Pennsylvania's Amish and Mennonite country. With the acquisition came editor Oliver Keller, who would continue to play a role in Block's newspaper chain even after Block sold the *New Era* in 1928 for $925,000 to the Steinman family, owners of the competing *Intelligencer Journal* and *News-Journal,* who had been fighting what they considered an unfair "invasion" by Block. In 1926, Block purchased the *Toledo Blade* for a reported $4.5 million. As with other newspapers that Block owned, he immediately made changes in the executive ranks and began ordering improvements of various kinds. He carried forward plans for a new building already underway when he bought the paper. As the years passed, the *Blade* became his particular favorite; he spent considerable time in Toledo, became well acquainted with its civic leaders, and editorially supported its hospitals, museums, and institutions. Significantly, he brought both of his sons, Paul Jr. and William, to Toledo to learn about the newspaper business. He also contributed many signed editorials, almost always placing them on the front page, in a pattern established by Hearst.

It is not clear when Hearst and Block first met and became friends, but by 1927 their relationship was firmly established in ways beyond the public eye. Not only was Block the special representative for many of Hearst's twenty-eight papers, but he also had had an affair during World War I with Ziegfeld Girl and actress Marion Davies, who would later gain fame as Hearst's mistress.[1] Even after Davies settled permanently into Hearst's life, the three remained good friends, often traveling together, and Block frequently visited Hearst's lavish California estate, the castle at San Simeon. The two men continued as business associates, and Hearst named Block the executor of his entire estate—a plan that went by the wayside because Block died before Hearst did.

The Hearst-Block friendship particularly served Hearst's purposes when in the 1920s he tried to break into the Pittsburgh newspaper market—the fifth largest in the nation at the time. His first overtures were toward the *Press,* but Scripps Howard was there ahead of him. Later, he turned to the Olivers to arrange for the purchase of the *Gazette Times* and the *Chronicle Telegraph.* Then Hearst learned that Arthur Braun was negotiating for the sale of the morning *Post* and the evening *Sun.* Braun made clear that he opposed Hearst's sensationalist kind of journalism and would not sell to him. Yet the sale did happen in 1927—because Hearst turned to his friend and fellow newspaper-chain publisher, Paul Block.

If the Pittsburgh purchases involving Hearst and Block remain puzzling to this day, so does the price involved. The best guess is that the purchases of the *Gazette Times,* the *Post,* the *Sun,* and the *Telegraph* involved ten million dollars.[2] The deal cast Block into disfavor with journalism critics, such as George Seldes, who particularly wondered in his *Lords of the Press* about the source of the Block purchasing money. Was it Hearst money—was Block the front man for Hearst's entrance into a market where he was not wanted?

Although there had been a reduction of Pittsburgh newspapers in 1923, in 1927 there still were five publications—two morning newspapers with Sundays (the *Gazette* and the *Post*); one evening with Sunday (the *Press*); and two other evenings (the *Sun* and the *Chronicle-Telegraph*). Advertisers' reluctance to make placements in so many newspapers—and the limited opportunity for circulation growth in a city of 675,000—indicated another round of mergers was in order.

In March 1927, Hearst sent Colonel Frank Knox to talk to Block about a joint venture into the Pittsburgh market. Knox, a New Hampshire publisher who had been a Rough Rider with Theodore Roosevelt in the Spanish-American War, had been recruited by Hearst for his *Boston American* and soon became his advisory executive. Block was enthusiastic about Hearst's idea, and this feeling was further boosted by approaches from another friend, Judge Elbert Gary, chairman of the board of U.S. Steel. Owning a newspaper as prestigious as the *Gazette Times* obviously appealed to Block. At the same time, Hearst was well aware that people hated him both for personal reasons and for his reputation of running newspaper monopolies, and so his chances of breaking into the market in Pittsburgh would be much enhanced through an alliance with Block. Although Braun's opposition to Hearst was clear, the *Post*'s proprietor considered Block "a man of human impulses, of high integrity and strong public spirit."[3]

The Knox and Gary overtures led to secret meetings throughout the Memorial Day weekend of 1927, held in Chicago as a convenient halfway point between Block's New York headquarters and Hearst's in California. In the sessions at Hearst's *Chicago American* and in Block's suite at the Drake Hotel, the two publishers worked out a plan. The first step would be for Block to buy Braun's *Post* and its kindred *Sun*, and Hearst the Olivers' *Gazette Times* and *Chronicle-Telegraph*. Once the transfer papers were signed, the second step would be for each publisher to make a trade of one paper. Hearst would take ownership of Block's *Sun* and merge it with his newly acquired *Chronicle-Telegraph* to form a newspaper called the *Pittsburgh Sun-Telegraph*. Block, in turn, would receive Hearst's *Gazette Times* and create a merged Pittsburgh *Post-Gazette*. The result would be three newspapers in Pittsburgh where there had been five—one six-day morning edition, Block's *Post-Gazette*, and two evening papers with Sunday editions, Hearst's *Sun-Telegraph* and Scripps Howard's *Press*.

This plan sounded good but had one major hitch: Block did not have the money he needed for his end of the purchase. With his recent acquisition of the *Toledo Blade*, he was cash poor. Then came the solution that cast a cloud of ambiguity over the entire transaction. With just a verbal agreement, Hearst secretly agreed to give Block the money he needed to complete the purchase of the *Post* and the *Sun*. It was implied that Block at any time in the future could pay up and own the paper outright. In the meantime, Block was to be owner, for all intents and purposes, carrying the unquestioned title and authority of publisher over the re-merged papers, with salary and some stock attached. Moreover, he had a fixed-term agreement for his special representative firm, Paul Block and Associates, to service both the *Post-Gazette* and Hearst's *Sun-Telegraph*. With everything in place, negotiations with the sellers began. Over the next two months, as the details of the sale were ironed out, life went on as usual for the staffs of the four newspapers. Efforts to chase down rumors here and there fizzled because the participants in the negotiations held their tongues as to who was buying from whom, which papers were involved, and if and when any purchase would occur.

The first alert came in the form of a bold-faced, eight-column headline in the Saturday, July 30, 1927, *Gazette Times:* "Hearst Favors Mellon President," over a story reporting an interview with Hearst by reporter Robert Ginter. This was a surprise because Andrew Mellon was an archconservative Republican and Hearst, at that time, was still backing liberal and Democratic causes. The *New York Times* speculated that this was a condition of Hearst's rumored entry into the Pittsburgh newspaper arena; others also believed that Hearst was trying to ingratiate himself with the powers-that-be in Pittsburgh. As the ensuing months passed, it became clear that Hearst, while publicly criticizing the pro-rich tax policies urged by Mellon, was indeed trying to help his business interests in the Pittsburgh community by soliciting Mellon's political backing.

On Monday, August 1, Block and a Hearst representative signed the papers for step one of the transaction. Minutes after the parties shook hands, they signed additional papers for step two, resulting in a Block *Post-Gazette* and a Hearst *Sun-Telegraph*. The parties hastened to produce explanations, some of which were more confusing than enlightening. For instance, Block and Knox denied that Hearst was really the owner of all four newspapers; Knox implied, but did not forthrightly say, that Hearst had not advanced any money to Block. Arthur Braun issued this statement: "Effective today the proprietorship of this newspaper passes from the present owners to Paul Block. Mr. Block has also bought the *Pittsburgh Sun*."[4] By March 1928, as matters settled down after the merger earthquake, the Audit Bureau of Circulations (ABC) figures were as follows: *Post-Gazette* (morning only), 225,128; *Sun-Telegraph* (evening) 191,916, (Sunday) 336,118; *Press* (evening) 219,825, (Sunday) 283,575. Eleven years later, when the Great Depression sand-bagged his finances, Hearst demanded that Block repay him the money for the *Gazette Times* purchase that he presumably had never furnished.

In many ways, the 1927 purchases of the Pittsburgh papers and the *Toledo Blade* represented the high point of Paul Block's newspaper career. By this time, Block had amassed a personal fortune that enabled him to own a mansion in Greenwich, Connecticut, complete with a nine-hole golf course and his own private railroad car, both of which he named "Friendship." A generous philanthropist, Block gave not only to Jewish organizations and causes but also to Catholic and Protestant charities, community centers, and college scholarships. In 1929, he made two grants of one hundred thousand dollars each to institutions where his sons went to school: one to finance the construction of a chapel building at Hotchkiss School, in Lakeville, Connecticut, the other to Yale University for establishing a foundation to promote the study of journalism.

Paul Block's proximity to the seats of power is particularly demonstrated by the role he played in the 1932 Democratic presidential nomination of Franklin D. Roosevelt. Hearst, an absolute isolationist, wanted the nomination to go to John Nance Garner of Texas. Block, Hearst's eyes and ears at the convention in Chicago, warned Hearst by telephone that if Roosevelt were stopped, the alternative would be Alfred Smith, the New York Catholic whom Hearst hated. After maneuvering during which Roosevelt accepted Garner as his running mate, Hearst switched California's forty-four votes to FDR, clinching the nomination. Eventually, both Block and Hearst turned against the New Deal and its governmental-intervention policies—Block excoriated many of Roosevelt's policies with front-page editorials. Yet Block and Roosevelt met occasionally, and on one such occasion at the White House in 1935, FDR told Block he was thinking of starting his own newspaper when he retired, with no editorials or advertisements—only news—and plumbed Block's knowledge of the dynamics of publishing. Throughout the years, Block maintained lines of communication into the Democratic camp as well as the Republican Party, with which he was more ideologically comfortable.

From the start, Block quickly made his imprint on the newly merged *Post-Gazette*. In the first issue, published on August 2, 1927, he issued

Front page of the
first issue of
*Pittsburgh Post-
Gazette*, August 2,
1927

this statement: "It will be our ambition to have the *Pittsburgh Post-Gazette* be a newspaper of which everyone may be proud. Its policies will
be independent and the newspaper will be of such high character as to
insure its welcome in every home." Block's first task was to deal with
excess staff, eliminating three hundred jobs, most outside the news/edi-
torial department. At the same time, Block began to devise changes in
the format to show that this was a new paper in fact as well as name.

In an effort to make the paper, as Block put it, more "peppy" than the predecessor *Gazette Times,*[5] he changed the look of the front page. Three days after Block took control, he ran an eight-column headline: "Lindbergh Arrives Today—Great Reception Planned," announcing a visit by Charles Lindbergh, whose solo, single-engine, trans-Atlantic flight to Paris had made him a phenomenal hero. Block already had a closer connection with Lindbergh than most, having served on the official New York City welcoming committee in June for the aviator's tremendous ticker-tape homecoming parade. This front-page display brought Block into conflict with Hearst, who reminded him of their understanding that the two papers would have distinct formats. The *Sun-Telegraph* would follow the same lines as Hearst's other twenty-five newspapers: heavy black headlines, big type, splashes of color, baseball box scores prominently displayed on the front page, unusual picture layouts, and sensationalist stories. In deliberate contrast, as the only morning paper, the *Post-Gazette* would adopt a more conservative, dignified look in an effort to appeal to a more upscale readership.

Block, however, had some misgivings about the paper's format being too conservative. He wanted to lead "thinking citizens," as he put it, into an independent Republican Party, and he feared the newspaper was looking too moderate. Hearst's own circulation director at the *Boston American,* after a week in Pittsburgh, gave his opinion that the *Post-Gazette* "would never sell or get any circulation looking as cold as it does." Block wrote to Hearst: "The above will give you an idea of why I have not made it look as conservative as even you might have had in mind. However, this does not mean I am not willing to change if you think it best."[6] That September, Hearst reiterated his position at a meeting in New York, and Block went along with him. Despite the circulation director's dire prediction, by October the *Post-Gazette* had a daily circulation of 234,238, the largest circulation to date of any Pittsburgh paper. Over the decade, Hearst and Block held many cordial discussions—a fact that would have surprised many Pittsburghers who assumed fierce competition between the two rival newspapers. The new publisher brought numerous technological innovations to the *Post-Gazette.* He ordered newsprint paper from Finland, which was both of a higher grade and less costly, creating savings, less breakage, and cleaner photographs. Thus the *Post-Gazette* could complete its daily run twenty to thirty minutes faster, with savings in overtime and supply costs. On the advertising side, Block took a step unprecedented in the Pittsburgh newspaper field by insisting that large local advertisers sign contracts for the purchase of a certain number of lines or pages of ads. The merchant was charged a lower rate if he used up the space and a higher rate if he did not. Although Block took the risk of being trapped in an unalterable contract, his salesmen did not have to pursue ad copy every day or week, and the advertising income was far more predictable. Within two weeks, his salesmen had 50 local contracts; eventually, they procured 120 national contracts. Block also raised the newspaper price from two cents to three without damaging circulation, despite the fears of skeptics within his staff. Indeed, by late autumn, due to the combination of these changes, Block's circulation had jumped to three hundred thousand, and had more advertising than any other morning paper in Pittsburgh's publishing history. The *Post-Gazette* was becoming one of the most successful and largest morning dailies in the country. Ironically, this success created problems for Block because if too many advertisers, bedazzled by *Post-Gazette* figures, deserted the *Sun-Telegraph*, that would damage his relationship with Hearst. So he often delayed publicizing the burgeoning figures, although shrewd advertisers could not help but notice what was happening.

Hearst became agitated over a particularly astute Block innovation—that of placing all of the comic strips on one page. Hearst had been more responsible than any other American publisher for cartoons and comic strips becoming one of the most popular forms of entertainment and highly effective circulation builders. He was quite clear about what comics should appear where in the paper and advised Block to insert something somewhere for everybody. He did not like to have them clustered on one page and telegraphed Block to say so. Block canvassed executives on both the editorial and business sides of the paper and found that most supported the single-page idea because it would give the reader who wanted comics a central place to find them, without irritating readers interested in having news and business pages free of such "clutter." So Block stuck with the format, gathering most of the comic strips on one page, but to smooth his relationship with Hearst, he bought two new comic strips—"The Gumps" and "Moon Mullins"— to be carried elsewhere in the paper.

Even though his advertising contract system was working well, local merchants argued that readers did not have time in the morning before going to work to read and respond to ads in the morning *Post-Gazette*.

In contrast, an advertisement in an evening paper provided time for home discussion and therefore started the cash registers ringing the next morning. Block's counterargument that an ad placed in a morning paper motivated customers for two days did not sell very well. Retailer Edgar Kaufmann placed a full-page advertisement every day on the back page of the first news section of the *Post-Gazette,* but Block noted that the store was also placing multiple ad pages in the evening and Sunday papers. This evening advantage continued in Pittsburgh long after evening papers everywhere else were folding.

Block's fast start was blunted by harsh luck. The autumn of 1927 was unseasonably cold and the following winter especially brutal. Retail store sales slipped because people were staying home and not shopping much, so many stores cut their advertising. Hearst began badgering Block, who was already concerned, about the hemorrhaging of money by the *Post-Gazette.* Outwardly, though, Block continued to display optimism, writing in the March 14, 1928, *Post-Gazette:* "But every sign seems to point to a revival of business this Spring, and already, the business in many industries is not only improving but breaking records." Certainly, the continuous climb of the stock market in those closing years of the Jazz Age fostered such expectations.

A shocking killing prompted one of the most important *Post-Gazette* crusades during Paul Block's tenure—a concerted attack on the Coal and Iron Police system. On Monday, February 11, 1929, the morning paper carried the headlines, "Coal police kick and beat man to death/ Two officers under arrest in death of farmer/Victim had drawn knife/ Dies from injuries received near barracks at Imperial." The story described how John Barcoski, age forty-one, a McDonald farmer and part-time coal miner, died after a fracas at a house on Pittsburgh Coal Company property. "Coal and Iron policemen H. P. Watts and Frank Slapikas had gone to the home of Bercoski's mother in law, Mrs. Anna Blussick, House No. 3, Santiago, to make purchases of liquor and to raid the place . . . Watts had been drinking . . . An argument ensued and Barcoski was taken toward the Coal and Iron barracks, fighting on the way. When they neared the barracks, Watts forced Barcoski against the building and began beating him over the head with his revolver."

This report forcibly brought to public attention a system repeatedly criticized by miners, steelworkers, and other labor groups. The Coal and Iron Police were men hired by the companies to "keep order," particularly during strikes. The anomaly was that Pennsylvania's governors commissioned them, which gave them a legal protection that caused a catch-22 for aggrieved workers. The police were private, on the one hand, and therefore protected against the political action possible if their bosses had been elected officials. On the other hand, they were quasi-government officials with immunities on that ground. Moreover, in a time when management was in ascendancy and organized labor was weak, the police were able to control not only the workplace but also corporation-owned property in company towns, of which Santiago was one.

Regular readers of the *Post-Gazette* might have been surprised to see the vigor with which the newspaper, considered friendly to business, took up the cause. On Tuesday, February 12, 1929, two days after the murder, the *P-G* editorialized:

Pittsburgh was shocked yesterday morning to read of the brutal clubbing to death of a farmer by three coal and iron policemen. The policemen claim that the farmer struck at one of them with a knife, following an altercation in a speakeasy. County detectives, following an investigation, declare that the farmer was unarmed, and that the officers were intoxicated at the time. . . . Whether or not there was justification for attempting to place the man under arrest only a thorough inquiry of the facts will determine. But even if the police officers are given the benefit of the doubt in this respect temporarily, and it is assumed that they were justified to that extent, there can be no satisfactory explanation for the vicious brutality which they displayed. . . . Nothing but the most careful and thoroughgoing investigation will satisfy an aroused public sentiment.

It is quite possible that the broader question of the proper regulation and restraint of special police forces will be brought up in the course of the investigation. While in fairness it must be said that an outrage by one individual or two individuals does not convict the entire force, there have been many instances of arbitrary abuse of power. There could be no better time to get at the facts without undue prejudice than the present when conditions in the coal fields are comparatively tranquil, and the tension existing two or three years ago has largely disappeared. In its broader phases, the question is one which should be of interest to the Legislature.

The next day the *Post-Gazette* reported that State Representative Michael Musmanno of Stowe Township had drafted a bill to abolish the system. Governor John Fisher, "known to be opposed to the present

Coal and Iron system," moved quickly and decisively to order an immediate investigation. The February 13 paper carried the full text of the Musmanno bill, which called for the repeal of an 1865 law "empowering railroad companies to employ police forces." On the first page of the second news section, the paper displayed "Scenes and figures in Coal Police murder," including a picture of Julius Bugay, "victim of a similar attack by Coal and Iron police in September 1927, as a result of which he was disabled permanently." The editorial page also carried a large, three-column cartoon by Cy Hungerford, who had been drawing for Pittsburgh newspapers since 1912, and had joined the *Post-Gazette* staff in 1927. The cartoon, titled, "The Land of the Free and the Home of the Brave," portrayed a man in a rough outfit—not a uniform—with the words "The Coal and Iron policemen" on his coat, with club in hand dragging a bag with a battered head sticking out.

Musmanno followed his abolition bill with a crusade, which eventually inspired a movie and a book, both called *Black Fury,* about the Coal and Iron Police and the case of John Barcoski. Musmanno was an attorney and legislator who would later go on to serve as a Pennsylvania Supreme Court Justice. By coincidence, he had rated prominent attention in the local news section of the February 4, 1929, *Post-Gazette,* a week before the murder of Barcoski, for publication of a book, *Proposed Amendments to the Constitution of the United States.* The article reported that Musmanno had spent five years writing the book, which so impressed Congress that it was adopted as a government document.

When Governor Fisher vetoed the Musmanno repeal bill, a new Cy Hungerford cartoon portrayed Fisher in the form of Lady Macbeth, wiping dripping blood from his hands. Behind him was shown the Musmanno bill, pinned to the floor by a dagger. The matter seemed to be settled when Gifford Pinchot, of the progressive faction of the Republican Party, was elected governor in 1930, having served a previous term from 1923–1927. He announced that there would be no more state commissions for Coal and Iron Police after the present set expired June 30, 1933. However, the law allowed sheriffs to appoint deputies who could be hired by the companies to perform the same services. So the reform pressure continued when the New Deal brought the Democrats to power in state government. On June 15, 1935, Democratic governor George Earle signed Act 156, abolishing the Coal and Iron Police for good. Perhaps not coincidentally, on that same June 15, miners held a huge parade in Waynesburg, Greene County. A year later, on June 7, 1936, the United Mine Workers Union launched efforts to organize the steel industry, starting with a parade in Rankin, a blue-collar Pittsburgh suburb. The eventual outcome was the formation of the United Steelworkers Union. On June 8, 1936, the *Press* quoted Michael Musmanno as saying, "This decision to accept industrial unionism is, unquestionably, one of the most important and forward-looking steps taken in labor history and it will lead to beneficent results in both fields of capital and labor."

By the time of the Barcoski affair, Paul Block had become a well-regarded part of the Pittsburgh scene, and the *Post-Gazette* was profitable. With his nine-newspaper chain and social and political friendships that included former president Hoover and President Coolidge, Block was at the zenith of his career. Then came the stock market crash of October 1929, and for him, as for so many others, the world changed immeasurably.

At first, Block was convinced that the setback was temporary and that a show of confidence by the nation's leaders would set matters aright again. Yet the solid financial footing of the *Post-Gazette*—and many other newspapers around the country—began to decline as the Great Depression undermined consumer spending and, therefore, businesses' willingness to advertise. Block sought ways to promote confidence: he sponsored a successful Thanksgiving Day benefit performance at the Stanley Theater for the city's unemployed, and used the *Post-Gazette* to hail a slight upsurge in Christmas season business, pointing especially to McCreery's stores as having hired more workers for the season than in 1929. The economic signs, however, went in the other direction once the Christmas shopping season was over.

Block began a slow slide into a personal depression that matched the downward curve of the Great Depression. His economic problems were compounded by his complicated business relationship with Hearst: how could he carry out what he believed was best for the *Post-Gazette* when he and Hearst disagreed? Distracted and restless, at times he had to act or speak out, regardless of what Hearst's reaction might be. In December 1930, the *Sun-Telegraph* published a front-page editorial by Arthur Brisbane, who was, by then, American's most famous editorial writer and a superstar in the Hearst system. Brisbane criticized the *Post-Gazette*'s endorsement in the governor's race of John M.

Hemphill, a liberal Democrat whose platform against Prohibition Block favored. What particularly stung Block was that Brisbane called this "a circulation mistake" because the election went to Pinchot, an energetic conservationist who also was a vigorous Prohibitionist. Block could not let that allegation go by. In a December 13, 1930, front-page editorial, he fired back: "You use the phrase 'circulation mistake.' It occasions some surprise because it is not our impression that the great list of newspapers, the William Randolph Hearst publications, with which you are so prominently associated, permits their editorial policies to be dictated by the circulation department. Certainly the *Post-Gazette* does not. But for your information, the *Post-Gazette*'s circulation exceeds by almost 50,000 that of the next Pittsburgh daily paper, and the last official report of the three papers showed that the gap was widening as compared with the previous six months average. If that is a mistake, we hope to make more of them."

As the Great Depression deepened, the pressures mounted on Block. In 1931, the Retail Merchants' Association of Pittsburgh, consisting of the eleven leading stores, decided to intimidate the *Post-Gazette* with the threat that if it did not lower its rates, the merchants would move all of their advertising over to the *Sun-Telegraph*. This must have created a dilemma for Hearst. He obviously welcomed the prospect of additional revenues for his paper at a time when he was already realizing an increase in circulation over his afternoon rival, the *Pittsburgh Press*. However, it would be a hollow victory if it hurt the *Post-Gazette* too much. In the end, Block lowered the rates, leaving historians to wonder whether he acted at Hearst's insistence, or on the basis of his own business judgment.

Despite Block's role in obtaining the 1932 Democratic presidential nomination for Franklin Roosevelt, his newspapers backed the reelection efforts of President Hoover. Block had grown quite unhappy with Roosevelt because of his treatment of Block's closest political friend, New York mayor Jimmy Walker. As governor of New York, Roosevelt had played a part in Walker's eventual resignation. Block's election stand was also based on his personal relationship with Hoover. His editorial support featured ebullient statements about the economy and its contemporary recovery, even though experiences with his own enterprises clearly suggested otherwise. In addition, Block—as well as Hearst—scorned Roosevelt's vague outline of proposed policies. In an April 4,

1932, *Post-Gazette* editorial, Block complained: "Nothing constructive is ever offered. Are we to follow vague and intangible promises which are impossible to fulfill?" On April 21, Block's editorial further urged Roosevelt to commit himself on such issues as the Prohibition question. Block remarked on June 29, 1932, that Roosevelt was "a pleasant, smiling cheerful Governor . . . but many doubt that he would be the forceful, aggressive, capable President that this country needs," and went so far on October 26, 1932, as to criticize FDR as a "dangerous radical, and a political experimentalist."[7] He was thrilled at FDR's bold, reassuring inaugural speech, but would not be as enthusiastic during the historic "First 100 Days" of the new administration, as Roosevelt initiated a cascade of radical new programs and increased federal spending that alarmed conservatives.

The year 1932 has been described by economists such as John Maynard Keynes as the "cruelest year" of the Depression. Certainly it was so for Block. With the exception of the *Toledo Blade,* which was benefiting from an infusion of automobile advertising, most of Block's newspapers were in deepening financial difficulties. His advertising business also was in trouble, thanks to a 40 percent drop in advertising between 1929 and 1933. Block began deferring decision making, and spent more and more time away from the office. He began to show signs of clinical depression—what then was called a nervous breakdown. Block would stay in bed for long periods in his Park Avenue apartment or in Greenwich. He would lie awake until after dawn, then sleep for much of the day, making it impossible for his business associates to reach him for crucial decisions until late in the day. He also complained of frequent stomachaches, a loss of energy, a feeling of guilt over the predicament of his enterprises, and difficulty in making even the most trivial decisions. He continued to ignore the cash shortages his companies were experiencing and the creditors to whom he owed money. Repeatedly, he called on such friends as Hearst and financial guru Bernard Baruch to write or telephone creditors to vouch for his good will and ability to pay up eventually.

In the midst of these worries, Block probably paid little attention to a sniping attack from Pittsburgh's society newspaper, the *Bulletin-Index,* under the headlines: "'Full of Sound and Fury—Signifying Nothing'/The *Post-Gazette* supplies us with a 'Monday Morning' crime wave." The story, published on February 18, 1932, read:

"Horrors!" cried Mrs. J. Ogleby Slackthorpe as she picked up her Monday morning *Post-Gazette,* "the city is being attacked by marauding bandits, the same thing we read about in China." And she called up Ogleby at his office, Slackthorpe, Slackthorpe and Dagshott, to rush a fleet of armored cars for the jewels and furniture, and to prepare to move to the ancestral estate, Slackthorpe-on-the-Youghiogheny, where they could barricade themselves in, or leave the country. . . .

For on this Monday Paul Block, "deus ex machina" of the nice *Post-Ga-zette* (or, as some Pittsburghers put it, little tin god in the machine, or out-of-town boss) had neglected to run his editorial against gangster pictures. And so the *Post-Gazette* editors . . . had made hey-hey with news of bandit attacks in Pittsburgh. Perhaps chuckling over the bogey they were using to frighten readers. . . .

Well, Monday morning is one time in the week when the alert afternoon papers can't beat the *Post-Gazette* on routine week-end news. Ergo, Pittsburgh must suffer the stigma of "gangster outrages" for dog-eared, flea-bitten stories that ordinarily would get buried somewhere on page seventeen.

Although the *Post-Gazette* historically was the least sensationalist of Pittsburgh's newspapers, gangsters such as Al Capone and bank robbers such as Bonnie and Clyde were all the rage with readers in the 1930s, famished for something exciting amidst the depressing economic news.

Certainly, Block had the latter much more on his mind. By the spring of 1932, his liabilities were nearing two million dollars. At that point, he sat down with his lawyer, Max Steuer, and urged him to write a letter to the major creditors asking them to wait until 1934 for their re-payments. Steuer urged Block to get his life in order in a letter of May 16, 1932, marked "Personal and Confidential," which read, in part: "I wish that you would make up your mind to be well. I do not personally consider that you are physically ill. The thinking requires your personal energetic attention. Your failing to give it is injuring you very seriously. You should be at your office and not talk about being sick. . . . I beg of you to make up your mind that nobody is going to consider friendship in this situation. . . . Nobody is your enemy. Nobody is unduly harsh. . . . Tell them [the creditors] what can be done, and then do it. I have the utmost confidence that you will be left in charge and that everything will work out all right, provided you will follow the suggestions I have tried to convey."[8]

Fortunately, Block followed Steuer's advice and began going to the office, although still complaining of his poor health and inability to sleep. He drew up a business plan and a schedule of small payments to the most insistent creditors. At the same time, his creditors realized that if they forced Block out of business, they would receive only a few cents on each dollar owed. So Block survived, helped, in part, by the election of Roosevelt and the policies the new president invoked. At first, Block was enthusiastic about Roosevelt's bold actions, such as the radio speech of July 24, 1933, which announced the launching of the National Recovery Act. Block immediately telegraphed the White House with a message that said: "Your speech tonight was the most human I have ever listened to [Stop] I commend you sir and congratulate the country."[9] Block was equally pleased when Prohibition was repealed. Roosevelt reciprocated by continuing to invite Block to the White House. By 1934, however, Block was starting to have misgivings and to turn away from Roosevelt. In editorial after editorial in the *Toledo Blade* and the *Post-Gazette,* Block took issue with Roosevelt: he opposed the Wagner Law, which strengthened organized labor's collective bargaining rights; urged Congress to limit the power of the president; expressed wariness about Roosevelt's massive rearmament and aid to the British; and came close to calling Roosevelt a liar when, in one of his "fireside chats" on the radio, the president said that the economic situation was getting better.

In late 1935, Block was becoming increasingly worried that Roosevelt was going to be renominated and possibly reelected the next year. In a scathing condemnation of the New Deal, Block told a Toledo Bar Association dinner on December 3, 1935, that "our President is surrounded by men just as dangerous and just as anxious to overthrow our democratic form of government as were the Mussolinis, the Hitlers and the Stalins who overthrew their form of government. . . . We must write and speak, yes, shout out and clearly explain to all who will listen, what these dangers are, so that the Frankfurter boys, the Tugwells, and the rest of the radical socialists and communists will be eliminated from public life." Asking members of the press to put down their pencils as he was about to say something "in confidence," Block went on to recount in a conversation in which he had engaged Roosevelt the previous May. The president, disgusted and discouraged that the U.S. Supreme Court had just found the National Recovery Act to be unconstitutional, told Block how British Prime Minister William Gladstone had "packed" a hostile House of Lords with additional members to dilute its influence after it had vetoed one of his major bills. Most of Block's audience was astonished by the insinuation that FDR might do something similar in the Supreme Court.[10] The press honored the publisher's request to keep quiet, but a member of the audience forwarded the Block's comments to Roosevelt, who was furious. Block, queried by FDR's press secretary, wrote saying he had not thought the May conversation was confidential. At that point, Block was no longer welcome at the White House. In the 1936 presidential campaign, Block strongly endorsed Kansas governor Alfred Landon.[11]

Meanwhile, Block continued to resist pressure by Hearst, who wanted to send one of two of his executives to "oversee" the operation of the *Post-Gazette*. Block pointed out that this course of action would undercut the belief of virtually everyone in Pittsburgh—advertisers, bankers, suppliers, readers—that he, not Hearst the silent backer, was the owner of the paper. Block also showed, using figures from across the country, that virtually every newspaper, especially morning papers, was having troubles. So-called "luxury advertising" for automobiles, higher-priced appliances, and financial services—the province of morning newspapers—was drying up. In the meantime, Block assured Hearst that he was making improvements and asked for sixty days to prove their worth. Wisely, he concentrated on furnishing financial resources to bolster the editorial content with solid reporting, well-known columnists, and appealing features. He also added wire services, including the *New York Times* Service, which he considered the best, so that by 1936, the *Post-Gazette* was using more wire-service reports than any other paper in the nation.[12]

At the same time, with strong, personally signed editorials and news exposés, Block criticized the local proliferation of slot machines, a taxi strike; and exorbitant freight rates affecting the coal industry. He campaigned for safer conditions for iron and steel workers and disparaged Pennsylvania's "blue laws," which prohibited such recreations as baseball games and concerts on Sundays. The paper also broke the story of a scandal in the Pittsburgh Department of Supplies, leading to the conviction of Mayor Charles Kline.

The newspaper also began paying more extensive attention to international issues. Block and Hearst had both been pro-German during World War I, and now Block tried to distance himself from this position. In an editorial that Block ran in both the *Post-Gazette* and the *Toledo Blade* on April 28, 1933, he suggested an international embargo on German products and money in order to check the rise of Hitler's dictatorship. The following year, in the summer of 1934, Block took his wife and two sons took a tour of Europe. In Paris, though, he found a sense of foreboding about another war. When he went to Germany, however, Block left his wife and children in France. Given that he had already written editorials condemning Hitler's government for attempting to destroy "religions and races, the stifling of free states and a free press," it remains a mystery why Block, a Jew, received not only access to Germany but cooperation from the government, especially in response to his request to meet Hitler. The latter appointment was cancelled at the last minute because President Paul von Hindenburg was critically ill and Hitler, as chancellor, had to be available to discuss the succession. In dispatches home, Block predicted that while the death of Hindenburg might help Hitler in the short run, he soon would be overthrown, to be followed by a military dictatorship and then a limited monarchy under a descendant of the Kaiser. Even though by that time Jewish-owned banks and other properties were being confiscated and Jews beaten on the streets, Block did not write specifically about these growing atrocities.

The publisher next went to Austria, where he had a private meeting with Chancellor Kurt von Schuschnigg, successor to Engelbert Dollfuss, who had been assassinated by the Austrian Nazis. Block rejoined his family in Rome, and had an audience there with Benito Mussolini. Block was quite impressed with the interview, reporting: "I cannot remember when I have had the privilege of talking so openly and frankly to a person of his rank. Certainly not with most of our executives in Washington." In his last article from Europe, commenting on Hitler and Mussolini, Block could not help but make some comparisons unfavorable to Roosevelt. When he arrived in New York at the end of August, he sarcastically remarked to interviewing reporters: "I was happy to note this morning that the Statue of Liberty was still here. I was afraid the New Dealers might have torn it down."[13]

On returning home, Block found that the Great Depression had undercut the circulation of Pittsburgh's newspapers. The ABC figures for March 1935 showed that the *Post-Gazette*'s numbers were down by over one hundred thousand copies since late 1927 to 194,516. The *Pittsburgh Press* showed figures of 168,874 for the evening edition and 254,565 for the Sunday, and the *Sun-Telegraph* was down to 151,624 for the evening edition, but had increased numbers of 362,809 for the Sunday edition.

The *Post-Gazette,* along with the rest of Pittsburgh, suffered a grievous blow with the St. Patrick's Day flood of 1936. During the worst flood in the city's history, houses were swept away and twenty feet of water in some downtown streets made skiffs and rowboats the only means of transportation. The story of the flood's approach and its path of destruction was reported by the newspaper as it developed, although slowly at first. On Friday morning, March 13, the paper's front page pictured a big watery scene, captioned, "Melting snows and rain cause second flood of season in Pittsburgh." The next day, however, the story was relegated to the second section's front page in a story headlined, "City will get relief from flood, cold/Rivers falling and temperature will rise today." It was accompanied by a picture, captioned, "Receding waters leave family homeless." Apparently, fears were lulled as nothing about the flood appeared on the front page on the morning of Monday, March 16, or Tuesday, St. Patrick's Day itself. By Wednesday, March 18, though, the picture had changed entirely, as evidenced by the huge headlines on the *Post-Gazette*'s front page: "River at 34 feet, still rises/ Downtown area under water/ Losses heavy, periled areas waiting blow." A *Post-Gazette* editorial that day hammered away at the need for action. While flood control in the Ohio River basin was neglected, it thundered, federal money was found for the "fantastic Passamaquoddy project in Maine to harness the tides" and also for the Florida ship canal.

On March 19, an editorial announced, "Because of flood conditions, and the complete failure of electric power, it was not possible for any newspaper to be printed in Pittsburgh [itself] today." It went on to declare that only through the cooperation of the *New Castle News* and the *Youngstown (Ohio) Vindicator* was the *Post-Gazette* able to maintain its

Aerial view of the Point during the flood of 1936
(Photo from the *Sun Telegraph,* reproduced in the *Bulletin Index;* Courtesy Carnegie Library of Pittsburgh)

record of 150 years of uninterrupted publication. The Block editorial continued:

The *Post-Gazette* takes this opportunity to thank the loyal men and women associated with us who have done such splendid work under the most trying circumstances. Their spirit has been a real inspiration; nothing could have been finer. Of course, it is unnecessary to say that all co-workers, including union men, who have been employed by us regularly under normal conditions, will receive full salary during this period. Whether or not they have all been able to do their usual jobs is not important; there is no question of their eagerness to do everything in their power to assist in this emergency and to assure Pittsburgh of consistent and accurate newspaper service no matter what the difficulties of the moment may be. PAUL BLOCK Publisher.

The March 21 edition returned to the issue of flood control, and featured an editorial cartoon by Cy Hungerford in which Pa Pitt asks Uncle Sam, "Now—are you thoroughly convinced we need adequate flood control in this neck of the woods?" In the same edition, the editors wearily noted that there was "no time for writing editorials," so the space usually allocated for that purpose was filled with Walter Lippmann's nationally syndicated "Today and Tomorrow" column. The

Cy Hungerford's cartoon of "Pa Pitt" arguing for adequate flood control
(Courtesy *Pittsburgh Post-Gazette*)

crusade for flood control was to be continued until the 1940s, when the first major element in Pittsburgh's postwar Renaissance was the building of dams and other control measures on the rivers draining into Pittsburgh.

Block's long-standing feud with Franklin Roosevelt took a bizarre but prizewinning turn in 1937 with one of American journalism's all-time scoops by the *Post-Gazette*'s reporter Ray Sprigle. Sprigle had established a reputation for unusual but interesting investigative reporting when, during a local mine strike in 1934, he had gone undercover as a miner and worked as a strikebreaker. His subsequent articles were so accurate and powerful that they drew praise from readers on both sides of the strike issue. In August 1937, while vacationing in Saratoga Springs, Block heard from Herbert Bayard Swope, former editor of the *World of New York* and a magnate in early-twentieth-century journalism, that Roosevelt planned to appoint U.S. Senator Hugo L. Black of Alabama to the U.S. Supreme Court. Swope reminded Block of a twenty-one-part series that had appeared in the *World* in the early 1920s, exposing the Ku Klux Klan as more than a small band of Southern white supremacists. Then Swope shocked Block by asserting that Black was a member of the KKK and, indeed, had been its candidate for the Senate in 1926. Swope was disgruntled that no newspaper was going after the rumor.

Block knew a news story when he heard it. Within minutes, he had phoned the *Post-Gazette* to relay the Swope rumor to Joe Shuman, the night editor, and told him to drop everything and dispatch Sprigle on the next plane to Birmingham "to get a story on Black's membership in the Klan."[14] No expense was to be spared, even if information had to be bought. Block believed that this story could validate his two years of warnings in editorials and speeches about Roosevelt's dishonorable intentions toward the Supreme Court. It was clear to Block that FDR was going to pack the high court after all, with a populist-progressive who had staunchly supported the New Deal. A story on the KKK connection could hurt Black's confirmation chances in the Senate, and Roosevelt's credibility.

Sprigle was a Republican, and, like Block, a strong critic of Roosevelt. Only four hours after Block's call, Sprigle was on an airplane heading for Alabama. His first few days in Birmingham gained him very little; many people he spoke to were sure of Black's connection to the Klan, but no one could provide any proof. In the meantime, the Senate confirmed Black, taking some of the steam out of Sprigle's enterprise. Eventually, the reporter found his way to the office of a disbarred lawyer, Jim Esdale, later described by Sprigle as "former Grand Dragon of the Realm of Alabama, The Invisible Empire, Knights of the Ku Klux Klan, the dreaded, hooded horde that ruled the Southland with scourge and noose and gun and torch and faggot, lord of the middle justice, the high and the low."[15] To Sprigle's surprise, Esdale's office was filled with reporters from around the country, but Esdale was not talking. Sprigle waited until that night to take a cab to Esdale's home. The lawyer let him in, but insisted in talking only about chickens. Esdale was about to set up his son with a new flock of Leghorns, and by some coincidence, Sprigle was not only a reporter, but also a chicken farmer in Moon Township. He offered some informed advice: forget the Leghorns—they are good for eggs but too skinny for eating—try White Wyandottes, the kind Sprigle raised at home. During the long evening, Sprigle did not mention Black, but Esdale agreed to meet again the next day.

Before that meeting, Sprigle found out that Esdale had been disbarred for setting up a phony corporation to handle bail bonds for his firm's own clients. When the two men sat down together, Sprigle delicately suggested that it was a shame such a thing had proved Esdale's undoing, especially when it could have been countered by a word from someone powerful like Hugo Black. "After all, you are responsible for the election of Hugo Black to the U.S. Senate."[16] This opened the floodgates. Esdale had asked Black for help, unsuccessfully, and for the next two and a half hours he talked at length about the ex-senator. The next morning, he opened his safe and dragged out a bundle of documents that proved Black's membership in the Robert E. Lee Klan from September 11, 1923, to his resignation July 9, 1925. Sprigle had the coup of a lifetime in his grasp, but Esdale did not want to let the documents get out of his hands. Realizing the importance of getting himself, his source, and the documents out of Alabama, Sprigle offered Esdale, his wife, and son an all-expenses-paid trip to New York City. The Esdales agreed, and Sprigle met them in New York and secured the documents he needed. A second trip to Alabama yielded more damaging material, including a document proving that Black had gotten a client acquitted of a racially-inspired murder by asking every witness brought before a Klan-affiliated judge and jury about his or her affiliation with Catholicism.

The six-part series of Sprigle's articles began on September 13, 1937, on the front pages of both the *Post-Gazette* and the *Toledo Blade*, accompanied by an editorial proclaiming: "When Senator Hugo L. Black's name was first presented for the Supreme Court bench, it was stated in the Senate and published in many newspapers that he had been elected as a Klan candidate. . . . The *Blade* [newspaper chain] has dug them [the facts] out and will present them in a striking series of six articles." Although the already-confirmed Black went on to surprise everyone as one of the most liberal justices of the twentieth-century court, the series earned the 1938 Pulitzer Prize for Sprigle and the *Post-Gazette,* its first.[17]

During World War II, Sprigle posed as a black-market meat operator to expose corruption in the war-rationing system. He later got himself committed to a mental institution to prove inhumane conditions. Finally, Sprigle disguised himself as a black man traveling through the south to produce an eye-opening twenty-one-part series in 1948. It is worth noting that Frank Hawkins, the editor of the *Post-Gazette*'s editorial page at the time and a southerner, criticized Sprigle's report as an example of "bounty hunting" by newsmen seeking journalistic prizes for "exposing the sins of Southerners against blacks":

Converting Sprigle into a black was the equivalent of converting Elizabeth Taylor into a gargoyle. No one in the South would ever have mistaken him for anything but a white with a Yankee accent trying to assay the role of a black. . . . Nothing out of the ordinary happened to him, of course, since no one could have taken his play-acting seriously or done anything to him even if he had been black unless he had broken the law. The story did little but eat up many columns of the *P-G*'s news space and provoke a rebuttal from Hodding Carter, publisher and editor of the *Greenville (Miss.) Delta Democrat-Times* and himself a Pulitzer Prize winner for his stand against racial injustice. I thoroughly disapproved of this silly venture into sensationalism, but it was out of my hands and I appreciated Bill Block's motives to combat racial injustice and, at the same time, establish a public-service reputation for the *P-G*.[18]

Sprigle died at age seventy-one on December 22, 1957, after a car wreck.

Later, Paul Block's son, William, made an interesting comment for an article on Sprigle in the newspaper's two hundredth anniversary edition on September 16, 1986. Then publisher of the *Post-Gazette,* William Block noted: "Sprigle was a great reporter, but I think he would be very unhappy in this business today. He never could get the other side of a story because it ruined the kind of investigative pieces he liked to do. Our reporting is a great deal more balanced today. . . . But the story on Hugo Black was accurate, above all. He got the dope, there's no doubt about it."

Not surprisingly, Roosevelt did not forgive and forget. A few months after the Hugo Black series appeared, Block was opening a new, sixty-five-thousand-square foot building for the newspaper at the corner of the Boulevard of the Allies and Grant Street. A decade earlier his presidential friend, Calvin Coolidge, had pressed the button to start the presses in a new plant for Block's *Toledo Blade,* and Block decided it was only right that the current president do the same at opening ceremonies for his Pittsburgh plant. FDR said no, however, and remained adamant even after Block tried numerous avenues of persuasion before the opening finally occurred on March 9, 1938. Apparently Block hoped against hope until the last, when he himself had to press the button. While he made no mention of the snubbed invitation in his speech at the gala opening, he told one partygoer, "If I had gotten just two or three words—'Congratulations on your new building'—or something about my courage in undertaking new construction these days, or something of that order . . ."[19]

By 1937, the Great Depression had caught up with William Randolph Hearst, forcing him to begin dismantling his empire. This gave Block the opportunity to finally obtain full ownership of the *Post-Gazette.* He scraped together some money of his own, transferred money from his other newspapers, and floated some bonds to come up with a final price that was estimated to be upwards of $2,500,000. The paper might have brought twice as much on the open market, but the sale was conducted in secret—neither Block nor Hearst wanted the public to know that Block had not been the full owner all along.

By this time the Great Depression and fierce competition had required Block, too, to divest himself of much of his empire, either by sales or by outright closure. His newspaper representative business had dwindled to serving only sixteen newspapers. By the end of 1939 he owned only the *Post-Gazette,* the *Toledo Blade,* and the *Toledo Times.* The *Post-Gazette* was doing well. John Troan, later editor of the *Pittsburgh Press,* recalls that when he arrived in Pittsburgh from Penn State in June 1939, the *Post-Gazette* was the daily with highest circulation, trailed by the *Press,* and, in third place, Hearst's *Sun-Telegraph.*[20]

By the start of the next decade, Block's health had gotten worse. He suffered intense pains in his stomach back, and legs that required daily injections of morphine. Some family members complained that many of his ills could be ascribed to hypochondria and depression; he was clearly dismayed when FDR was reelected in 1940 for an unprecedented third term. Block could have tried to discredit Henry Wallace,

Paul Block Sr. with first newspaper from new *Post-Gazette* plant
(Courtesy Carnegie Library of Pittsburgh)

FDR's running mate, by exposing a packet of letters that compromised Wallace as a member of a secret cult, but had backed away because FDR had threatened blackmail against the Republican presidential nominee, Wendell Willkie, and because in an interview with a reporter, Wallace laughed about the letters and contended that they were all lies. In that election year, Pittsburgh's newspapers had regained some circulation from the depths of the Great Depression, with the *Post-Gazette* climbing to 221,166; the *Press* to 214,269 (evening) and 335,934 (Sunday); and the *Sun-Telegraph* to 159,507 (evening) and 403,294 (Sunday).

In the years since his visit to Germany, Block had worried about at the ever-growing shadow of Adolph Hitler over Europe. As late as September 1939, however, when the war in Europe began with Hitler's invasion of Poland, Block continued to be ambivalent about any intervention by the United States. On April 16, however, Block published one of the most important editorials of his career, announcing that he had changed his mind and now thought it was imperative to send aid to

England. It was the first editorial in the country that expressed outright support for becoming Britain's ally. Ten days later, on April 26, Block wrote another editorial, commending his old publishing friend Frank Knox, now Roosevelt's Secretary of the Navy, for endorsing Block's previous editorial regarding England. At a meeting of the American Newspaper Publishers Association in New York, Knox had publicly cited the editorial to underline the fact that the war was "plainly *our* war."[21] As it turned out, these were the last such position-paper editorials that Block ever wrote. Later that spring, Block and his wife Dina visited Hearst at San Simeon, where the two old friends reminisced over old times and discussed the present. Hearst reasserted his isolationist beliefs but conceded that involvement in the war was likely.

Paul Block's condition was finally diagnosed at the Cornell-NYU Medical Center as pancreatic and liver cancer, with no hope of a cure. On Sunday morning, June 22, 1941, the sixty-five-year-old died. Block's death made headlines across the country. More than five hundred people attended the funeral, making it one of the largest funerals in Temple Emanuel El's history. Along with family, friends, and a host of employees—current and past—were Herbert Hoover, Alfred E. Smith, Edgar Kaufmann, and William Randolph Hearst. At one o'clock in the afternoon of June 24, the exact moment of the funeral, newspaper employees at the *Post-Gazette* and the *Blade* ceased all activity in a moment of silence for Paul Block.

Chapter 10

The Next Generation

A GLASS OF MILK provided a dismaying introduction to 1946 Pittsburgh for the William Block family. Fresh from five years of Army duty, Bill—as friends and associates knew him—finally had the chance to take personal charge of the *Post-Gazette*. With his wife Maxine and twenty-two-month-old son William Jr., he had arrived from Chicago by train at 7:00 a.m. on a warm August day and gone to the Schenley Hotel in Pittsburgh's Oakland section.

Block opened all the windows in the room and ordered breakfast. The tray arrived almost immediately, complete with a glass of milk for the baby. However, by the time Maxine had the child cleaned up and ready for breakfast, a film of soot had settled on the glass of milk. Maxine shuddered. "My God, do we have to live here?" Block answered, "This is where the job is."[1]

This story is symbolic of a Pittsburgh where the air pollution was such that car headlights often were needed at midday, and where men working downtown often brought an extra shirt to change into before going out to lunch. Corporate magnate Richard King Mellon had realized that he could not hope to attract capable executives to such a dismal and unhealthy atmosphere. In response to this situation, he worked with other top-level executives during the war years to create an

William Block

organization, the Allegheny Conference on Community Development, to be ready to tackle postwar Pittsburgh's many problems. These included flooding, air and water pollution, and a decaying Golden Triangle—the romantic name for downtown Pittsburgh, where the Monongahela and Allegheny Rivers join to form the Ohio—abutting a tangle of railroad yards, warehouses, and slum houses.

The story also demonstrates Block's determination to forge ahead with managing the newspaper he had inherited from his father. Andrew Chancellor, a former *P-G* city editor, believed this is one reason for the ultimate survival of the *Post-Gazette*. "[Bill Block] actually lived here, not running the show from somewhere else. So that even though the paper was part of a chain, it in effect was a locally owned newspaper."[2] On that depressing first morning, Block probably did not realize the difficulties his newspaper would go through in the decades ahead, or how much he and the *Post-Gazette* would be caught up in many civic

When the news of the Japanese surrender reached Pittsburgh on August 14, 1945, crowds streamed into the streets. Fifth Avenue, as seen from the Smithfield Street corner, became a solid mass of people; on the Warner Theater marquee, *The Valley of Decision*, with Greer Garson and Gregory Peck, based on Marcia Davenport's best-selling novel set in Pittsburgh.
(Photo by James W. Ross, *Pittsburgh Post-Gazette*; Courtesy Carnegie Library of Pittsburgh)

improvement endeavors to overcome Pittsburgh's disadvantages. The city had barely gained ground during the Depression and World War II, despite its vital role in the armament effort. Pittsburgh's population had grown only negligibly of late, from 669,817 in 1930 to 671,659 in 1940. This would change little in the next decade, though reaching a historic high of 676,806 in 1950. On the surface, matters looked promising. All three Pittsburgh newspapers had gained circulation during the war. The *Post-Gazette* had grown from 221,160 readers in 1940 to 254,525 in

1946. The *Sun-Telegraph* had seen similar gains: the evening edition had grown from 159,407 to 201,098 over the same six years, and the Sunday edition from 403,294 to 559,478. Ominously for the *P-G*, the *Press* had grown most of all. The daily had risen from 214,268 to 255,375, and the Sunday edition soared from 335,930 to 440,600.

While the war years had been good for newspapers, thanks to the public's hunger for news from the battlefronts, the Block newspapers had been in an almost leaderless situation since the death of Paul Block Sr. That 1941 event had left the diminished Block empire in an awkward position. Although both sons had been grounded in newspaper operations by their father, neither was immediately available to take over the business. Bill was in the army for a five-year term of service, and Paul Jr., within months after his father's death, was laid up in a Massachusetts hospital with a leg fracture suffered in a skiing accident, making him ineligible for service in the armed forces. Besides, his real interest was in organic chemistry and not journalism. Indeed, at the time of his father's death, he was in New York obtaining his doctoral degree in chemistry at Columbia University.

Shortly after Paul Jr. moved to Toledo in 1942 to take charge of the *Blade,* he was appointed to an industrial fellowship on iodine at the Mellon Institute in Pittsburgh. While that position enabled him to keep an eye on the *Post-Gazette,* it meant the Block interests were virtually on hold for several years. After the fellowship ended, he and his wife made their home in Toledo, and Paul moved the headquarters of all the Block concerns there.

Holding matters together at the newspapers during those war years were Grove Patterson (1881–1956) in Toledo and Oliver Keller (1898–1968) in Pittsburgh. Keller was brought to Pittsburgh by Paul Block Sr. from Lancaster, Pennsylvania, at the time of the 1927 merger to be editor and general manager. Keller was a graduate of Williams College and had served as an Army officer. Bill Block later recalled Keller's decisive editorial presence, evidenced in an incident with Paul Block: "[Paul] traveled here to urge Keller to support Dave Lawrence for mayor in 1945. Keller absolutely refused—he was a rock-ribbed Republican, something that fitted well with my father's positions. Keller also was turned off on Lawrence because of an alleged gravel scandal in the past that put a little black mark against Lawrence in Keller's eyes. My brother expressed his dismay and unhappiness with Keller, but that was that."[3]

The *Pittsburgh Press* endorsed Lawrence, in part because Ed Leech, its strong-minded editor and an ardent proponent of smoke control, believed Lawrence was the best bet for acting on that problem. That 1945 election, which Lawrence won, was the last time the *P-G* did not endorse him. By the next election in 1949, Bill Block was sufficiently impressed by Lawrence's demonstrated ability to work with Mellon and the Allegheny Conference in furthering the Renaissance to express support.

When Bill Block arrived in Pittsburgh, he well knew he faced difficulties taking up his new role as a publisher. Having been out of the newspaper business for five years, he expected to do some retraining and work in various departments, especially editorial, where he felt he had little experience. However, just a few days after his arrival, he was shocked to learn that Keller was leaving. It seemed that Keller and a group of Pittsburghers had an opportunity to buy a radio station in Springfield, Illinois. At that point in 1946, Block faced the difficult choice of whether to hire a new general manager or to take on that responsibility himself. He recalled, "Probably mistakenly, I tried to do the job. Because we were operating on such a narrow margin, I thought, 'Why not do it?' I had a lot to learn. I had no administrative experience and made a lot of mistakes. It was a very competitive situation." He chose as his editor Andrew Bernhard, who had come to the *Post-Gazette* in 1945 from the *Brooklyn Eagle,* where he had been managing editor for four years. After army service in World War I, Bernhard had gone to work in Paris for the *Chicago Tribune* before leaving for Brooklyn. Block describes him as "not a man of strong views, but sophisticated and worldly, one who handled people well." He adds, "I was a novice and feeling my way, and I depended a lot on Andy and on Joe Shuman, my managing editor."[4] Block named Frank Hawkins, who had arrived from Georgia in January 1946, to head the editorial page. The *Post-Gazette* had more than seven hundred employees at that time, including ninety in the news and editorial departments. The staff included people of various ethnic, economic, and religious backgrounds. There were, however, no African American employees, other than custodians.

Under Keller's direction, there had been two wartime-related price increases, to four cents on September 14, 1942 and to five cents on June 3, 1946. Helping to boost circulation was the *Post-Gazette*'s early "bull-dog" edition that came out at 7:00 p.m. the night before the main morning edition. This provided readers with all of the results of the baseball games that afternoon.[5] In the days before television and widespread air-conditioning, people sat on their porches in warm weather, and vendors could go down residential streets and sell the bulldog *Post-Gazette*. Not surprisingly, then, circulation was strongest in the summer months.

However, the *Post-Gazette* faced the "Sunday problem." The two competing papers, the *Sun-Telegraph* and the *Pittsburgh Press,* each had Sunday papers in addition to their evening editions. With news-print tight after the war, the two papers could increase their advertising rates on Sunday, which provided enough money to cover their increased expenses. Without a Sunday paper, the *Post-Gazette* could not go that route. In 1949, the *P-G* and the *Press* dailies had about the same circulation, around 280,000, while that of the *Sun-Telly* (as it was nick-named) hovered around 200,000. All three dailies sold for five cents.

"One thing we began to realize was that unless we got in the Sunday business, we didn't have a chance," Block recalled. "For example, when we raised our price to seven cents for outlying areas, the other papers were able to keep the rate at five cents and make up the difference in Sunday prices. We didn't have that leeway." The *Sun-Telly*'s Sunday figure was 548,595, while the *Press*'s was 482,489. Then in 1949, two proposals emerged that seemed to provide a pathway forward. The *Chicago Tribune*'s news service made a proposal concerning comics, a strong component of any newspaper's appeal. "The *Tribune* had been unhappy for a long time at playing second fiddle in the *Sun-Telly* to Hearst's own King Features. While their comics were included, they didn't get the big play that the King Features comics did. The *Chicago Tribune*'s contract with the *Sun-Telly* was expiring. They came to us and said they understood we were talking about starting a Sunday paper. 'If you'll sign with us, we will leave the *Sun-Telly*. But you must make up your mind before our contract expires.'"[6]

At the same time, the *Post-Gazette*'s newsprint supplier, the Abitibi Company, found that because of the 1949 recession, it could supply extra newsprint for the first time since the war. "Those two coincidental offers put us in a position that we had to do it then or not at all. So we decided to go ahead with a Sunday paper,"[7] Block stated. That would require increasing the size of the news and editorial staff by about a third. City editor Shuman was made Sunday editor and put in charge of recruiting the additional personnel. The *Post-Gazette* found itself scooped on the news of a forthcoming Sunday edition by the opposition *Press* in a January 25, 1949, story by reporter John Troan, later to be *Press* editor. He recalled, "That was my first contact with the *Post-Gazette*. Afterward, Mr. Block saw me and said, 'You tell Mr. Leech [editor of the *Press*] he wrote a pretty good story.' I didn't care either to affirm or deny that."[8]

As part of the arrangement, the *Post-Gazette* had to buy many new features for its Sunday paper and it spent $250,000 promoting them. Longtime reporter Alvin Rosensweet remembered arriving to start work in 1949 and seeing a helicopter atop the *Post-Gazette* building—part of the promotional efforts headed by Fred Lowe.[9] Troan remembered two giant searchlights knifing the sky. One of the searchlight operators told him, "A man stopped in to see us tonight and said he picked up our beam on the other side of Canonsburg [twenty-five miles away]. He couldn't get over it."[10] The purchases of new features, in a maneuver that baffled even insiders like Frank Hawkins, included taking from the *Sun-Telegraph* some of its top King Features comics, including "Dick Tracy." The latter coup prompted the *Press*'s Leech to spread the rumor that the comic detective would be the editor of the *P-G* Sunday paper. Before long, the *Press* revved up its Saturday coverage to undercut the *P-G*'s Sunday edition.

Part of the preparation for the initial March 27, 1949, issue included a breakfast with the strange name of "Wayzgoose." Somewhere, Lowe had run across a bit of journalistic history from earlier centuries in London where a master printer decided to entertain his printers on August 24. The printer fetched the name—probably no relation to goose—from somewhere to mark the time in London's latitude when printers would have to begin working by candlelight. Other master printers copied the idea, which usually included a banquet and often an excursion into the country. Later, London's shopkeepers took up the idea, providing an August banquet for the printers. Lowe, in staging a Wayzgoose, did not have the printers in mind. Instead he invited Pittsburgh's elite to a banquet on the seventeenth floor of the William Penn Hotel to mark the advent of the Sunday edition upon which so much of the *Post-Gazette*'s money and hopes rested.

Despite all of these preparations, the Sunday venture was not to succeed. Under Shuman and his assistant, James Alexander, who had been brought in from Ohio, the first twenty-four-page tabloid showcased a story on nearby McKeesport that took up almost the entire Sunday magazine. Reporter Alvin Rosensweet was sent to Wheeling, West Virginia, where he stayed two weeks to do a ten thousand–word story on that racy city—gangsters, crime, politics, society, and all. It never ran. Rosensweet remembers learning that Block had warned Shuman to hurry up and get such stories published because he knew the Sunday edition was failing. Even as early as July, people were being let go, including some who had left their jobs and sold their homes in other cities.[11]

"Unfortunately," Block later admitted, "we did very poor planning. We decided to try to imitate the other Sunday papers, to put in everything they had, and charge the same rates. They ganged up on us and warned distributors in outlying areas that they had better not handle the *P-G*."[12] Chancellor also remembered that there was a lot of sabotage, such as "bundles thrown away, not even opened." Block elucidated, "Even though we got a little advertising support, we soon realized we were losing money and dragging the entire *Post-Gazette* down." The Sunday edition was closed down on November 27, 1949.[13]

In 1950 the *Post-Gazette* faced additional troubles as it was caught in the first of an interminable string of strikes by the production unions across the succeeding decades. The teamster and mailers unions went on strike at all three Pittsburgh papers, forcing a suspension of publication from Monday, October 2, through Friday, November 17. The circulation of all three papers was hurt, but the strike was particularly damaging for the *P-G*, which was still recovering from the Sunday-edition fiasco.

Bill Block explained: "The Teamsters insisted on having a man at the bottom of each pressroom chute, thus duplicating the mailer already there. That was totally unnecessary. The *Press* caved in first; it didn't want trouble, especially if it was just against the *Press*. The *Sun-Telly* had only two chutes, so readily agreed. Our circulation manager resisted, we took a short strike, and then we gave in. We could least afford the additional payroll. That was the day of strong muscling."[14]

The *Post-Gazette* made its unhappiness clear in a November 18 article written by Frank Hawkins:

The newspaper business, like the building industry, is subject to the most appalling and irresponsible featherbedding practices. Because it has become big business, it is considered fair game by labor unions. Costs have reached such astronomical proportions that a newcomer is seldom able to meet competition long enough to get a toehold. As a result, the most successful operators get bigger and lesser lights go out

Well, readers may say, that's tough on you newspaper boys but why weep on our shoulders? What does it mean to us?

It means plenty to every citizen of the U.S. The implications of a monopoly trend in the newspaper business are alarmingly clear. The press is the only private commercial enterprise that enjoys a constitutional guarantee of freedom [the First Amendment] . . . Government was expressly forbidden from denying the press that freedom—the right to publish—which can be denied, willy-nilly by private pressure groups. . . . The point is that economic pressures in the industry resulting largely from union demands have established a monopoly trend wholly contrary to the intent of the founding fathers.

Just as the *Post-Gazette* got up and running again after the strike, Pittsburgh was blanketed by the worst winter storm in its history, the

On Thanksgiving Day, 1950, Pittsburgh was paralyzed by a record thirty-six-inch snowfall, marooning cars and blocking transit vehicles. (Photo by W. F. Mahon; Courtesy *Pittsburgh Post-Gazette*)

record-breaking thirty-six-inch snowfall on Thanksgiving Day. Because streets were impassable, Block called off preparations for the Saturday edition—marking the first time in the *Post-Gazette*'s thirty-three years that it did not publish on Saturday. The *P-G* did not publish on Sundays, so it was Monday morning when the *Post-Gazette* resumed production with an edition full of pictures of a city at a complete, white-sheathed standstill.

One untoward result of the turn-of-the-decade turmoil for the *P-G* was that on October 20, 1952, it was forced to raise its prices outside Allegheny County from five cents to seven cents for the daily and from forty cents to forty-two cents for a home delivery subscription each week. The accumulation of problems resulted in a decrease in circulation—by 1955 the *P-G* had only 258,480 readers.

In those years, the *Post-Gazette* and the other city newspapers were caught up in the remarkable downtown renewal effort that became known as the Renaissance. It was a model widely watched by other industrial cities facing pollution problems, not to mention major downtowns everywhere hit in the postwar era by decaying properties, transportation problems from the burgeoning of automobile traffic, and the rise of competition from suburban malls and other amenities of growing outlying communities.

In the midst of planning for the Renaissance, however, Pittsburgh was struck an industrial blow—little noticed at the time but with consequences that became highly evident three decades later. That setback was the federal government's termination of the "Pittsburgh Plus" pricing plan that had given the Steel City an edge for half a century. The Pittsburgh Plus system required steel plants anywhere in the United States to bill customers of rolled-steel products at a Pittsburgh-base price, plus the cost of freight from Pittsburgh to the destination, regardless of where the product was manufactured. Thus, a Chicago customer ordering a shipment of steel from the nearby U.S. Steel plant in Gary, Indiana paid the same price as if it had been purchased in Pittsburgh. Obviously, that put competing mill towns at a competitive disadvantage against Pittsburgh steelmakers. Presumably, Pittsburgh steelmakers had been able to establish this advantage quite early and had amassed the economic and political power to maintain the edge.

Through the decades, Pittsburgh's competitors fought the Pittsburgh Plus system in the federal system, while Pittsburgh newspapers predicted market chaos if it were abandoned. During the war, no one wanted to tamper with steel production, but shortly afterward, the fight against base-point pricing began again. In 1948, the U.S. Supreme Court upheld a Federal Trade Commission ruling forbidding the practice in the cement industry. That decision put the final nail in the coffin for base-point-pricing in any industry, including steel.[15] In the midst of the changing steel industry, the Renaissance project proved to be a lifesaver for Pittsburgh. It received almost absolute support from Block, Leech, and other leaders of the press on grounds that the need for drastic change was so great. The Renaissance paired a strongly Democratic political organization with leaders of Pittsburgh businesses, who were largely Republican. On one side was Mayor David Lawrence, who ran a well-oiled Democratic "machine." (Lawrence disliked the words "boss" and "machine," which the media frequently applied to him and his government, respectively.) Lawrence was willing to risk unpopularity to get results.

On the other side was the Allegheny Conference, led by Richard King Mellon, a business baron with enormous clout, but personally shy and retiring—"like a teller, showing up every morning in his office," as Andrew Chancellor described him.[16] Just as Lawrence was willing to look past political barriers to support efforts of his Republican adversaries, the business community responded in kind. The result was an unusually powerful alliance that could get things done. Interestingly, Mellon and Lawrence almost never met in person, preferring to handle negotiations through trusted envoys.

The inspiration for the Allegheny Conference had come during the war. Mellon had been asked to come to Washington, D.C., to head the government's transportation effort. At that point, he had realized he could no longer personally run all of the various elements of his business and industrial empire—the Mellon Bank, the Union Trust Bank, Gulf Oil, the Aluminum Company of America, Koppers, and others. In trying to recruit highly capable executives at top salaries, however, he ran into a roadblock: they did not want to move to polluted, problem-beset Pittsburgh. Even if they did, their wives balked: "Take Pittsburgh and we're divorced," was the colloquial story in Pittsburgh's inner circles. Mellon realized he either had to do something about Pittsburgh or move the headquarters of his companies elsewhere. Fortunately for Pittsburgh's future, Mellon chose the former, and in 1943 formed the

Allegheny Conference. From the very beginning, the conference's clout came from two simple rules. Only the top person in a particular firm could be a member of the policy-setting executive committee, and, second, if he was not at a meeting, his firm lost a vote. He could not be represented by a subordinate, although that was common practice on many community boards. With this arrangement, a CEO's company could be committed on the spot.

Block and other top newspaper executives were placed on the sponsoring committee—"window-dressing," in Block's words, for the real decision makers. "There was a feeling that the only people who could run it were bankers and industrialists. There was a suspicion of newspapermen." However, Block formed a close friendship with Wallace Richards, Mellon's advisor on city planning and the "imaginative idea man for Pittsburgh's Renaissance." The media effectively broadened the two-sided business/government relationship of the Renaissance into a triangle. In an analysis by Andrew Chancellor, the newspapers made up the third, narrowest, bottom side of the isosceles triangle—"no TV then, and radio didn't count!"—and provided the news articles, features, and supportive editorials to persuade the public of the sometimes distasteful steps necessary for revitalizing the city. The *Post-Gazette* and the *Pittsburgh Press* were particularly aggressive; the *Sun-Telegraph* did what it could; "but it was a Hearst newspaper, you know," Chancellor commented, meaning that it was both conservative and not as interested in local affairs. As various governmental authorities were established—urban redevelopment, parking, public arena—the newspapers seldom raised questions. At one time, the *Post-Gazette* library files had more than fifty clipping files about the Renaissance, including five files of buttressing editorials.[17]

A story from much later, during the tenure of editor Frank Hawkins, illustrates the "understanding" between the media and the Renaissance leadership. Plans for creating Point State Park included razing the old Point and Manchester bridges and replacing them with the Fort Pitt and Fort Duquesne bridges. The old bridges were still extant when Donald Miller, a young reporter at the time, interviewed a *New York Times* writer who suggested making the Manchester Bridge across the Allegheny River into a facsimile, complete with shops, of the Ponte Vecchio. Miller recalls, "Frank was absolutely furious with me for any suggestion about saving the Manchester Bridge. 'We've been trying for twenty-five years to finish the Point,' he dressed me down."[18]

The first item on the Allegheny Conference agenda was flood control, made particularly urgent by the St. Patrick's Day flood of 1936. Even businessmen and newspapers who were generally resistant to federal programs realized that only the national government could finance and build the necessary upriver dams. Preparatory action in the late 1930s had been put on hold because of the war, which meant a postwar political push by Pittsburgh Democrats and Republicans alike was needed to crank up the program again. The newspapers were "yelling about that." Not the least of the problems was that the Kinzua Reservoir behind a dam scheduled for the Allegheny River in northern Pennsylvania would swamp land owned by Native American of the Seneca tribe. Given the mood of the times, the Pittsburgh reaction was a dismissive "oh, those poor Indians trying to use a paper signed by George Washington."[19]

The second item on the agenda was tackling downtown decay. In 1946, the newly elected Lawrence established the Pittsburgh Urban Redevelopment Authority, using legislation passed the year before by the state. A key Lawrence aide, John P. Robin, was named the first executive director. As strategies evolved, old plans were revived for simultaneously clearing the Point and forming a state park. The visionaries in both the Mellon and Lawrence camps, however, saw an opportunity to stretch governmentally initiated development beyond the park. They hoped that a section of the triangle would be transformed into a completely different business district with tall, privately owned office buildings. This constituted a wholly new concept in Pittsburgh's government, the results of which would have profound significance well beyond Pittsburgh itself. In both theory and practice, government—whether by kings or popularly elected leaders—has always had the right to condemn private property for public purposes. Called "the right of eminent domain," the legal exercise was necessary to obtain land for highways, schools, public buildings, parks, and the like. However, taking property from one set of private hands and transferring it to another set of private hands was quite something else. The key, as planners presented it, was "slum clearance," that is, condemning and razing deteriorated property for the public good, and placing the land in the hands of

Allegheny Conference on Community Development leaders review a picture of the Point. Left to right: Richard K. Mellon, Edward Magee, executive director of the ACCD, John T. Ryan, chairman, and Carl B. Jansen, board chairman of the Dravo Corporation.
(Courtesy *Pittsburgh Post-Gazette*)

private owners who would put it to better uses. That was the core of the "Pittsburgh Package," a set of ten bills drafted by Mellon and Lawrence attorneys and submitted to the Pennsylvania Legislature. As historian Michael P. Weber has explained, these bills "concerned such diverse matters as county refuse disposal; creation of a city parking authority; creation of a city department of parks and recreation; extension of county smoke control laws to railroads; establishment of a county transit and traffic study commission; completion of the Penn-Lincoln Parkway, a vital link into the city; and broadening of the city's tax base to include sources other than real estate."[20]

The reaction of Pittsburgh's newspapers to the Renaissance is epitomized in the coverage of a significant date in that renewal effort. On May 18, 1950, the day the first building was demolished to make way for the development of Point State Park and Gateway Center, the *Post-Gazette*'s front-page headline read, "Work on Point Park Launched: First of Old Buildings Torn Down at Site." The *Pittsburgh Press*'s headline read, "Point Wrecking Job Starts." James Duff, the governor of Pennsylvania, gave the signal for a one-ton wrecking ball to smash into

Cy Hungerford's cartoon of James Duff with hammer pounding "Old Point Buildings" and the headquarters of former U.S. Senator Joseph Grundy
(Courtesy *Pittsburgh Post-Gazette*)

a 103-year-old, unnamed, two-story red brick warehouse. Duff, fresh from a convincing victory two days before in the Republican primary, shared the platform with Democrat Lawrence and other dignitaries. The ceremony was watched by a crowd of two thousand, including hundreds of schoolchildren who had been given a holiday. Also present were marching bands from Carnegie Institute of Technology and the University of Pittsburgh.

On that milestone day in Pittsburgh history, the newspapers gave as much attention to Duff's primary election victory and to a strike affecting suburban bus lines as to the demolition event that followed years of planning and legal activity and presaged years more of razing and building in the Golden Triangle. The *Post-Gazette*'s venerable cartoonist, Cy Hungerford, combined the two events, picturing Duff with a hammer pounding at two targets—"Old Point buildings" and "Ruins of Grundy's

Headquarters." The latter referred to Duff's defeat of former U.S. senator Joseph Grundy, founder of the Pennsylvania Manufacturers Association and a high-tariff exponent. The *Pittsburgh Press*'s lead story commenced: "Gov. James Duff began another major operation this afternoon at Pittsburgh's Point. Fresh from wrecking the Republican Old Guard in Tuesday's primary, the New Guard leader touched off the demolition for the thirty-six acre Point Park." The *Sun-Telegraph* devoted just six paragraphs to its front-page story under the headline, "Lowering the Boom! Duff Signal Starts Project Near Point." None of the stories mentioned Mellon, perhaps because the industrial leader preferred to fulfill a description frequently applied to him—that he liked to operate in the background.

The *Sun-Telegraph*'s editorial page ignored that presumed "day of days" entirely, carrying instead a typical Hearst editorial titled "The Tyranny of Liberalism," linking "Radicalism, Socialist Labor Government, and Socialist 'Welfare State.'" This, of course, was a far cry from Hearst's early day espousal of many reformist causes that others had labeled "socialist" and worse. Of the three Pittsburgh papers, only the *Post-Gazette*'s editorials dealt directly with the importance of the Point ceremony: "For nearly a century civic leaders have been dreaming of creating a park on the Forks of the Ohio River, where the City of Pittsburgh was born. That dream will near reality today when workers start clearing condemned structures from the thirty-six-acre park area. . . . When Gov. Duff signals the start of demolition, he will set in motion a chain of events which, within the next few years, will literally change the face of the historic Point."

Although flood control and urban redevelopment were necessary to revitalize Pittsburgh, an equally important item on the Allegheny Conference's agenda was the problem that had confronted William Block and his family on that warm August day in 1946—smoke pollution. Smoke had been a problem in the region for hundreds of years. In 1782, John Bernard described Pittsburgh this way: "On approaching Pittsburgh we were struck with a peculiarity nowhere else to be observed in the States: a cloud of smoke hung over it in an exceedingly clear sky, recalling to me many choking recollections of London." In 1807, Christian Schultz, who had previously praised the city's "charming" situation, said: "The first entry into Pittsburgh is not equally agreeable to every person, as the sulphurous vapour arising from the burning of coal is immediately perceptible."[21]

As Pittsburgh's industries developed, smoke came to be equated with prosperity and was even defended as good in itself. In an 1868 *Atlantic Monthly* feature on Pittsburgh, James Parton, who described the city as "Hell with the lid off," also observed that the average Pittsburgher insists "that the smoke of bituminous coal kills malaria, and saves the eyesight . . . the smoke, so far from being an evil, is a blessing . . . and it destroys every property of the atmosphere that is hostile to life. . . . All this is comforting to the benevolent mind." Nevertheless, Parton noted sarcastically "that the fashion of living a few miles out of the smoke is beginning to prevail among the people of Pittsburg. Villages are springing up as far as twenty miles away, to which the business men repair, when, in consequence of having inhaled the smoke all day, they feel able to bear the common country atmosphere through the night."[22]

During this period, the *Gazette* was resolutely pro-smoke. In 1866, the Allegheny Court of Common Pleas ruled that John Huckenstine, a Northside brickmaker, could not burn bituminous coal because it caused harm to his neighbors and their property. When Huckenstine appealed to the Pennsylvania Supreme Court, the *Gazette* took his side. The July 11, 1871, paper called Huckenstine's neighbors "wealthy property owners" living in "comfortable and costly houses" with grounds made beautiful by "money, taste, and the skills of the landscape gardener." The *Gazette* went on to accuse them of seeking to destroy industry itself. Later in the year, the newspaper downplayed the value of domestic cleanliness and comfort in comparison to the benefits of industry. An October 27, 1871, editorial dismissed prospects for smoke reduction through steam heating from central plants, and decried efforts to exchange the city's "hearth stones" for a life made labor-free by "no dirt, no coal smoke" and "no dust from fires." The Pennsylvania Supreme Court reflected that praise-the-smoke attitude when, in 1871, it overturned the 1866 injunction against Huckenstine. In its opinion, the court declared that the "single word" smoke described "the characteristics of . . . [the] city, its kind of fuel, its business, the habits of its people and the industries which . . . [gave] it prosperity and wealth."[23]

A turning point in the conflict came in the early 1880s with the advent of clean natural gas from wells within the city. The skies were clearer, and evidence multiplied that natural gas made better iron, steel, and glass than bituminous coal. Unfortunately, the local gas supply was quickly depleted.

By the end of the century, although the industrial sector, including workers, continued to think in terms of "smoke means jobs," a growing community of professionals and businessmen complained about the cost of smoke to retail merchants and its effects on Pittsburgh's parks and architectural showpieces. Pittsburgh's first organized antismoke movement, the Ladies' Health Protective Association (LHPA), began in 1889, using as its model a New York City group founded to combat impure water, inadequate garbage disposal, and smoke. It included some of the most wealthy and prominent women in Pittsburgh. Yet during its five years of existence, the LHPA usually relied on men to speak for it in public meetings. The organization's strategy was to stress the health risks caused by pollution, thus sidestepping the labor-related arguments that had long hindered opposition to Pittsburgh's smoke. The LHPA spearheaded passage of a smoke ordinance in 1892, but it only covered residential suburbs and exempted mill districts.

As pressure continued to build, industrialists also began to address the issue of smoke. In 1899, Andrew Carnegie led the Chamber of Commerce to appoint a Committee on Smoke Abatement, consisting of engineers and manufacturers. By 1906, this committee had drafted an ordinance that prohibited the emission of dense smoke for more than eight minutes an hour. The Carnegie initiative may have induced—or released—some Pittsburgh newspapers to begin extensive crusading on the subject. For instance, the *Pittsburgh Sun* published more than fifty-five antismoke articles in one six-month period in 1906. The *Gazette Times,* the *Dispatch,* and the *Post* together published more than twenty articles criticizing smoke during the same period. On June 22, 1906, the *Sun* complained, "more clothing has been ruined than could be purchased with the monetary returns from the sand and gravel gathered at that point" and exhorted, "An anti-smoke ordinance is demanded at once." A year later, on July 3, 1907, the *Sun* claimed credit for inspiring city councilmen to develop a new, stronger antismoke ordinance, passed in that year. The Pittsburgh Chamber of Commerce announced support for smoke regulation, calling it necessary to "increase our industrial prosperity," and, at the request of the mayor, helped select the chief smoke inspector.[24]

In the meantime, attitudes among Pittsburgh's leaders took an interesting turn after the 1908 publication of a landmark sociological study, "The Pittsburgh Survey," funded by the Russell Sage Foundation. Its six volumes criticized the city for its low level of social provision and organization in contrast to its high level of industrial efficiency. In a reaction similar to the one after the Johnstown Flood, even reform-minded businessmen and club women rallied to a defense of Pittsburgh against such attacks by outsiders.

In 1911, after the courts had declared the 1907 ordinance unconstitutional, the mood at the *Gazette Times* had changed to the extent that a March 10 editorial entitled "Help the Anti-Smoke Bill," urged taking the battle to the state level: "The city administration is determined to make a strong fight on behalf of the bill that has been introduced [to] empower cities to regulate the smoke nuisance, and its hands should be upheld by the people of Pittsburgh. . . . The courts have recently declared invalid the local antismoke ordinance under which a vigorous campaign against the evil was conducted. . . . It was generally admitted that under the original ordinance the situation was considerably bettered. . . . This, then, is the question that confronts us: is the improvement in conditions not only to cease, but are we to go back to our original status and be deservedly called the Smoky City?"

Three months later a bill introduced by Representative Horace McClung of the East End was passed and signed into law. However, it was an imperfect solution, in that it exempted mill heating and puddling furnaces. Despite continuing problems, Pittsburgh activists, officials, and newspapers were eager in the years that followed to inform the world about every indication of improvement in the smoke situation. For instance, the *Gazette Times*, in a December 7, 1922, article called "Pittsburgh Model of Spotlessness," quoted the *Cleveland Plain Dealer*'s recognition of Pittsburgh's 80 percent reduction in smoke, which proclaimed, "What Pittsburgh has done Cleveland intends to do."

Whatever successes these articles proclaimed, Pittsburgh housewives faced with laundry hardships and businessmen trying to keep clean shirts knew that the air was still filthy. Another major push came in the late 1930s when Councilman Abraham L. Wolk began a crusade for new legislation, forming a strong alliance that included the Civic Club, the Allegheny County Medical Society, and the League of

Women Voters. His effort was given new impetus when St. Louis passed a tough smoke-control ordinance, after a 1939 campaign by the *St. Louis Post-Dispatch.* Mayor Cornelius Scully and the City Council dispatched Dr. I. Hope Alexander, Pittsburgh's health director, to see what was happening in that Missouri city. Gilbert Love, a *Pittsburgh Press* columnist, publicized the St. Louis experience and argued on January 31, 1941, that "thousands of prospective citizens . . . have been lost to Pittsburgh because they did not like the idea of living and bringing up their families in atmospheric filth." Mayor Scully and the council visited St. Louis in February 1941. Finally, the council passed a stiffer smoke-control law based on the simple but effective St. Louis policy. Under its provisions, consumers had to use smokeless fuel, or else install "fuel-burning equipment which has been found to prevent the production of smoke."[25] In contrast to previous legislation, private homes and multiple-dwellings with less than six units would have to comply.

Then came Pearl Harbor and all bets were off as the nation strained every industrial sinew to provide the materials with which its fighting men and women could confront the Axis powers. So it was only at war's end that the Republican business elite combined with Democratic Mayor Lawrence to launch another major attack on smoke control, with the *Pittsburgh Press* playing a leading role. To this end, a United Smoke Council was formed, soon to become an affiliate of the Allegheny Conference. That group supported Mayor Lawrence's decision to require industry, railroads, and commercial buildings to comply with Pittsburgh's smoke-control law by October 1, 1946, and residential buildings by October 1947. In turn, Lawrence depended upon the Allegheny Conference and, specifically, its founder, Richard Mellon, to deal with obstructionism by the coal and railroad companies, especially in the state legislature.

A particular key was the Pennsylvania Railroad, which at that time was one of the most powerful forces in Pennsylvania politics and, through its lobbying prowess, in the state legislature. A Harrisburg story had it that on one occasion at the end of a legislative session, the presiding officer announced: "The Pennsylvania Railroad having no further business at this session, it is adjourned."[26] The "Pennsy" created considerable consternation when it announced its opposition to a proposed law for Allegheny County, which might mean a costly switch from coal to diesel locomotives. Bill Block and the *Post-Gazette* entered the picture at that point. Block later explained:

One of the bills called for eliminating three magic words from the powers given the county in the county smoke-control code. The words were "except the railroads." An official of the Pennsylvania Railroad's Central Division announced that the railroad was going to oppose the eliminating of the three words and, moreover, planned to pay no attention to any Pittsburgh ordinance on the subject. The *Pittsburgh Press* had a hot editorial condemning that stand, and so did we in an editorial on a Friday. We got a call from the man who headed the Western Division of the railroad who said he would like to come in the next day and talk to us. We told him we didn't work that day [since the *Post-Gazette* did not have a Sunday edition]. So they came in on Sunday, a whole troop. We told them the people of Pittsburgh were determined to control the smoke situation. We suggested that they go to the Smoke Council and make the best deal they could. Which is what they did, such as bargaining to be allowed to emit a certain amount of smoke in any given hour. Actually, the passage of the legislation helped them with the coal customers, one of their major hauling customers, because they could say they had no choice but to cut back on coal use. As a matter of fact, of course, in that era they were switching to diesel fuel anyway.[27]

Another story, probably partly apocryphal, has it that when Mellon learned that the Pennsylvania Railroad intended to lobby against the smoke-control bill, he summoned representatives of the railroad to come to meet him in Pittsburgh. When they arrived in Mellon's office, they found arrayed in chairs around the room the CEOs of the various Mellon enterprises. Mellon reportedly told the railroad executives that "we"—sweeping his arm around the room—had decided to move their shipments to other railroads. The next day, as if by magic, the Pennsy's lobbyists in Harrisburg let it be known they no longer were opposing the Pittsburgh legislation. Politicians to this day marvel at this exhibition of the magnate's "raw power."[28]

Much harder and riskier was the Lawrence administration's task to persuade citizens to abandon the practice of shoveling bituminous coal into their furnaces. The best option was to switch to natural gas, but at the time there was not enough of that resource available in southwestern Pennsylvania. Another was to change either to disco—a treated coal—or to hard (anthracite) coal. The third option was to install stokers—mechanical, screw-type devices that could load soft coal into furnaces and thus decrease smoke emissions. All were costly. Relief finally came in 1947 when the government-built Big Inch Pipeline from Texas was privatized as a natural-gas carrier, making the commodity available to householders at reasonable rates.

The financial pressure on many householders had political repercussions. For one, it persuaded City Council on October 1, 1947, to give an extra year of grace before the new law on household heating went into effect. The *Post-Gazette* editors were sufficiently concerned over the inevitable battle a year later that they reassigned Andrew Chancellor from the editorial page to find out whether there was enough low volatile coal available in order to counter arguments on that score. He discovered there was plenty of it and wrote five front-page articles that appeared the next March, which represented the resources and the aggressiveness of the newspapers in supporting the smoke-control effort.[29]

The problems of pollution were powerfully brought home to southwestern Pennsylvania in Donora, a town in the Monongahela Valley thirty-five miles south of Pittsburgh. Donora's billowing smokestacks had always been seen as a sign of prosperity, until Wednesday, October 16, 1948. On that night, an unusual temperature inversion clamped down a layer of dense air like the lid of a metal pot, trapping smoke and gas from the local iron and zinc works operated by U.S. Steel's American Steel & Wire Company. Citizens, used to smoke, went about their business despite a blanket of fumes so dense that visibility was near zero. On Friday, October 18, the town of 14,000 held its annual Halloween parade and on Saturday groped through the fog to watch a high school football game. That night, however, fire alarms shattered the eerie stillness as a deluge of calls from suffering people alerted officials to the fact that the whitish smog, laced with sulfur dioxide, was burning the eyes of the townspeople and attacking their lungs. By the time the skies began to clear on Sunday, 20 people were dead and some 6,000 were ill—1,440 of them seriously.

A lengthy investigation by the U.S. Public Health Service found that, although the company had followed the prescribed procedures, the zinc works were not shut down completely until most of the harm was done. American Steel and Wire paid individual, out-of-court settlements that ranged from one thousand to thirty thousand dollars, but the company never admitted responsibility. The incident helped push Pittsburgh's cleanup and state anti-pollution laws passed in 1955, formulated in response to the Donora incident. In a retrospective article of October 29, 1998, the *Post-Gazette* declared, "When the U.S. Clean Air Act was passed in 1970, the impact of smog on Donora was a key issue in congressional debates."

Even the Donora tragedy did not convince some Pittsburgh citizens of the importance of the smoke-control efforts. In the 1949 mayoral election, a campaign by Councilman Eddie Leonard threw a scare into Lawrence's re-election hopes. Leonard, head of the plasterers' union and a vigorous opponent of the smoke-control laws, had been the only councilman in 1941 to vote against the smoke-control ordinance. He contended that "the little Joes" were forced to pay the price of smoke control in extra expense and inconvenience while the railroads and big industries were allowed their own sweet time to install new equipment.

As the September Democratic primary approached, Leonard was running stronger than expected. The Central Labor Union, made up of representatives of the AFL locals, announced its support of him as an alternative to Lawrence. The CIO stayed in Lawrence's camp only after Philip Murray, its president, obtained a promise that a CIO representative, Pat Fagan, would fill the next vacancy on City Council. A *Press* article of June 22, 1949, reported that at a Twelfth Ward fundraiser, Leonard lashed out at Lawrence: "He is a prisoner of the royal family of high finance. Under the guise of cooperation he helped big business capture both political parties. . . . A coalition of Daveycrats and conservative Republicans [has] detoured the Democratic program from its liberal course." Lawrence revved up party regulars at every level to work as if their jobs depended on the outcome. He even persuaded President Truman to come to Pittsburgh on his behalf for a Labor Day rally, where, as the *Post-Gazette* reported on September 2, 1949, the president praised him as one of the "greatest Democrats of our day and a great municipal leader." As noted above, this was the first time that the *Post-Gazette* endorsed him. Block remembered, "I got to know Dave Lawrence well and admired him a great deal. From the time Keller left, we always supported Lawrence."[30] Lawrence won the Democratic nomination by a margin of 60 percent—75,838 to 53,206—but he would never again have a closer race, as he lost seven wards and ran behind three of the five organization candidates.

The Leonard effort marked the high tide of opposition within the city's political system to smoke-control. Eventually, the public became enthusiastic. Chancellor recollected, "Now, for a change, on Fifth Avenue you could see the top of the Cathedral of Learning [at the University of Pittsburgh]. People were saying, 'My God, this city is looking better.'"[31] The dramatically visible success of smoke control helped to build widespread support for the entire Renaissance effort. In 1957, efforts to include the county succeeded as Allegheny County government absorbed the Pittsburgh Health Department, which had been enforcing the city ordinances, leading to the establishment of the County Bureau of Air Pollution Control.

Thus was completed the penultimate smoke-control effort. The word "penultimate" is appropriate because while the laws and ordinances of the 1940s coped with household smoke, it was not until the 1970s that local activists, aided by new federal laws, were able to secure the abatement of industrial smoke pollution—not many years before the closing of many mills for economic reasons cleansed the skies in a bitter reminder of the old slogan, "Smoke means jobs."

Chapter 11

Race and
Government

———◆◆◆———

IN THE 1950S, Pittsburgh and its newspapers were caught up in the issues of race relations, Communism and the anti-Communism movement, and the pressures of coping with increased suburbanization. In that decade, the *Post-Gazette* was pushed toward yet another merger whose fallout forced the paper into a lifesaving, though humbling, joint operating agreement with its remaining rival.

In 1955, the civil rights revolution in the south gained national attention when Rosa Parks refused to move to the back of a Montgomery, Alabama, transit bus. The unrest had hit Pittsburgh earlier, even though for decades the local black community had been noted for its apathy regarding political issues. This struck many observers as an anomaly, considering that the *Pittsburgh Courier,* which published both a local and a national edition, had the largest circulation of any black newspaper in the country. Known especially for its vigorous advocacy of civil rights, the *Courier* had an outstanding staff of writers and a stellar photographer, Charles "Teenie" Harris. Its editor, Robert Vann, had had a national impact when in 1932 he had urged black voters to turn the picture of Abraham Lincoln to the wall, a metaphorical request for the community to break its sixty-five years of support for the Republican

Robert L. Vann,
publisher of the
Pittsburgh Courier
(Courtesy *Pittsburgh
Post-Gazette*)

Party in order to vote for Franklin D. Roosevelt and a transformed Democratic Party favorable to the black cause.

The *Courier* frequently criticized its home community for political apathy. Arthur Edmunds, who came to Pittsburgh in 1960 to head the Urban League of Pittsburgh, later told an interviewer that he arrived from Des Moines filled with expectations of finding a militant community based on having read the *Courier* for years, but was surprised to discover the reality was quite otherwise.[1] A black middle class had developed in Pittsburgh, but the only professional positions open to African Americans were as social workers assigned to recruit and help in the adjustment of black migrants. Not until 1948 was the first black physician permitted to practice at a local hospital—Montefiore, which had been established in 1908 by Jewish doctors who had been similarly

Pittsburgh Courier photographer Charles "Teenie" Harris poses with a photograph of himself from the 1950s.
(Photo by Harry Coughanour; Courtesy *Pittsburgh Post-Gazette*)

excluded from Pittsburgh's hospitals. In general, until the civil rights upsurge in the 1960s, the story for Pittsburgh's African Americans was bleak, despite the growth of the community's population and of institutions geared to attack racial injustice. In restaurants, blacks found salt in their coffee, pepper in their milk, and overcharges on their bills; in department stores, they were not permitted try on clothes; and in downtown theaters, they were refused admission or were sent to the balcony. African Americans were confined to certain sections of the stands at Forbes Field when they attended Pirates baseball games. Despite the 1887 public accommodations law, downtown hotels usually turned away black guests. In the 1920s, the region's Ku Klux Klan boasted seventeen thousand members.

Pittsburgh's African Americans had developed an impressive set of institutions that included the *Courier;* two outstanding, black-owned baseball teams in the Negro Baseball League, the Pittsburgh Crawfords and the Homestead Grays; local chapters of the NAACP and the Urban League; and numerous strong churches—forty-five in the Hill District alone. The Aurora Reading Club and the Loendi Club of Pittsburgh were two of the nation's oldest and most distinguished black women's and men's social clubs, while the city's Frogs Club hosted an annual week of fun and festivities that attracted revelers from around the country. Pittsburgh was a notable leader in the field of jazz, nurturing, more than any other city of its size, world-class musicians, including Kenny Clarke, Billy Eckstine, Roy Eldridge, Errol Garner, Earl "Fatha" Hines, Lena Horne, Billy Strayhorn, Maxine Sullivan, and Mary Lou Williams. The two Crawford Grill restaurants and the Flamingo Lounge in the Hill District were part of the circuit for national jazz figures, and white as well as black audiences flocked to the shows. As the district's fame spread, Claude McKay, a leading poet of the Harlem Renaissance, called the intersection of Wylie Avenue and Fullerton Street in the Hill the "Crossroads of the World."[2]

There were several reasons for the lack of political involvement. One, seldom cited, was the attitude of Pittsburgh's mainstream newspapers to African American concerns, which was indifferent at best, and hostile at worst. One amateur historian, Walter Worthington, has traced attitudes in Pittsburgh back to colonial times, when southwestern Pennsylvania was, for a time, part of Virginia, which embedded the slaveholding culture and its attitudes in the region before it was allocated to Pennsylvania.[3] In its early years, the *Gazette* had carried advertisements about runaway slaves for years before becoming an advocate of the abolitionist cause. Clearly, the greatest evidence of hostility to blacks was the approval by Pennsylvania voters on October 9, 1838, of a constitutional amendment stripping blacks of the right to vote. The *Gazette*'s response was equivocal. The *Pittsburgh Post* in the nineteenth century had a similar outlook when it came to issues of race; the paper did not extend its pro-labor, pro-workingman support to African Americans. Instead, it ridiculed their organizations and meetings, as well as the efforts of all abolitionists.

Similar attitudes persisted in Pennsylvania after the Civil War, even though Pittsburgh was dominated by the Republican Party—the party that had abolished slavery, extended citizenship to former slaves, and given black males the right to vote. As historian Laurence Glasco has pointed out: "In 1872 the Democratic *Pittsburgh Post* lampooned Republicans hypocrisy in posing as friends of Negroes when blacks in Republican Allegheny County 'could not be admitted to the orchestra, dress or family circle of the opera house, could not purchase a sleeping berth on any of the railroads that leave the city, could not take dinner at the Monongahela House, Hare's Hotel, or any A No. 1 restaurant,' and could not even enter the Lincoln Club, 'except as a waiter.'"[4]

Even though Pittsburgh's black population grew from twenty-five thousand in 1910 to fifty-five thousand in 1930, it tended to be too geographically scattered to have political impact. The growth, mostly from the south, had been made possible by the demand for workers in the mills. The traditional labor supply was diminished when World War I cut off immigration from Europe and again later when Congress passed laws limiting immigration from eastern and southern Europe. African Americans settled in different neighborhoods around the city, which prevented the isolation that thwarted black hopes in so many northern cities, but also diluted their ability to influence elections. Not until 1930, for example, did African Americans comprise half the population of their single largest neighborhood, the Hill District immediately east of downtown.

Further restricting political opportunities for blacks was the system by which Pittsburgh City Council seats were contested on an at-large basis, meaning that candidates had to win citywide. In the late 1940s, David Lawrence, a powerful and politically savvy Democratic mayor, established a distributive system, satirized by the media as "the Balkan succession," which ensured council representative of diverse ethnicities and affiliations. There was no law on the subject or any guarantee for a group to have representation; Lawrence's authority was such that whatever he and his top aides decided became an incontestable reality. It was only after the organization built by Lawrence and carried on by his successor Joseph Barr was badly battered in 1969 by the election of Peter Flaherty that this system fell apart. By 1985, diversity on the council was no longer assured. In 1987, the council—supported by the *Post-Gazette*—successfully advance a referendum for the election of council members by districts, rather than at-large. That gave Pittsburgh's African Americans, though geographically scattered, enough concentrated clout to successfully campaign for seats on the council on a regular basis.

Many of the leaders of Pittsburgh's African American community, including Vann of the *Courier,* had national aspirations and interests. Daisy Lampkin, a successful fundraiser for the local NAACP branch, was enlisted to travel the country on behalf of the organization. Attorney Homer Brown, longtime head of the local NAACP, had made a political breakthrough in being elected to the Pennsylvania House of Representatives. These achievements were important to the community, but also had the effect of removing these figures from the daily give-and-take of Pittsburgh politics. Still, as a legislator in Harrisburg, Brown helped to bring about civil rights successes at the state level. In 1937, Brown convened state hearings on the hiring practices of the Pittsburgh Board of Public Education, which continued to refuse to hire African American teachers, even though the system had been desegregated since 1875. These hearings cleared the way for a lawsuit against the board by two black attorneys. Before the year ended, the board had hired its first African American instructor, Lawrence Peeler, to teach music. In 1939, Brown scored another victory when he helped gain passage of a public accommodations law, amending and strengthening the 1887 act. However, two *Courier* staffers, reporter Edna Chappell and photographer Charles "Teenie" Harris, sought service at a number of local eating establishments and found massive noncompliance with the 1939 act. This foreshadowed the much more publicized Southern lunch counter sit-ins in 1960.

Pittsburgh's newspapers made some small efforts to reflect the shift in local attitudes in the twentieth century—the *Post,* for example, launched a special column on African American issues during the World War I period. Yet racist language and other problems remained. John T. Clark, who in 1918 became the Pittsburgh Urban League's first executive secretary, "repeatedly took the newspapers to task for referring to Negro women as 'negresses'—a form, he said, that is generally restricted to designating the female of an animal species, as in 'tigress' and 'lioness'—and, with disarming tact, added that since newspapers had difficulty finding stories to print about 'Colored people' who were not criminals, 'it might not be a bad idea to add to your staff, composed of hundreds of men, a young Colored man as a reporter.'"[5]

Little changed after the 1927 merger of the *Post* and the *Gazette,* as is evidenced by the lack of coverage of African Americans in sports. The Pittsburgh Crawfords started as a loose organization for casual games, but later was bankrolled by Gus Greenlee, owner of the Crawford Grill restaurants, into a team that produced five eventual Hall of Fame members—Satchel Paige, Josh Gibson, "Cool Papa" Bell, Oscar Charleston, and Judy Johnson. When Greenlee resurrected the National Negro League, the Crawfords and the Homestead Grays, run by Cumberland "Cum" Posey, made Pittsburgh the national center of black baseball. The newspapers' sports pages, however, did not reflect this stellar period in Pittsburgh's athletic history. The Crawfords and Grays were relegated to the box-listed Sandlot results, along with such company as the Ingram team in the Methodist League.

On Thursday, July 4, 1935, the emphasis on the main sports page was on a Pirates game, plus a story reporting the reaction of Pirate great Honus Wagner to the death of umpire Hank O'Day. The page also carried a four-inch story that announced: "Pittsburgh's biggest holiday baseball attraction takes place today at Greenlee Field with the Homestead Grays battling their local Colored National League rivals [the Crawfords], the first time this season in three games. . . . Today's [two] games have stirred so much interest that the management has arranged to handle the largest crowd that has ever jammed the Bedford Avenue enclosure." Yet in the five sports pages on July 5, the only report of these games appeared in the small type of the Sandlot results: "Crawfords 6, Homestead Grays 3" and "Crawfords 8, Homestead Grays 6." There was also a three-inch story in small type announcing that the Grays and Crawfords had arranged to play a nine-game series together over a period of six days, throughout Pennsylvania and the eastern part of the country. Finally, on Monday, the newspaper managed to provide its readers with a one-paragraph story of a Crawfords-Grays game in Harrisburg, along with a box score, quite in contrast to the ample coverage given Pirates games over the weekend.

During the same week, however, the *Post-Gazette* included some coverage of African Americans athletes involved in certain other sports, particularly boxing. Roy McHugh, former sportswriter for the *Pittsburgh Press,* has noted that boxing was a sport of major appeal in the 1930s, with Pittsburgh a boxing center second only to New York City.[6] A July 3 story publicized a forthcoming fight between "Anson Green,

Homestead colored destroyer, [and] Joe Smallwood of Wilmington."
On July 5, the *Post-Gazette* made a noteworthy announcement, although it may have been tarnished for some by language typical of the
time. It read: "Louis will tell story of life in *P-G*. Joe Louis, the talk of
the pugilistic world and rated by many fans as a coming world heavy-
weight champion, has furnished story of his rise, and the first of 10 articles by Louis will be printed in the *Post-Gazette* Monday. Watch for
the entertaining details of this 21-year-old boy who has come to the top
within a year."

On the same day, the sports page carried a story that presaged one of
the great feats in athletic history, Jesse Owens's four gold-medal victories in track at the 1936 Berlin Olympics. Similarly, the coverage was
marked by language of the time: "Colored stars may dominate Berlin
Games. Dusky shadows are being cast athwart the coming Olympic
games by the greatest crop of colored track and field athletes ever developed in the United States, or, for that matter, anywhere else in the
realm of competitive sport." The story went on particularly to cite
Owens, "the Ohio State flyer," as a college sophomore "whose exploits
surpass anything else in track and field athletics this year."

After William Block took over the *Post-Gazette* in 1946, the paper
gradually became more responsive to African American concerns. Also
during that period, Pittsburgh civil rights groups led the nation in the
use of picketing of businesses. In the Christmas season of 1946, K.
Leroy Irvis arrived in the city to work for the Urban League, and quickly
set in motion a campaign to pressure downtown department stores into
hiring black women as sales clerks.[7] Mayor Lawrence began a weekend
round of negotiations between the advocacy groups—Urban League,
the NAACP, the Allegheny County Committee for Fair Employment
Practices and others—and the department stores, Kaufmann's,
Gimbels, Frank & Seder, Joseph Horne Company, and Rosenbaum's.
The effort, however, proved fruitless, and picketing began on Monday,
December 9. As the *Courier* reported in its next weekly edition, dated
December 14, 1946, "The campaign swung into high gear Monday when
groups of white and Negro citizens paraded before downtown department stores in a 'poster wall' designed to bring the issues before the
general public in the most dramatic manner possible." The *P-G* chose
to put a story and picture on an inside page of its December 10 issue. It
reported that pickets had started on Monday, December 9, at 11:00 a.m.,

were then recalled while a mayor-brokered session took place, and were sent back out after that conference finally broke up shortly after 2:00 p.m. Accompanying the story was a news photograph of "Pickets on Patrol," carrying signs urging the stores to change their hiring practices. The *Sun-Telegraph* also reported the story, but the *Pittsburgh Press* did not, probably because Ed Leech, the paper's editor, was hostile to the cause. The *Pittsburgh Catholic* weighed in with a statement, pointedly backed by Bishop Hugo Boyle and also published by the *Courier,* noting that the stores had been running large ads pleading for help to meet the unexpected demand and yet were turning away black applicants. Mayor Lawrence was furious with the picketers, and under pressure from the department stores, the Urban League fired Irvis—temporarily as it turned out. Except in the *Courier,* the matter dropped out of the news. After the first of the year, the stores quietly began hiring black women, beginning with Frank & Seder and Rosenbaum's.

The treatment of African Americans by Pittsburgh's newspapers was not much improved in the years that followed. In all of the Pittsburgh newspapers, according to attorney Wendell Freeland, if an African American was reported to have committed a crime, no matter his true address, he was listed as coming from the Hill District. Freeland later said that he did not look for sympathy in a Scripps Howard paper, because "the *Press*'s heroes statewide were unfriendly to blacks," but he did expect better of the *Post-Gazette,* partly because he had worked with William Block in the Urban League. Freeland also noted that the *Post-Gazette* endorsed him in 1962 election for state representative over a white incumbent.[8]

Efforts to desegregate public facilities in Pittsburgh—the Highland Park swimming pool in particular—also drew negative reactions from the media outlets. As reported in the August 23, 1948, edition of the *Press,* a group called "Young Progressives for [Henry] Wallace" set out that summer to establish "the rights of Negroes to swim at Highland Pool." A biracial group appeared on Sunday afternoons, only to be quickly confronted by an angry white crowd. On August 22, sixteen members of the group were arrested, including Nathan Albert, who eventually was convicted of inciting to riot, fined, and sentenced to the Allegheny County Workhouse.

Albert was described by the media as secretary of the Squirrel Hill Club of the Communist Party and the "ringleader" of the protest at the swimming pool. The *Press* had a field day linking race, Communism, and riots, and continued to do so for several years. For example, on February 18, 1950, the *Press*'s headline read: "Highland Pool Red Riot Cost City $8,000/Commies Call Tune at Taxpayers' Expense." The news story began: "Pittsburgh taxpayers found out today how much it costs to finance a successful Communist 'incident.' The bill for rioting at the Highland Park swimming pool in 1948 came to a cool $8,000 for extra police protection alone." The quoted figure was the cost for more than 150 city policemen, some in swimsuits, assigned to the pool to maintain order and "to escort Negroes from trolley stops a quarter mile away from the pool."

Still, isolated efforts at the pool continued, making the assignment of recognition for the eventual breakthrough problematic. Varying groups gave credit to the NAACP, the Urban League, and the garbage workers' union. In the summer of 1951, the Urban League took the lead under its new executive secretary, Alexander J. Allen, who had arrived in 1950 from the Baltimore Urban League. Once in Pittsburgh, as historians have noted, Allen put himself at risk to take a stand on the swimming pool issue: "While lifeguards sat idly by, a gang of a hundred white teenagers ejected Allen from the pool, hurling racial slurs at him. Police assured Allen that he 'had a perfect right to use the pool' but refused to guarantee his safety."[9] Frank Bolden, retired city editor of the *Pittsburgh Courier*, later recalled the role of the NAACP in resolving the issue. In July 1951, he covered a Monday session in which a group of NAACP leaders met with Mayor Lawrence and notified him of their intention to file a lawsuit unless safe desegregation of the pool could be promised. Lawrence was quite angry, describing all that he had done for the black community but proclaiming that he had no intention of breaking the color line at swimming pools. He assured Richard F. Jones, one of the leaders, that if the suit were filed, the mayor would make sure Jones never became a Common Pleas Court judge. "He kept his word. Dick never made judge," Bolden noted.[10]

Within fifteen minutes after the failed meeting, the NAACP filed a suit. More efforts to desegregate the pool ensued, with Leech and the *Press* continuing to complain that the expense of providing extra police protection during the "swim-ins" was needlessly costing the taxpayers. The police effort proved to be sufficiently effective, however, that by September, the NAACP asked that the suit be dropped.

Mayor David L. Lawrence signs the city's Fair Employment Practices Commission into law, December 5, 1992, as leading supporters look on. (Courtesy Carnegie Library of Pittsburgh)

A key to progress in that era was the presence of both whites and blacks working together in interracial alliances. In 1952, Pittsburgh passed a Fair Employment Practices ordinance; in 1955, the city government established a Commission on Human Relations to process citizen complaints; and in 1958, Pittsburgh became the second city in the nation to enact a fair housing ordinance. It made a difference when someone with the stature of Leland Hazard, vice president of Pittsburgh Plate Glass, could ask his fellow white Pittsburghers: "Is it possible that no Negro musician is qualified for a chair in the Pittsburgh Symphony? Is it possible that there is only one Negro educator qualified to be a Pittsburgh public school principal?"[11] On the electoral scene, Homer Brown left the state legislature in 1950 and was elected judge of the Allegheny County Court of Common Pleas, which made him the first local African American elected to a countywide office. In 1954, Paul F. Jones became the first African American elected to Pittsburgh City Council since the 1880s, and in 1958, K. Leroy Irvis was elected to the state legislature—twelve years after he had been fired by the Urban League for demonstrating in front of the downtown department stores

Judge Homer
Brown
(Courtesy *Pittsburgh
Post-Gazette*)

—and would eventually become Speaker of the Pennsylvania House of Representatives.

The African American community was hit hard in the 1950s by a plan to combine an eastward extension of Pittsburgh's Renaissance effort with a cleanup of the blighted Lower Hill. The neighborhood included Italians and other ethnic groups in addition to African Americans, but its black establishments, including nightclubs featuring eminent musicians, made it the center of African American community life in Pittsburgh. Yet the housing and facilities in the area were substandard, and the Renaissance leadership believed it best to remove those structures and replace them with cultural buildings. The designation of 106 acres and 1,300 structures as a blighted area appropriate for razing created serious conflict within the city. In Pittsburgh and around the nation, critics of the urban renewal process saw the plan as an attempt

K. Leroy Irvis,
Speaker of the
Pennsylvania
House of Repre-
sentatives
(Courtesy: K. Leroy
Irvis Archival
Collection at the
University of
Pittsburgh)

to remove or relocate African American residents. The effort, however, had the continued backing of the city's newspapers, and the plan proceeded to its completion, including the construction of a new Civic Arena in the 1950s.

In 1955, at the insistence of Bill Block, the *Post-Gazette* became the first mainstream Pittsburgh paper to hire an African American reporter. Regis Bobonis had earned a journalism degree at Duquesne University and went to work for the *P-G* on September 1, at the age of thirty. He covered both city and suburban assignments until December 17, 1962, when he left to become executive editor of the *Pittsburgh Courier*.

The sports pages began to reflect the change in the national climate as, for example, Jackie Robinson began to play Major League Baseball. Frank Bolden later credited this shift in Pittsburgh's newspapers to two reporters: Al Abrams of the *Post-Gazette* and Harry Keck of the *Sun-Telegraph*.[12] A particularly noticeable event occurred in 1955, when the *Post-Gazette,* on both its editorial and sports pages, firmly made its civil rights position clear in the situation involving Bobby Grier, the Sugar Bowl, and the governor of Georgia. Grier was an African American fullback on the Pitt Panthers football team whose 1955 season was so successful it was invited to the 1956 Sugar Bowl. The announcement of the bowl invitation and its acceptance by Pitt was front-page news on November 23, the day before Thanksgiving, accompanied by a report that this event would bring some $160,000 into the university's cash box. The previous Saturday, in a driving snowstorm, the University of Pittsburgh had defeated Penn State 20-0 at State College, with Grier scoring the final touchdown. Next came the news that Georgia Tech had been chosen to oppose Pitt in the New Year's event in New Orleans. The usual sports-advance stories followed, such as a November 28 headline notifying readers: "Georgia Tech big and fast but Pitt doesn't fear 'em." Then, in the December 3 issue, came a bombshell: "Race issue tangles bowl game. Negro fullback will play or Pitt won't go." Governor Marvin Griffin of Georgia had asked that Grier be banned from the game, and that spectators in the Tulane Stadium where the game was scheduled be completely segregated. Pictures of both Griffin and the firmly resisting Charles R. Nutting, acting Pitt chancellor, accompanied the story. Griffin was one of a group of southern governors resisting the U.S. Supreme Court's 1954 and 1955 rulings on school desegregation. The article quoted him as declaring: "The South stands at Armageddon. The battle is joined. We cannot make the slightest concession to the enemy in this dark and lamentable hour of struggle. There is no more difference in compromising integrity of race on the playing field than in doing so in the classroom. One break in the dike and the relentless seas will rush in and destroy us."

The editorial in that issue of the *P-G*, headlined "Governor Griffin's bigotry," read: "Good people everywhere, north and south, should ignore the rantings of Georgia Governor Marvin Griffin. In demanding that Georgia Tech be kept out of the Sugar Bowl game on New Year's day if the University of Pittsburgh uses a Negro player, he is hurting nothing but Georgia Tech and his own unenviable reputation. Governor Griffin is hopelessly behind the times. On at least two occasions, University of Georgia football teams have played against Negro players. And colored players are found on the rosters of professional baseball teams in the Deep South as elsewhere throughout the nation. . . . Surely the majority will have the courage to tell Gov. Griffin to take his bigotry deep back into the piney woods from which he came."

A sports column by Al Abrams that day was equally pointed: "The south stands at Armageddon indeed. We would rather see the University of Pittsburgh pull out of the Sugar Bowl than submit to the views of narrow-minded, bigoted and vicious groups who are hundreds of years behind the times." Abrams noted that both universities had accepted the invitation in good faith, that Sugar Bowl officials had made plans "knowing the situation full well," and that Tulane University had welcomed the players, Grier among them, to use one of its dormitories. Abrams asked readers to remember the heart of the issue: "last but not least, the innocent victim of the furor, young Grier, a fine boy who is a credit to his race and the University."

The *Post-Gazette* had no Sunday edition, but on Monday, December 5, the front-page headline read, "Georgia Tech bowl OK hinted." On the editorial page, a Cy Hungerford cartoon entitled "Georgia's All-American Ass" portrayed Griffin as a donkey kicking into the air a receptacle labeled "Sugar Bowl game," while the stands, labeled "Georgia Tech's cheering section," yelled "Block that kick!"

The next morning, a headline reported, "Georgia allows Pitt bowl game. Regents reject governor's request on segregation." Hungerford's cartoon that day portrayed a football player, with the words "Pitt vs. Georgia Tech" on his sweater, stiff-arming a donkey named Governor Griffin, underneath a caption that read "Bowled Over." The main sports story the next day was headed, "Bobby Grier and his Pitt teammates drill."

Alas, the Sugar Bowl story did not have a fairy-tale ending for Pitt and Grier. The *Sun-Telegraph* ably summed up the Sugar Bowl story with "Pitt loses controversial 7-0 decision. Interference call on Grier decisive." Nevertheless, it was a moral victory for Pitt. In a column entitled, "Won everything but game," *Sun-Telegraph* sports columnist Harry Keck wrote that "through it all, Bobby Grier, the first Negro ever to play in the New Orleans Classic, was both the hero and in a way the 'goat' of the defeat. Each time he entered the lineup, he was applauded and he definitely broke the ice for his race as much as Jackie Robinson did in 'big league baseball.'"

Almost two years later, the *Sun-Telegraph*'s George Kiseda launched a crusade to have the Army-Tulane game scheduled for November 16, 1957, shifted from New Orleans to West Point because of a 1956 Louisiana law prohibiting integrated seating at sports events. In an August 24 sports column, Kiseda wrote that in a conversation with Lieutenant

Cy Hungerford's
cartoon, "Georgia's
All-American Ass"
(Courtesy *Pittsburgh
Post-Gazette*)

General Garrison H. Davidson, superintendent at West Point, he was
told, "we made our contract four years ago and we're going to honor it."
Kiseda commented: "It will be the first breakthrough in an unofficial
boycott that has existed among northern colleges since the Louisiana
State Legislature last year passed a law barring interracial sports competition and integrated seating. No Northern colleges have sent their
football and basketball teams into Louisiana since then. The University
of Pittsburgh was the first to announce its position, withdrawing as a
possible candidate for the Sugar Bowl football game." Kiseda noted that
the University of Wisconsin had also canceled a two-year football contract with Louisiana State University. Two days later, he wrote: "The

U.S. Military Academy presumably represents all the people. It seems to me that the Academy is under no obligation to honor a contract that was legally conceived but now can be honored only by violating the Constitution."

Kiseda was so incensed about the situation that he sent copies of his columns, along with a personal letter, to U.S. Representative James Fulton, a moderate Republican from the Mt. Lebanon suburb of Pittsburgh, who promptly replied, "Certainly admire your courage and think they are wonderful. Am placing them in the Congressional Record today and will send you copies. Am also contacting White House immediately protesting football game in New Orleans on November 16, and strongly urging its cancellation. What is use of civil-rights law by Congress if Army disregards civil rights and cooperates in their repression." That brought the matter to the attention of President Eisenhower and of the Pentagon; the latter finally overruled the administration at the Military Academy to order the game played at West Point. Officials at both schools were not amused, as the income from the stadium at West Point, which accommodated twenty-eight thousand spectators, was far less than it would have been from a game in the New Orleans stadium, which sat eighty thousand. Nevertheless, it was a significant event in the same season that saw the school integration crisis in Little Rock, Arkansas, which eventually required President Eisenhower to send in Army troops to enforce the law.

An Associated Press story in the September 17, 1957, edition of the *Sun-Telegraph* was the newspaper's only reference to the outcome of the dispute. Kiseda, in retirement in Los Angeles, recalled with regret that the *Sun-Telegraph's* sports department was not permitted to comment on the victory. "We were never allowed to get the credit we deserved," Kiseda said. He made it clear that the people who forbade him to follow up on the issue were not his immediate bosses, sports editors Davis J. Walsh and later Harry Keck, but, rather, superiors within the newspaper itself—but not the Hearst chain. After the Army-Tulane affair, those superiors told Kiseda to stop writing about segregation on the sports pages.

As evidence of the backing he received from the sports editors themselves, Kiseda cited his coverage of a basketball team from St. Francis College (Loretto, Pennsylvania) in the Carousel Tournament in Charlotte, North Carolina. The Frankies had won the tournament by beating Fordham in the finals. Kiseda and Beano Cook, at that time a freelance sportswriter, hitched an airplane ride back to Pennsylvania with the team on New Year's Day, 1959. Unfortunately, icing forced the plane to make an emergency landing at three o'clock in the morning in Winston-Salem. There, the Reverend Sebastian Soklic, dean of students, had to tell the team that the white players would be housed overnight in a hotel but that the black team members would have to go to "a new hospital for Negroes" as there were no hotel rooms for them. In his account, published in the January 2 *Sun-Telegraph,* Kiseda wrote that team captain Jack O'Malley's specialty was "making big plays that win games. O'Malley made the big play this time. 'Father,' he said, 'if all of us can't go to the hotel, none of us will go. We're a team. We'll stay right here.'" The entire team slept on benches until the plane was fixed. Kiseda, wary of the shutdown he had received for his previous desegregation stories, checked with Keck before filing the story. Keck told him to go ahead, despite the consequences. "That's the kind of backing I got from within the sports department," Kiseda remembered. His article read: "St. Francis won its greatest game in Winston-Salem, not Charlotte, when it refused to bend to Jim Crow." There were no repercussions from that particular story.[13] It is worth noting, however, that when the *Sun-Telegraph* was merged with the *Post-Gazette* in 1960, neither the *P-G* nor the rival *Pittsburgh Press* chose to hire Kiseda. O'Malley, the team captain featured in the story, turned down a chance to play with the Detroit Pistons in the National Basketball Association and became a Pittsburgh parish priest highly active in peace and justice causes. One of his later assignments was that of labor chaplain for the Pennsylvania AFL-CIO.

In 1964, the *Post-Gazette* took the lead in pushing for advances in housing for African Americans in Pittsburgh. The *P-G* published a series of articles outlining the travails of Kenneth L. Hawthorne, a young, black public relations professional at Gulf Oil Company, as he sought to purchase a house in the Virginia Manor section of Mt. Lebanon, an upscale suburb. The articles prompted an investigation by the Pennsylvania Human Relations Commission and a set of hearings at the Allegheny County Courthouse. As recounted in a November 23, 1965, *Post-Gazette* article, a commission report described how a realtor had tried to prevent a white couple from showing their house to Hawthorne. Joe Shuman, managing editor at the paper, headlined the article, "A Matter of Complexion." The hearings also included testimony from a Jewish woman who said that when she and her husband sought to buy a house in Virginia Manor, a saleswoman said, "There is more or less 'a gentleman's agreement' against selling to a Jewish person." Hawthorne first settled in Scott Township and later moved to Mt. Lebanon. On May 24, 1966, bias charges against two realtors in the Hawthorne case were dropped. At that point, the general counsel for the commission said the report had become anti-climactic because of "the magnificent coverage" given by the news media to the whole affair.

These changes in the *Post-Gazette*'s approach did not go unnoticed among readers accustomed to the conservative paper of the 1930s. In a recent interview, William Block reflected: "I've always been that horrible term—liberal. More than my editors. I was to the left of Frank Hawkins and John Craig. When I got back in 1946, I veered our editorial policy more to the center. We've been liberal in connection with civil rights; conservative on economics. That is my personal feeling and the road that we followed." Block also related: "A lot of people who read the *P-G* were incensed that we were veering to the middle of the road—or, in their opinion, to the left. One who wrote me vitriolic letters was Alan Scaife, a man very protective of the Mellon money that he had married into."[14]

Alan Scaife was not a person who could be easily ignored. A fifth-generation member of an old Pittsburgh industrial family and a graduate of Yale's Sheffield Scientific School, Alan Magee Scaife had married Sarah Cordelia Mellon, the daughter of industrialist and banker Richard Beatty Mellon, and the sister of Richard King Mellon, kingpin of the Renaissance effort. Among Scaife's many contributions to Pittsburgh's civic life was his service on the board of trustees of the University of Pittsburgh, beginning in 1931, when he was only thirty-one years old, and assuming its presidency from 1949 until his untimely death from a heart attack on July 25, 1958. His death was regarded as a keen loss within Pittsburgh's leadership. Scaife's rift with Block foretold events that would occur more than three decades later when his son, Richard Mellon Scaife, by then publisher of the *Greensburg Tribune-Review* and a staunch conservative, would launch a Pittsburgh edition of his newspaper to challenge the *Post-Gazette*.

Alan Scaife was not the only person upset with the direction in which Block was guiding the newspaper, even though under Block, the

Post-Gazette endorsed Republicans for the presidency three times in a row—Thomas Dewey in 1948 and Dwight Eisenhower in 1952 and 1956. (In the following two elections, the *P-G* endorsed Democrats: John F. Kennedy in 1960 and Lyndon Johnson in 1964.) Yet the *Post-Gazette* often supported presidential actions by men it had not endorsed. When President Truman, for example, fired General Douglas MacArthur during the Korean War, creating a storm in Congress and throughout the country, the *Post-Gazette* backed the president. The newspaper lost some advertising as a result.

Some of Block's political ideas had been revealed when he backed the Marshall Plan for reviving Western Europe after the war and supported the establishment of the North Atlantic Treaty Organization (NATO) as a military bulwark against Soviet Union expansionism. The front page of the *Post-Gazette* on April 5, 1949, carried a two-deck banner headline about action taken the day before in Washington, D.C.: "12 Nations Sign Atlantic Pact/ Truman Offers Peace Assistance." Accompanying the story was a cartoon by Cy Hungerford depicting a nonspecific person wielding a sword-like object labeled "War," which then tapered into a pen for signing the treaty. Peeking through a window was Josef Stalin. The caption was "The Pen is Mightier than the Sword," and the text above the cartoon read, "We Hope." The lead editorial for the day, "An Historic Alliance," asserted, "There are few Americans who believe in these days of supersonic planes and atomic weapons that we can remain aloof from world affairs. That being true, we must be prepared to participate in them. . . . The Atlantic pact, we believe, offers the best hope."

Another political crucible came out of the McCarthy era, when, from 1950 to 1954, U.S. Senator Joseph McCarthy, made headlines with speeches claiming high numbers of Communists were at work within the State Department and the Defense Department. "In the McCarthy era, we were very troubled," William Block recalled. "I got very involved, mostly in influencing our editorial opinion." Block remembered especially the role played by Matt Cvetic, who was "an informer for the FBI, looking for subversives, mostly in the labor movement. Pittsburgh was important to the Allied military effort, providing 60 percent of the steel used. There was a good deal of concern about what trouble left-wing members of labor union might cause. Cvetic appeared before the House Un-American Activities Committee and told the whole story of

Cy Hungerford's
cartoon, "The Pen
is Mightier than
the Sword"
(Courtesy *Pittsburgh
Post-Gazette*)

his being an informer. That ended Cvetic's income [from the government], so he began making speeches for pay around the Pittsburgh area. He hooked into Roy Harris, a symphony composer, and his wife Johanna for alleged Communist affiliations."

The Harrises had come in 1951 to the Pennsylvania College for Women (Chatham College after 1954) on a five-year, twenty-five-thousand-dollar per year grant from the A. W. Mellon Charitable and Educational Trust. In 1952, Harris was asked by Carnegie Technical Institute and the College for Women to serve as executive director of the First Pittsburgh International Festival of Music. A man of strong ego and many enthusiasms, Harris was excited by the idea of the festival, especially if it featured music composed by himself and his contemporaries.

The newspapers in Pittsburgh and elsewhere hailed the festival as part of the city's Renaissance and a musical counterpart to the biennial

International Art Exhibit at the Carnegie Institution, with which it was scheduled to coincide. The *Sun-Telegraph* was particularly effusive. A front-page story on April 18, 1952, written by Charles W. Prine Jr., declared: "A week-long international festival to be held next November, concurrent with the International Art Exhibit will focus on Pittsburgh as one of the world's great cultural centers. . . . Civic, industrial, and educational leaders are hailing the festival as one of the most important cultural developments in Pittsburgh's history. . . . Mayor Lawrence said that 'we are making this industrial capital one of the world's great cultural capitals.'" A *Post-Gazette* editorial, published on April 25, was equally enthusiastic. "In all, ear as well as eye will find unusual artistic satisfaction next fall. The twin festivals, one of modern color and the other of modern sound, should considerably enhance the growing cultural prestige of this city." Nationally, the festival received remarkable attention, including an estimated 160 columns of general news coverage, 6 columns of editorial comment, 20 columns of society news, and 30 columns of musical criticism.

Occasional negative comments were heard: Harris was criticized by some new music enthusiasts for exercising tight control of the repertoire and refusing to program "controversial works." That was a most interesting censure considering that Harris had scheduled such composers as Paul Hindemith, Arthur Honegger, Aaron Copland, Darius Milhaud, Igor Stravinsky, Béla Bartók, and Sergei Prokofiev, not to mention Arnold Schoenberg, Alban Berg, and Olivier Messiaen. The objections were an early sign of the tangent classical music was to take for decades in the direction of the atonal-composition model of Schoenberg and beyond, a direction Harris did not favor.

Far more serious, however, were the charges brought forward by Cvetic. During World War II, on November 16, 1944, a U.S.-Soviet friendship dinner was held at the Waldorf in New York to which Winston Churchill, George Marshall, Dwight Eisenhower and other worthies sent greetings. At the time, Soviet Russia was a staunch ally in the war against Hitler's Nazi Germany. Harris wrote a piece of music, "Ode to Friendship," for the occasion. On the basis of this, Cvetic attacked him as pro-Soviet. At this point, State Supreme Court Justice Michael Musmanno—the colorful political figure who had led the fight against the Coal and Iron Police and later was a presiding judge at the 1946

Nuremberg trials of leading Nazis—joined the outcry, persuading the state Veterans of Foreign Wars to condemn Harris and trying (unsuccessfully) to convince the American Legion in Pittsburgh to do the same. The *Post-Gazette* defended the composer, but the other Pittsburgh newspapers reacted differently.

A *Pittsburgh Press* article of November 26, 1952, carried the headlines: "Musmanno calls for repudiation/Asks Harris to take back praise of USSR/Urges people not to applaud Harris 5th Symphony/Dedication March 13, 1943 when Russia an ally." The *Press* went on to insist, "Of course, there is still time for Roy Harris to prove his devotion to American ideals of freedom if he will do what Beethoven did following the writing of the Third Symphony, the immortal 'Eroica.' Beethoven had dedicated this number to Napoleon Bonaparte as a great man, but when Bonaparte seized absolutist power in France, made himself a dictator and unleashed a horrible European war, Beethoven tore up the dedication sheet and inserted into the symphony the now famous 'March Funebre' for all dictators." Two days later, on November 28, the *Press* carried a story headlined: "Audience rejects pleas to snub Harris symphony/Listeners refuse Musmanno's request to 'sit on hands' after playing of work." On the same date, the *Post-Gazette* carried a cartoon by Cy Hungerford called "A little too big to handle." It showed a small figure of Musmanno crying, "Sit on your hands" unavailingly as huge hands labeled "Symphony Audience" clapped vigorously. The *Sun-Telegraph,* eager to pursue Hearst's anti-Communist crusade, printed a November 30 headline that read: "Echo of Music Festival/Harris blasted by Cvetic, Musmanno and Gunther." The article quoted State Superior Court Judge Blair F. Gunther as saying, "A deep, disfiguring injury has been inflicted upon this community by the rendition of the Roy Harris Symphony. . . . The shame of playing this number, with its unchanged Communist implications, must tragically remain as a red scar on the face of Pennsylvania."

Bill Block later recounted:

The A. W. Mellon Trust, which was financing a three-year composer-in-residence at Chatham College for Roy Harris and a pianist-in-residence for his wife Johanna, became nervous and hired Charles Kenworthy, chief trial lawyer for the Reed Smith firm, to do a complete investigation of Harris's life. Harris stood up to Musmanno and therefore got our editorial support.

Kenworthy checked out Harris's entire life. It turned out he was completely apolitical, had no interest in anything political. Anyway, Charlie hosted a meeting at his Carlton Hotel apartment with Musmanno and invited me to sit in. Charlie walked back and forth, as was his style, and told Musmanno everything they had found. Musmanno, in his usual flamboyant way, protested: "But Charlie, I've got these papers here, all these accusations and papers!" Kenworthy suddenly reached over and grabbed the papers out of Musmanno's hands. They were blank! Later, I asked Kenworthy, "How did you know that?" He replied, "I've been practicing law long enough to know when somebody is faking."[15]

The Harrises continued their careers elsewhere, unaffected by the Pittsburgh controversy.

Chapter 12

The Joint Operating
Agreement

———◆———

URING THE 1950s, the competitive picture among Pittsburgh's
newspapers was becoming more focused, making for a particularly uncertain period for the *Post-Gazette* in the wake of the collapse of
its 1949 Sunday-edition effort. The circulation had dropped from a high
of 280,000 in 1950 to 258,480 in 1955. Block later explained the intricacies of the situation: "The *Press* was growing rapidly in advertising volume at the expense of the *Sun-Telegraph*. We were growing in advertising volume, but not so rapidly as the *Press*. But we, too, were growing at
the expense of the *Sun-Telegraph*." One bright spot recalled by Block
was a coup with the Kaufmann's department store: "I went to see Irwin
Wolf at Kaufmann's and was able to persuade him to switch 200,000
lines of advertising from the *Sun-Telly*. Not only was there a revenue
gain for us, but it was important for others because it signified a loss of
confidence by Kaufmann's toward the *Sun-Telly*."[1]

The *Sun-Telegraph*, however, had an advantage that Block wanted
—a Sunday edition. He later recounted: "I tried to talk the Hearst
people into forming a combination with us, either a morning edition or
a Sunday together. But Hearst had died in '51, and there was a hiatus
where no decisions were being made by the Hearst organization." A
resolution, however, was in sight. Block explained that by this time the

Sun-Telegraph was coming to its end: "They were declining rapidly both on Sunday and daily. The *Press,* which had a great deal of newer equipment, was in a position to give later news, better distribution, and was killing them on Sunday. Finally, the Hearst people realized that they couldn't carry on. We went into a negotiation with them, which resulted in our purchase of the *Sun-Telegraph* and a trade of buildings. We thought that we needed their presses to put out the Sunday. I believe that we paid them one million dollars and agreed to share profits for ten years, if there were profits." The purchase was completed on April 24, 1960.[2]

This transaction came as a complete surprise to *P-G* employees. They were summoned to a meeting on the first floor of their Second and Grant building where Block, standing on a chair, announced that the *P-G* had bought the *Sun-Telegraph* and that the whole establishment would be moving down Grant Street to the *Sun-Telegraph* building, which had new presses. "Naturally, you move the people to the presses," was one employee's reaction.[3]

The deal, however, did not work out well for the *Post-Gazette.* The 1960 census showed a decline in the city's population for the first time, down to 604,332 from the highpoint 1950 figure of 676,806. In addition, the *Sun-Telegraph* building proved to be impossibly inefficient. "The new pressroom was fine, but all the rest of it was like a rabbit warren; it was difficult and expensive to operate in," Block remembered. The building was not air-conditioned, and became so stiflingly hot that at times during its history, staff members broke windows to admit cooler air. *P-G* veterans who lived through that period have memories of how distressing it was to work in "the old *Sun-Telly* barn," with its rattling windows and its city room of dirty pine. In addition, there was the problem of merging the two staffs, including people with overlapping specialties.[4]

Employees were adjusting not only to a new environment, but to new technology, as well. Before World War II, newsroom employees trained in taking Morse code received wire news and typed it for transmission to linotype operators in the composing room. In 1951, the Associated Press and the United Press International introduced teletype machines that produced printed material that could be marked up by copy editors and sent to the composing room. Yet even with the teletypes, problems remained concerning proofreading for accuracy, and especially of the stock tables where precision was mandatory. About the time of the *Post-Gazette*'s move to the old *Sun-Telegraph* building, the Associated Press developed a tape that could be fed directly into the linotype machine, bypassing human operator problems. That, of course, created further printers-union concerns about cutbacks in jobs, with consequent labor unrest.

The staff plunged immediately into publishing a Sunday edition. Jim Alexander was named Sunday editor and the proven abilities of managing editor Joe Shuman in designing special sections were put to work. By that time, Andrew Chancellor was city editor, succeeding Jim Ross, who one evening slumped over dead at his newsroom desk. Chancellor, in World War II a Navy lieutenant with duty off Normandy, Southern France, and Okinawa, returned to his hometown of Pittsburgh to join the *Bulletin-Index* magazine. There he wrote a major article bannered, "Can the press be free in Pittsburgh?" detailing the way department stores removed ads over articles they disliked. That brought him to the attention of the *P-G* where he went to work in 1946.

Despite the working conditions, the *Post-Gazette* continued its coverage, including full treatment of the historic 1960 presidential election in which John F. Kennedy managed to defeat Vice President Richard Nixon. Reporter Alvin Rosensweet, who, with photographer Don Bindyke, was assigned to cover Senator Kennedy's forays into neighboring West Virginia, recalled an interesting anecdote about that campaign. Bindyke was under explicit orders from Joe Shuman to get a picture of Kennedy and his wife Jackie together. Bindyke was able to do that at the McClure Hotel in Wheeling, but in one of the horror stories for any photographer, the picture did not develop. Unfortunately, Bindyke had bought his film at a drug store instead of a good camera shop.[5]

In the 1960 transition, the *Sun-Telegraph*'s logo, the Hearst eagle, was gradually reduced until finally it disappeared. The *Post-Gazette* nearly met the same fate. Block discovered that just having the new presses was not enough. To gain needed revenue, he tried a subscription price increase, the first in eight years. On November 14, 1960, the *Post-Gazette* raised its daily rate to seven cents outside the immediate area, though the price remained at a nickel within the city. Block explained the decision this way: "We were trying to build city circulation, and so we didn't touch that price. But the price increase didn't help our

On March 30, 1962, President John F. Kennedy hosted a luncheon at the White House for Pennsylvania editors and publishers. William Block is seated on the president's immediate left. (AP Wire Photo; Courtesy of the *Pittsburgh Post-Gazette*)

total circulation. The Press passed us in total circulation daily and had far more in the city."[6]

In 1959, before the merger, the *Post-Gazette* was selling 273,328 papers (the *Sun-Telegraph*'s figure was 178,715 and the *Press*'s 306,707). In April 1960, the newly merged *Post-Gazette* had 404,907 subscribers. Within a month that figure fell to 313,755 and by December it was down to 306,033. The Sunday figures dropped from 366,647 in April to 338,615 by the end of the year.

Block sadly recalled: "I did not realize how badly off their [the *Sun-Telegraph*'s] Sunday had become. Instead of the Sunday helping us, it actually dragged us down, and our losses increased. It soon seemed incumbent on us to see if Scripps Howard was interested in working out a joint operating agreement."[7] A joint operating agreement, or JOA, was an arrangement that sprang up in numerous cities as a way to maintain competition by saving the weaker of two surviving newspapers from extinction. The stronger paper would take over circulation, distribution, advertising, composing, and printing—everything except news and editorial functions—for the weaker paper, thus allowing the continuation of competing voices in the marketplace of ideas.

Such a merger had already occurred in twenty cities nationwide, and involved six Scripps Howard newspapers. Because of antitrust questions, the JOA concept ultimately failed to withstand court challenges; the U.S. Supreme Court ruling ruled against it in 1969. In 1970, however, Congress passed the "Newspaper Preservation Act." Introduced by U.S. Senator Carl Hayden of Arizona, the law provided that such agencies are legal if one of the papers involved is unlikely "to remain or to become a financially sound publication." Thus, the law acquired the nickname, the "failing newspapers act."

Paul Block Jr. handled the Blocks' overtures to the Scripps Howard organization on the possibility of a JOA, while William Block stayed in Pittsburgh to keep the sinking *P-G* afloat. The Blocks had one important lever in the negotiations—the fact that they had a seven-day paper. It was to the advantage of Scripps Howard to reach an agreement that would leave it with the only Sunday edition. Finally, a satisfactory agreement was worked out in the fall of 1961. The *Press* would handle all of the *Post-Gazette*'s affairs, except news and editorial functions, out of its plant on the lower end of the Boulevard of the Allies, and would print the *Post-Gazette* on the *Press*'s seven Hoe presses, which had a maximum capacity of ninety-six pages. The *Post-Gazette* gave up its Sunday edition as well as its bulldog (evening-before) edition, which had helped keep it in circulation competition for so long. The fourth floor of the *Press*'s building was renovated for use by the *P-G*'s editorial department, with a separate entrance and elevator at 50 Boulevard of the Allies. The news and editorial workers remained at the old *Sun-Telly* building until that transformation was completed.

The JOA agreement was written to last until December 31, 1999, with the right of renewal. Either party could terminate the agreement if the Agency fell into a deficit. The *Press* would collect all revenues, which were put into a common fund to be divided 80-20, with the *Press* receiving the larger share because of its profitable Sunday edition and its larger daily circulation. As to the disposition of properties, the Hearst interests sold to the city the former *Post-Gazette* building at Second and Grant for which it had traded its properties farther north on Grant Street. The Second and Grant building became the city's police headquarters. The Blocks later sold the old *Sun-Telly* building to the Pittsburgh Urban Redevelopment Authority, which was gathering land parcels in that Grant Street area for what eventually became the site of the U.S. Steel Building.

Block made it clear to the staff that they had to make this transition or else the *Post-Gazette* would go out of business. The last Sunday edition of that era's *Post-Gazette* was published on November 12, 1961.

The successive failures of the Sunday-edition initiatives had brought the *Post-Gazette* to this pass. In a strange way, however, those setbacks contributed to its continuing survival. The *Sun-Telegraph* began losing circulation after it had been wounded by the *P-G*'s 1949 Sunday effort, ultimately causing its sale to the Blocks. The 1960 effort made the *P-G*'s JOA overture to Scripps-Howard more enticing because it left the *Press* with the only Sunday edition in town.

The trick now, after more than a decade of traumatizing experiences, was to maintain the traditions of the *Post-Gazette* in a more constrained environment where many of the keys to success—circulation, advertising, quality of printing and of delivery—were in the hands of others.

Frank Hawkins, who became the editor of the *Post-Gazette* in 1965 after two decades on the editorial page, has vividly described the situation at the *P-G* after the joint operating agreement with Scripps Howard took effect.

In order to accommodate both Pittsburgh papers under one roof, Scripps Howard converted the fourth floor of the *Press* building into quarters for the *P-G* news and editorial department. . . . While we were more comfortably housed in the *Press* building in much more attractive surroundings [than in the old *Sun-Telegraph* Building], I suffered frustration because we were no longer masters of our own house. There was no longer any way by which we could pull ourselves up by our own bootstraps because we couldn't reach the straps. I knew from my contacts with *Press* personnel that they were making no serious effort to sell the *P-G* lest they weaken their own advertising and circulation. They were particularly zealous in protecting the Sunday edition, which is the big revenue producer.

Hawkins also explained how the *Post-Gazette* was constrained concerning "many things we wanted to do and couldn't." He wanted an op-ed page but "that would have taken away from an already too restricted news space. Similarly, we knew how to get out a Sunday edition, with its various sections and supplements, but our hands were tied." Hawkins said that he consistently argued for use of color, both spot and full, "But we were held to the use of spot color, and that only when

some advertiser was using it and we could ride its coattails. Rarely were we permitted the use of full four-color because it entailed additional production costs which the *P-G* didn't control."

For Hawkins, the frustrations became especially burdensome after he succeeded Andrew Bernhard upon his retirement as editor on June 15, 1965. "Just as Bernhard as editor had continued to function, in effect, as managing editor, so did I continue to do what I had long done and what was traditionally the role of a newspaper editor, to write and to supervise the newspaper's opinion function. But I was also now responsible for the whole non-advertising content of the paper. I had to assume responsibility not only for the paper's various departments but also for its syndicated material. That included the features, like comic strips, various columns, puzzles, serialized articles, book condensations, etc." Making matters more difficult, the slow, agonizing falloff in circulation continued; at the time Hawkins took over as editor, the figure was 250,928, representing a drop of one-sixth since the time of the merger.

Another result of the JOA was to formalize the publisher-in-residence at the *Post-Gazette,* occasioning these comments from Hawkins:

The *Pittsburgh Post-Gazette* team in 1975: James E. Alexander, managing editor; publisher William Block Sr.; and Frank Hawkins, editor (From Stefan Lorant, *Pittsburgh: The Story of an American City,* Author's Edition, 1964; Courtesy Rowman and Littlefield Publishers)

My situation differed from that of many editors in that I had a publisher on the premises (unlike editors of chain newspapers) and since most business matters were handled by the joint operating agency, Block could devote much of his time to the news and editorial operations of the *P-G*. He was closely involved in all personnel decisions. And, of course, he had to settle with the *Press* any problems arising under the agency contract. He also had other business interests, including radio and television properties in Pittsburgh and elsewhere. These duties took him away from Pittsburgh often, and in his absence, I carried the responsibility. In fairness, it must be said that he gave me a free hand and never did any second-guessing, even when I was wrong. . . . He was, in fact, known to the staff as a soft touch, and if he had a failing, it was in permitting employees to come to him directly with their requests or complaints rather than go through the chain of command. The effect was to vitiate the authority of his executives. By and large, however, the *P-G* was a happy shop.[8]

Block's management style is also evidenced by a story remembered much later by Tim Menees, a Seattle reporter who in 1974 had decided to become an editorial cartoonist. A four-page tabloid-size collection of his recent cartoons caught Block's eye, and Block arranged to have Menees come to San Francisco for an interview. Block was clearly interested, but explained why he was not ready to make a commitment: "Cy Hungerford has been here in Pittsburgh for years. I'm not going to force him to retire. This is his life, and it would kill him." Menees was impressed. "As much as I wanted the job, I thought, 'Wow! If this is the attitude of the owner of the paper it must permeate the place. He must care about people so much that he's not going to farm out an elderly employee just to get new blood.' It was the exact opposite of the horror stories of guys getting cut in their fifties and sixties."[9] When Hungerford, in his late eighties, decided to reduce his workload in 1976, Menees was hired to produce, at first, three of the six cartoons a week. Hungerford died in 1983.

The JOA allowed Block and his wife Maxine ample time for community affairs, and they were particularly interested in the cultural and health and welfare fields. Bill Block served on the board of the Pittsburgh Symphony, and later became involved with a program that brought symphony musicians, who at the time had only thirty-two-week contracts and were seeking ways to supplement their income, to visit and work with children in public schools. The program was incorpo-

Cy Hungerford,
cartoonist, at his
desk
(Courtesy *Pittsburgh
Post-Gazette*)

rated as a non-profit organization, Gateway to Music, which Bill Block headed for a number of years. Bill and his wife Maxine amassed a first-class collection of art objects and helped establish a new Glass Center, opened in Pittsburgh in 2001. Additionally, Block was a member of a committee to study the reconstruction of the Federation of Social Agencies—the planning agency that presented the social welfare needs of the community to the Community Chest. Because of this experience, Block was asked in the 1960s by Mayor Joseph Barr to chair a committee to develop a social plan for the city's urban redevelopment ventures. Block was also active with the Golden Triangle Association, a coalition to promote downtown, which he led for a term.

In the postwar period, William Block and his brother Paul Block Jr. expanded Blade Communications Inc., with new acquisitions beyond those their father had made. Both men were quite conservative on that subject. William wrote: "Both of us were concerned about the trouble that Father had gotten into during the Depression, when he had owned a number of newspapers and because of debt and the fact that in the Depression business got so very bad, he had to divest most of his acquisitions. Paul was especially conservative about acquisitions. He'd seen all the trouble and the difficulty of financing the estate, and he was just unalterably opposed to us getting into too much debt. . . . We have not ever tried to get the maximum financial return, as so many of the bigger chains do. In fact, I don't think that Paul or I were really businessmen. We had very little training in business management. Both of us probably had more interest in the editorial side of the paper and not as much interest in the business side."[10]

The Blocks' acquisitions in the broadcast media began in 1931, when Paul Block Sr. purchased WWSW, a radio station in Pittsburgh. Its major assets were an anchorman named Rege Cordic and a contract to broadcast Pirates baseball. Much later, in order to obtain a channel to heighten the power for the 250-watt station, Paul Block Jr. hired a Washington radio lawyer, Paul Segal. While Segal was able to obtain a highly desirable channel of 970 on the AM dial, the Federal Communications Commission permission was quite restrictive in order to protect stations in Buffalo and Ashtabula, Ohio, already on the dial at 970. The Blocks had to build a complicated array of antennas directed to the south, but blocked to the north. When the FCC in 1949 finally authorized the permit, a costly earth-moving project on a site north of Pittsburgh was necessary. The station proved to be profitable until the growth of television eventually brought a third television station into the Pittsburgh market. WWSW had an excellent FM channel, but even as radio stations began moving into that medium, the Blocks waited "because it obviously was going to take time to build an acceptance for FM and for radio sets to be sold that could receive FM."[11] After trying various formats to be competitive, the Blocks tired of that battle and sold the station in 1984.

Meanwhile, as the television age blossomed, the Blocks applied for Channel 11 at Paul Segal's suggestion. That set off a complicated set of negotiations with other contenders, the Westinghouse Corporation and the Brennan Family, owners at the time of radio stations WKQV and WJAS, respectively. The Blocks and the Brennans joined together in an equal partnership and finally got Channel 11 on the air in 1957. The arrangement was that the Blocks would run the station, with Oscar Schloss and Bob Mortensen as managers. The first major decision was whether to affiliate with the established NBC or with the struggling new ABC network (Channel 2 had already taken CBS). The partners chose NBC, leaving ABC for the third emerging station, Channel 4, which, as WTAE, soon became the second-ranked station in viewer numbers. Channel 11, as WIIC (later WPXI), was ranked third, though it always was profitable. The Blocks began having trouble with their partners, however, and in 1964 both families sold their interests in the station to Cox Broadcasting Company.

Out of that disputed transaction came a new and highly profitable venture for the Blocks. J. Leonard Reinsch, head of Cox Broadcasting, told Bill Block, "You know, there's a new thing coming along, cable, and this is something you ought to get into. What we ought to do is to organize some companies to get franchises for cable. I'd like to tie in with the *Post-Gazette* and the *Blade* in Toledo."[12] As a result, two companies were established in 1964, one in Pittsburgh and the other in Toledo; the Blocks were 55 percent owners and the Cox chain held a 45 percent share. Matters went well in Toledo, where the city government rather quickly granted the necessary franchise, making it possible for the Blocks to establish their company, called CableSystem. The Toledo enterprise contracted with Ohio Bell, but, in the words of Bill Block, "The system built by Bell Telephone was a disaster, and we ended the relationship and set out to build our own system."[13] From that point, the company went on to acquire cable systems in Monroe, Michigan, and Sandusky, Ohio.

The story was different in Pittsburgh. First, efforts to gain the necessary City Council approval dragged on and on. Then the FCC ruled that one company could not own both a television station and a cable system in any one city. So, because of its Channel 11 ownership, Cox had to back out of the partnership with the Blocks. Bill Block's efforts to interest Time, Inc., in a joint enterprise were to no avail. He then partnered with Telecommunications, Inc. [TCI], and with John Sengstacke, who owned the *Pittsburgh Courier.* However, the city set difficult franchise requirements, and Warner Communications and its partners won the franchise. Ironically, Warner began losing money with the system it had built in Pittsburgh and sold it to TCI, but by that time the Blocks were out of the picture.

The Blocks used the money received from the sale of Channel 11 to purchase two newspapers. The first, acquired in 1964, was the *Red Bank (N.J.) Register*. Not only were the terms right, but the Block brothers were nostalgic about Red Bank because their boyhood summers had been spent nearby. The purchase eventually put a strain on the Block enterprises, however, because a fire devastated the *Register* plant, except for the pressroom. Even sending the twenty-eight-year-old Bill Block Jr. on a resuscitation mission ultimately did not work, and the paper was finally sold on his recommendation in 1982 to the Capital Cities chain.

The second purchase, of the *Monterey (Calif.) Peninsula Herald*, came about because Bill Block Sr. pursued a tip and visited Colonel Alan Griffin, the owner. After Griffin had described his experiences in both World Wars, he began discussing the newspaper, which none of his heirs was interested in owning. He told Block that he would never sell to Scripps Howard, Hearst, Knight-Ridder, or the owner of the *San Francisco Chronicle*, Richard Thierot, whom he hated. Block then asked directly, "Do you see any reason why you wouldn't sell to me?" Griffin paused before replying gruffly, "Well, I don't know why not."[14] The transaction was completed in 1967.

While Bill Block Sr. and Paul Block Jr. were of one mind about those two purchases, the brothers later disagreed as to whether there ever had been a thought of selling the *Post-Gazette*. In Bill's recollection: "It probably would have been a very wise thing had we decided after World War II to sell the *Post-Gazette* and buy something else in a more stable market with the proceeds. But we were terribly loyal to what father had built, and it was difficult psychologically to dispose of an enterprise he had worked so hard to keep. Paul later said that he had wanted to sell the *Post-Gazette*, but I had opposed the sale. He may have made a casual remark about selling, but certainly there was never any serious discussion to that effect." Block also recalled another disagreement: upon learning that a small paper in Lancaster, Ohio, just outside Columbus, was for sale, Bill visited Lancaster and began urging the purchase. "Paul put thumbs down on it, and so we never followed up on it. I think the paper has doubled its circulation since, because it's

getting the benefit of the growth of the Columbus area." Despite their disagreements, Paul's death in 1987 came as "a great blow" to Bill, bringing to the fore a realization of how well they had worked together and how much he had depended upon his brother's counsel. "When you've known someone all your life and worked closely with him and know his idiosyncrasies, his good points and his bad, there is a terrible void that is left when that person passes away."[15]

In 1967, two years after Frank Hawkins became editor of the *P-G,* a parallel era began downstairs at the *Pittsburgh Press* when John Troan became editor after a distinguished career as a reporter in the science and medical fields. Troan, the tenth child (six died in infancy) of an anthracite coal miner, had garnered a job with the *Pittsburgh Press* immediately upon his graduation from Penn State in 1939. After combat duty in the U.S. Navy in World War II, he returned to the *Press* and presently became its medical reporter. In one of the greatest "scoops" of all time, Troan broke the news that Dr. Jonas Salk at the University of Pittsburgh Medical Center had developed a polio vaccine. Troan had interviewed Salk before a University of Pittsburgh fundraising dinner on May 12, 1952, and had heard Salk say, almost casually, that he would soon begin

The *Pittsburgh Press* team in 1975: editor John Troan with executive editor Leo Koeberlein (From Stefan Lorant, *Pittsburgh: The Story of an American City,* Author's Edition, 1964; Courtesy Rowman and Littlefield Publishers)

tests of a polio vaccine on human beings. Troan's *Press* story of May 13, published around the world, was officially corroborated three years later when an official announcement about the vaccine was made on April 12, 1955, to a jam-packed auditorium that included 158 newsmen from across the world.

Because of that coup, Troan was hired as a science editor for the Scripps Howard chain and relocated to Washington, D.C. In 1966, he returned to Pittsburgh to be associate editor of the *Press*; a year later he succeeded W. W. "Wally" Forster as editor. Troan said he took the position with the understanding that Leo Koberlein, his chief rival for the job, would be the executive editor, the "inside man," handling the day-to-day running of the paper, while "I took care of the budget, relations with Scripps Howard, editorial policy, and did outside liaison with the Pittsburgh community."[16] Koberlein had made his name by assuming leadership as Forster's health declined. Troan and Koberlein began integrating the *Press*'s editorial staff, something the *Post-Gazette* had already started in 1955. The two editors also began moving women into positions of management, including the promotion of Madelyn Ross, who would later become managing editor.

As editor, Troan's philosophy was along these lines. "I tried not to offend big blocks of readers. If somebody is criticizing the Pope, you don't put it on the top of page one. And I wanted stories written so that a parent getting the *Press* would have no compunction about leaving it on the coffee table for the children to read."[17] Yet world events were evolving in such a way that it would soon become more difficult to shield readers from tragic violence.

Chapter 13

Turbulent Times

——◆——

TWO MAJOR EVENTS in the late 1960s changed the lives of Pittsburgh's residents and influenced newspaper coverage. The first was the rioting of 1968 in the wake of the assassination of civil rights leader Dr. Martin Luther King Jr. The second was the election in 1969 of maverick Democratic politician Pete Flaherty, who began to dismantle Lawrence's Democratic political machine and its Renaissance partnerships with the mostly Republican leaders of the city's industries and businesses.

Pittsburgh, at first, escaped the "urban disturbances" of the mid-1960s that engulfed the Watts district of Los Angeles, then Newark, Detroit, Chicago, and Rochester. Although the city seemed peaceful, in March 1968 a prescient series of articles appeared in the *New Pittsburgh Courier,* in which staff writer Carl Morris noted that local militants, watching other cities' riots on television, were rumored to be planning a "B-Day" or "Burn Day" for May 1968. There is no evidence that either the *Post-Gazette* or the *Press* paid any attention to these warnings. The "Burn Day" would arrive earlier than predicted because of the assassination of Dr. King on April 4. While rioting broke out immediately that Thursday night in many cities, Pittsburgh remained relatively calm until Saturday night.[1]

On April 5, the morning after King's death, the *Post-Gazette* head-lined both the assassination and the news that President Johnson had delayed a trip to Honolulu, where he had scheduled a review of the Vietnam War with his advisers. A headline on the second page reported, "Negroes erupt in some cities." The *Press* featured "Ode to a Martyr," written by Pulitzer Prize–winning poet Gwendolyn Brooks. It also re-ported that Jack Howard, president of Scripps Howard, had announced that the newspaper chain was offering a twenty-five-thousand-dollar reward for information leading to the arrest and conviction of King's assassin.

As tensions mounted, both the *Post-Gazette* and the *Press* urged calm. The *P-G* editorialized on April 6: "The stark finality of death sometimes blinds us to the spiritual riches bequeathed us by a life well-lived. The specter of new civil strife stalks the land. Dr. King's ideal of human brotherhood has been shadowed by fear and hostility. . . . But when the race has wearied of bloodshed and cruelty it may turn once more to the vision of Martin Luther King, a vision as practical as it is sublime." The leading department stores, Gimbels, Horne's, and Kauf-mann's, ran a full-page advertisement: "We join in mourning the un-timely passing of a distinguished citizen. We pray that all who labor for the fulfillment of American life will be inspired by his objectives." On Sunday, April 7, the *Press* declared: "But before there can be further progress in any direction, there must be discipline and order."

David Craig later recalled that when he became director of public safety in the administration of Mayor Joseph Barr, there was a realiza-tion of the need to reach out to different groups beyond City Hall's comfortable relationship with the business community. Craig's depart-ment set up a "Red Vest Brigade"—young African American men who were deputized as peacekeepers to patrol neighborhoods. That program may have helped when anger mounted in the black community, as did Craig's ability to call upon leaders such as Father Charles Owen Rice, best known as the "labor priest." It also helped that many African American leaders, with the support of Mayor Barr, swung into action to allay pent-up anger within the community. State Representative K. Leroy Irvis, who had organized the department store picket two decades earlier, dispersed a large crowd in the Hill District which had sur-rounded two policemen, and later persuaded a group of angry young men not to get themselves killed in order to vent their frustrations. Out of respect for Irvis, young rioters posted guards around his Centre Avenue apartment. On the North Side, the Reverend Jimmy Joe Robinson was credited with keeping young men busy and out of trouble during that violent weekend. A former Pitt football star and pastor of the Bidwell Presbyterian Church, Robinson had previously worked with young gangs and groups such as the "Black Rangers." African American policemen, including "Muggsy" Moore, later Pittsburgh police chief, and Harvey Adams, later head of the Pittsburgh Public Housing Authority's police force, informally aided him.

The civil rights leadership decided that the best way to ease the pressure was to stage a protest march on Sunday, April 7—Palm Sunday—from the Hill District past the Civic Arena in the razed Lower Hill and into downtown. Police officials were aghast at the idea, particularly when the relative calm came apart on Saturday night with looting and burning throughout the Hill District. There were predictions that not a window downtown would be left unbroken. Yet David Craig, backed by Barr, agreed with the black leadership that a peaceful outlet for emotions was absolutely vital. An integrated group of leaders led a long column of black protesters into downtown between walls of policemen and the march proceeded peacefully.

On Monday, April 8, the *Post-Gazette* reported: "In seven hours yesterday afternoon, [things] went from worse to bad. . . . At the worst, through the sunshine hours, the well-known streets above the Civic Arena were witness to fire bombings, bottle and rock throwing, looting and near anarchy. . . . With sunset it improved to just bad. . . . Street sounds were those of the clomp-clomp-clomp of boot-clad feet as more than 1,000 Pennsylvania National Guardsmen moved into positions at every intersection." The article also highlighted the protest march on Palm Sunday, including a huge picture by *P-G* photographer Harry Coughanour of a long line of marchers wending past Chatham Center to Sixth Avenue. The story read: "An estimated 3,000 persons of all ages and creeds marched from the Lower Hill to Point State Park yesterday afternoon in memory of slain civil rights leader Martin Luther King. The march began 30 minutes late after a tense confrontation between march leaders and squads of blue helmeted city police at the assembly point, Center Avenue and Crawford Street, just above the Civic Arena. . . . David W. Craig, director of Public Safety, originally told the leaders . . . that he 'cannot permit your safety and the safety of this city to be

Children walk through the Hill District on Palm Sunday, 1968, as smoke billows behind them during the unrest and violence following the assassination of civil rights leader Dr. Martin Luther King Jr.
(Courtesy *Pittsburgh Post-Gazette*)

endangered.' . . . Even as the police and Negro leaders stood but yards apart, fire engines were driven through lanes in the growing crowd to bear firemen to various fires that erupted in the Upper Hill."

The *Post-Gazette* carried additional pictures, farther back in the section, including one captioned: "Looters cart their plunder from a Center Avenue grocery store unmolested." A story reported: "'Let the looters

Smoke from the Mainway Super Market fills the air as violence erupts in response to Dr. King's assassination. (Courtesy *Pittsburgh Post-Gazette*)

go!' was the word city police got from owners of stores in the Hill District yesterday when police officials told them their stores were being plundered by roaming gangs. Far from being apathetic, the store owners were just acting realistically, police said, and realized that stopping the looters by force could only lead to further trouble." What they did not expect, the story went on to relate, were the fires the gangs would set. Fernand Auberjonois, foreign correspondent for both the *P-G* and the *Toledo Blade,* reported that Europe was stunned by the violence of the post-assassination disorders that had erupted in so many American cities.

The *Press* that Monday also carried extensive coverage of both the looting, "189 fires, 700 held," and the march, "3,000 march to a dream, a song." Under the heading, "Mobocracy must end," the paper editorialized: "No one can deny that serious injustices continue to exist in this country. . . . If democracy is to survive, if we are to get on with the job of making it work better and more justly, we must first safeguard it from being subverted by merciless mobocracy."

On Tuesday, April 9, the *Post-Gazette* philosophized:

Much as civic leaders may have hoped for a continuation of Pittsburgh's relative tranquility, no one should have been surprised by the turmoil that has erupted. We had been warned many times by responsible observers that it could happen here. Now that it has happened, the urgent objective must be to guard against a larger tragedy, to protect life, to prevent further injuries and destruction. . . . As Pittsburghers consider the disorder and destruction that have come to their own city, they should avoid blanket condemnation based on skin color. They should acknowledge that gross racial injustices still exist here. And they should greatly intensify their efforts to equalize opportunities in employment, in education and in housing—not as a reward for the vocal hostility and violence of the few but as the just due of the majority of black people who have tried to keep their faith in our system and who for the most part suffer in silence.

Editorial cartoonist Cy Hungerford commented on the situation with a cartoon called "A Sad Day for America," in which the memorial of Dr. King, engraved with the word "peace," was shadowed by a dark cloud labeled "violence."

While the efforts of Irvis, Robinson, Craig, and other leaders saved lives, the looting and 415 fires resulted in an estimated one million dol-

Cy Hungerford's cartoon, "A Sad Day for America" (Courtesy *Pittsburgh Post-Gazette*)

lars in property damage. The Hill District was especially affected as the mayhem there destroyed much of the business district and eventually drove many merchants out of the Hill or out of business altogether.

In Pittsburgh, the riots roused a new sense of urgency within the city's leadership. The Allegheny Conference on Community Development began switching its emphasis to programs that would alleviate some of the problems that had surfaced. Robert Pease, then the Conference's executive director, remembers taking such business leaders as Henry Hillman to meetings with African American community activists, whom Pease had come to know when he was executive director of the city's Urban Redevelopment Authority.

The protest movement flared up again in Pittsburgh in 1969 with marches and sit-ins to pressure contractors for the new U.S. Steel Building on Grant Street to hire more African American workers. Nationally, however, the riots of 1968 marked the end of the integrated phase of the civil rights movement, already being challenged by the rise of the "black power" movement symbolized by Stokely Carmichael. The emphasis of protest groups on picketing against the war in Vietnam also drained manpower from the previous emphasis on civil rights. Moreover, although the laws that King and others had sought were on the books, and the War on Poverty had been launched in the inner cities, these seemingly made little difference in the daily lives of poor blacks, calling into question the effectiveness of interracial coalitions and such civil rights tactics as marches and demonstrations. The racial isolation of the black community increased as whites continued to leave for the suburbs. The shrugging off of alliances with whites also paralleled a "do for yourself" movement on the part of African Americans.[2]

Meanwhile, another momentous development for Pittsburgh was taking place on the political scene. When Mayor Barr in 1969 decided not to run for reelection, the Democratic organization chose and endorsed Harry Kramer, a judge in the Orphans Court division of the Allegheny County Court of Common Pleas. In a daring move, a young city councilman, Pete Flaherty, decided to run against Kramer in the Democratic primary. Before Flaherty, the mayoral elections were usually controlled by behind-the-scenes maneuvering to obtain a consensus before a public vote was taken. Flaherty made a name for himself by loudly opposing last-minute budget-making, insisting that a city which was spending so many millions a year should take longer to figure out how it was going to deal out its money and how it was going to raise it. Flaherty also objected to a new tax that the city administration, in its scramble to avoid another increase in the real estate tax, imposed on hospital bills and college tuition fees. To the surprise of many, in the May 20, 1969, primary, Flaherty won.

In part, this outcome resulted from disarray within the Democratic organization, some of it caused by reform efforts pushed by people whom Mayor Barr had moved into key positions in his administration. For example, David Craig agreed to move from solicitor to public safety director only if he had complete control over the top positions in the agency. Employees up to the lieutenant level were under the authority of civil service; Craig wanted authority over everyone above that, and Barr agreed. Craig recalls: "The ward chairs were befuddled when they heard that from Barr. . . . Of course, party unity is built up by political favoritism. So we lost a useful coin in the political realm."[3]

For Republicans, this evidence in the primary election of disorder among the Democrats looked like a heaven-sent opportunity to capture the mayor's seat, especially with a solid candidate, lawyer John Tabor. Flaherty bulldozed them, too, though, with a campaign built on the slogan that he was "nobody's boy." That double-trumped Tabor's opening campaign ploy of challenging "Pete" to "win without the machine," which Flaherty did. Nor was Tabor able to gain ground by repeating Kramer's primary-campaign assault on Flaherty for attacking urban renewal and community programs.

By the end of the campaign, the *Pittsburgh Press* was supporting Flaherty. In an October 16, 1969, editorial, "The Next Mayor," the *Press* said, "All big cities are in a heap of trouble—financial, social, criminal and other kinds. . . . The *Press* believes Mr. Flaherty is more likely to persuade the man in the street to gain the broad base of support any mayor so desperately needs to give any large city today. That's why the *Press* favors his election." The *Post-Gazette* felt otherwise, as expressed in an October 30, election-eve editorial, "New Leadership for the '70s." The *P-G* declared: "This city is ripe for political change. The Democratic Party has mobilized its government for the last 35 years. Over the last 15 years, while the city was losing some 100,000 in population, the city payroll was more than doubling. The cost of political inbreeding runs high." Although the city would be assured of at least a partial change with Flaherty, the *P-G* reasoned, "the Democrats would still occupy City Hall and the political climate would not be materially affected. For a deeper and more meaningful change, Pittsburghers should elect the Republican candidate, John K. Tabor. That would put a different party in control and restore to the city some semblance of two-party government." As it turned out, Tabor garnered only 62,860 votes against 118,936 for Flaherty—a demoralizing defeat for the Republicans.

Yet Pittsburgh voters were clearly ready for a change, and Flaherty provided it, in spades. To the dismay of Democratic leaders, labor unions, and the business community, Flaherty lived up to his "nobody's boy" slogan. The door to the mayor's office was no longer open, angering and embittering those who had assumed that once the campaign was over, the new mayor naturally would reach out to various constituencies. His stance signaled the end of the City Hall–business alliance that had made the Renaissance possible.

For reasons seemingly beyond the control of politicians and businessmen alike, Pittsburgh's population continued to slip, falling from 604,322 in 1960 to 520,069 in 1969.

Flaherty proved to have an uncanny ability to gauge the public pulse, enabling him to take controversial positions and still retain his popularity. For example, in January 1971, five city plumbers refused to drive trucks formerly assigned to members of teamsters unions. The plumbers were sent home. Protest spread among the workers, as nearly one thousand employees suddenly became "ill." Flaherty called it an illegal strike and refused to talk until the unions ordered members back to work. Judge Loran L. Lewis of the Allegheny County Court of Common Pleas issued an injunction ordering the city to begin collecting garbage immediately from certain institutions where it constituted a health hazard. The city's two newspapers were undergoing a pressmen's strike those first weeks in January, so that it was not until publication recommenced January 18 that the *P-G* was able to carry this report by Tom Hritz, City Hall reporter, on what had happened on January 12: "Mayor Flaherty finally made another move. Publicity-wise, it was a coup. Otherwise, it was ridiculous. Early in the morning, the mayor and [four] of his department heads rented a number of trucks and went out and began collecting the garbage from the institutions cited in Judge Lewis's court order. Television and radio reporters gobbled up every morsel of the incident and Flaherty's popularity among the taxpayers went up about 1000 percent." The unions rushed to blockade the city's garbage transfer station in the West End, but Flaherty outfoxed them by going instead to a sanitary landfill in Washington County. Ultimately, Judge Lewis acted as a mediator and then issued a back-to-work order.

Events outside the confines of the city were also making headlines. The nationwide protests against the Vietnam War came close to home when four students were killed on May 4, 1970, at Kent State University in Ohio, including Allison Krause of the Pittsburgh suburb of Churchill. The *Post-Gazette* published a May 6 editorial, entitled "Tragic Fruits of Violence," which read, in part:

The fatal shooting of students at Kent State University by National Guardsmen is the sort of tragedy all too likely to occur where both sides in a confrontation behave badly. It should be a sobering reminder of the necessity of restraint both by public officials and by people who are protesting the war or any other issue. . . .

Had the Guardsmen, no matter what their provocation, reacted in a better trained and more responsible manner, however, the killing of four students and the injury of others could have been avoided. . . . [But] attacking police and/or troops is, like bull baiting, a dangerous sport in which even the innocent bystander can suffer. . . . People who oppose the president's policy can in a free and democratic manner express their dissent to their elected representatives. They can demonstrate and they can strike. But they cannot be allowed to destroy property and to disrupt and endanger the lives of their fellow citizens if this republic is to survive.

The divisions created in American society by the Vietnam War were mirrored in the *Post-Gazette*'s editorial board. The editor of the editorial page, John Lofton, increasingly had been at odds with Frank Hawkins about the war. The rift had come to a head with the *Post-Gazette*'s endorsement of U.S. Senator Hugh Scott for reelection while Lofton was away. Lofton felt that, as editorial page editor, he should have made the decision. His superiors felt quite otherwise. Hawkins, in particular, was irked because he had only reluctantly agreed to grant Lofton's repeated request for the title of editorial page editor, which he wanted in order to enhance his position in the National Conference of Editorial Writers (NCEW). It would be fifteen years before anyone was given that title again. The upshot was that Lofton decided to leave the *Post-Gazette* for a teaching position at the University of Pittsburgh. He later moved from Pittsburgh to become an editorial writer with the *St. Louis Post-Dispatch*.

On May 14, 1971, came the second strike of the year, one of a seemingly interminable string of strikes—six in all—in the early half of the 1970s. Although the *Post-Gazette* was not the intended object of the strike, it automatically became a victim under the joint operating agreement because its editions could not be printed or distributed. That strike, presaged by deliberate composing room slowdowns that made it difficult for the staff to get the editorial page into print on time, was part of a struggle across the country as newspaper managements sought to move from "hot type" to "cold type." The former referred to slugs of type created by linotypes; the latter referred to a newer photographic process. The advantage for management, but a crisis for the work force, was that this new process would eliminate a great many jobs. The Pittsburgh strike, involving all members of the Newspaper Guild, lasted until August 29, 1971. September 9 was set as the date to resume publication after gearing up again, but on that date, the building service employees' union and Teamsters Local 211 went on strike. Those strikes were settled on September 14, and publication resumed September 20.

That four-month strike was torture for editorial writers, interfering with their ability to comment on such momentous 1971 events as President Nixon's opening dialogues with Communist China, his wage-price freeze, the death of Nikita Khrushchev, and the opening of Heinz Hall as the new home of the Pittsburgh Symphony Orchestra. Department heads and those others who were "exempt" from inclusion in the Newspaper Guild were not eligible for certain strike benefits that the guild provided for its members. A few key reporters also were retained on the payroll, even though they were members of the guild—the paper had to be ready for action when the strike ended. Many staffers augmented their guild strike-benefits by going to work for television and radio stations, which added reporters to fill the news vacuum.

Just after the strike had ended, the *Post-Gazette* and the city of Pittsburgh played host to a convention of the National Conference of Editorial Writers. The NCEW convention was a great success, due in part to several unplanned events. For one thing, the Pittsburgh Pirates baseball team made it to the World Series, which was played the same week as the convention. Guests of the NCEW conference stayed at the same hotel, the Pittsburgh Hilton, where the competing teams were housed, so they shared in all the excitement. The games themselves, between the Pirates and the Baltimore Orioles, necessitated rearranging the convention schedule at some points so that NCEW attendees would not miss an inning.

Another bonus was the unexpectedly contentious nature of the convention's opening ceremony, usually a pro forma affair. Only at the last minute could Calvin Mayne of the *Rochester (N.Y.) Times-Union* persuade Mayor Pete Flaherty to appear. A mayoral welcome was customary wherever a NCEW convention met, but instead of making the dull, inoffensive speech typical of such occasions, Flaherty uttered some critical remarks about the city's media. He said they would support him were he not questioning three projects dear to the city's urban redevelopment leadership—Three Rivers Stadium, the proposed convention center, and Skybus, a new, driverless rail form of rapid transit. Flaherty said that he was not opposing these projects, but making sure city residents got equitable treatment when it came to paying for them. A *Post-Gazette* article of October 14, 1971, called "Mayor Blames His Press Ills on Three Projects," reported Flaherty as stating: "While the press has not smiled on me in this city, they would lend their support to me if I supported these three projects—projects that will require huge outlays of public money and heavy annual tax subsidies." Asked about the infrequency of his press conferences, Flaherty declared: "The problem is that the press speaks of communication when what they mean is support for their programs."

That presentation prompted another unscheduled event. After the mayor left, Bill Block rose from the audience to offer a rebuttal. As reported on October 14, 1971, Block asserted that the *P-G* favored building a convention center but felt the mayor's choice of a South Side site was a poor one; although the cost of Three Rivers Stadium exceeded first estimates, the stadium was still good for the city; Flaherty's opposition to Skybus was blocking the imagination needed to develop an improved rapid transit system; and the *P-G* had vigorously supported him on such major issues as his efforts to cut the city payroll in the face of stiff opposition from the municipal employee unions.

The final years of the Hawkins era at the *Post-Gazette* were filled with national and international news, including the Yom Kippur War of 1973, the subsequent oil crisis which brought long lines at the gasoline pumps, and Watergate. The *Post-Gazette* drew particular attention, however, over its endorsement in the 1972 presidential race. At a heated conference in the publisher's office, it became clear that both Block and Hawkins intended to endorse President Nixon for reelection.[4] Block also, however, requested a counter-editorial to accompany the endorsement. The *Post-Gazette* editorial page on October 24, 1972, thus carried a unique combination of texts. In the regular editorial slot on the left-hand side, Hawkins endorsed Nixon, though he did not attempt to portray the president as a saint:

More than any presidential election campaign within our memory, this year's is focused more on what is wrong with the candidates than on what is right. . . . That makes a choice much more difficult than if one candidate could be portrayed as Galahad and the other as Lucifer. . . .

From Mr. Nixon's long record in public service emerges the portrait of an unlovable and not always credible professional politician who is, nonetheless, skillful and competent. Despite his streak of huckersterism, he gives us a greater sense of confidence than we can find in the amateurish and strident campaigning of Senator McGovern.

This is the first time in his three races for President that the *Post-Gazette* is endorsing Mr. Nixon. On balance we feel that, despite his shortcomings, he should remain in the White House for another four years. Given a clear mandate of the voters and a better hold on Congress, we believe that the President can go far to redeem his pledges.

Down the right-hand of the page ran the unsigned counter-editorial, entitled, "Presidential Choice: An editorial dissent"

Because of a division of opinion within the editorial board of the *P-G* on whom to endorse for president, the dissenting board members were asked to express their view, which follows:

. . . We believe that nearly a decade of political opportunism and a brutal, unjust war have made Americans forget that they are one people, with the right and the capacity, given the proper leadership, to respect each other and to feel proud and confident toward their future as a nation united by the best qualities that human nature has to offer. . . .

Mr. Nixon did not create the race issue around which busing has spun poisonous clouds of hate and fear. But he exacerbated it. . . . If Mr. Nixon deserves at least a modicum of praise in some areas of foreign policy, we hope that no man in the U.S. Presidency ever again will allow the good name of the office and of the nation and people for which it stands to be sullied by seeming to turn his back on such a national disgrace as the "Watergate affair." . . . He [McGovern] will, we believe, turn his country away from overreliance on the military and overgenerosity to those who least need it and back to a temperate internationalism and a responsibly human concern for the masses of people who live in his—and our—nation.

The page also included a Cy Hungerford cartoon, "In the Middle of a Flood," portraying Uncle Sam on an elephant with a Nixon head and long nose, saying, "It's no time to swap an elephant for a Donkey!" The elephant was chasing a donkey with a McGovern face and long ears in a flood entitled "The world—Vietnam and National Problems." Two years later, when the Watergate scandal fully unfolded, it was a disillusioned Hawkins who wrote the *Post-Gazette* editorial that it was time for Nixon to go.

Strikes continued to plague the *Post-Gazette* and the *Press* during the mid-1970s. The fourth and fifth strikes, both by Teamsters Local 211, stopped work briefly from January 3 to January 5, 1974, and again from March 31 to April 4, 1974; publication in the latter case resumed only on May 16. Block continued to reassure the temporarily pared-down crew that the JOA was in place for another quarter-century, at least until 1999, ensuring the *Post-Gazette*'s survival for at least that long. On one labor front, however, matters came to a head across the country as major newspapers worked out a three-point "buy-out" bargain with typographer union locals to make possible the transition to the new technology and the consequent slimming of printers' ranks. The settlement amounted to recognition by each side of the long-range concerns of the other. That pattern set by the *Washington Post,* the *New York Times,* and other newspapers of various sizes was the basis for an agreement Scripps Howard made with Pittsburgh's Typographical Union Local 7 during yet another strike.

That agreement did not affect the teamsters, who struck again in the summer of 1975, from June 27 to July 25. The settlement of that strike, however, brought relative peace for the *Press* and the *Post-Gazette* for the next seventeen years. The succession of strikes took a damaging toll, especially in terms of circulation. Every time there was a strike and subscribers went without a paper, a large number did not resubscribe when the paper was back in operation. The *P-G*'s circulation had dropped from 234,345 in 1970 to 196,077 in 1975. The *Press,* too, had been hurt, with its daily circulation tumbling from 346,230 in 1970 before the strikes to 270,025 in 1975. Its Sunday circulation fell from 741,267 in 1970 to 662,243 in 1975. Provisions in the labor contracts hurt, too. During the ten-year period from 1965 to 1975, the *Post-Gazette* instituted three price increases. On May 6, 1968, the price went from seven cents to ten cents, or fifty cents a week for home delivery; on August 3, 1970, the price for home delivery went to sixty cents a week; on October 22, 1973, during the oil crisis, the daily price went to fifteen cents and the home delivery price rose to ninety cents a week. In each case, the teamsters were guaranteed against any loss of earnings.

The knowledge that Hawkins was approaching his sixty-fifth birthday in 1976 led to speculation as to whether he would be retiring and, if so, who would be his successor. William Block himself settled the matter by hiring of John Craig of Wilmington, Delaware, to be his assistant. It quickly became apparent that Craig was the incoming editor, just as it was likewise apparent that Hawkins had not been involved in the process and was not very happy about that. Block later explained:

I always picked the executives, leaving the hiring for the newsroom mostly to Joe Shuman. At that point I didn't see anybody internally for the job of editor. I met Craig in Philadelphia in 1976 and found him to be a pretty lively guy. His history was one of considerable independence. A man of considerable energy, he had worked for the Duponts and he resigned—or was fired—from the Wilmington paper where he had worked as reporter, editorial writer, managing editor, and editor, climbing the whole rung. I didn't check with the Dupont people, because they certainly weren't on his side. I brought him in as assistant to me, where he got acquainted with the community and with the staff. True, I didn't consult with Frank. I don't think he was too fond of Craig. But things were ready when Frank retired—I wasn't pushing him; he had decided to retire. I was fond of Frank and would not have pushed him.[5]

Craig had these recollections of the process: "I got in touch with a headhunter, Hilton Wasserman, and through him got in touch with Bill Block. I talked with Paul Block Jr., also. We met in Philadelphia in the Berkeley Hotel in the spring of 1976. I felt comfortable with the opportunity. I had wanted to operate in the Northeast. Frank Hawkins didn't know about my selection, nor did [managing editor] Bill Deibler, who many thought was in line for the job. The first they knew was when they saw a [Block-placed] notice on the newsroom bulletin board.[6]

Before Craig actually took the editor's seat in September 1977, he spent considerable time visiting other newspapers to learn from their operations. Even though he sat in on some staff meetings, his visits to the *Post-Gazette* were intermittent and seldom on a personal get-acquainted basis. So there was some apprehension within the staff. Even though Hawkins could be brusque and even cold at times, he was courtly and had been a known quantity when he—like his predecessor Andrew Bernhard—took the editor's chair. Neither had rocked the boat. Would Craig be different?

Chapter 14

Catching Up

———◆———

J OHN CRAIG's evaluation of the *Post-Gazette* when he became editor in 1977 was, to put it charitably, that it was behind the times. He felt it was still traumatized by the long string of strikes it had endured in the early 1970s. Furthermore, management seemed too intimidated by its 1960 joint operating agreement with Scripps Howard and the *Pittsburgh Press* to make operational changes, especially those that required spending more money.

Much needed to be done internally, and Craig believed it could be. The *Post-Gazette* had many assets that could be built upon: "It was very rarely that I would talk to anyone who would say, 'I don't read the *Post-Gazette*,'" he said. However, Craig felt that both the *P-G* and the *Press* had fallen behind national newspaper trends, such as in suburban coverage and typography. Already, for example, his old newspaper in Wilmington had moved into zone editions to extend circulation to outlying areas. "Here I found only one reporter, Ken Fisher, working a telephone to cover everything outside of Pittsburgh. And the *Press* was old-fashioned, too, with no suburban operations."[1] Failure to move ahead in that direction in the 1960s had left the field open to suburban papers and powerful competitors in neighboring county-seat towns such as the *Washington Observer-Reporter*, the *Greensburg Tribune-Review*, the *But-*

John J. Craig,
editor (right), with
publisher William
Block Sr.
(Courtesy *Pittsburgh
Post-Gazette*)

ler Eagle, and the *Beaver County Times.* Craig also felt embarrassed by
what he considered the old-fashioned character of features such as Joe
Browne's folksy "Our Towne" column and Mike Kalina's restaurant coverage. To him, they seemed like something published at the end of
World War II.

Typography was another area where Craig felt both papers were
quite behind the times. One initial move he made was to "remove all
the clutter" around the *Post-Gazette*'s flag—the newspaper's name
across the top of the front page—and to reset it in an antique German
typeface. In graphics, he found the practice of doctoring photographs
by airbrushing them to be heretical. Here was an instance, he argued,
where changes could be made without spending a lot more money, in
order to end what he considered an operation "completely isolated from
the larger world journalistically." He pushed for a general improvement
in graphics, well before the revolution that occurred in 1982 when the
Gannett chain introduced *USA Today,* which used graphs and maps to
enliven its stories.

Craig set upon a deliberate path of bringing minorities onto the staff by drawing from an Urban Journalism Workshop for minorities run by Professor Samuel Adams of Kansas State University, using a program of newsroom internships, and working to promote copy messengers into copy-reading or reporting tasks. Craig hired Al Donalson, an African American reporter from the *Press,* to be an assistant city editor, a supervisory-level position.

The loose ethics practiced in some areas of the paper bothered Craig. The sports department, for example, followed a custom universal in American journalism at the time, by which Pittsburgh's professional teams paid travel expenses, including food and lodging, for the writers covering them. Moreover, sportswriters were utilized as scorers by the Pirates and paid fifty dollars a game. That system faltered when *Pittsburgh Press* writer Don Donovan's call of a "hit" instead of an "error" cost Pirates pitcher Bruce Kison a no-hitter on June 23, 1979, producing acrimony on all sides. The Pirates won 7-0, but Kison's complaint about being "robbed" of a Hall of Fame opportunity brought the scoring practice to public light. The *Post-Gazette*'s Charles Feeney was required immediately to quit performing that role. John Troan of the *Press* announced, "We would like to invoke the ban right now, but it would be unfair to the league for us to change the rules in the middle of the season." Donovan was allowed to finish the season as a scorer, and the *Press* compensated him for the income he subsequently lost. The system of "freebies" for reporters extended much further: staff attended Pirates games paying only the sales tax on the tickets, and movie and television companies often paid for entertainment or trips. In 1974, television critic Win Fanning was photographed receiving a handful of dollars when attending a screening in New York. As it happened, the television industry considered it easier to hand out cash for such expenses as taxis, rather than going through the rigmarole of requiring expense accounts. Bill Block was appalled at the harmful publicity, however, particularly when CBS's *60 Minutes* featured the incident, and Fanning was nearly fired. Craig was disturbed at the sight at Christmastime of a truck backing up to the *Post-Gazette* for a writer to take home all the "gifts" from corporations he covered. Craig's efforts at improving ethical standards got a strong helping hand from Bill Deibler, the managing editor, who persuaded leaders of the Newspaper Guild to accept some changes in the contract to make possible more stringent rules on the subject. Deibler, as a correspondent to the state legislature some years before, had created an uproar among his colleagues in Harrisburg by urging a rule against accepting gifts from politicians and lobbyists. Deibler's sense of integrity had been upset by seeing correspondents' desks in the Capitol Press Room piled high with gifts of liquor, turkeys, hams, and the like in November and December. His success in this cleanup endeavor did not endear Deibler to many of his associates.

At first, Craig made few staff changes—to the surprise of those who feared there might be a housecleaning. He kept Jim Alexander as managing editor and Gerard "Gerry" Patterson as city editor. Gradually, he brought in new people, some the best and brightest from the *Pittsburgh Press* and from outside the city. Craig noted with satisfaction that *Press* staff were willing to come to the *P-G,* but almost no one left the *Post-Gazette* for the *Press.* Over the years, however, there often was unease as Craig, in the interests of what he called "creative tension," would periodically shake up the staff or the organizational chart, and otherwise alter routines. More than once he would put two people in a single job slot and leave them to "fight it out" for the ultimate appointment, adding to what his critics considered both inefficiency and insecurity.

Craig rather quickly abolished the traditional women's page, feeling it was outmoded in an era of rising feminism. The "Seen" column remained, however. Written by Jim Richardson, a hairdresser at Kaufmann's store, the column was a roundup of the names of prominent people glimpsed at charity and other social events. Though the subject of snickers by some ardent feminists and others, the column proved to be popular and widely read, even by those who insisted they would not be caught dead reading it.

A few years earlier, the *Pittsburgh Press* had challenged the ban on the use of male and female distinctions in classified advertisements for employment. The Pittsburgh Commission on Human Relations ruled out such differentials in September 1969. The *Press* appealed, contending this was not a matter of discrimination but of usefulness to job seekers. The Pennsylvania Commonwealth Court denied the appeal, but the Pennsylvania Supreme Court reversed that ruling, upholding the *Press*'s position. The case then went through the federal courts, and the U.S. Supreme Court had the last word: want ads by gender were forbidden, and all newspapers had to comply.

Craig was surprised to find that in a city surpassed only by New York and Chicago in the number of corporate headquarters, the *Post-Gazette* business page had only two staffers. One, Jack Markowitz, was essentially a columnist; the other, Maurice "Sully" Sullivan, handled the pages containing stocks and other business statistics. Enlarging that staff became a priority, because by that time, American business journalism was following the *Wall Street Journal*'s pattern of serious investigation into business matters, rather than running affirmative articles that sometimes were little more than rewritten press releases from the businesses themselves.

During this period, the *Post-Gazette* introduced another succession of price increases. Mail subscription prices in all zones were raised on September 5, 1977. Partly because of the steep inflation during the early years of the Carter administration, the daily price went up on April 2, 1979, to $0.20, home delivery increased to $1.20 per week, and commissions for the Teamsters per one hundred copies sold rose from the previous $0.25 to $0.275. Other price increases were inaugurated until by 1985, the price for home delivery was $1.50. Circulation that year was 174,391. One result of this pattern was that on March 17, 1986, a total of 3,701 mail subscriptions were cut off because of mailroom costs that were excessively high and could not be reduced any other way. During that period, the *Press*'s daily circulation declined more slowly—from 270,075 in 1976 to 267,158 in 1980 and to 245,832 in 1985.

The circulation problems of both the *Post-Gazette* and the *Press* certainly were not helped by the continued decline of Pittsburgh's population. Even though some of those who left the city moved to the surrounding suburbs, the core city's 1980 census was still alarming in that it showed a population of 423,928, nearly one hundred thousand less than the 1970 figure of 520,069. Not long after, another devastating factor, the loss in the early 1980s of nearly one hundred thousand industrial jobs in the region due to the demise of steel mills and other related plants, caused a further drop in the city's population.

This decline of the steel industry occasioned sharper reporting than either management or labor was used to. The *Post-Gazette,* however, as baffled as anyone as to a remedy in a world with a surplus of steel, continued to advocate free-trade policies as in the best long-run interests of America and the world. The *P-G* was unimpressed with a sideshow purporting to represent the interests of the steelworkers facing unemployment. The Denominational Ministry Strategy (DMS—later DMX) was formed by a small group of radical clergy and labor leaders who used disruptive tactics developed by Saul Alinsky, a Chicago labor activist. The DMS particularly targeted the Mellon banking system, contending it had failed to invest in the Monongahela Valley, resulting in widespread unemployment. The group's tactics included putting fish in Mellon safety deposit boxes to rot and smell. The organization also perpetrated guerrilla warfare tactics on churches attended by captains of industry and commerce, such as Shadyside Presbyterian. On Sunday night, December 16, 1984, as congregation members ate a Christmas pageant dinner, four men wearing gas masks burst into the room and hurled balloons filled with dye and skunk water at the diners, including children. The incident received wide coverage in the days that followed. On Tuesday, December 18, a *P-G* headline writer could not resist a pun: "Police on scent of skunk water bombers." An editorial the following day, called, "A skunk-like act," expressed disgust with the whole DMS approach:

So it has come to this. Now, more than ever, it is time to ask some pertinent questions. Just what sort of a cause is it that must be advanced in this way? Surely a noble cause does not require its followers to cover their faces. And surely the fact that intruders wore gas masks like furtive cowards is no coincidence.

What is the point of denouncing "corporate evil" when at least some of those who would rail against it are apparently prepared to condone such outrageous behavior? Where is the decency? How, in God's name, does this help? . . .

After all, the intruders came to a church that had had unwelcome visits before and they left skunk oil—which has become almost the symbol of the recent protests. Indeed, although they denied all knowledge of it later, protesters and some sympathetic clergy just happened to be around the church when the intruders came in. One final question: Does making little children cry help the unemployed?

The following Easter the activists, accompanied by actor David Soul, carried scrap iron to the church. At that point, the DMS lost whatever support it had previously garnered.

Under the Craig regime, the *P-G* took a more critical view of urban renewal projects, in contrast to its virtual cheerleading for any and all urban redevelopment proposals during the Renaissance. Questions were asked and objections reported, often to the bewilderment and consternation of architects, builders, and especially officials arranging financing. Even before Craig's arrival, some community leaders wondered why the *Post-Gazette* had turned into such a skeptic, undermining hopes of bringing to fruition projects that they considered to be in the interest of the community.

The sports pages also changed under Craig, who brought in new writers from both the *Press* and elsewhere. Throughout the nation, though, sportswriting was already changing as a genre. American journalism was entering a new era in which the transgressions, as well as the praiseworthy activities, of individual athletes were reported. Gambling, sexual philandering, wife-swapping, drug use—all had become as much a part of the coverage as batting averages, touchdown records, and United Way appearances. Gone was the day when sportswriters concealed the off-the-field antics of such idols as Babe Ruth and Ty Cobb. Not every reader appreciated this.

Craig made fewer changes to the editorial page, though he envisioned his role differently than Hawkins had: he would be writing few editorials, as he intended to spend his time supervising changes in the rest of the paper. At the same time, he took charge of the editorial board's morning conferences in a way that Hawkins had not, by introducing the subjects he felt deserved comment before going around the room to ask the input of others. Craig also restricted letters to the editor, so that individuals were limited to a maximum of four published letters each year (an exception was made for public officials responding to letters aimed at them). The new policy encouraged writers who had seen the same people's views appear repeatedly and assumed there was no room for newcomers. Even for frequent writers, the policy put a premium on being published and improved the overall quality of the page.

Craig battled for additional op-ed space for letters and more syndicated columns, part of his struggle for a larger "newshole"—a term for the portion of the newspaper allocated for the news department after advertisements have been placed. Frank Hawkins had wanted an op-ed page but had felt stymied by the JOA. For the *P-G,* any hopes of enlarging the newshole would mean persuading the Blocks to spend more, as well as bargaining with *Press* executives since they handled all the advertising.

To Craig, this state of affairs underlined the "complete sense of hopelessness" he felt at the *Post-Gazette* concerning relations with the Scripps Howard officials at the *Press.* "Scripps Howard was in charge, and we could do little about it. I completely resisted this, maybe because of my personality. We had the edge because we were the morning paper, and morning papers elsewhere were enlarging. But the *P-G* would just pay its bills and go along. If you looked at that dispassionately, it meant a steady decline—and at a time when morning newspapers elsewhere were enlarging."

The problem in Pittsburgh, as Craig saw it, was that the *Press* was behaving as though it were a monopoly, and set prices accordingly. The *Press* would set advertising rates to suit itself and allocate space so that "we had no ads in the *P-G* to speak of," Craig recalled. In fairness, however, the succession of strikes had hampered the joint operation. After each strike, circulation for both papers fell below pre-strike levels. Also, when Gimbel's closed its downtown store in September 1986, the papers lost five million dollars in annual advertising revenues. Even though that was only 3 percent of the total, there was no way such a loss could be made up.

Hanging over the *Post-Gazette* was the question of what would happen when the JOA ran out in 1999. Craig thought the paper should prepare itself to meet this challenge by utilizing the huge asset of being a morning paper in good repute, rather than letting it depreciate. He wrote a detailed report outlining ways he felt the newspaper could situate itself for life after 1999. This document had four parts—circulation, advertising, financial, and a summary—each buttressed by a host of figures comparing the *Post-Gazette* with the *Press,* plus comparisons with neighboring county papers and similar JOAs across the country. Craig's report stated that, although the *P-G* still had "strong appeal in its primary market, . . . there were much better investments during the 1980s than the *P-G,* if making money was the goal." For both papers, the future looked bleak.

Craig then listed six possible courses of action, including eliminating the *Post-Gazette,* reducing it to a weekly or invoking similar contraction measures, and maintaining the status quo with continuing uncertainty and damage to staff morale. Only a sixth possibility appealed to him: "Get ready to operate an a.m. paper on our own. Advantage: Control our own destiny. Disadvantage: Where to get cash flow; also increased tensions with Scripps Howard's Pittsburgh managers likely, if not inevitable." To move in that direction, Craig outlined, the *P-G* management would need to—

- Learn about our business. Why advertisers do and do not use *P-G*, and why people do or do not purchase the *P-G*.

- Improve the editorial product, which means spending more money on space. First, to improve the daily national and international news report, which is not as good as the *Press*'s; second, to improve the *P-G*'s daily TV, sports and business reports, which are as good or better than the *Press*'s, but not as good as they should be.

- Hold the line on rates . . . until we can be assured of equality on money expended on circulation promotion for the two dailies.

- Promote the paper. Get past public confusion about the independence of the two newspapers. Why is the *P-G* not promoted regularly in the Sunday *Press*?

- Diversify the business.

- Expand local support. Because of Bill Block's leadership, the *P-G* enjoys a significant advantage over the *Press* when it comes to being seen by community leaders as an enterprise that is of Pittsburgh and for Pittsburgh. The *Press* for all its economic clout has a bit of a carpetbagger's image, largely as a result of Scripps Howard policies.

To Craig's dismay, no one paid attention to his position paper. However, it would later prove useful in the antitrust hearings before the U.S. Justice Department during the 1992 merger effort. The problem of obtaining a larger newshole turned out to be somewhat less intractable than Craig feared. Over the years, the *P-G* managed to acquire more space from Scripps Howard, partly because of the addition of the zone editions and the concomitant new advertising revenue.

The *Post-Gazette* and the *Press* were both faced with how to handle the news of the extraordinary events occurring at Three Mile Island. At three o'clock in the morning on March 28, 1979, Pat Boyle, the *Press*'s Harrisburg correspondent, got a tip from one of his sources that "something big"—no specifics yet—had happened at the nuclear power plant at Three Mile Island on the Susquehanna River just south of Harrisburg. Boyle relayed the information to the Pittsburgh office, where it lay dormant until Leo Koberlein, executive editor, glanced at the memo. Koberlein scribbled the response, "Let the wires handle it," meaning the *Press* would obtain its information from the wire services. That is how the *Press* proceeded, apart from a story by John Taylor of the Harrisburg bureau and an article by Dolores Frederick, science writer, on the reaction at the Duquesne Light Company's Beaver Valley Power Plant at Shippingport, northwest of Pittsburgh. In contrast, the *Post-Gazette* sent Stuart Brown, Mike Moyle, Al Neri, and Carolyn Freeman to Harrisburg to augment the work of Ed Jensen, the *P-G*'s Harrisburg correspondent. Even this fell far short of the galvanic activity ordered at the *Philadelphia Inquirer* by its dynamic executive editor, Gene Roberts, who immediately reserved an entire motel near the nuclear site to house a staff of more than a dozen reporters, photographers, and copy readers to handle every possible detail of what developed into a milestone event in the history of nuclear power—a near-meltdown of an atomic reactor. The effort paid off handsomely when in 1980 the *Inquirer* won the Pulitzer Prize in the local news category for its coverage of the event.

Much of the credit for the changes that came at the *Press* is given to two individuals, first, Madelyn (Maddy) Ross and, subsequently, Angus McEachran. Ross, a native Pittsburgher, came to the *Press* from journalism training at Indiana University of Pennsylvania and the Ph.D. program at the University of Pittsburgh, plus three summers interning at the *Press*. When she began to work full-time in 1972, she "felt the *Press* was on a downward slide—awful, considering the talent of the people here. The morale was terrible. We talked about sports but not how to cover it. I was a complainer. I wanted to work for a great newspaper, but didn't want to leave Pittsburgh. So what was the choice? When there was an opening for something different, I would volunteer. First, for the zones. And for features. Without realizing it, I was putting myself through a sort of management training."[2] In 1974 she attended a three-day writers' workshop at the *St. Petersburg (Fla.) Times*, headed by writer Peter Clark. When she came back and suggested holding similar workshops to editor John Troan and managing editor Ralph Brehm, they agreed, with two conditions: she must do it on her own time, and they wanted to be present. The latter apparently was in line with Scripps Howard worries that letting staffers get together for any purpose might lead to forming a Newspaper Guild chapter like the one at the *P-G*. A notice went up about a brown-bag luncheon and writing session in a third floor conference room. The response—a jam-packed room—surprised everyone. Ross handed out an article by Gay Talese of the *New York Times* and asked for comments. One staff member remarked: "If we wrote this piece, it would never get into the *Pittsburgh Press*." That led to a discussion of rules and restrictions at the paper, but people left the session with an exhilarated feeling.[3]

Ross recalled that after the meeting, a group of reporters met informally about what to do next. "We decided to throw out all the rules. Use brand names if we want to. Quote sources not usually allowed. Let the editors save us from ourselves, if necessary." So that no one would feel left out, Ross sent out summary messages to everyone, including the editors. She gave full credit to Troan and Brehm for letting matters take their course. The brown-bag lunches continued, with the ground rules understood all around. Ross recalled, "You checked your title at the door. At the meeting, all were equal. We had clerks telling Ralph Brehm he was full of bull. By declaring it that way, it worked. We started out with gripes and ended up with joy. In the newsroom you began finding people talking about journalism—not about a game but about covering the game." Quite as important, the break-the-rules pact among certain reporters was working. "Nothing bad happened. We soon began seeing stories published where the reporter had broken the rules. The editors were sensitive, cutting some things out but leaving others in." Gradually, the focus of the lunches expanded, and questions were posed such as: Why not more flamboyant magazine pieces? Why do we use photographers as taxi drivers? Ross sensed that "you could feel morale starting to grow. People were talking: we're really not as bad as we thought."

Troan retired in 1982 and Scripps Howard brought in Angus McEachran, who was noted in the trade for allegedly having once hurled a typewriter through a newsroom window in exasperation. At the *Pittsburgh Press*, however, he had the reputation of being straightforward and unequivocal. McEachran brought a different style to running the editorial page. Of course, both he and Troan followed the policy on national matters set by the Scripps Howard editors in Cincinnati. Local editors were allowed to override these policies to some extent, if they felt it was in the local paper's best interests. All Scripps Howard papers, however, had to run the same endorsement editorials in national elections. McEachran had daily meetings with the editorial writers, whereas Troan had held one or two a week, filling in with smaller sessions around his desk when necessary. Troan edited every editorial, no matter who wrote it, wanting to put his stamp on it; McEachran "saw" them. Troan valued explanatory editorials; McEachran wanted to have a clear, sharp voice on every issue. Each editor had favorite issues— Troan often campaigned against those he called "payjackers," members of Congress and of the state legislature who raised their own salaries, sometimes in devious ways. McEachran's particular interests were ethics and the First Amendment.

The development of a McEachran-Ross regime proved to have a remarkable impact on the newspaper's place in Pittsburgh journalism. When Ross approached McEachran soon after he arrived, she found out that her superiors had been sending her summation memos to Scripps Howard headquarters in Cincinnati where they were copied and sent out to all the newspapers in the chain. At that point, Ross was special projects editor, heading the *Press*'s investigative reporting endeavors. Within a year, McEachran named her managing editor. Ross recounted: "When Angus looked around for an M.E., for someone knowing the whole operation, someone seen as a leader in the newsroom, he found me—a combination of Mother Teresa and Attila the Hun." Furthermore, McEachran assured her that he would help her get things done. The upshot, Ross said, was that her ideas "got legs and resources, and we started to take off. People here no longer thought Edsels, but Rolls Royces. There was no stopping us—we were still on the march when the [1992] strike hit us." By 1991, the *Press*'s daily circulation was 226,188; and the Sunday circulation was 555,676.

The fruits of the McEachran-Ross team became spectacularly evident when the *Press* won the Pulitzer Prize two years in a row. The first, the winner in 1986 for specialized reporting, was a an investigative series on the organ transplant field, written by Mary Pat Flaherty and Andrew Schneider and closely edited by Ross herself and by Matthew Kennedy, special projects editor. McEachran's only stipulation was that every quote had to be pinned to the person saying it—no easy out such as "a knowledgeable source said." The reporters protested that it would make it impossible to nail down some of the details, but McEachran insisted. The research, which uncovered greed, favoritism, neglect, and criminality in the illegal sale of organs, often procured from poor people, took the reporters to such places as India and Japan, at an ultimate fifty thousand–dollar cost to the *Press*. The series, which ran November 3 to 8, 1985, had a particular resonance for Pittsburgh transplant-surgeon Dr. Thomas Starzl, who had put the University of Pittsburgh Medical Center on the world map in that field. Moreover, University of Pittsburgh was, at that time, at the center of a controversy regarding whether scarce organs should be kept for hospitals in the region where they were "harvested," or, as Pitt preferred, sent where they were needed most. This controversy has continued into the twenty-first century.

The second *Press* Pulitzer was awarded in 1987 for a series by Andrew Schneider and Matthew Brelis on the previously ignored problem of airline pilots flying while intoxicated. It highlighted a flawed and dangerous air travel system that allowed sick and drug- and alcohol-impaired pilots to take the controls in some of the nation's biggest airliners. The award encompassed editorials and editorial cartoons that accompanied the series, which ran from September 21 through December 21, 1986, and was guided to completion by city editor Flora Rathburn and Madelyn Ross.

The irony was that the *Press* should have won a Pulitzer twenty years earlier, had it handled its entry correctly. The story concerned the 1966 "Mountain Man" kidnapping of a seventeen-year-old girl at Shade Gap in the central Pennsylvania mountains. For eight days, May 11–18, 1966, the nation followed the ordeal of Peggy Ann Bradnick, kidnapped from her home by Bill Hollenbaugh, who led law enforcement officials a chase across the adjacent hills. The *Press* sent Scott Rombach and Ralph Brehm to cover the event. They rode over to the Huntingdon area with Butler County peace officers whom Rombach knew from his days with the *Butler Eagle*. Rombach was right at the scene when Hollenbaugh was flushed out of a cabin and killed in the ensuring firefight. In two bylined May 18 stories for the *Press,* Rombach personalized the event: "Hollenbaugh was firing out over our heads—we were in a little gap that was actually lower than the troopers behind us—and the troopers were winging shots back and we were caught in the middle. . . . When I looked at Hollenbaugh, he started to topple. When he fell, Peggy Ann came running out to me and I grabbed her. She was hysterical, crying and saying, 'Thank God! Thank God! I'm safe! I'm safe!'" Rombach's stories were carried on the United Press International wire service and utilized by scores of papers, including the *Chambersburg (Pa.) Public Opinion,* whose reporter also had been following the story. Both papers entered the Pulitzer competition, the

Chambersburg paper in the local news category for individual effort and the *Press,* for some reason, in the public service category. In those years, the Pulitzer committee was not allowed to switch entries from one category to another that it thought more appropriate. As a result, on the day of the Pulitzer announcement, Rombach's compatriots in the newsroom saw him pounding his fists on the wire machine in the utmost frustration. The Pulitzer had gone to Robert V. Cox of the Chambersburg paper for stories that had relied heavily on Rombach's firsthand accounts. Rombach was so angry over his superiors entering his stories under an inappropriate category that he resigned and went to work in the public relations department of the Jones & Laughlin steel company.

In 1987, the *Post-Gazette* provided a striking example of how a newspaper can change long-held editorial views. Since 1911, the *P-G* had supported the at-large elections of Pittsburgh City Council members. However, after the demise of Mayor Lawrence's "Balkan succession" system, by which different ethnic and interest groups were guaranteed at least one seat on the council, the representation of African Americans had dwindled from two seats to one, and then to zero when William Robinson failed to win reelection in 1985. Bill Block thought it was wrong for a group that composed 24 percent of the city's population to have no representative on Council. He led the editorial board to a consensus that the newspaper's policy of three-quarters of a century should be changed. In such cases, there are three ways to go about making the change known to the readership. One is to write editorials that gradually slide the paper to the new position, hoping that no one will notice. The second is to write an editorial abruptly setting forth the new position, without explanation—again hoping most readers will not realize a significant shift has taken place. The third is to acknowledge openly the change and explain the reasoning to the readers. The *Post-Gazette* chose the third route, editorially calling for a change in procedure so that council members would be elected by district. When the council held a referendum on this issue in the 1987 primary election, the *P-G* published a May 18, election-eve editorial, urging voters to approve it in order to open the way for better neighborhood representation, more diverse political representation, and more minority members of the council. The referendum mandating the change passed two to one. Ironically, in that same primary, a black candidate, Otis Lyons Jr., won a seat on a citywide basis, coming in fourth of the five top Democratic winners. The practical outcome of the referendum was that henceforth the council always had at least two, and often three, African American members.

In other political matters, the *P-G*'s views sometimes prevailed and sometimes did not. Editorial efforts aimed at influencing mayoral races did not fare so well. First, there had been the Pete Flaherty fiasco for the *Post-Gazette* in 1969. Then, when Flaherty was called to Washington, D.C., in 1977 to join President Jimmy Carter's Justice Department, little-known council president Richard Caliguiri, age forty-six, took the mayor's chair on what everyone thought was an interim basis. Many assumed that once Flaherty was gone, the way would be open for Tom Foerster, chair of the Allegheny County Board of Commissioners, to fulfill his dream of becoming mayor. Caliguiri, however, did not see things that way. He stayed out of the Democratic primary, which Foerster easily won. Meanwhile, Caliguiri steadily gained popularity through a street-repaving campaign and by working with an attention-starved business community to launch a downtown revitalization through skyscraper building that came to be known as Renaissance II. In the November general election, he ran on a "Pittsburghers for Caliguiri" independent ticket, although the Foerster forces claimed this was unfair if not actually illegal. In its election-eve editorial of November 7, 1977, the *P-G* enthusiastically endorsed Caliguiri: "Mayor Caliguiri has done a most workmanlike job since taking over after Pete Flaherty resigned to join the U.S. Justice Department in Washington. Pittsburgh is now on the move, with action on street paving and repair and the completion of the Market Square renovation being specific evidence that Mr. Caliguiri can get things done." Caliguiri defeated Foerster and continued in office, winning two more elections, and becoming one of the most beloved mayors in Pittsburgh history before he died on May 6, 1988, from amyloidosis, a disease in which the body accumulates deposits of abnormal proteins, causing irreparable damage.

Once again a Pittsburgh City Council president, Sophie Masloff, took the mayor's seat. Going into the primary election, City Controller Tom Flaherty was endorsed by the Democratic organization, and Councilman Frank Lucchino was the clear favorite of the business community. State Representative Tom Murphy was a maverick who was not afraid of tangling with the Democratic leadership in the state legislature. The *Post-Gazette,* never impressed with Masloff, became alarmed that Murphy might cut sufficiently into Lucchino's vote to reelect the incumbent mayor. In almost frantic tones, the *P-G* urged Murphy to come to Lucchino's aid, or at least back off of his own effort. One editorial of May 10, 1989, argued, "If you want to change the cast of characters at city hall, shake up the bureaucracy and circumscribe the influence of inveterate political operators, . . . vote for Frank Lucchino on Tuesday. If you want to keep things much as they are, vote for Mayor Masloff—or for Byrd Brown, Tom Flaherty or Tom Murphy, which accomplishes the same thing by a different name." Murphy did not acquiesce to the *Post-Gazette*'s appeal. Moreover, Masloff proved to be more popular that expected, particularly with women. She took 28 percent of the vote to win the primary, which was tantamount to an eventual general-election victory in a heavily Democratic community. Tom Flaherty, incidentally, ended up in fifth place in the six-candidate race, evidence of the increasing hollowness of endorsements by the Democratic Party.

In 1992, the *Post-Gazette* finally won a Pulitzer for the first time since Ray Sprigle had received the 1938 award for his series on the Ku Klux Klan connections of Hugo Black. It was awarded to photographer John Kaplan in the feature photography category for a series of photo and text essays on the diverse lifestyles of seven twenty-one-year-olds. Published over a six-month period starting in July 1991, the series was edited by Mark Roth, assistant managing editor for news.

On the morning the Pulitzers were to be announced, Craig grew increasingly pessimistic as the hours passed with no word. So when the news came over the wires, the newsroom was unprepared. Woodene Merriman, assistant to the publisher, quickly garnered some company money from Ray Burnett, the business manager, and sent clerk Karen Scott to a nearby liquor store to buy champagne. The *P-G* went all-out in savoring the triumph, including sending its top executives to New York for the official awards ceremony. Thus, it was in a New York hotel on a Monday morning, just before the main Pulitzer luncheon event at Columbia University, that John Craig received the startling news that would change everything.

Chapter 15

The 1992 Strike

THE NEWS THAT startled Craig was that the teamsters had gone on strike against the *Pittsburgh Press,* thus also bottling up the *Post-Gazette* because of the joint operating agreement. Craig skipped the Pulitzer Prize luncheon and hopped an airplane for Pittsburgh to manage the new crisis, which involved immediately paring the staff to a skeleton crew as during the strikes two decades earlier. Thus began a management-labor clash that would receive national attention as interested parties watched the effectiveness or failure of contrasting strategies.

Craig was not the only person surprised by the turn of events that would ultimately completely change the Pittsburgh newspaper scene. Maddy Ross, managing editor of the *Press,* said that with all the improvements of the recent years, hopes were high at first that the strike would be short. "No one thought it would end the way it did," she recalled.[1] Because the newsroom was nonunion, having once again fended off the Newspaper Guild the year before, all 220 editors, reporters, photographers, and copyreaders were kept on the job.

The old proverb held in this instance, however: the left hand did not know what the right hand was doing. The Scripps Howard management had decided it was time to trump the teamsters for good. William Burleigh, general editorial manager for Scripps Howard at the time, later emphasized that the problems were not with the Blocks but with the teamsters in particular and the other *Press* unions in general. "The labor costs through union contracts that were far too liberal kept diminishing the profitability of the whole operation. There was featherbedding throughout the whole operation, wasteful practices not directed to improving the delivery of newspapers. We were hamstrung. It was not a question of Scripps Howard being parsimonious. Wages were way above average for newspapers in the United States. But because of the stranglehold of union contracts, when you looked at all American newspapers, we were overspending [in Pittsburgh] for circulation and underspending for editorial operations."[2]

One factor cited by analysts was the fact that Scripps Howard had gone public on June 3, 1988—meaning that an organization that had gotten complacent now had to pay attention to Wall Street and the demands of stockholders for a fair return. This theory is an oversimplification, however, according to Richard Boehne, director of communications for E. W. Scripps, as the overall company is now known (Scripps Howard is an operating subsidiary). A more rigorous approach had started in the 1960s when professional management was brought in to the company. Up to that point, a member of either the Scripps or the Howard family had been in charge, "with a willingness to accept some things that the public wouldn't tolerate." The new management began tackling problem areas one by one, selling the *Cincinnati Post* in 1977 to the Gannett chain; ending a JOA in Cleveland in 1980 in order to sell the *Cleveland Press* to an industrialist, who later closed it; and ridding itself of United Press International in 1982 to Media News Corp. Attention would then have turned to the *Pittsburgh Press*, whether or not Scripps Howard had gone public. Burleigh elaborated, "Wall Street was happy with us, because the whole company was reasonably profitable. But that didn't reflect the company's wishes because, while we were faring well at the other papers, we weren't doing well in Pittsburgh because of the stranglehold by the teamsters. Pittsburgh was never earning back for its shareholders a fair return on the dollar. Better to put that money into a savings and loan account and earn better interest. Ideally, we wanted to be in Pittsburgh for the long term, so something had to be done."[3]

That "something" began to center on the December 30, 1991, end of the corporation's three-year contract with the teamsters. Direct negotiations would be handled by Jimmy Manis, general manager of the *Press*. Joe Pass, attorney for the teamsters and seven other of the eleven unions at the *Press*, was on the brink of taking a long-awaited vacation in Europe with his wife and two daughters. Indeed, Pass thinks that that may have been one reason why Scripps Howard decided to move when it did, thinking that with Pass gone, the unions might find it difficult to get their act together. If so, that strategy was foiled when Pass put off his departure for a day. Pass was still in Pittsburgh on the night a Scripps Howard move set in motion a long-planned change.

Although the specific timing was unexpected, the labor unions had begun making plans for a long strike on July 9, 1991, when a group that became known as the Newspaper Unity Council met in Joe Pass's office on the Monongahela waterfront, two blocks from the *Press* building.[4] Present were Joe "Jo-Jo" Molinero, president of Teamsters Local 211, and other union representatives, including Thomas J. McGrath, from the Washington headquarters of the International Brotherhood of Teamsters; and Harry Tkach, from Newspaper Guild 61, *Post-Gazette*.[5] The minutes of the meeting report that the tone was set immediately when Bill Metz of the Communications Workers of America urged the unions to "try to get support around the city," and to bear in mind the fate of the *Post-Gazette*. At the next Unity Council meeting on October 1, Thomas McGrath suggested that plans should be made to put out a union newspaper in the event of a strike, which he believed might come at the end of the teamsters' contract on December 31. J. E. Pietkiewicz of the mailers' union asked, "What if they lock us out?" Pass replied, "We will tell them we will go with the old agreement. Then we collect unemployment compensation."

On October 22, Scripps Howard announced its plan to cut its teamsters' payroll by moving to a "depot arrangement," which would use adult carriers only, making it possible to deliver bundles of papers to centralized depots rather than to the homes of the 4,500 youth carriers. Manis asserted that the teamster force could be cut from the 628 people employed under the existing 1989 labor contract to 178.[6]

Joe Molinero maintained that the system the *Press* was proposing would not work with less than two hundred teamster drivers. (It was also evident to union officials that it would be politically suicidal for any president to agree to cut nearly three-fourths of his members.) Molinero held that it was impossible to evaluate the demand until the proposed new depot system was laid out, but that at least 378 positions would be needed to maintain it—meaning no more than 250 layoffs.

Molinero was drawing on his long experience in supervising the delivery system before he took over the teamsters' leadership from the famed Teddy Cozza. The U.S. Justice Department had been constantly on the trail of Cozza—a hardheaded, rambunctious man in the mold of such teamster presidents of the postwar era as Jimmy Hoffa—and, finally, on May 9, 1991, had succeeded in having him thrown out of the teamster leadership on grounds of links with organized crime figures. Because Molinero was a much calmer individual than Cozza, Scripps Howard may have thought him a patsy who could be swept aside to make way for the depot plan. Not only did Molinero know the delivery system inside out, however, but he also felt that the teamsters had already made a significant number of cost-saving concessions for Scripps Howard in their 1989 contract.

At Unity Council meetings in December, decisions were made to contest the proposed abandonment of youth carriers. There was talk of union members giving up part of their pay to subsidize the carriers. McGrath suggested that in addition to proposed Unity Council "Unions Together" buttons, there be a separate button for the preservation of the youth carriers—in black and gold, the colors of Pittsburgh's professional sports teams. He also proposed securing many names for a unity letterhead, including the steelworkers, teachers, firefighters, transit workers, and clergy, with Monsignor Charles Owen Rice, the famed "labor priest," specifically mentioned.

The contract deadline passed with the arrival of the new year, and still no lockout or strike occurred. On January 1, 1992, the *P-G*'s single copy price at newsstands, coin boxes, and corner outlets was increased from twenty-five cents to thirty cents. At a January 8 session of the Unity Council, a lengthy list was formulated of things to do "if the company keeps pulling our chain to get us to go out on strike." Some expressed worries about involvement in the *Post-Gazette*'s annual Dapper Dan Rally, a local charity event. McGrath insisted, "We are not attacking the *P-G*. We are trying to help it." Two meetings later, the subject came up again. After Molinero insisted, "Our fight is not with Bill Block," Sonny Shannon of Pressmen's Local 9 said, "I'm willing to concede." George Curtin from AFL-CIO's national headquarters was designated as coordinator for the Unity Council—one of the first indications that the Pittsburgh impasse was gaining attention within the national labor movement. For the first time, the group included a woman, Ann Mecklin of the AFL-CIO.

On January 23, the council approved a letter to advertisers on a letterhead containing such names as that of Lynn Williams, president of the steelworkers' union, and signed by Molinero, Jim Lowen from Printers' Local 7, and Shannon. The text of the letter read: "We are currently involved in a bitter labor dispute with the *Pittsburgh Press*. . . . Contrary to what the *Press* might tell you, this dispute is not about modernization of production or restructuring of distribution. This is about corporate greed versus dignity and fair play for workers. . . . [T]he *Press* has engaged the services of a notorious union busting firm from out of state, plans to fire 4,500 youth news carriers who provide home delivery; refused to continue a long standing medical insurance plan for employees, while [moving] to reduce retirees' health coverage; and demanded the elimination of fully two-thirds of all newspaper drivers' jobs. . . . Please help us! STOP THE PRESS."

On February 11, the Unity Council learned that the Reverend Michael Szpak, religion-labor coordinator for the AFL/CIO's Department of Organization and Field Services, would be coming in at the end of the month. In the March 20 issue of the *Pittsburgh Catholic* weekly, Monsignor Rice predicted dire consequences if Scripps Howard had its way: "The *Press* will become, in essence, a low-pay modern equivalent of the old sweat shop with worker security a thing of the past. If there is a strike, permanent scabs will be hired. It seems that a strike-breaking cadre is in preparation. What we have in the making is a social and economic revolution that goes beyond a labor defeat. Corporate ruthlessness knows no bounds. A possible casualty will be the *Pittsburgh Post-Gazette* which, under a joint operating agreement has its printing, circulation and advertising handled by the *Press*."

On April 7, the Pittsburgh City Council passed a resolution backing the youth carriers. The pressure was ratcheted upward by a letter of April 14 to Manis from Michael L. Pulte, chairman, president, and C.E.O. of Joseph Horne Co., a major department store, expressing worries about the possibility of a strike and "the prospect of being drawn into your dispute by virtue of our advertising in the *Press*. We certainly do not wish to become a target of a boycott by our own customers, many of whom are union members or sympathetic to union causes." In keeping with customary newspaper practice, no notice of these events appeared in the news or editorial pages of either the *Post-Gazette* or the *Press.*

John Craig, editor of the *Post-Gazette,* issued a letter to the staff on March 20: "I came back from a week in Florida studying the future of newspapers at the Poynter Institute convinced that the newspaper could be doing a great many more things to help itself and that its biggest problem is me. Management has not been using the *P-G's* most important asset, the entire staff, as effectively as it could." He announced that he had set up an all-day meeting for Saturday, April 11, at Froggy's, a restaurant near the newspaper building, "to discuss what can be done." From that meeting came a number of ideas, some of which unexpectedly were put to use to keep the *Post-Gazette* visible when the strike occurred five weeks later.

Unknown to the staff, the *Post-Gazette* management during the previous two years had been having its own difficulties with Scripps Howard. If the unions complained that Scripps Howard kept moving the goal posts, the Blocks felt frustrated in trying to find out where the goal posts actually were. Bill Block had written to Jimmy Manis, the general manager of the *Press,* in an October 22, 1990, letter: "Before the *Post-Gazette* approves an increase in the single copy price from 25 cents to 35 cents, we would like to receive the following information: Dollars to be spent in the coming year for the daily *Press* and the *Post-Gazette* for television advertising, radio advertising, billboards or other forms of advertising, as well as carrier and dealer promotions. We also request written assurances from you that the *Post-Gazette* will be treated equally in all types of promotions, including contests, price reductions, bonus coupons and other similar types of price offers." A year later, John Craig was informed by staffers that no significant effort had been made by the *Press* to solicit ads for a new real estate section. At that point, William Block Jr. stepped in from his office in Toledo, suggesting in an October 23, 1991, letter to Manis that advertising rate cards and promotion efforts should be restructured to "treat the *Press* and *P-G* equally in both effort and dollars expended . . . The *P-G* will be permitted to promote in the *Sunday Press,* and vice versa." He also touched upon the possibility of a strike, given the difficult negotiations going on with the teamsters. "In a strike situation that could shut down both papers, if one paper can be printed, both papers will be printed and distributed, either separately or together, to all *P-G* home delivery customers and single copy outlets, even if it has to be delivered during daylight hours or with the *Press*."7

Manis responded on October 25, pointing out that the joint operating agreement was silent on the subject of combination advertising or combination rates, but added: "However, in line with our obligation to use our best efforts to sell advertising space in the [*P-G*], we have, over the years, offered discounts to evening or Sunday *Press* full-rate advertisers to entice them to also advertise in the *Post-Gazette*." Despite such conciliatory words, the key thrust of the Manis letter was this paragraph:

You have offered to work with me to improve the overall performance of the JOA. While I am always willing to listen to your suggestions, the JOA states in paragraph 4, "From and after the effective dates of this agreement, the *Press* shall control, supervise, manage and perform all operations involved in printing, sell and distributing the Newspapers, shall determine the edition times, page sizes and cut offs of the Newspapers, shall purchase newsprint, material and supplies as required, shall solicit and sell advertising space in the newspaper, shall collect the Newspapers' circulation and advertising accounts receivable which have come into existence after the effective date of this agreement, shall make all determinations and decisions and do all acts and things necessarily connected with the foregoing activities."

In Scripps Howard's view, this paragraph was all that was needed to set the record straight. To the Blocks, it seemed like a schoolmarm scolding an impertinent child, rather than a partnership effort for the good of all concerned.

At an October 31 meeting involving Manis and the two copublishers of the *Post-Gazette*, Bill Block Jr. and John Robinson Block, the subject of a potential strike surfaced anew. According to Bill Block's minutes:

I said that in a strike condition, if the *Press* is printed, the *P-G* should be printed the same day, even if they were part of one product. Manis said initially that one product with neither name on it would probably be printed. He made no promise that the *Press* would not be printed without the *P-G*. . . . I showed Manis his classified rate card, which included six pictures of the *Press* and one of the *P-G* and told him those pictures guide the advertiser toward the *Press* more than the *P-G*. He made no promises (but later told me he had acted on that the following day). . . . I told Manis that "best efforts" to promote the *P-G* would mean using Pittsburgh's best medium, the Sunday *Press.* He said that would be up to the *Press's* editor, Angus McEachran—who later told me he didn't want to run *P-G* ads.

Just what the phrase "best efforts" meant was a key to the friction. On April 27, 1992, Bill Block Jr. wrote directly to Scripps Howard's Burleigh, citing several instances where Blade Communications Inc. felt that Scripps Howard was not fulfilling its "best efforts" obligation under the JOA. That resulted in a two-hour meeting on May 11 in Pittsburgh involving Burleigh, Manis, and Bill Block Jr., where *P-G* editor John Craig took notes. After Block laid out the *P-G's* complaints, Craig wrote: "Burleigh did almost all the talking for Scripps Howard. He began by making the general observation that the tone of Bill's [April 27] letter . . . made him uncomfortable." The Craig minutes conclude: "The rest of the meeting, about 20 minutes, was taken up with a review of the Agency's plan to introduce circulation depots. Burleigh and Manis made it clear during this discussion that they were not going to permit the Teamsters to avoid the issue until the fourth quarter of 1992. They said that one way or another the issue would be joined well before that."

That proved to be the understatement of the year. On the same day, May 11, the Unity Council sent out notices of two meetings for the coming weekend. The first would be held at noon on Sunday, May 17, at the David Lawrence Convention Center for all union members of the *Press* and the *Post-Gazette,* at which "all questions will be answered and rumors laid to rest." The second gathering would be "a major labor rally on May 18 [a Monday] at 6 p.m. in the park across from the *Press.*" The *Press* management countered with an announcement that on May 18 it would start its new depot delivery system with two of its planned thirty depots, one in the West End and the other in Moon Township (near the Greater Pittsburgh International Airport) and explained that youth carriers would be replaced by adult carriers.

At that point the roof fell in. As reported in the Monday edition of the *McKeesport Daily News* under the headline, "Teamsters Strike Pittsburgh Newspapers," the Pittsburgh Press Company was quoted as saying that the strike "was an over-reaction to planned changes in the distribution system for the *Pittsburgh Press* and the *Post-Gazette.* . . . 'Strikes benefit no one—not employees, not subscribers, not advertisers, not the company, and certainly not the community,' said Jimmy E. Manis, vice president and general manager of the Press Co. 'Unfortunately, the Teamsters have chosen a variety of tactics to void meaningful negotiations and the result is today's strike action.'" The article explained that "the city's afternoon newspaper was not published today and most editions of the morning paper were not delivered due to a strike by delivery drivers. About 600 members of Teamsters Local 211 walked off the job shortly after 9 p.m. yesterday. The strike began as delivery of the morning *Post-Gazette* was beginning. William Deibler, managing editor of the *Post-Gazette*, said his paper was caught off guard by the strike declaration."

The Scripps Howard decision to implement the new depot system suddenly on May 17–18 allowed the teamsters to argue with federal and state officials that even though they refused to carry out the new distribution plan, they were not responsible for the strike. Instead, they contended, Scripps Howard was to blame because it was breaching the still existing 1989 contract with the union. That constituted an "unfair labor practice" under the rules of the National Labor Relations Board (NLRB), thus amounting to a lockout.

It quickly became evident that the top management of Scripps Howard was prepared for the strike. The assumption on all sides was that once a settlement was reached, the *Press* would be back in business, working with humbled unions. The *Press* adopted a business-as-usual attitude, maintaining on the payroll all 220 members of the *Press*'s non-union staff of reporters, photographers, and supervisors to put out a weekly, the *Allegheny Bulletin*. Meanwhile, not surprisingly, the newspapers surrounding Pittsburgh did their utmost to capitalize on the situation, as did Pittsburgh's television and radio stations.

The *Post-Gazette*'s management was in much more of a quandary than the *Press*'s. Its destiny was out of its hands. Under the JOA, labor negotiations were the sole prerogative of Scripps Howard. There was also the realization, particularly at Blade Communications headquarters in Toledo, that a long strike would badly damage the balance sheet. The impulse, therefore, was to throttle back operations entirely in order to spend as little money as possible. John Craig, however, in cooperation with John Robinson Block, came up with a different response: do everything possible to keep the *Post-Gazette* visible in the community at large, as well as to subscribers. Like the *Press*, the *P-G* was looking beyond the strike. It was particularly concerned with strengthening its position for the end of the JOA in 1999, when as the morning paper it would have a strong card to play if it maintained a strong front in the meantime. To that end, the *Post-Gazette* developed a whole range of activities to convince the public, including advertisers, that it was alive and well, building on ideas fortuitously developed in the April 11 all-day staff meeting at Froggy's.

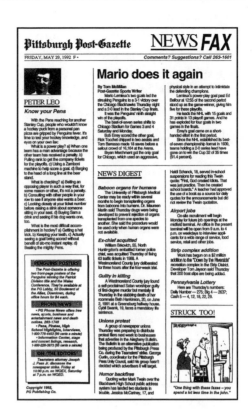

Pittsburgh Post-Gazette Fax edition from Friday, May 29, 1992, with Peter Leo column and a Tim Menees cartoon (Courtesy *Pittsburgh Post-Gazette*)

Within days after the strike began, the staff launched a *P-G* Fax edition, a newssheet sent out to a wide range of citizens and businesses. The first Fax edition went out on May 20, with the headline, "Maintaining the News Flow," and tight sections labeled "Business," "City/State," and "Obituaries." By May 26, *Post-Gazette* News Fax contained a humor column by Peter Leo, entitled "Just the Fax, Ma'am," a sports column by Ron Cook, a digest of news, and a political cartoon by Tim Menees. Angus McEachran, editor at the *Press,* sourly observed in the *Allegheny Bulletin* that "a fax machine is wonderful for a church bulletin, but I don't think it serves up the news very well."

The Fax edition played up columns by Leo, Cook, Sally Kalson, Tom Hritz, and Bruce Keidan. Sometimes, the edition spotlighted sports, at other times television, and also finance. On June 2, it printed a large picture of the celebratory Pittsburgh Penguins, who had won their second consecutive Stanley Cup. The same edition described how the *P-G* Fax was going out to businesses, convenience stores, hospitals, and other news organization, and included a toll-free telephone number for obtaining news, sports, and entertainment information, "a device logging about 100 calls an hour." It also announced plans to produce radio news and a television news program. Craig called this the "media factor."[8] The effort received attention in the June 6 issue of *Editor and Publisher* magazine, the "bible" of American journalism. It reported that half of the one hundred thousand copies of the *P-G* Fax were going to Port Authority Transit, Pittsburgh's public transit system, and the other half to thirty-one 7-11 convenience stories, where readers could pick them up at no cost.

The *Post-Gazette* opened a radio news service, headed by veteran editor and reporter Bill Moushey, selling news to some thirty radio stations. Craig and the staff continued their weekly television show, "The Editors," on Pittsburgh's public television station, WQED. Finally, the *Post-Gazette* initiated a town-crier system: men and women dressed in colonial-era costumes went into Market Square and suburban malls to shout "Hear Ye! Hear Ye!" and the headlines of the day—outfits and practices hearkening back to the *Gazette*'s beginnings two centuries earlier. Usually, the headlines concerned local matters, plus Bill Clinton's developing presidential challenge to President George H. W. Bush. At one point the criers heralded a new book revealing that Princess Diana had attempted suicide five times, which the *P-G* was faxing to readers a chapter a day.

These activities were designed to give the impression that the *Post-Gazette* was here to stay, regardless of the strike outcome. Moreover, they provided real reporting work for the skeleton staff of twenty to thirty. Laid-off workers were brought back on a rotating basis to supplement that crew from time to time. This not only augmented the income of many *P-G* personnel but also helped keep the workforce intact for the return to publication. Despite these efforts, an alarming headline appeared in the June 4, 1992, edition of *USA Today*: "Strike Imperils *Post-Gazette*." The article quoted an industry analyst: "The handwriting is on the wall. The *Post-Gazette* is not going to be with us over the long haul."[9]

On June 25, the Labor Unity Council printed the first edition of its own newspaper, which announced itself as "A Publication by Pittsburghers for Pittsburghers." A box at the bottom of the page explained: "Who We Are. The *Greater Pittsburgh Advertiser* is an interim newspaper published by the Pittsburgh Newspaper Unions Unity Council. It will be published weekly during the labor dispute with The Pittsburgh Press Company. Once the dispute is ended, so will publication of the *Advertiser*. We will provide coverage of local news and sports. We are

Pittsburgh people—all union members—who are publishing a paper for Pittsburghers and residents of the Tri-State District." Later, after objections from a small weekly in Washington County called the *Advertiser*, the Unity Council changed the name to the *Greater Pittsburgh Newspaper*. On May 29, 1992, the *Valley News Dispatch* reported that William Brown, international representative of the Newspaper Guild, had been brought in to run the *Greater Pittsburgh Newspaper*, whose free circulation of 325,000 would match that of the *Press's Allegheny Bulletin*. Delivery would be by teamsters and youth carriers, in contrast to the *Bulletin's* distribution by mail. Brown, a former publisher of newspapers in Pennsylvania and Wisconsin, had helped start *Citizens Voice* during a protracted guild strike against the *Wilkes-Barre Times Leader*. To the surprise of many, the new labor newspaper was able to obtain advertising, including an insert from the Monroeville Mall. To labor leaders, this was proof that their strategy was working, with no backlash from the teamsters' perennial bad image in the eyes of the general public.

Understandably, events were wearing down the nerves of the Blade Communications executive board—Bill Block, his son Bill Block Jr., and the twin sons of the late Paul Block Jr., John Robinson Block and Allan Block. Bill Block Jr. was increasingly concerned about the hit that the company was taking from the strike, perhaps as much as thirty million dollars in lost revenue, including two million dollars for its share of the skeleton operations during the strike. Bill Block Sr. later related that the strike cost Blade Communications one million dollars a month—"a terrific drain on a small organization."[10] Among alternatives discussed was that of offering to sell the *P-G* to Scripps Howard. At one point, according to John Robinson Block, sentiment in favor of a sale was three to one. He recalls his brother Allan telling Craig, "The *Post-Gazette* has been published for the last time." John Robinson interjected, "The hell it has!" While some family members thought a sale would bring one hundred million dollars from Scripps Howard, John Robinson thought that under the circumstances caused by the strike, the figure would be closer to twenty million dollars. Finally, Allan swung over to the side of his twin, "probably as a favor to me," John Robinson believes, creating a two to two impasse. Not everyone in the Block family remembers the course of events that way; some maintain that the family was never divided. Bill Block Sr. says his goal was not to sell but "to get back into production." Bill Jr. is equally insistent: "I have no memory of any serious discussion of selling the *P-G* by the executive committee of BCI."[11]

Seven weeks into the strike, the one hundredth anniversary of the bloody Homestead strike bolstered the unionists' cause. The Unity Council was amused when the *Press's Allegheny Bulletin* expressed displeasure at organizers of the Homestead Strike Centennial who explained they had cut off contact with the *Press* "as long as they continued to treat their employees in the same manner that Andrew Carnegie and Henry Clay Frick did with their workers a century ago."

In addition, the Unity Council put out occasional flyers, such as one in late May headed: "What happened to the *Press* and *Post-Gazette?*" It asserted: "First . . . we think they want to trade us in for low-wage, part-time hourly workers who get no health insurance, no vacations, no nothing. Second, we think the Press Co. wants to put the *P-G* out of business altogether, giving the *Press* a monopoly in town—and the freedom to raise per-copy prices and ad rates as high as they want. . . . Apparently nothing will stand in the way of the company craving for ever-greater profits (Scripps-Howard made $72 million last year)." *Editor and Publisher* magazine, on June 6, 1992, quoted lawyer Joe Pass on the second contention, giving as the Scripps Howard motive: "According to the JOA, if the *Press* loses money for two years in a row, it can escape the agreement and win the Pittsburgh market for itself." The *E&P* story then quoted a rebuttal by Randall Notter, spokesman for the *Press:* "There is absolutely no truth in that."

As the strike rumbled on, the Unity Council developed what it called the "Frontlash," bringing in Deborah Reed, national campus organizer for the AFL-CIO, at a cost of $2,334 for airfare, lodging, and meals for four weeks. The rationale was described in the June 9 minutes of the Unity Council: "It is apparent that community outrage over the paper's abandonment of the youth carriers can be effectively mobilized to add to a more speedy, just resolution of the strike." Reed also was assigned to mobilize students at midwestern colleges "if the strike goes into the fall."

The Golden Triangle Association of downtown merchants expressed concern about the lack of death notices because of the strike, bemoaning, "not being able to know who died is giving us a bad reputation." *U.S. News and World Report* also mentioned that Pittsburgh readers were particularly missing the obituaries during the strike. Father Szpak announced that an interdenominational prayer service would be held on June 30 at St. Pamphilus, a Roman Catholic church in the Beechview section of Pittsburgh, with the theme "Peace through Unity." All three major television networks covered the service, prompting plans for a candlelight prayer vigil involving clergy to be held in front of the *Press* building.

Union activity continued near the *Press* building itself, but strikers for the most part stayed on the sidewalk across the Boulevard of the Allies to avoid charges of mass picketing. A list of "Dos and Don'ts" issued by the Unity Council counseled: "Don't congregate in groups larger than two or three. Don't walk back and forth ["patrolling" in labor parlance]. Don't use the word picket. Handbill advertising is legal. Picketing is not. It is illegal to even threaten to picket. *Don't use the word picket.*" Still, negotiations were going nowhere, with each side blaming the other.

Both the *Press* and the *Post-Gazette* were becoming concerned that the strike might continue into August and early September, costing them lucrative pre-school advertising. That presumably prompted Scripps Howard to take the next bold step—resuming publication with strikebreakers, or "scabs." The Unity Council first learned of this from a newspaper reporter in New England, who told them that an outfit named MADI was advertising in the Boston area for men to deliver packages of not more than one hundred pounds in a region somewhere within seven hundred miles of Boston. The labor leaders soon ferreted out that MADI stood for Massachusetts Alternative Delivery System, headed by Boston lawyer Robert Katz. At the same time, the Council got word that the Vance Security Company (Vanco) of Oakton, Virginia, known as an organization of police types that often abetted strikebreaking efforts, was involved. The unionists quickly put two and two together—delivery drivers plus protection. With that information, they warned Pittsburgh Police Chief Earl Buford that Scripps Howard was probably going to bring strikebreakers to Pittsburgh and that Vanco was noted for using "thugs and shady characters" in its operations. The word about Scripps Howard's plan also went out to labor union members of all kinds, as well as to the activist groups the Unity Council had been cultivating. Reports in the media helped to raise the alarm. The *Wall Street Journal* of July 15 suggested that a showdown could be precedent-setting and quoted analyst John Morton, of Lynch, Jones & Ryan, as saying of the company's move: "It really throws down the gauntlet to the Teamsters. . . . It raises the specter that the Teamsters are going to be squeezed out and won't get back in." At the same time, the *P-G* Fax edition reported that *Press* officials had said publication of the two newspapers would resume with or without the unions as early as July 24.

At the Unity Council's July 21 meeting, Thomas McGrath reported that MADI was recruiting in Boston, Hartford, and "even in Erie." He urged, "There should be a mass demonstration immediately." The tension mounted as Scripps Howard pasted newsprint covers over the first-floor windows of the *Press* building, where its high-powered printing presses were located. Crowds began gathering around the *Press* building, determined to prevent delivery trucks driven by strikebreakers from leaving via the exit ramps from the building. Many sported "Stop the Press" buttons. The front-line volunteers were instructed to lie down and not resist arrest so as not to create a riot that could be captured by television cameras and used to turn public opinion against the union cause. Inside the building, employees of both papers felt the tensions of a siege. A Scripps Howard official described people crawling on the floor past windows for fear of projectiles being hurled through them.

On Sunday evening, July 26, the rumble of the presses was heard behind the blacked-out windows. Then, heralded by the shout, "Here they come!" the trucks began rolling down the exit to the street. Protesters lay down in front of the trucks; the vehicles stopped short of hitting the prone bodies. When the police began arresting the protesters and taking them, without interference, to nearby paddywagons, others surged forward to take their places and were arrested in turn.

Union attorney Pass hurried to police headquarters to begin bail procedures. To his surprise, the sergeant in charge insisted, "We don't have anybody here that you are talking about." Then he added, "There's been a jail break." Actually, there was a series of "jail breaks." A few blocks away from the *Press* building, the door of each paddywagon somehow opened and the prisoners "escaped."

As it turned out, however, the biggest farce of the evening was that no papers had been printed in the *Press* building at all, and the delivery trucks were empty. Instead, Scripps Howard had printed the edition elsewhere, trucked it to Pittsburgh in tractor-trailers, and delivered it to

customary places of sale in Pittsburgh and environs using Plymouth Acclaims, chosen for inconspicuousness. Nevertheless, some of the vehicles were spotted by unknown assailants, who smashed their windows and threatened the drivers. Scripps Howard officials had no doubt that the "unknown assailants" were striking unionists.

The purpose of the publishing effort, union officials surmised in their caucuses, was to get a foot in the door and persuade subscribers and especially advertisers that the Pittsburgh newspapers were back in business. Once that was established, the strikebreaking effort could be made at the *Press* plant itself.

If that was the intent, it backfired. Many sales outlets refused to accept the bundles of papers. Union members and some angry subscribers took them down to the seething scene on the Boulevard of the Allies and threw them at the *Press* entrance. Most important, there was no indication that advertisers were coming to the rescue. To the surprise of staffers at both the *Press* and the *Post-Gazette,* Scripps Howard abandoned the effort, making no further effort to publish.

On July 26, 1992, Teamster 211 president Joe Molinero and other protesters led thousands down the Boulevard of the Allies to denounce the *Pittsburgh Press*'s attempt to publish in defiance of striking workers. (Photo by John Beale; Courtesy *Pittsburgh Post-Gazette*)

The *Post-Gazette,* of course, was involved because it would have been next to publish—a Tuesday morning edition—had the *Press* ploy succeeded. The Blocks, however, were never consulted about the strikebreaking decision to resume publication, and by the time they learned of it, there was nothing they could do. Craig later recalled, "We had the worst of both worlds. They [Scripps Howard] decide we are going to publish. We have a lot of union members that we want to hold onto, who are not going to cross a picket line, so it created a hell of a problem for us. But as good soldiers, we decided to go along. We were taking a lot of PR grief, and then they pulled the plug within 48 hours. I was disgusted."[12] Bill Block Jr. told the August 21 *Pittsburgh Business Times,* "I think it's too bad the drivers saw fit to stop the *Post-Gazette* and *Press* from publishing. And I also think it's too bad the police weren't more effective in upholding the law."

Scripps Howard went to the Allegheny County Court of Common Pleas for an injunction to stop mass picketing, but union attorneys successfully relied on a Pennsylvania law forbidding the use of strikebreakers from outside the state. Under the law, a company may itself hire replacement workers but not employ another company to do it for them. The *Press* had no better luck when it went to the federal courts to have two specific sections of the state strikebreaker law thrown out on grounds that federal law pre-empted them. U.S. District Judge Donald Ziegler refused the request. A report in the August 5, 1992, *Greensburg Tribune-Review* stated that Scripps Howard was spending ten thousand dollars a day for its lawyers.

Not surprisingly, the Unity Council had its biggest turnout ever on July 28, with thirty-two participants, or about three times the usual number, including representatives from such disparate union locals as the laborers and the asbestos workers. The atmosphere was celebratory.

The failure to publish had not escaped attention elsewhere. The *Boston Herald,* where the first cryptic advertisement for replacement workers had appeared, supported the *Press.* On July 29, 1992, under the headline, "Steel Town Thugs," the *Herald* castigated everyone from Mayor Masloff "right on down to talk-show callers and lots of Pittsburghers [who] joined in condemning the *Pittsburgh Press.* . . . Shame on them. Shame on a city that would rather go without a newspaper than read newspapers produced by journalists and workers who refuse to be intimidated by Local 211 of the most infamous nest of corruption in U.S. labor history, the International Brotherhood of Teamsters." *Editor & Publisher* magazine and the *Washington Post* printed detailed accounts. The latter, on August 9, quoted Ben Fischer, a professor of labor studies at Carnegie Mellon University and a former steelworkers' union executive, who said that he could use this event as a model on which to base a whole twelve-unit course on what not to do during a strike, such as using non-Pittsburghers as replacements. He also said the outcome had less to do with union clout—as the teamsters maintained—than with empathy for those about to be put out of work. The *Washington Post* further reported that Manis, at a mid-July news conference, had contended that the Press Company was not advertising for replacement drivers, only to be embarrassed the next day when a classified ad in the *Boston Herald* to that effect surfaced. The *Press* thereupon said it had not misled anybody because the ad was not from the *Press* but from the company hired to recruit drivers.

In its August 6–12 issue, the alternative weekly *In Pittsburgh* quoted Pittsburgh labor leader Rosemary Trump as saying, "The unions have been able to touch upon the basic issue. It's about trying to preserve a middle class in America—to keep a middle-class income for working Americans." In the same issue, columnist Huntley Paton noted with wonder that the *Press* had caved in, partly because of "the staggering area-wide wave of emotion against the *Press,* which, rightly or wrongly, was tarred and feathered as the bad guy. . . . The Press Company said it didn't consider its decision to stop publishing a victory for labor. Please. It was a mind-blowing, blitzkrieg-style victory for labor—and it surprised even the Teamsters." The weekly also quoted an anonymous reporter who made the interesting point that the *Press* had refrained from tearing down the teamsters' image with references to the union's history of alleged mob connections and the lack of productivity among the drivers. On January 18, after the strike, the *Post-Gazette*'s labor reporter Jim McKay made this same point. "The *Press* had plenty of ammunition but failed to fire the shots. The drivers were highly paid, averaging $43,097 in wages, overtime and guaranteed bonuses, and some worked shifts short enough to provide time to hold other jobs. Benefits and other costs pushed the typical compensation package to $58,179."

Scripps Howard executive Burleigh agreed in retrospect that the publishing chain made a major mistake in not appealing to the memories of the general public by pounding harder through every media source on the unsavory history of the teamsters.[13] A decade later, Scripps Howard officials acknowledged the thwarted effort to publish was the turning point. One, who asked not to be identified, recalls that in a meeting of top executives at the Cincinnati headquarters "I saw something I'd never seen in business before—grown men crying, weeping out of frustration and bitterness and loss at realizing the game was over, that we were going to lose a fine newspaper." There was no hint of this outside the executive suite, however, and the unions continued the pressure, building on the July strikebreaking effort to enlist more support from the churches and activists.

As the end of September approached, new worries arose. The Christmas shopping season, a crucial source of revenues for the newspapers, was approaching. Grapevine rumors from Scripps Howard headquarters suggested that another strikebreaking effort to resume publication was in the works. Worse, mediation efforts by Bernard DeLury, head of the federal Mediation and Conciliation Services, had come up dry.

By Thursday, October 1, when DeLury's talks broke off, the teamsters, though insisting that 378 positions were needed to deliver newspapers, had agreed to settle for 368, thereby cutting 260 positions. Scripps Howard, which had begun by demanding 450 layoffs, had offered to settle for only 275. This fifteen-position gap proved unbridgeable—neither side would budge. The union charged Scripps Howard with bad faith and a hidden agenda; Scripps Howard accused the union of being unresponsive.

The afternoon of that same Thursday, Bill Block Jr. in Toledo got a call from Cincinnati suggesting he be in his office the next morning for an important message. In a conversation with his father in Pittsburgh, the two indulged in the obvious speculation that Scripps Howard had finally agreed to a settlement with the teamsters.

The message the next morning, October 2, came as a thunderbolt to everyone. Scripps Howard was giving up and was willing to sell the franchise. First Boston, an investment banking firm, would be handling the sale as a consultant, the broker, in effect. The Block organization was being informed in case it might be interested as a potential purchaser. Bill Block Jr. later admitted that he almost fell to the floor in astonishment. He and his father, who reacted similarly, quickly decided to tell Scripps Howard that they indeed were interested.

Ostensibly for tax purposes, Scripps Howard wanted the sale to be completed by December 31, in the same year as the costly strike. That meant the Blocks had less than three months to settle the strike; come up with a suitable financial package; and get the approval of the U.S. Justice Department's Anti-Trust Division to abandon the JOA. For *Post-Gazette* employees, the news was an unexpected miracle. The only concern was whether the Blocks could pull off the purchase. Rumors swirled that Richard Scaife, publisher of the *Greensburg Tribune-Review,* was also interested in the purchase. In the *Press* newsroom, however, as the incredible news filtered in, there was angry disbelief. The mouse was swallowing the elephant: how could that be after all those months of anxiety, all those reams of stories gathered, written, and stockpiled for the return to publication, all those efforts the year before to aid Scripps Howard's battle against Newspaper Guild unionization? Would *Press* staffers be recruited by the *Post-Gazette* or some other news outlet in the Pittsburgh area, or would they have to move somewhere else? Managing editor Maddy Ross began conducting classes on writing resumes. One group of *Press* staffers decided that if Pittsburgh were to retain two newspapers, they should launch an effort for an Employee Stock Ownership Plan (ESOP).

The Blocks turned to their law firm, Reed Smith, for negotiations with the labor unions, to be handled by Leonard Scheinholtz and Scott Zimmerman. "We didn't realize how complex these things would be," Zimmerman later recalled. "Some agreements were over a hundred years old. Some were written by lawyers but others by guys with a fourth grade education. They were difficult to understand and voluminous. On the other hand, we weren't familiar with these contracts or how people functioned under labor contracts. . . . We trusted these unions. Not because we wanted to but because we had to. They acted in a very responsible manner."[14]

Union lawyer Joe Pass said that from the first, "We wanted the Blade people more than anyone else. We had been dealing with them through the Guild. Harry Tkach pointed out that they were decent people. We recognized they were good people to deal with, better than anyone in the business. And, besides, the *Post* was already there."[15] The conciliatory mood was set in the first real negotiating session. After the opening remarks, the labor leaders called a break to meet separately. They were amazed that the *P-G* negotiators were so willing to listen to their side and to meet at least halfway in order to wrap up settlements.

Numbers were the crux of the dispute. Zimmerman quickly determined that 50 percent of the distribution jobs were being handled by teamster members and 50 percent by independent contractors who were not members of the union: "I learned that those independent contractors could be terminated. Some didn't even have contracts; others had contracts decades old. The whole business was quite archaic."[16]

The solution seemed simple: eliminate the independent contractors and give their work to the teamsters. Also, drop the youth carriers, as newspapers across the nation, worried about keeping customers and advertisers happy, already had done. From the union side this meant abandoning the very crusading pivot around which the Unity Council had built so much of its public appeal during the strike with parents, social activists, and many subscribers—but they agreed to it anyway. At that point, the *P-G* was ready to accept Molinero's considered estimate that it would take 338 teamsters to do the whole job—a reduction of 260 employees, rather than the 285 that Scripps Howard had sought. After the teamsters' contract was completed, it took only five days more for agreements to be reached with the other unions.

That was cause for celebration, and the Unity Council decided to hold one on the Tuesday before Thanksgiving at Rico's, a North Hills restaurant in a wooded setting about ten miles north of Pittsburgh. It proved to be unprecedented in more ways than one. For one thing, the company negotiators were invited to attend. The second innovation happened by chance. Ray Burnett, involved in the negotiations as the *P-G*'s business manager, was having a conference with Bill Block Sr., when he said he needed to leave in order to attend the dinner at Rico's. Block asked Burnett whether he thought it would be all right if he attended. Burnett blinked a moment and said he was sure it would be.

When Block and Burnett entered a private dining room at Rico's, "mouths dropped open." Then the entire room of union men scrambled to its feet to give a long round of applause for Block. More than one attendee said he could never have imagined such a gathering in all the years of negotiations with Scripps Howard. Burnett smiled as he recalled: "The labor guys were drinking imported wine, while Bill and I were drinking beer."[17]

The Blocks developed a satisfactory financial offer by the December 15 deadline. It included twenty-five million dollars in cash, which Blade Communications borrowed from lending groups led by PNC Bank and including Mellon Bank; twenty-five million dollars in preferred stock, which Blade Communications later quietly bought back for less than that price; and the *Monterey (Calif.) Herald,* one of the company's prized possessions, valued at fifty million dollars.

The bone of contention with U.S. Justice Department approval was the creation of a monopoly situation. Reed Smith attorneys had to make the case for abandoning the JOA, whose purpose had been to keep Pittsburgh a two-newspaper town. They argued that a newspaper monopoly in Pittsburgh was unavoidable. They urged the Justice Department to look at the situation as it existed in the autumn of 1992, rather than in the previous January. Based on the demographics of readership across the nation and of Pittsburgh in particular, try as anyone would, it was impossible to retain two newspapers. One way or another, whether with the Blocks or someone else, only one newspaper would come out of the wreckage.

Another purpose of this "single-survivor" argument was to counter the ESOP effort by a group of *Press* employees, led by reporters Lawrence Walsh and Bernie Cohen. Adding to the pressures for early action was troubling evidence that the independent dealers, by now fully aware that they were being excluded, were bringing political pressure both locally and in Congress to derail the deal. With the George H. W. Bush administration in its waning days, and with Richard Scaife's clout within Republican circles—by that time Scaife had expressed outright interest in buying the *Press*—there was the possibility that the politicians might prevail over the professionals in the Justice Department.

On December 30, the Justice Department telephoned Reed Smith to ask about a rumor, heard through a *Tribune-Review* source, that the seeming adversarial relationship between the Blocks and Scripps Howard was a sham, and that the whole scenario had been a collusion to flout the JOA. To the *Post-Gazette,* this last-minute rumor seemed as if it could be a sign of the Scaife intervention they had feared all along. There followed a flurry of calls offering to submit telephone logs, minutes of meetings between the two newspaper groups, and any other evidence that could disprove the rumor. On the afternoon of December 30, the word came that the *Post-Gazette*'s purchase of the *Press* had been approved.

While relief and jubilation flooded the *Post-Gazette,* the mood that Wednesday afternoon in the *Press* newsroom was somber. Walsh recalled, "Bernie (Cohen) and I went up to the fourth floor to shake hands in congratulation all around. We thought that was the end of a bitter day; we turned out the lights."[18]

Sorrow upon sorrow piled up on McEachran. The first was closing his *Pittsburgh Press* office on December 31 and saying goodbye to the people whom he had led in doing so much to improve the quality of the paper. He was relaxed as he took a plane to Greenville, South Carolina, for a short visit with family before going to Athens, Ohio, to be an editor-in-residence at Ohio University's E. W. Scripps School of Journalism. When McEachran stepped off the plane, he was met with an urgent message to call Scripps Howard executive Burleigh. From Burleigh he learned the tragic news that Leon Linder, the editor of the *Memphis Commercial-Appeal* and a friend of his from their earliest Scripps Howard days, had just died, two hours after being struck by a hit-and-run driver on his way home from a New Year's Eve party. The numbed McEachran suspected what was coming next. Burleigh asked him to change plans and go to Memphis to succeed Linder. He agreed, his expectations of a relaxed season in academe dashed.

Meanwhile, the *Post-Gazette* management, having conquered the biggest mountain, still had some foothills to cross—getting back into production as soon as possible.

Chapter 16

Moving Forward

◆—◆—◆

T HE BIG MOMENT came on a Sunday night less than three weeks later, when the first edition of the next day's January 18, 1993, *Pittsburgh Post-Gazette* rolled from the presses. It was the culmination of eighteen days of exhaustive work by all concerned to so quickly publish a merged paper with an organization that had been idled eight months.

To mark the occasion and set the tone for the years ahead, a big party was held at the Hilton Hotel, attended by more than six hundred community leaders. In the *Post-Gazette* press room, Bill Block Jr. took the first of 315,000 copies off the press and handed it to a group of teamsters, who had rented green tuxedos, at their own expense, as part of the honor of delivering that first copy one hundred yards to Bill Block Sr. in the Hilton lobby. To rousing cheers, as white balloons bearing the newspaper's name dropped from the ceiling, the elder Block held the issue up for the television cameras and announced with a wide grin, "We're back!" A similar picture of Block as chairman was played at the bottom of the page, along with a pledge to the readers of independence and fair play, over the signatures of copublishers William Block Jr. and John Robinson Block.

That first edition's front page carried the headline "U.S. Lashes Out at Iraq" over a story reporting that missiles had been fired at a nuclear

William Block Jr.   John Robinson Block

site, and a story about the imminent inaugural of President Clinton, "Tracing a Path to the Presidency." Inside were two stories by labor writer Jim McKay on the unions' victory in "knocking out the *Press*," and the lead editorial, "Back in Business/And Why You Should Feel Free to Give Us the Business."

When the Justice Department had approved the merger in December, the *Post-Gazette* had decided to resume publication no more than three weeks later in a Monday morning edition. Bob Higdon, then general manager, remembers, "We weren't ready to wade into a Sunday jungle the first thing."[1]

Basic decisions had to be made about the paper's identity. Would the name of the *Press* be kept in any form? Most believed that a triple name would be cumbersome, so it was decided to stick with *Post-Gazette*, evoking the two most historic newspaper names in the region.

What about the company color? The *Press* trucks, in which the *Post-Gazette* had been distributed, were yellow and black. That had to be changed. Given today's emphasis on the environment, general manager Higdon thought green would be an appropriate, politically correct color for the reborn newspaper and sold the rest of management on the idea.

The return of advertising was a key to the startup. After the tentative agreement with Scripps Howard was made, the *P-G* began contacting major advertisers. "Automotive, real estate, department stores—all had been affected by the strike. We got most of it back immediately, except for pre-print ads [inserts]. We began taking classified ads after the first of the year," Higdon said. A particular loss was the Giant Eagle supermarket chain, a four million–dollar annual account, as it went to television and other venues.

One of the hardest tasks was to acquire the customer lists, because so many had been held by independent dealers who were dealt out in the *Post-Gazette*'s contract with the teamsters. "Only about 40 percent of our customers were known from lists actually in *P-G* hands," Higdon explained. "Often we learned a name only when people called asking where their paper was." Eventually, the company obtained and controlled all the subscription lists.

The *Post-Gazette* decided that aggressive, multimedia advertising and public relations were critical. Under the slogan, "The Morning of a New Era," the paper offered home-delivery customers free copies for thirteen days, while the *Post-Gazette* town criers handed out free papers at downtown locations during the first week.

After the acquisition of the *Press*, circulation declined slightly, from 458,575 Sunday and 248,687 daily in early 1993, to 452, 815 and 248,289 in 1995, and 408,102 and 245,624 in 2003. In part, this paralleled the continued decline of Pittsburgh's population—from 1990 to 2000, census data showed a decrease in residents from 369,879 to 334,563

As editor-in-chief, John Craig made an early decision that no one from the *Press* would be added to the editorial board. In the news and photography departments, all previous *Post-Gazette* staffers would be retained. So far as integrating former *Press* employees into the system, Craig decided on somewhat of a layered-cake method, making sure that persons from both staffs were represented at the various levels. Some choices, however, could not be avoided—for example, did the paper need two political cartoonists? In this case, it was decided that the answer was yes—both the *Press*'s Rob Rogers and the *Post-Gazette*'s Tim Menees were retained. Their cartoons ran on alternate days, and rotated on Sundays between the editorial page and the op-ed page. Rogers was syndicated nationally, and his local commentary was concentrated in a weekly panel called, "Brewed on Grant." The strip fea-

Rob Rogers's 1998 cartoon from the "Brewed on Grant" series, in which waitress Rosie kids Mayor Tom Murphy about ways to make the city more attractive to tourists (Courtesy *Pittsburgh Post-Gazette*)

tured Rosie, a typical Pittsburgh waitress on Grant Street in downtown Pittsburgh, wisecracking with customers—including government officials—about Pittsburgh's cultural and political plans and controversies. Menees satirized the city's institutions and foibles so well that many of his images became recognizable popular icons, such as his depiction of Pittsburghers' habit of placing lawn chairs on the street to reserve parking spaces.

Craig named Madelyn Ross, managing editor from the *Press*, to the same position at the newly merged *P-G*. Among her other credentials, Ross was experienced at putting out a Sunday paper, something the *Post-Gazette* had not done for more than three decades. Ultimately, 81 of 212 *Press* reporters and editors were added to the *P-G*'s newsroom. The *Post-Gazette*'s full-time roster at the end of 1992, before the merging of work forces, had been 129. At the end of 1993, there were 212 full-time employees, and an additional 22 administrative, clerical, library, and part-time staffers. By 2000, the total staff had risen to 293. The roster of non-editorial staff, however, fell by 230 between 1992 and 2000.

Tim Menees's 2002 cartoon, "The Official Pittsburgh 4th of July Guide," satirizes
the quirks of Pittsburgh life, such as the restrictions placed on alcohol sales by the
Pennsylvania Liquor Control Board.
(Courtesy *Pittsburgh Post-Gazette*)

This large cut in advertising, circulation, and production employees
was part of the agreement with the teamsters.

Creating a smooth working relationship in the news department
proved to be a challenge because of longstanding elements of mutual
disdain. While *Press* people traditionally thought that the *P-G* staffers
were too free and easy, the *Post-Gazette* people considered the *Press*
people willing subjects of some kind of a humorless military dictatorship. Craig and Ross decided to institute a cooperative pattern by sending *P-G* reporter Jones and Roddy from the former *Press* staff to cover
the Clinton inaugural.

In the end, it took a community tragedy on September 8, 1994, to
unify the factions. On a slow Thursday night, people around the city
desk were startled when seasoned reporter Johnna Pro began weeping
after fielding a phone call. "There'll be no one alive?" she asked, her
voice breaking. Thus the *Post-Gazette* staff learned that in nearby Bea-

A law-enforcement official stands watch as members of the press get their first look at the crash scene of USAir flight 427, Sunday, September 11, 1994. The USAir crash occurred Thursday night six miles away from the Pittsburgh International Airport as the seven-year-old plane was preparing to land.
(AP photo/George Widman; Courtesy *Pittsburgh Post-Gazette*)

ver County, USAir flight 427 from Chicago had crashed on its way to the Greater Pittsburgh International Airport. All 131 passengers aboard —mostly Pittsburghers—were killed. In one of its finest hours, the *Post-Gazette* marshaled all of its resources into covering the tragedy. Everyone from feature writers, to copyreaders to sportswriters was thrown into the task. The result was one of the outstanding feats of Pennsylvania journalism: on Sunday, September 11, three days after the tragedy had occurred, the *Post-Gazette* published page after page of information, with biographical information about every single person aboard, and comments from bereaved relatives and neighbors. The experience of intense cooperation and the shared sense of pride knit together the staff in ways never before achieved.

Inevitably, there were questions about how much Pittsburgh and the region had lost with the demise of the *Press* and the resulting one-newspaper situation. Both newspapers had been largely supportive of civic endeavors, including major building developments. The demise of the *Press,* however, meant the end of John Troan's "payjackers" campaign against salary increases for legislators. The *Post-Gazette* favored merit selection for judges, while the *Press* had championed a continuation of elections. The major differences between the papers had been on matters of national policy, including presidential endorsements.

The emergence of the *Pittsburgh Tribune-Review* certainly helped to mute the "monopoly opinion" criticism. The *Trib's* birth was connected with a number of lawsuits and countersuits that followed the *Post-Gazette* into the 1990s. In one such suit, the *Post-Gazette* found itself on the same side as its usual rival, Scripps Howard, facing Richard Scaife, publisher of the *Greensburg Tribune-Review.*

On January 8, 1993, Scaife sued both newspaper chains in the Westmoreland County Court of Common Pleas, claiming they had colluded to deny him a fair chance of acquiring the *Press.* He contended that the two chains had covertly worked out a handover, and that Scripps Howard's offer to sell was actually a sham. Scaife asserted that Scripps Howard had denied his bid even though, at $125 million in cash, it came in higher than those submitted by the *Post-Gazette,* the *Washington Post,* and the *Buffalo News.* Scaife's claim proved to be unpersuasive with Judge Daniel J. Ackerman, however, because there was no record of the bid. Finally, in January 1998, on the brink of a jury trial, an out-of-court settlement of undisclosed terms was reached.[2]

Even though Scaife failed to acquire the *Press,* he was determined to break into the Pittsburgh market. In December 1992, he had launched a Pittsburgh edition of the *Tribune-Review.* There was friction within the organization, however, as the newsmen at Greensburg considered Pittsburgh an interloper draining off resources, and the Pittsburgh staff felt cramped for finances and disliked having to conform to Greensburg's procedures. The *Post-Gazette* did its best to characterize the Scaife paper as an outside enterprise.

In 1992, Ed Harrell, president of the *Tribune-Review* company, approached a veteran newsman, Lee Templeton, a private newspaper consultant, about starting a daily in Pittsburgh. The two had worked together in New York in the Newspaper Advertising Bureau, an organization sponsored by the newspaper industry to promote the use of newspapers as an advertising medium. Templeton bluntly told Harrell,

"You don't want to do that." The new paper would have to have 30 percent coverage in key zip code areas, at a time when second newspapers
were dying all over the country. Advertising would be a problem, too,
Templeton explained. Although it would be natural to suppose that advertisers would welcome a second newspaper, because reduced prices
would result from competition, having a second paper in fact involves
negotiations and transactions costs they do not like—such as the extra
money required to lay out different ads for each paper.[3]

Despite his own warnings, Templeton joined the *Pittsburgh Tribune-
Review* on April 1, 1994. His first decision was to make the Pittsburgh
product as independent of Greensburg as possible. The *Pittsburgh Tribune-Review* built a new, highly electronic plant with two press lines
in Marshall Township, north of Pittsburgh. Moreover, new policies
evolved within the Scaife chain. While material gathered by any of
the Scaife properties—Johnstown, Connellsville, or Greensburg—was
available to all, the Pittsburgh paper was not required to use it and thus
dilute its "hometown" emphasis. In 1997, Templeton hired as editor
David House, a man who knew the hallmarks of a metropolitan paper
and how to put them in place.

The Pittsburgh paper began investigating stories such as the shaky
aspects of the city's finances of the city of Pittsburgh—a detailed outline of "why the city is bankrupt and won't get better," in Templeton's
words. The fact that Mayor Tom Murphy in the 2001 Democratic primary won by only seven hundred votes is proof, Templeton felt, that the
Tribune-Review has had an impact on Pittsburgh politics that belies its
relative youth. By 2003, the *Tribune-Review*'s Sunday edition circulation
was 182,803 and its daily figure was 120,318.[4]

Whether or not the *Post-Gazette* was spurred by the *Tribune-Review*,
it certainly did not stand still. In 1998, the *P-G* won its third Pulitzer
Prize ever, and the second in the decade. The Pulitzer Prize for spot
news photography was awarded to the *P-G* for "Trek of Tears," a special
photo section photographed and written by Martha Rial. Chronicling
three weeks among Rwandan and Burundian refugees in Tanzania, it
was published in the *Post-Gazette* on January 16, 1997. In reporting the
award, the *P-G* splashed across its April 15, 1998, front page an eight-
column photograph of a winding column of refugees in a barren African landscape, many carrying all of their worldly goods in bundles on
their heads. It symbolized, in eerily dramatic fashion, the heartbreaking

story for the tens of millions of refugees around the world who were, in the twentieth century, driven out of their homes by wars, civil strife, and genocide, as well as by natural disasters and economic turmoil.

In its science coverage, the *Post-Gazette* followed the shift at the University of Pittsburgh Medical Center from the 1980s emphasis on organ transplants to biological therapy. The latter involves stem cells, regenerative medicine, and fashioning new organs out of tissue. Similarly, the newspaper diligently covered Carnegie Mellon University's groundbreaking efforts in computer science, as well as its leadership in the robotics field in advancing from stationary to mobile robots.

The business page inaugurated periodic Benchmarks surveys in 1996 in order to compare Pittsburgh to fourteen similar metropolitan areas. This was part of a significant improvement in the newspaper's business coverage during the decade. On specific days each week, special attention was paid to investments and to the "New Pittsburgh" of dot-coms and other innovative industries.

In 1999, Marilynn Uricchio was transferred from movie critic to head a new "Seen" column. She envisioned not just a society page in

Pulitzer Prize– winning photo by Martha Rial shows Rwandan Hutu refugees with as many possessions as they could carry along the road near Benaco Junction after being turned back by Tanzanian soldiers. December 1996. (Courtesy *Pittsburgh Post-Gazette*)

Page from *Post-Gazette* Benchmarks special section, May 17, 1998 (Courtesy *Pittsburgh Post-Gazette*)

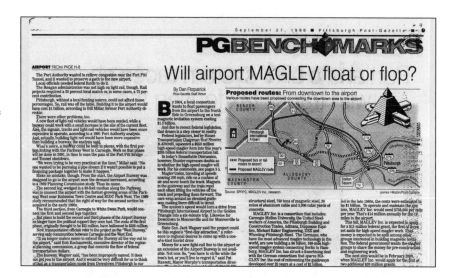

the traditional sense, but a feature that would bring new faces into the picture alongside old wealth and heads of corporations. "Seen" began to showcase many lesser-known causes—food banks, autism, other special needs—whose events often did not get into the newspaper, let alone in a glamorized fashion. John Craig conceded that, in retrospect, the earlier abandonment of daily "society coverage," partly in response to feminist egalitarianism, proved to be shortsighted.[5]

During this period, the *Post-Gazette*'s editorial page expressed support for various new restructuring and construction projects facing the region: reorganization of county government under a "home rule" charter; the construction of a new convention center; North Shore development, including new stadiums for football and baseball; and riverbank development. The backing of these projects promoted by the business community represented the continuation of a tradition that went back to the earliest years of the *Gazette*. However, the *Post-Gazette* also supported efforts to combat air and water pollution that often put the newspaper in conflict with industrial interests. In the realm of local government, the *P-G* devoted dozens of editorials to promoting the transformation of Allegheny County's governing body from a three-person commission to a single executive. In an April 7, 1993, piece, the paper pointed out that twice in the 1970s it had supported county home-rule measures that were defeated by the voters, and exhorted: "The 21st century is upon us. If Allegheny County is to move forward, it needs the advantage of home rule to let it chart its course." The paper continued its support through legislative passage of an enabling act, subsequent selection of a charter-writing committee, and the winning campaign for voter approval.

The *Post-Gazette* also championed the construction of a new terminal at Pittsburgh International Airport, and leaned heavily at times on USAir, the principal client, to cease its resistance. As fate would have it, because of the 1992 strike, the *P-G* had to cover the successful opening of the new terminal in abbreviated form—the October 1 Fax edition enthusiastically described the inaugural arrival of 118 passengers on USAir flight 620 from San Diego.

The construction of new stadiums for the Pirates and for the Steelers came only after rigorous debate in which the *P-G*'s editorial staff found itself under attack by populist groups and on the losing side of one tax referendum. Pittsburgh was trying to keep major-league teams in a small market, under the constant threat that the teams might move to eager and more lucrative Sunbelt cities. In 1985, a consortium of local corporations bought the Pirates from the Galbreath family; ten years later, Kevin McClatchy, of a California newspaper family, purchased the team, backed by a group of investors including the *Post-Gazette*. The Pirates contended, however, even under new ownership, that in order to stay in the city, they would need a new stadium. The state legislature created a referendum for the November 4, 1997, ballot, which proposed a half-cent sales tax in Allegheny County and ten adjacent counties to help fund new stadiums for the Pirates and the Steelers, increase the size of the David L. Lawrence Convention Center, and aid economic development projects in the eleven participating counties. The *P-G* went full-throttle in support of the tax, arguing in a June 15, 1997, editorial: "The question for southwestern Pennsylvanians is, are they willing, like people in competing regions, to maintain the kinds of facilities that support major-league teams? And, are they willing to back a mechanism that will do not just that, but at the same time invigorate other major regional assets and create economic opportunities across 10 counties? If they are, then there's a modest proposal they should be considering in the voting booth this November." The voters, however, resoundingly defeated the proposal. That brought more scrambling in the legislature by Mayor Murphy and other civic leaders, resulting in what critics considered a sleight-of-hand "midnight maneuver" to push through funding for separate stadiums for both professional sports teams. This "Plan B" for stadium financing—floating a bond issue through a combination of state financing, contributions by the Regional Asset District, and money from the teams themselves—would poison local politics as anti-tax groups and skeptical citizens argued that the citizens' will expressed in the 1997 referendum had been disregarded.

The *Post-Gazette* also argued, along with many civic and business leaders, for efforts to improve downtown Pittsburgh's Fifth Avenue and Forbes Avenue corridor. Plans for a mall-type development in the heart of downtown ran into resistance by historic preservationists and small retailers in the affected area. The *P-G* published editorial after editorial promoting the project, particularly hailing decisions by the Lazarus and the Lord and Taylor department store chains to open stores downtown. In a December 25, 1998, editorial titled "The Right Mix," the *P-G* counseled: "In the end, the whole district must be attractive—to both the eye and the wallet. And it will best do that if it can combine a neighborhood of popular retailers with the uniqueness and diversity of Pittsburgh." When Lord and Taylor announced plans to use the former Mellon Bank building on Smithfield Street, the March 20, 1999, *Post-Gazette* published an article by Patricia Lowry, its architecture critic, urging that executives "be sensitive to both the historic nature of the structure and the place it holds in the city's collective sentiment." By July 17, 2003, in the wake of a Lord and Taylor announcement that it would be closing its downtown store, the editorial board summarized that "our beloved Downtown isn't in bad shape" but "Fifth and Forbes is in trouble." The problem was compounded as Lazarus in early 2004 announced that it, too, was closing its taxpayer-subsidized downtown store.

In interesting contrast, another part of downtown, on the Allegheny River side of Liberty Avenue, continued to have success after success as a burgeoning cultural district. In 1971, Henry J. Heinz II guided the conversion of the Loew's Penn Theater into Heinz Hall, a performing venue for the Pittsburgh Symphony Orchestra. In succeeding years, the Stanley Theater was converted into the Benedum Theater for opera, ballet, and traveling Broadway shows, and the Pittsburgh Public Theater moved from the North Side into a new O'Reilly Theater downtown. The Fulton Theater was converted into the Byham Theater, and these buildings, along with other cultural amenities, transformed an area that once had been a haven of pornography shops and blighted buildings. The *Post-Gazette* hailed each project, including the razing of the David Lawrence Convention Center and the erection of its replacement, a daring postmodern building with its face turned to the Allegheny River. The new center seemed to represent a realization by Pittsburgh's leadership of the scenic worth of its once industrially oriented rivers. Along the same lines, the embattled stadium efforts achieved success in many a skeptical eye by their designs, which were open to the river. The *P-G* continued to promote the idea of retail and housing in the vicinity of the new PNC baseball park and the Heinz football stadium, and to push for a light-rail extension from downtown to the north shore, via a tunnel under the Allegheny. In a March 19, 2003, editorial, the *Post-Gazette* expressed satisfaction that the Federal Transit Administration had restored a "recommended" designation to the light-rail extension, calling it "a worthy transit project, and Pittsburghers should rejoice that it's gotten a green light again."

In international affairs, the *Post-Gazette* continued to maintain a free-trade policy, with a major exception—ambivalence concerning tariffs on steel imports. A key statement came in a June 27, 1994, editorial responding to a study by the Economic Strategy Institute that recommended tough sanctions against foreign producers who dump their steel in the United States: "We tend toward the more moderate view that trade management should be limited to the extent possible, but we also recognize that intervention is warranted to level the playing field." On December 11, 2001, the *P-G* sought a balance: "The long-term goal, in our view, should remain the same: the establishment of clean global competition in steel, with neither foreign nor domestic producers receiving special deals from their governments." When the George W. Bush administration in 2002 imposed a scale of tariffs on steel products up to 30 percent, the newspaper commented that the action "provides an opportunity for the American steel industry to put its house in order, to work itself into shape to be competitive on the world market without tariff protection."

In the wake of the collapse of the Soviet empire, the *Post-Gazette* shared the ensuing uncertainty on the questions of war and peace. When Iraq invaded Kuwait in 1990, the *P-G* backed President George H. W. Bush's 1991 war on the grounds that he had worked with the United Nations in assembling a coalition of powers. In turn, that led to ambivalence when the second President Bush in 2003 invaded Iraq on a largely unilateral basis. In a March 20, 2003, editorial commenting on the launching of the attack, the *P-G* urged: "What needs to be done now is to get the conflict over with quickly and efficiently, with minimum loss of life, for the military people involved and for the Iraqi people themselves. Then the United States and its few faithful allies can seek to build a good peace, in Iraq, in the Middle East region. We pray that God will cup His hands around our brave men and women as they seek to do their best for our country." The newspaper continued to urge the Bush administration to bring the United Nations more fully into the picture as nation-building efforts after the defeat of the Iraqi army ran into deadly resistance from insurgent groups.

In terms of endorsements for political office, the *Post-Gazette*, as it had done for many years, continued to support candidates from both parties. Where the candidates had equal value in the editorial board's opinion, the preference might go to a woman or a minority candidate to help achieve a balance in political leadership. The *P-G* endorsed Republican Dick Thornburgh for governor in 1978 over former Pittsburgh mayor Peter Flaherty, and backed Thornburgh again in 1982. The paper supported Republican William Scranton Jr. over Democrat Robert Casey in the 1986 gubernatorial election, but selected incumbent Casey over Republican challenger Barbara Hafer in 1990. The *Post-Gazette* twice endorsed Republican Tom Ridge for governor, in 1994 and 1998. In 2002, it backed a Democrat, Ed Rendell, former mayor of Philadelphia.

The same propensity was shown in the U.S. Senate races, in which the *P-G* backed Republicans such as Hugh Scott, John Heinz, and, in later races, Arlen Specter. However, the paper selected Democrat Harris Wofford over Dick Thornburgh in the special election after Heinz's untimely death in a 1991 airplane accident. Twice (unsuccessfully), the newspaper opposed Republican Rick Santorum, who upset Wofford in 1994 and overcame Representative Ron Klink in 2000.

As to the presidency, the *Post-Gazette* had a long policy of boosting Republican presidential nominees, stemming from the days of Paul Block Sr., but abandoned this trend in 1960 with the endorsement of John F. Kennedy. From that election onward, the *P-G* has continually backed the Democratic nominee for president, with only one exception:

the 1972 endorsement of incumbent Richard Nixon over the Democratic challenger, Senator George McGovern.

In the 1990s, the *Post-Gazette* pioneered in an important revolution in the field of newspaper production—pagination. Pagination is the ability to create an entire page in the computer and send it directly to image setters. The hard copy of stories, ads, and photographs is digitized, and the image setter receives the digital information and develops it into a plate for printing. Michael Pearson arrived from San Francisco in 1995 to become director of systems and technology, and immediately noted that all of the *Post-Gazette*'s computers were threatened by the potential Y2K nightmare. Scripps Howard, which had operated the production side under the JOA until 1992, had spent virtually no money on computers; so they were still of 1970s vintage. Blade Communications realized that, for more reasons than one, it had to replace all of the *Post-Gazette*'s computer systems. That cost nearly four million dollars for equipment and training. It also required renovations of the various floors at the *Post-Gazette,* including transforming the old, cold-type backshop by taking out the bulky, obsolete equipment and creating an open work environment. Part of the process was establishing image archiving for the *Post-Gazette* library (the "morgue" in old-time newspaper parlance), a step that only about 5 percent of the nation's newspapers with circulations over one hundred thousand had taken at the time. When production in the wee hours of New Year's Day 2000 went ahead without a Y2K glitch, Cuban cigars were broken out to celebrate.

With pagination, as in the old days, the advertising department decides where the ads will go. If a page has no ads on it, it is transmitted immediately to the image setters. If it has advertisements, it goes back to the ad department, which puts in the ads and then forwards it to the image setters. Pearson explained that devising a way to handle display advertisements from local sources was difficult because "you are dealing with somebody's creative genius" in devising catchy formats. That is why the *Post-Gazette* decided on the two-step arrangement for pages containing advertisements—ad department to news department back through ad department—so that knowledgeable people would be handling "their" material in each case to avoid errors. A major advantage of pagination is that these professionals can see the complete page as it will be when printed.[6]

Technology has also revolutionized newspaper photography. Digital cameras can be plugged into a laptop computer or a telephone system to send pictures directly into the *P-G* computer system, where the photo editors can pick and choose. The system is used not just for out-of-town photographic shoots but also, because of the speed and ease factors, for transmitting pictures from baseball and football stadiums just across the Allegheny River from the *Post-Gazette* plant.

The new equipment transformed every department, from news to display advertising to classified advertising. The press and delivery departments also were renovated in important ways. Michael Tomasieski, director of production, said that the most important was the installation in 1997 of seven Flexographic printing units at a cost of twenty million dollars. These presses use a raised image plate like the old letterpresses, but the ink is water-based, not oil-based as in older presses. The new system suits everyone because it produces clarity, is environmentally friendly, and eliminates the annoying oil-based ink that smeared readers' hands.[7]

In February 2003, the newsroom leadership changed hands when John Craig retired as editor. David M. Shribman, at the age of forty-eight, joined the newspaper as executive editor. He came to the *P-G* from the position of Washington bureau chief for the *Boston Globe*, where he had won a Pulitzer Prize in 1995 for specialized reporting. A 1976 graduate of Dartmouth College, Shribman worked at the *Buffalo News*, the *Washington Star*, the *New York Times*, and the *Wall Street Journal* before serving a ten-year stint with the *Globe*. John Robinson Block continued to lead the editorial page, and his cousin William Block Jr. served as chairman of the board, having succeeded his father William Block Sr. in that role.

At the turn of the millennium, the Blocks decided to change the corporate name of its various enterprises from Blade Communications Inc. to Block Communications Inc., highlighting that their interests now stretch beyond the onetime *Toledo Blade* flagship. At the time of the change, the corporation's holdings included fifteen communications companies nationwide—the *Pittsburgh Post-Gazette*, the *Toledo Blade*, Buckeye Cable System, Buckeye TeleSystem, Monroe Cablevision (sold in 2002), Erie County Cablevision, Metro Fiber and Cable Construction, KTRV-TV, WAND-TV, WDRB-TV, WLIO-TV, Commu-

Newsboys greet guests as they enter the Senator John Heinz Pittsburgh Regional History Center for the "Block Party," September 27, 2000.
(Courtesy *Pittsburgh Post-Gazette*)

nity Communication Services, Corporate Protection Services, Access Toledo Internet, and WFTE-TV.

The Block family also decided to commemorate the one hundredth anniversary of Paul Block Inc., which had launched its empire in 1900. Community leaders were invited to join in an October 11, 2000, celebration held at the Senator John Heinz Pittsburgh Regional History Center in the Strip District. The affair was called "The Block Party," highlighting the family and business name, and also evoking the neighborhood parties held in many parts of Pittsburgh. The name reinforced for Pittsburgh the importance of the *Post-Gazette* in the life of the city and the region as the twenty-first century began. The centennial observance also indicated some answers to the question: Why did the first newspaper west of the Alleghenies, the *Gazette,* outlast all of its competitors—more than fifty across the years—to be more than two centuries later the sole native survivor?

Over the centuries, an array of gifted editors and financially astute executives, aided by timely purchases and mergers, made the difference for the *Gazette* and its successors against more flamboyant competitors. It survived, in part, because it did a good job of covering the news. In the later part of the twentieth century, the *Post-Gazette*'s status as a family owned, privately held newspaper also allowed it to survive on

William Block Sr.,
Karen Block
Johnese, and
William Block Jr.
at the "Block
Party"
(Courtesy *Pittsburgh
Post-Gazette*)

thinner profit margins than a publicly held company subject to the demands of stockholders. Joe Pass, lawyer for many of the newspaper unions serving the *Post-Gazette,* remarked: "I can't help but feel that the *P-G* survived because it remained a family business, not pulled by the shareholders. It could make quicker decisions. When we did negotiations with the *Post-Gazette* and went to Bill Block, we could get decisions. With Scripps Howard, there was a layer and then another layer. They could deliver but not as quickly. It led to a lot of frustrations across the years. It's a lot easier when you don't have to keep going to someone else to make your case."[8]

Building on the past and on the reputations of former editors and owners, Paul Block Sr. and his son Bill earned a reputation for integrity even among those who disagreed with their editorial policies. These included business groups who felt Bill had veered too far from the Republican principles of his father, as well as progressive political groups who felt he had not shifted enough. Neither Republicans nor Democrats were happy with the *P-G*'s habit of endorsing candidates of both parties. To local Republicans, the paper seemed too often to be uncritically supportive of officials elected by an overwhelmingly Democratic electorate; to Democrats, the constant uncovering of misbehavior by public officials amounted to harassment of the party and a refusal to support the overall agenda. Nor was everyone pleased with the *Post-Gazette*'s support of the civil rights movement and of school desegregation. Roman Catholics had trouble with the *P-G*'s pro-choice stance on abortion, partly because they felt it represented too close an alliance with Pittsburgh's Protestants. Jews were upset with the newspaper's emphasis on the rights of Palestinians in the struggle that frequently convulsed the Middle East.

The newspaper set up mechanisms, however, to air differing viewpoints. For instance, the *Post-Gazette* went out of its way to publish syndicated columnists whose views on abortion, Israel, and school desegregation ran directly opposite to its editorial positions. The *P-G* also gave preference in its "Letters to the Editor" column to those critical of its news coverage and editorial positions. On the editorial board, the wry joke was that the best way for a letter writer to ensure his or her missive would be printed was to write on the general theme: "Wrong again, *Post-Gazette!*"

To be sure, the *Post-Gazette*'s conservatism on economic issues and its opposition to some of the causes dear to labor created resentment. In contrast, the *Pittsburgh Press* deliberately sought to appeal to blue-collar readers, even though this often did not extend to support of their political causes. Yet, in the 1992 showdown, labor unions unable to reach agreements with the *Press* and its Scripps Howard ownership came quickly to terms with the *Post-Gazette*. Although both papers were part of chains, the *Post-Gazette* managed to seem "local," while the *Press* was "carpetbagger." In great part, this was because longtime publisher Bill Block lived in Pittsburgh and was deeply involved in community affairs.

From the Whiskey Rebellion to the Gulf War, from the Johnstown Flood to the crash of USAir flight 427—whenever Pittsburghers have needed or wanted the news, the *Post-Gazette* or one of its predecessors has been there to cover it. Winning in business, as in sports, often turns as much on the mistakes of others as on one's own prowess; that and plain dumb luck. An awestruck Bob Higdon, who represented the Blocks in the crucial 1992 labor negotiations, suggested that the *Post-Gazette* survived "because there is a God." Time and again the mistakes of others and luck combined with the shrewdness of owners and editors and the trust they had earned from the people of Pittsburgh to ensure that the original *Gazette* and its successors would endure.

NOTES

Chapter 1: The Beginning

1. Marder, *A Hugh Henry Brackenridge Reader*, 9.
2. Andrews, *Pittsburgh's Post-Gazette*, 11, quoting "Extracts from the Journal of Arthur Lee," *The Olden Time* 2 (1847): 339.
3. Baldwin, *Pittsburgh*, 113.
4. Ibid.
5. Andrews, *Pittsburgh's Post-Gazette*, 23.
6. The Maryland Historical Society confirms the attribution of this quote to William L. M. Pinckney.
7. Baldwin, *Pittsburgh*, 116.
8. Warner, *A History of Allegheny County*, 657.

Chapter 2: The Whiskey Rebellion

1. Reese, *Flavor of Pittsburgh*, 15, quoting James Veech, *Centenary Memorial of the Planting and Growth of Presbyterianism in Western Pennsylvania and Parts Adjacent*, 1876.
2. Phillips, *The Cousins' Wars*, 179.
3. Baldwin, *Whiskey Rebels*, 142–45.
4. Baldwin, *Whiskey Rebels*, 162.
5. Andrews, *Pittsburgh's Post-Gazette*, 41.
6. Warner, *A History of Allegheny County*, 657.
7. Stevens, *Albert Gallatin*, 82–83.
8. Baldwin, *Whiskey Rebels*, 205.

Chapter 3: Competition

1. Andrews, *Pittsburgh's Post-Gazette*, 19–20.
2. Andrews, *Pittsburgh's Post Gazette*, 46. Baldwin, like Andrews, cites August 6, 1800, as the starting date for the *Tree of Liberty* (*Pittsburgh*, 178), but Killikelly records the date as August 4 (*History of Pittsburgh*, 496).
3. Quoted in Andrews, *Pittsburgh's Post-Gazette*, 34. The microfilm archives at the Carnegie Library of Pittsburgh have a gap from March 1803 to August 1805.

4. Quoted in Andrews, *Pittsburgh's Post-Gazette,* 51–52.

5. Reiser, *Pittsburgh's Commercial Development,* vii.

6. Baldwin, *Pittsburgh,* 164.

7. Some sources relate that the *Commonwealth* was first published in 1804.

8. Historians consider the *Commonwealth* and the *Statesman* direct predecessors of the *Pittsburgh Post,* which was established in 1842 and was a direct ancestor of the *Post-Gazette.* A fuller description of the growing proliferation of newspapers in Pittsburgh in that era can be found in chapters 3 and 7 of Andrews, *Pittsburgh's Post-Gazette.*

9. The *Gazette's* circulation numbers at that time cannot be determined from existing documents.

Chapter 4: An Editor for a Contentious Era

1. Andrews, *Pittsburgh's Post-Gazette,* 62.

2. Andrews, *Pittsburgh's Post-Gazette,* 108.

3. Baldwin, *Pittsburgh,* 262–63.

4. Andrews, *Pittsburgh's Post-Gazette,* 81.

5. Wilson, *Standard History,* 849.

Chapter 5: The *Post* Arrives

1. Between 1845 and 1847, White had three co-owners in succession: Z. H. Costen, Matthew M. Grant, and Benjamin F. Harris.

2. Andrews, *Pittsburgh's Post-Gazette,* 132

3. Andrews, *Pittsburgh's Post-Gazette,* 141.

4. Andrews, *Pittsburgh's Post-Gazette,* 146, quoting the *Gazette* of January 1, 1856.

5. Andrews, *Pittsburgh's Post-Gazette,* 143.

6. Baldwin, *Pittsburgh,* 222–23.

7. *Pittsburgh Press,* September 16, 1936.

Chapter 6: The Civil War

1. *Pittsburgh Dispatch,* quoted in Killikelly, *History of Pittsburgh,* 422.

2. Andrews, *Pittsburgh's Post-Gazette,* 148.

3. Ibid.

4. Baldwin, *Pittsburgh,* 313.

5. For more on the cultural impact of Sanitary Fairs and other contributions by women during the Civil War period, see Jean Thomas, "Music of the Great Sanitary Fairs."

6. *Post,* April 14, 1863.

Chapter 7: Reconstruction, Railroads, Riots

1. Andrews, *Pittsburgh's Post-Gazette,* 185.

2. Andrews, *Pittsburgh's Post-Gazette,* 189.

3. Family records of Mary Ellen Leigh of Pittsburgh, great-granddaughter of Joseph Lare and retired *Post-Gazette* journalist.

4. *Post-Gazette,* August 21, 1934, as quoted in Andrews, *Pittsburgh's Post-Gazette,* 293–94.

5. Andrews, *Pittsburgh's Post-Gazette,* 200.

Chapter 8: The Twentieth Century Opens

1. Steffens, *The Shame of the Cities,* 107.

2. Andrews, *Pittsburgh's Post-Gazette,* 267.

3. Tarr and Yosie, "Critical Decisions," 71–72.

4. Tarr and Yosie, "Critical Decisions," 72.

5. Women's Suffrage clippings, January 5, 1913.

6. *Pittsburg Leader,* February 18, 1912.

7. Andrews, *Pittsburgh's Post-Gazette,* 268–69.

8. Credit for the creation of "Pa Pitt" is disputed. J. Cutler Andrews ascribed the image to Burgoyne (*Pittsburgh's Post-Gazette,* 255), and in "Worthy Tribute to 'Town Poet," *Gazette Times,* April 8, 1911, Burgoyne is reported to have claimed authorship: "On November 5, 1895, Father Pitt was born. He was my offspring." However, in "Father Pitt in Cartoons," *Index,* October 6, 1906, author Raymond Gros wrote: "Before [Pa Pitt's] advent the cartoonists of Pittsburgh, who are all gallant young fellows, represented the city by the figure of a maiden 'Miss Pittsburgh' . . . a self-respecting 'sweet-thing,' who must ignore scandals, and be above the little vexations of common life. It was then that Fred Johnston, of the *Leader,* had an inspiration. Without warning he banished Miss Pittsburgh from his cartoons and introduced in her stead Father Pitt, and there arose in all the editorial rooms a concert of sadness and joy: "Miss Pittsburgh is dead—long live Father Pitt!" The Web site of the Pennsylvania Department of the Carnegie Library of Pittsburgh explains: "In his various forms, Pa Pitt was never the property of any one newspaper or institution. Over the years Pa Pitt served the interests of several editorial cartoonists, but perhaps the most definitive representation and certainly the one still most familiar to many Pittsburghers is Cy Hungerford's portly, good-natured old Colonial." http://www.clpgh.org/locations/pennsylvania/papitt/ (accessed June 4, 2004).

9. It was only after the newspaper industry established the Audit Bureau of Circulations in 1914 that circulation figures could be trusted. The various Pittsburgh newspapers signed on in 1918.

10. Emery, Emery, and Roberts, *The Press and America,* 165, 219.

11. Ibid., 207, 308.

Chapter 9: The Block and Hearst Deal

1. The chronology of these affairs is quite tangled, varying from one biographer to another. For one version, see Brady, *The Publisher,* 169, 183–87.

2. Brady, *The Publisher,* 348.

3. *Post-Gazette,* August 2, 1927.

4. Brady, *The Publisher,* 348.

5. Brady, *The Publisher,* 349.

6. Brady, *The Publisher,* 351.

7. Brady, *The Publisher*, 405.

8. Brady, *The Publisher*, 401.

9. Brady, *The Publisher*, 415.

10. Brady, *The Publisher*, 434–35.

11. Brady, *The Publisher*, 441–44.

12. Brady, *The Publisher*, 404.

13. Harrison, *The Blade of Toledo*, 247–48.

14. Sally Kalson, "Chickens Had Role in Sprigle's Pulitzer," *Pittsburgh Post-Gazette*, September 16, 1986.

15. Ibid.

16. Ibid.

17. For more on this story, see Brady, *The Publisher*, 453–460.

18. Hawkins, *That Was Hot Type*, 35.

19. Brady, *The Publisher*, 460–61.

20. John Troan, interview by author, July 26, 2001.

21. Brady, *The Publisher*, 479.

Chapter 10: The Next Generation

1. Block, *Memoirs*, 83.

2. Andrew Chancellor, interview by author, December 6, 2000.

3. William Block, interview by author, September 9, 2000.

4. Block, *Memoirs*, 84; William Block, interview by author, June 5, 2001.

5. All major league games were played in the afternoon at that time, and all but the St. Louis teams were in the east.

6. William Block, interview by author, June 5, 2001.

7. Ibid.

8. John Troan, interview by author, July 26, 2001.

9. Alvin Rosensweet, interview by author, September 21, 2000.

10. John Troan, interview by author, July 26, 2001.

11. Alvin Rosensweet, interview by author, September 21, 2000.

12. William Block, interview by author, June 5, 2001.

13. Andrew Chancellor, interview by author, December 6, 2000; William Block, interview by author, June 5, 2001.

14. William Block, interview by author, September 14, 2000.

15. *FTC v. Cement Institute et al.*, handed down April 26, 1948. U.S. Reports 683, volume 333.

16. Andrew Chancellor, interview by author, December 6, 2000.

17. Block, *Memoirs*, 122–26, 175–76; Andrew Chancellor, interview by author, December 6, 2000.

18. Donald Miller, interview by author, August 12, 2000.

19. Andrew Chancellor, interview by author, December 6, 2000.

20. Weber, *Don't Call Me Boss*, 240.

21. Gugliotta, "How, When, and for Whom Was Smoke a Problem," 111.

22. Ibid., quoting James Parton, "Pittsburg," *Atlantic Monthly* 21 (January 1868): 17–19.

23. Gugliotta, "How, When, and for Whom Was Smoke a Problem," 113–14.

24. Lubove, *Twentieth Century Pittsburgh*, 47–48.

25. Ibid., 116.

26. Hawkins, *That Was Hot Type*, 42.

27. William Block, interview by author, September 14, 2000.

28. John Grove, associate director, Allegheny Conference, interview by author, June 1971.

29. Chancellor still prefers the term "smoke-control effort" to newer terms such as "environmental enhancement." Andrew Chancellor, interview by author, December 6, 2000.

30. William Block, interview by author, September 14, 2000.

31. Andrew Chancellor, interview by author, December 6, 2000.

Chapter 11: Race and Government

1. Arthur Edmunds, interview by author, July 1971.

2. Glasco, "Double Burden," 76.

3. Walter Worthington, interview by author, November 9, 1997.

4. Glasco, "Double Burden," 73.

5. Bush, *Daybreakers,* 73.

6. Roy McHugh, interview by author, September 2000.

7. The Urban League's history, *Daybreakers: The Story of the Urban League of Pittsburgh,* edited by Esther L. Bush, wrongly dates the department-store campaign to 1947; that mistake has been repeatedly copied in retrospective articles since.

8. Wendell Freeland, interview by author, November 11, 2000.

9. Historical Society, *Beyond Adversity.*

10. Thomas, *Witness,* 140.

11. Glasco, *To Make "Some Place Special,"* 5.

12. Frank Bolden, interview by author, December 7, 2001.

13. George Kiseda, interview by author, September 13, 2001.

14. William Block, interview by author, September 14, 2000.

15. William Block, interview by author, June 5, 2001.

Chapter 12: The Joint Operating Agreement

1. William Block, interview by author, September 14, 2000.

2. William Block, interview by author, September 14, 2000; Block, *Memoir,* 86.

3. Andrew Chancellor, interview by author, December 6, 2000.

4. William Block, interview by author, June 5, 2001; Donald Miller, interview by author, August 12, 2000.

5. Alvin Rosensweet, interview by author, September 9, 2000.

6. William Block, interview by author, September 14, 2000.

7. Ibid.

8. Hawkins, *That Was Hot Type,* 51–54.

9. Tim Menees, interview by author, December 8, 2000.

10. Block, *Memoirs,* 169, 172.

11. Block, *Memoirs,* 94.

12. William Block, interview by author, June 5, 2001.

13. Ibid.

14. Block, *Memoirs,* 113–15.

15. Block, *Memoirs,* 173, 168, 167, 174.

16. John Troan, interview by author, July 26, 2001.

17. Ibid.

Chapter 13: Turbulent Times

1. Unfortunately, copies of the local edition of the *New Pittsburgh Courier* for that period were lost in a creditor's takeover. The national edition is available on microfilm at the Carnegie Public Library in the Oakland section of Pittsburgh. Issues of the national edition for April 1968 give surprisingly little attention to the unrest following the assassination of Martin Luther King Jr. anywhere, let alone in Pittsburgh.

2. Glasco, *To Make "Some Place Special."*

3. Thomas, *Fortunes and Misfortunes,* 46.

4. The *Toledo Blade* under Paul Block Jr. endorsed the Democratic candidate, Senator George McGovern.

5. William Block, interview by author, September 14, 2000.

6. John Craig, interviews by author, January 4, 2001, and January 18, 2001.

Chapter 14: Catching Up

1. Throughout this chapter, statements attributed to John Craig are taken from two interviews conducted by the author on January 4 and January 18 of 2001.

2. Madelyn Ross, interview by author, December 8, 2000. All statements in this chapter attributed to Ross are taken from this interview.

3. Lawrence Walsh, interview by author, July 18, 2001.

Chapter 15: The 1992 Strike

1. Madelyn Ross, interview by author, December 8, 2000.

2. William Burleigh, interview by author, October 6, 2001.

3. Richard Boehne, interview by author, October 31, 2001; William Burleigh, interview by author, October 6, 2001.

4. Minutes of Unity Council meetings, various letters, and other relevant documents quoted in this chapter were made available by attorney Joe Pass.

5. Other union leaders present were Samuel Mahfood, Teamsters Local 211; Dick Nussbaumer, Platemakers 24; J. Talerico, Paperhandlers 5; Sonny Shannon, Pressmen 9; Jim Lowen, Printers 7; Tom Moore, Engineers 95; Jack Yoedt, Service Employees International Union 29; Bill Metz, Communication Workers of America; James Elnyczky, International Association of Machinists; and J. E. Pietkiewicz and Danny Zorich, Mailers 22.

6. Asked by the author for an interview to present his side of the situation, Manis replied in writing, "Thanks but no thanks. I have no desire to be a part of a book about the *P-G.*"

7. Personal correspondence of William Block Jr. quoted in this chapter was made available by the Block family.

8. *New York Times,* May 31, 1992.

9. The *USA Today* article of June 4, 1992, went on to explain: "Neither newspaper will discuss how operating profits are split, but a 1989 report by Merrill Lynch media analyst Lauren Fine says that of the first $4 million, 66% goes to Scripps, 34% to Blade [Communications]. Scripps gets the next $3.8 million. Of the next $2 million, 73% goes to Scripps, 27% to Blade. More than that, Scripps gets 70%, Blade 30%."

10. William Block, interview by author, September 14, 2001.

11. John Robinson Block, interview by author, February 10, 2001; William Block, interview by author, September 27, 2001; William Block Jr., interview by author, August 17, 2001.

12. John Craig, interview by author, November 19, 2001.

13. William Burleigh, interview by author, October 6, 2001.

14. Scott Zimmerman, interview by author, October 6, 2000.

15. Joe Pass, interview by author, September 26, 2000.

16. Scott Zimmerman, interview by author, October 6, 2000.

17. Ray Burnett, interview by author, October 12, 2000.

18. Lawrence Walsh, interview by author, July 18, 2001.

Chapter 16: Moving Forward

1. Bob Higdon, interview by author, November 24, 2000. All statements in this chapter attributed to Higdon are taken from this interview.

2. Richard Scaife declined to be interviewed for this book.

3. Lee Templeton, interview by author, May 29, 2001.

4. Ibid. The Audit Bureau of Circulation does not break out the Pittsburgh edition's figures separately from the Greensburg edition's figures.

5. John Craig, interview by author, January 18, 2001.

6. Michael Pearson, interview by author, September 19, 2000.

7. Michael Tomasieski, interview by author, September 19, 2000.

8. Joe Pass, interview by author, September 26, 2000.

BIBLIOGRAPHY

The newspapers consulted are part of the microfilm collection of the Pennsylvania Department of the Carnegie Library of Pittsburgh, Oakland. The collection includes major Pittsburgh newspapers from 1786 to the present, with the exception of a gap between March 1803 and August 1805. Most *Post-Gazette* articles from 1998 to the present are also available online at http://www.post-gazette/search.

Alberts, Robert C. *Pitt: The Story of the University of Pittsburgh, 1787–1987.* Pittsburgh: University of Pittsburgh Press, 1986.

Andrews, J. Cutler. *Pittsburgh's Post-Gazette.* Boston: Mt. Vernon Press, 1936.

Apelt, Brian. *The Corporation: A Centennial Biography of Unites States Steel Corporation, 1901–2001.* Pittsburgh: Cathedral Publishing, 2000.

Baldwin, Leland D. *Pittsburgh: The Story of a City, 1758–1865.* 1937. Reprint, Pittsburgh: University of Pittsburgh Press, 1970.

———. *Whiskey Rebels: The Story of a Frontier Uprising.* 1939. Reprint, Pittsburgh: University of Pittsburgh Press, 1992.

Block, William Sr. *Memoirs of William Block.* Toledo: privately printed by William Block Jr., 1990.

Brackenridge, Henry Marie. *History of the Western Insurrection, Commonly Called the Whiskey Rebellion, 1794.* 1859. Reprint, New York: Arno Press, 1969.

Brady, Frank. *The Publisher: Paul Block: A Life of Friendship, Power, and Politics.* Lanham, MD: University Press of America, 2001.

Bush, Esther L., ed. *Daybreakers: The Story of the Urban League of Pittsburgh, The First Eighty Years.* Pittsburgh: Urban League, 1999.

Bynum, Mike, et al. *Greatest Moments in Pitt Football History.* Nashville: Athlon Sports Communications Inc., 1994.

Demarest, David P., Jr. *The River Ran Red: Homestead 1892.* Pittsburgh: University of Pittsburgh Press, 1992.

Dolson, Hildegarde. *Disaster at Johnstown: The Great Flood.* New York: Random House, 1963

Duffy, John. "Smoke, Smog and Health in Early Pittsburgh," *The Western Pennsylvania Historical Magazine* 45 (June 1962), quoting John Bernard, *Retrospection of America 1797–1811* (New York, 1887), 182.

Emery, Michael, Edwin Emery, and Nancy L. Roberts. *The Press and America: An Interpretive History of the Mass Media.* 9th ed. Boston: Allyn and Bacon, 2000.

Field, Alston G. "The Press in Western Pennsylvania to 1812." *Western Pennsylvania Historical Magazine* 20 (December 1937: 231–64.

Findley, William. *History of the Insurrection, in the Four Western Counties of Pennsylvania.* Philadelphia: 1796.

Glasco, Laurence. "Double Burden: The Black Experience in Pittsburgh." In *City at the Point: Essays on the Social History of Pittsburgh,* edited by Samuel P. Hays, 69–109. Pittsburgh: University of Pittsburgh Press, 1989.

———. *To Make "Some Place Special": The Civil Rights Movement in Pittsburgh.* Pittsburgh: Freedom Corner Forum, 2001.

Greenwald, Maurine, and Margo Anderson, eds. *Pittsburgh Surveyed.* Pittsburgh: University of Pittsburgh Press, 1996.

Gugliotta, Angela. "How, When, and for Whom was Smoke a Problem in Pittsburgh?" In *Devastation and Renewal: An Environmental History of Pittsburgh and its Region,* edited by Joel A. Tarr, 110–125. Pittsburgh: University of Pittsburgh Press, 2003.

Harrison, John M. *The Blade of Toledo: The First 150 Years.* Toledo: Toledo Blade Co., 1985.

Hawkins, Frank N. *That Was Hot Type.* Privately printed.

Hays, Samuel P., ed. *City at the Point: Essays on the Social History of Pittsburgh.* Pittsburgh: University of Pittsburgh Press, 1989.

Historical Society of Western Pennsylvania, Museum Program Division. *Beyond Adversity: African Americans Struggle for Equality in Western Pennsylvania, 1750–1990.* Pittsburgh: Historical Society of Western Pennsylvania, 1993.

Killikelly, Sarah Hutchins. *The History of Pittsburgh: Its Rise and Progress.* Pittsburgh: B. C. & Gordon Montgomery Co., 1906.

Lorant, Stefan. *Pittsburgh: The Story of an American City.* Lenox, MA: Author's Edition, 1964.

Lubove, Roy. *Twentieth-Century Pittsburgh.* Pittsburgh: University of Pittsburgh Press, 1996.

Marder, Daniel, ed. *A Hugh Henry Brackenridge Reader, 1770–1815.* Pittsburgh: University of Pittsburgh Press, 1970.

McCullough, David. *The Johnstown Flood.* New York: Simon and Schuster, 1968.

McHugh, Roy, et. al. *Pittsburgh Characters—Told by Pittsburgh Characters.* Greensburg, PA: The Iconoclast Press, 1991.

Nasaw, David *The Chief: The Life of William Randolph Hearst.* Boston: Houghton Mifflin, 2000.

Parton, James. "Pittsburg." *Atlantic Monthly* (January 1868).

Phillips, Kevin P. *The Cousins' Wars: Religion, Politics, and the Triumph of Anglo-America.* New York: Basic Books, 1999.

Ray, John Watson. *A History of Western Pennsylvania.* Erie, PA: self-published, 1941.

Reese, Ralph H., ed. *The Flavor of Pittsburgh.* Pittsburgh: Pittsburgh Diners' Guild and Allegheny County Chapter, Pennsylvania Association of Retarded Citizens, 1976.

Reiser, Catherine Elizabeth. *Pittsburgh's Commercial Development, 1800–1850.* Harrisburg: Pennsylvania Historical and Museum Commission, 1951.

Ruck, Rob. *Sandlot Seasons: Sport in Black Pittsburgh.* Urbana: University of Illinois Press, 1987.

Schroyer, Will, and Maxine Schroyer. *The Scaife Company and the Scaife Family.* Pittsburgh: Scaife Co., 1952.

Schultz, Christian. "Extract from Schultz's Travels." Monthly Bulletin of the Carnegie Library of Pittsburgh (April 1902–June 1902), 180.

Schulz, Constance B., and Steven W. Plattner, eds. *Witness to the Fifties: The Pittsburgh Photographic Library, 1950–1953.* Narrative by Clarke M. Thomas. Pittsburgh: University of Pittsburgh Press, 1999.

Seldes, George. *Lords of the Press.* New York: J. Messner, 1939.

Smith, Helene. *The Great Whisky Rebellion: Rebels with a Cause.* Greensburg, PA: MacDonald-Sward Publishing Company, 1994.

Steffens, Lincoln. *The Shame of the Cities.* New York: McClure, Phillips & Co., 1904. Reprint, New York: Hill and Wang, 1992.

Stevens, John Austin. *Albert Gallatin.* Boston: Houghton Mifflin, 1883. Reprint, New York: AMS Press, 1972.

Sword, Wiley. *President Washington's Indian War: The Struggle for the Old Northwest, 1790–1795.* Norman: University of Oklahoma Press, 1985.

Tarr, Joel A., and Terry F. Yosie. "Critical Decisions in Pittsburgh Water and Waste Water Treatment." In *Devastation and Renewal: An Environmental History of Pittsburgh and its Region,* edited by Joel A. Tarr, 64–88. Pittsburgh: University of Pittsburgh Press, 2003.

Thomas, Clarke M. *Fortunes and Misfortunes: Pittsburgh & Allegheny County Politics, 1930–95.* Pittsburgh: Institute of Politics, 1998.

———. *They Came to Pittsburgh.* Pittsburgh: *Pittsburgh Post-Gazette,* 1983.

Thomas, Jean Waters. "Music of the Great Sanitary Fairs: Culture and Charity in the American Civil War." PhD diss., University of Pittsburgh, 1989.

Tifft, Susan E., and Alex S. Jones. *The Trust: The Private and Powerful Family Behind the New York Times.* Boston: Little, Brown and Company, 1999.

Troan, John. *Passsport to Adventure.* Pittsburgh: Neworks Press, 2000.

Vile, John R. *Encyclopedia of Constitutional Amendments, Proposed Amendments, and Amending Issues, 1789–1995.* Santa Barbara: ABC-CLIO Inc., 1996.

Warner, A. *A History of Allegheny County, Pennsylvania: Including Its Early Settlement and Progress to the Present Time.* Chicago: A. Warner & Co., 1889. Reprint, Butler, PA: Mechling Associates, 1998. Page references are to the 1998 edition.

Weber, Michael P. *Don't Call Me Boss: David L. Lawrence, Pittsburgh's Renaissance Mayor.* Pittsburgh: University of Pittsburgh Press, 1998.

Wilson, Erasmus. *Standard History of Pittsburg, Pennsylvania.* Chicago: The Goodspeed Publishing Company, 1898.

Women's Suffrage clippings file. Pennsylvania Department. Carnegie Library of Pittsburgh, Pittsburgh, Pennsylvania.

INDEX